How many manga titles have you purchased in ... titles?
(please check one from each column)

MANGA	VIZ Media
☐ None	☐ None
☐ 1 – 4	☐ 1 – 4
☐ 5 – 10	☐ 5 – 10
☐ 11+	☐ 11+

How much influence do special promotions and gifts-with-purchase have on the titles you buy?
(please circle, with 5 being great influence and 1 being none)

1 2 3 4 5

Do you purchase every volume of your favorite series?

☐ Yes! Gotta have 'em as my own ☐ No. Please explain: ______________________

What kind of manga storylines do you most enjoy? **(check all that apply)**

☐ Action / Adventure	☐ Science Fiction	☐ Horror
☐ Comedy	☐ Romance (shojo)	☐ Fantasy (shojo)
☐ Fighting	☐ Sports	☐ Historical
☐ Artistic / Alternative	☐ Other ______________________	

If you watch the anime or play a video or TCG game from a series, how likely are you to buy the manga? **(please circle, with 5 being very likely and 1 being unlikely)**

1 2 3 4 5

If unlikely, please explain: ______________________

Who are your favorite authors / artists? ______________________

____

What titles would like you translated and sold in English? ______________________

____

THANK YOU! Please send the completed form to:

VIZ media

NJW Research
42 Catharine Street
Poughkeepsie, NY 12601

Your privacy is very important to us. All information provided will be used for internal purposes only and will not be sold or otherwise divulged.

LOVE MANGA? LET US KNOW!

☐ Please do NOT send me information about VIZ Media products, news and events, special offers, or other information.

☐ Please do NOT send me information from VIZ Media's trusted business partners.

Name: _____

Address: _____

City:_____ State:_____ Zip:_____

E-mail: _____

☐ Male   ☐ Female   Date of Birth (mm/dd/yyyy): ____/____/____   (Under 13? Parental consent required)

What race/ethnicity do you consider yourself? (check all that apply)

☐ White/Caucasian   ☐ Black/African American   ☐ Hispanic/Latino

☐ Asian/Pacific Islander ☐ Native American/Alaskan Native ☐ Other: _____

What VIZ Media title(s) did you purchase? (indicate title(s) purchased) _____

_____

What other VIZ Media titles do you own? _____

_____

Reason for purchase: (check all that apply)

☐ Special offer   ☐ Favorite title / author / artist / genre

☐ Gift   ☐ Recommendation   ☐ Collection

☐ Read excerpt in VIZ Media manga sampler   ☐ Other _____

Where did you make your purchase? (please check one)

☐ Comic store   ☐ Bookstore   ☐ Grocery Store

☐ Convention   ☐ Newsstand   ☐ Video Game Store

☐ Online (site:_____)   ☐ Other _____

ZATCH BELL!™

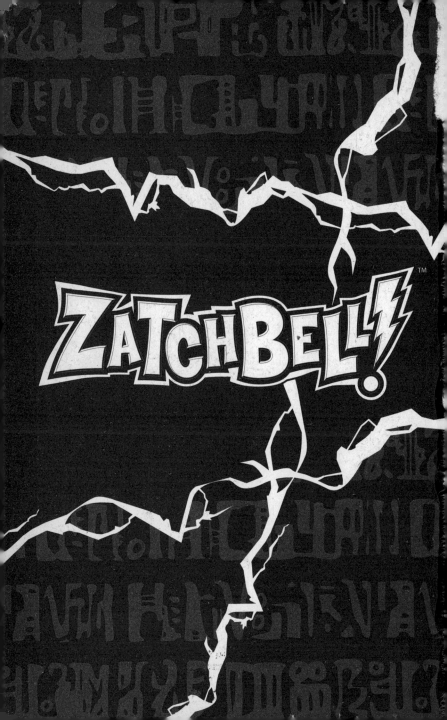

ZATCH BELL!
Vol. 5

STORY AND ART BY
MAKOTO RAIKU

English Adaptation/Fred Burke
Translation/David Ury
Touch-up Art & Lettering/Melanie Lewis
Design/Izumi Hirayama
Special Thanks/Jessica Villat, Miki Macaluso,
Mitsuko Kitajima, and Akane Matsuo
Editor/Frances E. Wall

Managing Editor/Annette Roman
Director of Production/Noboru Watanabe
Vice President of Publishing/Alvin Lu
Sr. Director of Acquisitions/Rika Inouye
Vice President of Sales & Marketing/Liza Coppola
Publisher/Hyoe Narita

Printed in the U.S.A.

Published by VIZ Media, LLC
P.O. Box 77010
San Francisco, CA 94107

10 9 8 7 6 5 4 3 2 1
First printing, January 2006

www.viz.com
store.viz.com

STORY AND ART BY
MAKOTO RAIKU

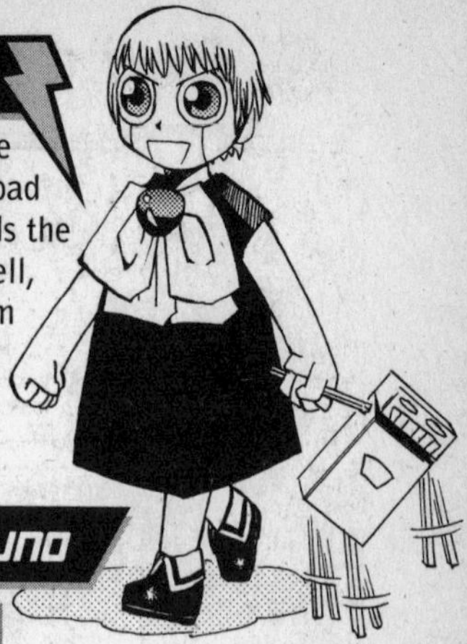

Zatch Bell

A mamodo kid who came to help Kiyo reform his bad attitude. When Kiyo holds the red book and reads a spell, lightning bolts shoot from Zatch's mouth. His past in the mamodo world is shrouded in mystery...

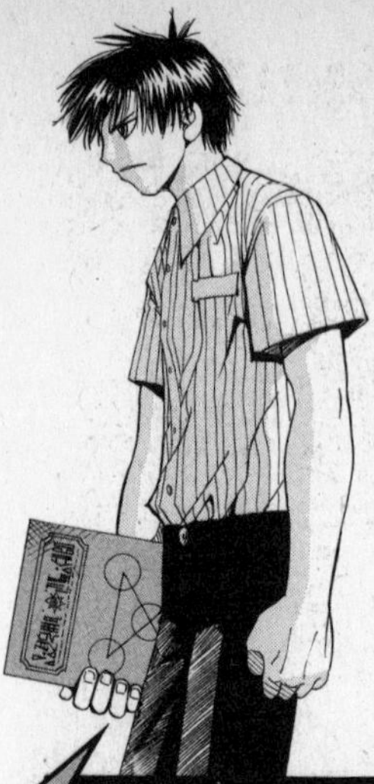

Kiyo Takamine

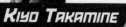

An aloof student with a keen intellect, Kiyo doesn't fit in—but now Zatch is here, and all that's starting to change!

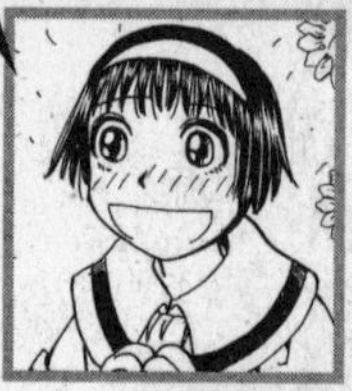

Suzy Mizuno

A classmate who likes Kiyo, Suzy is always getting in trouble.

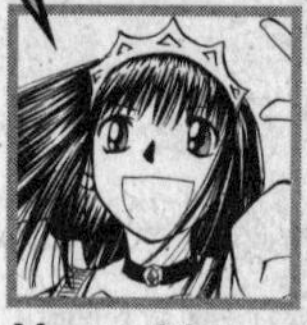

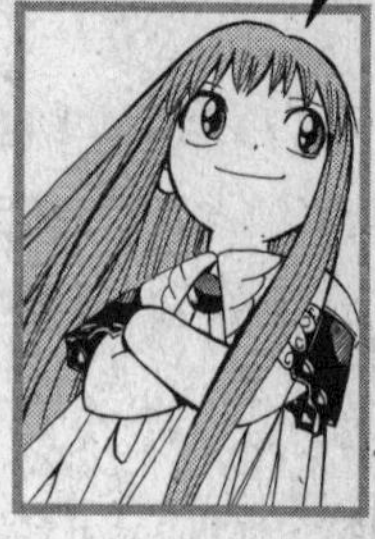

Megumi & Tia

Megumi is a superstar pop singer and the human partner of Tia, a mamodo girl. Zatch and Kiyo saved their lives, and now the four have become friends.

Hana Takamine

Kiyo's mother, nice but strict.

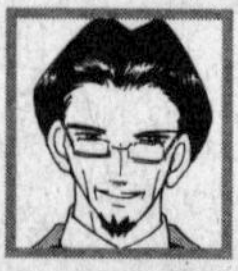

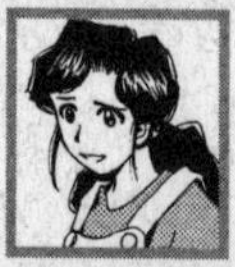

Seitaro Takamine

Kiyo's father, an archaeology professor at a university in England.

Hiroshi Yamanaka

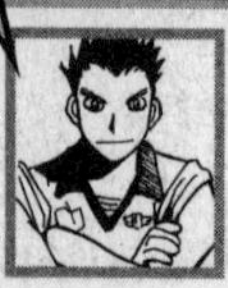

On the baseball team.

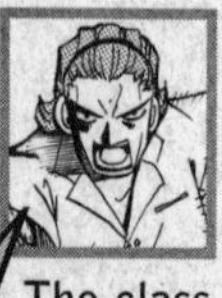

Kane

The class bully.

Mamoru Iwashima

A funny guy.

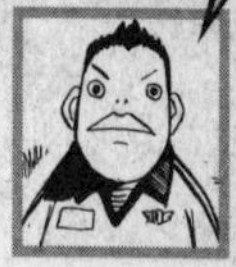

Zatch's Past Opponents

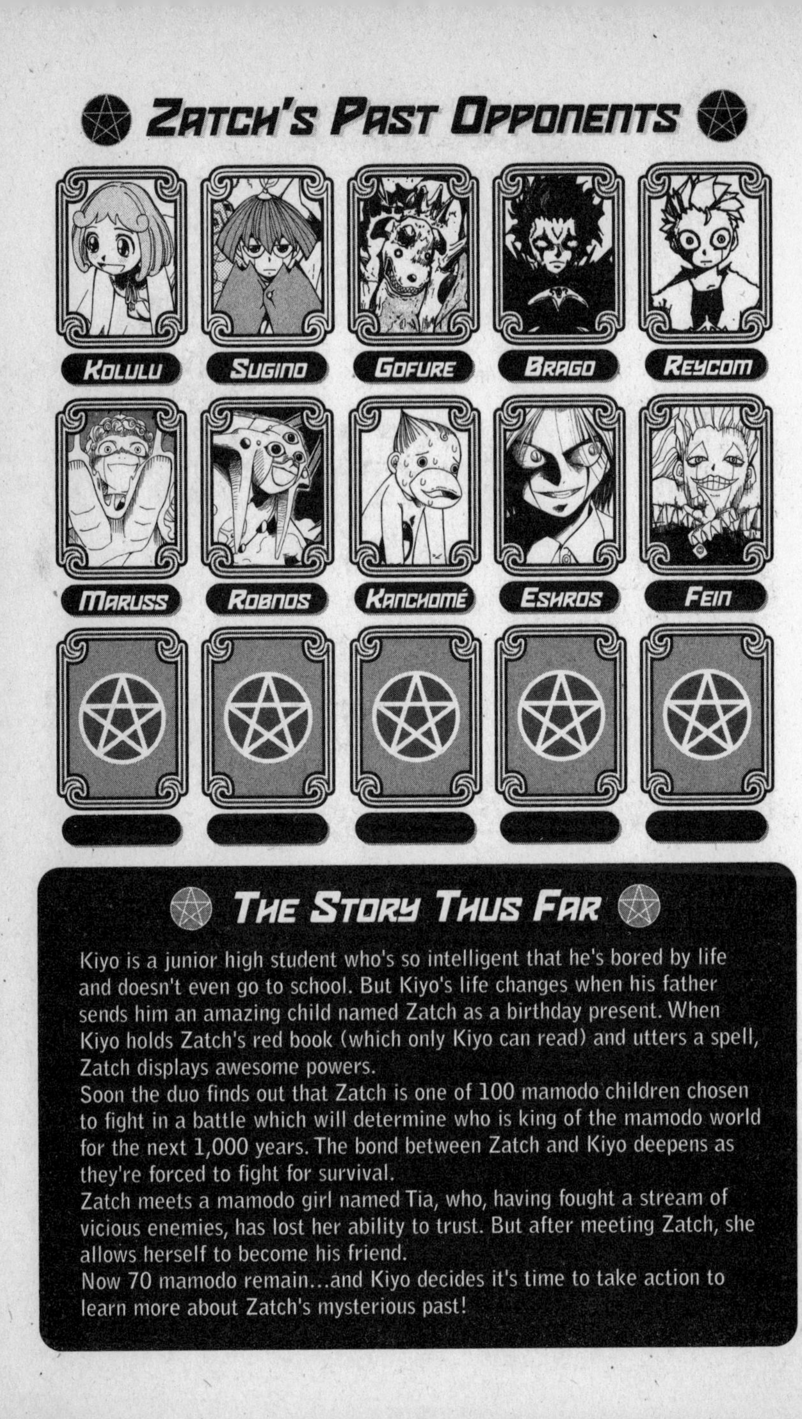
Kolulu
Sugino
Gofure
Brago
Reycom
Maruss
Robnos
Kanchomé
Eshros
Fein

The Story Thus Far

Kiyo is a junior high student who's so intelligent that he's bored by life and doesn't even go to school. But Kiyo's life changes when his father sends him an amazing child named Zatch as a birthday present. When Kiyo holds Zatch's red book (which only Kiyo can read) and utters a spell, Zatch displays awesome powers.

Soon the duo finds out that Zatch is one of 100 mamodo children chosen to fight in a battle which will determine who is king of the mamodo world for the next 1,000 years. The bond between Zatch and Kiyo deepens as they're forced to fight for survival.

Zatch meets a mamodo girl named Tia, who, having fought a stream of vicious enemies, has lost her ability to trust. But after meeting Zatch, she allows herself to become his friend.

Now 70 mamodo remain...and Kiyo decides it's time to take action to learn more about Zatch's mysterious past!

ZATCH BELL! 5

CONTENTS

LEVEL 39: Kiyo's Summer Break

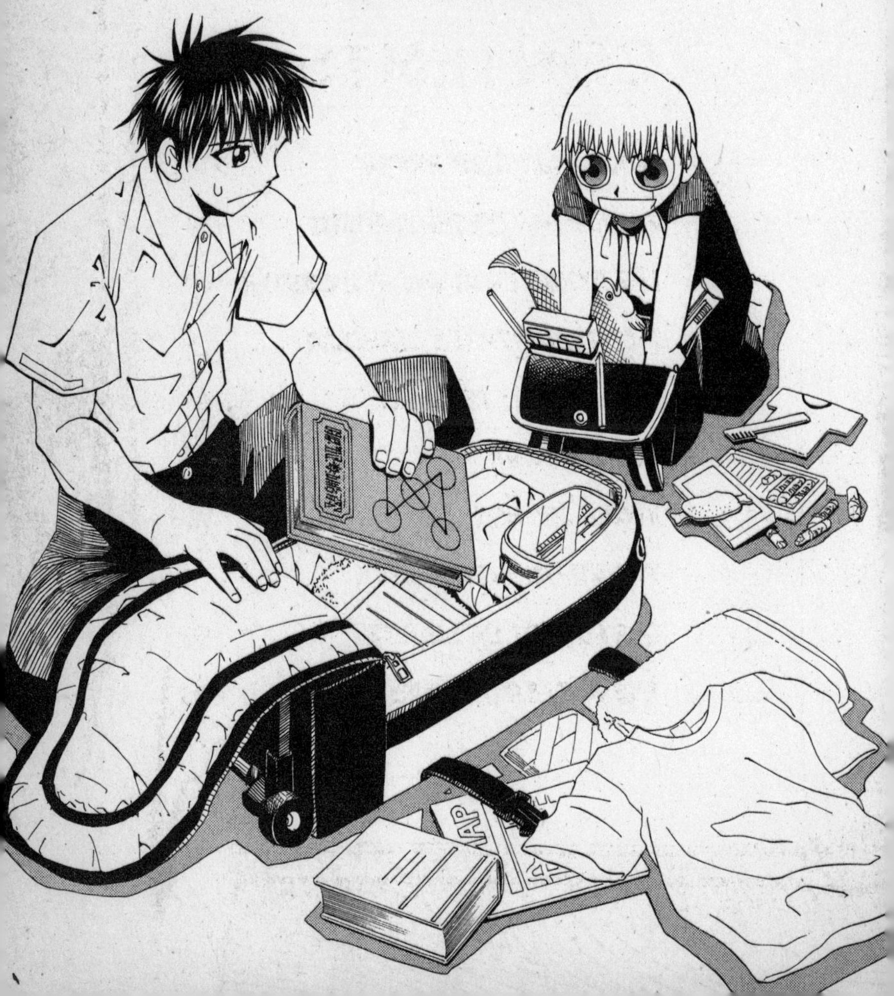

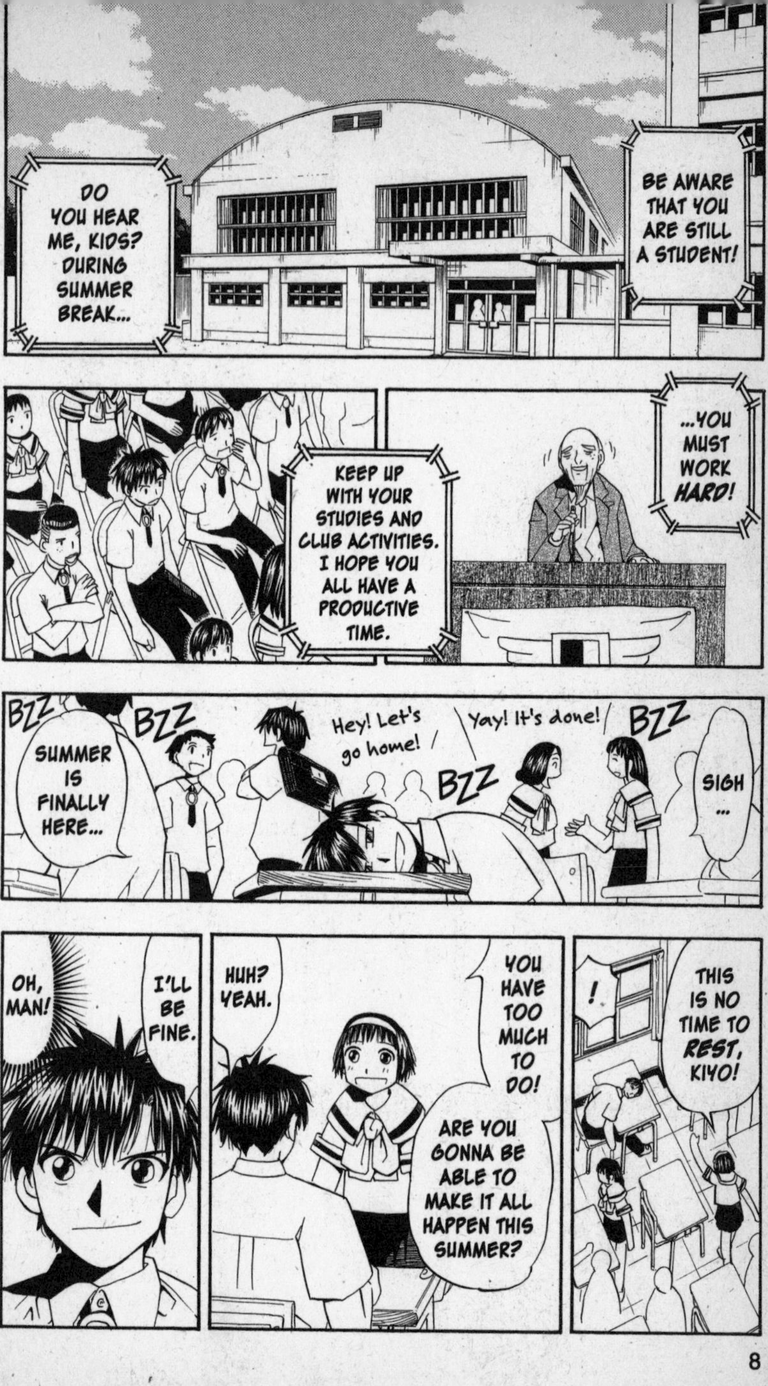
BE AWARE THAT YOU ARE STILL A STUDENT!
DO YOU HEAR ME, KIDS? DURING SUMMER BREAK...
...YOU MUST WORK HARD!
KEEP UP WITH YOUR STUDIES AND CLUB ACTIVITIES. I HOPE YOU ALL HAVE A PRODUCTIVE TIME.
SIGH ...
BZZ
Yay! It's done!
BZZ
Hey! Let's go home!
BZZ
SUMMER IS FINALLY HERE...
BZZ
!
THIS IS NO TIME TO REST, KIYO!
YOU HAVE TOO MUCH TO DO!
ARE YOU GONNA BE ABLE TO MAKE IT ALL HAPPEN THIS SUMMER?
HUH? YEAH.
I'LL BE FINE.
OH, MAN!

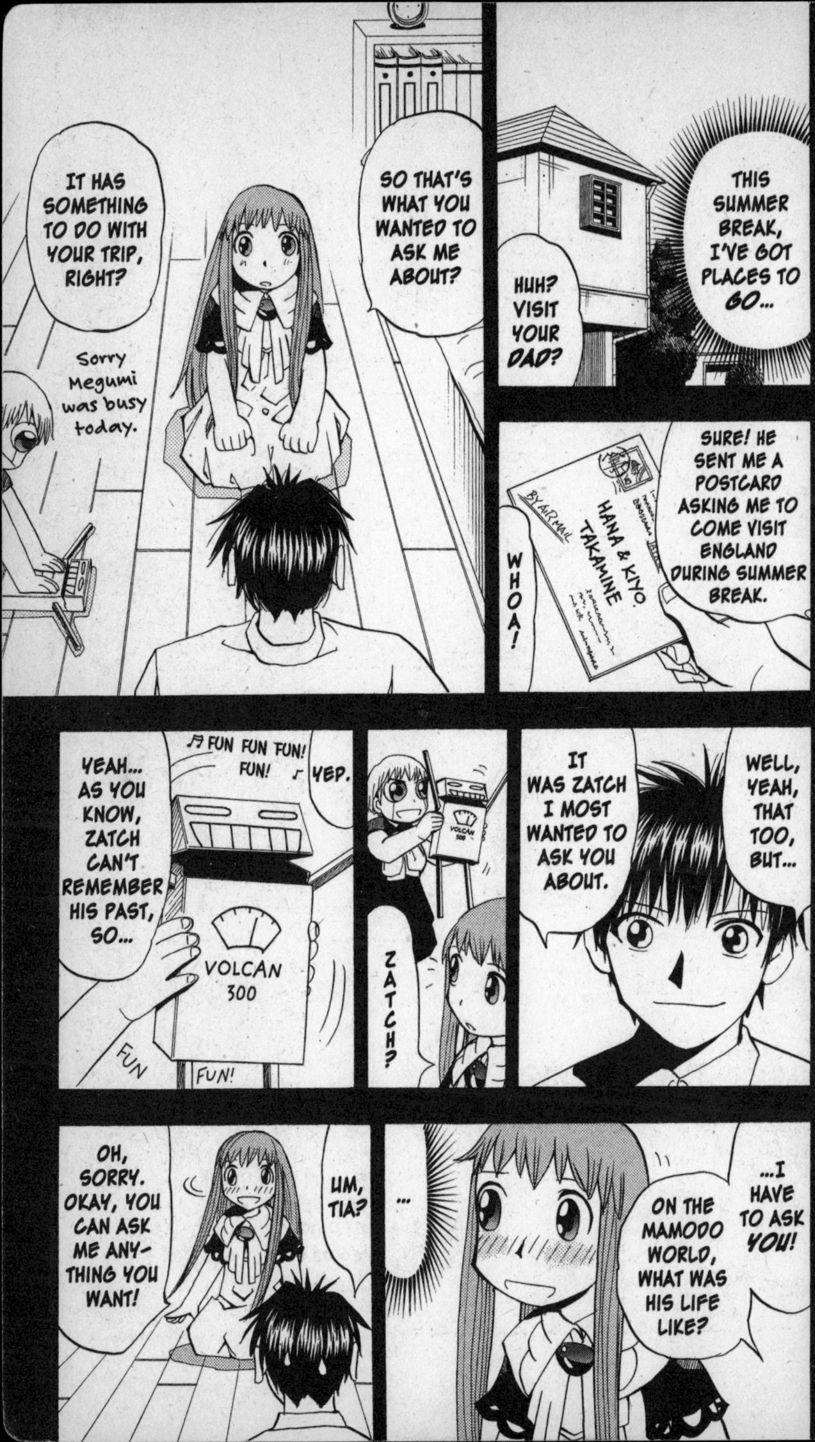
THIS SUMMER BREAK, I'VE GOT PLACES TO GO...
HUH? VISIT YOUR DAD?
SURE! HE SENT ME A POSTCARD ASKING ME TO COME VISIT ENGLAND DURING SUMMER BREAK.
WHOA!
BY AIR MAIL
HANA & KIYO TAKAMINE
SO THAT'S WHAT YOU WANTED TO ASK ME ABOUT?
IT HAS SOMETHING TO DO WITH YOUR TRIP, RIGHT?
Sorry Megumi was busy today.
WELL, YEAH, THAT TOO, BUT...
IT WAS ZATCH I MOST WANTED TO ASK YOU ABOUT.
YEP.
VOLCAN 300
ZATCH?
FUN FUN FUN! FUN!
YEAH... AS YOU KNOW, ZATCH CAN'T REMEMBER HIS PAST, SO...
VOLCAN 300
FUN
FUN!
...I HAVE TO ASK YOU!
ON THE MAMODO WORLD, WHAT WAS HIS LIFE LIKE?
...
UM, TIA?
OH, SORRY. OKAY, YOU CAN ASK ME ANYTHING YOU WANT!

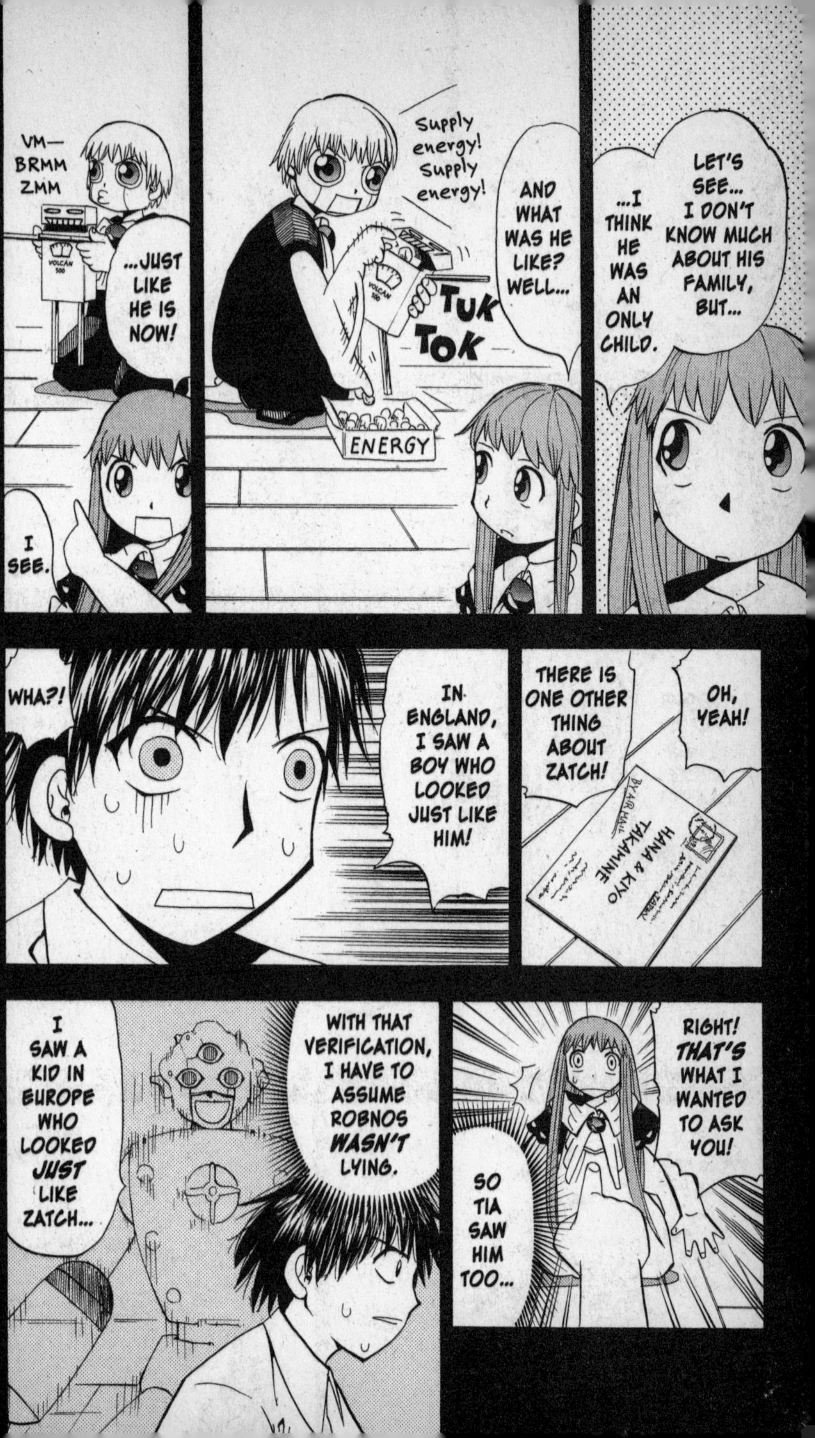
LET'S SEE... I DON'T KNOW MUCH ABOUT HIS FAMILY, BUT...
...I THINK HE WAS AN ONLY CHILD.
AND WHAT WAS HE LIKE? WELL...
Supply energy! Supply energy!
TUK TOK
ENERGY
VM— BRMM ZMM
...JUST LIKE HE IS NOW!
I SEE.
OH, YEAH!
THERE IS ONE OTHER THING ABOUT ZATCH!
BY AIR MAIL
HANA & KIYO TAKAMINE
IN ENGLAND, I SAW A BOY WHO LOOKED JUST LIKE HIM!
WHA?!
RIGHT! *THAT'S* WHAT I WANTED TO ASK YOU!
SO TIA SAW HIM TOO...
WITH THAT VERIFICATION, I HAVE TO ASSUME ROBNOS *WASN'T* LYING.
I SAW A KID IN EUROPE WHO LOOKED *JUST* LIKE ZATCH...

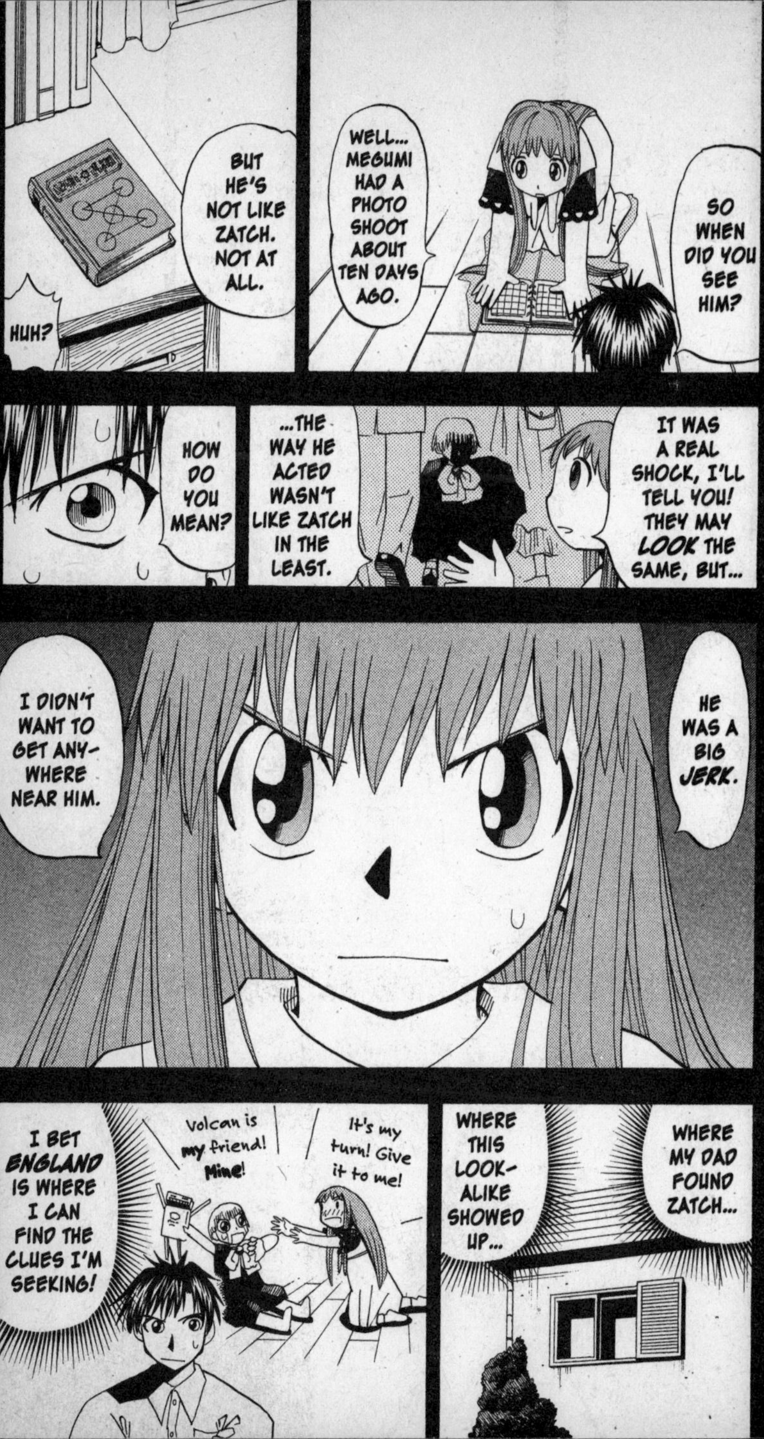
SO WHEN DID YOU SEE HIM?
WELL... MEGUMI HAD A PHOTO SHOOT ABOUT TEN DAYS AGO.
BUT HE'S NOT LIKE ZATCH. NOT AT ALL.
HUH?
IT WAS A REAL SHOCK, I'LL TELL YOU! THEY MAY LOOK THE SAME, BUT...
...THE WAY HE ACTED WASN'T LIKE ZATCH IN THE LEAST.
HOW DO YOU MEAN?
HE WAS A BIG JERK.
I DIDN'T WANT TO GET ANY-WHERE NEAR HIM.
WHERE MY DAD FOUND ZATCH...
WHERE THIS LOOK-ALIKE SHOWED UP...
It's my turn! Give it to me!
Volcan is my friend! Mine!
I BET ENGLAND IS WHERE I CAN FIND THE CLUES I'M SEEKING!

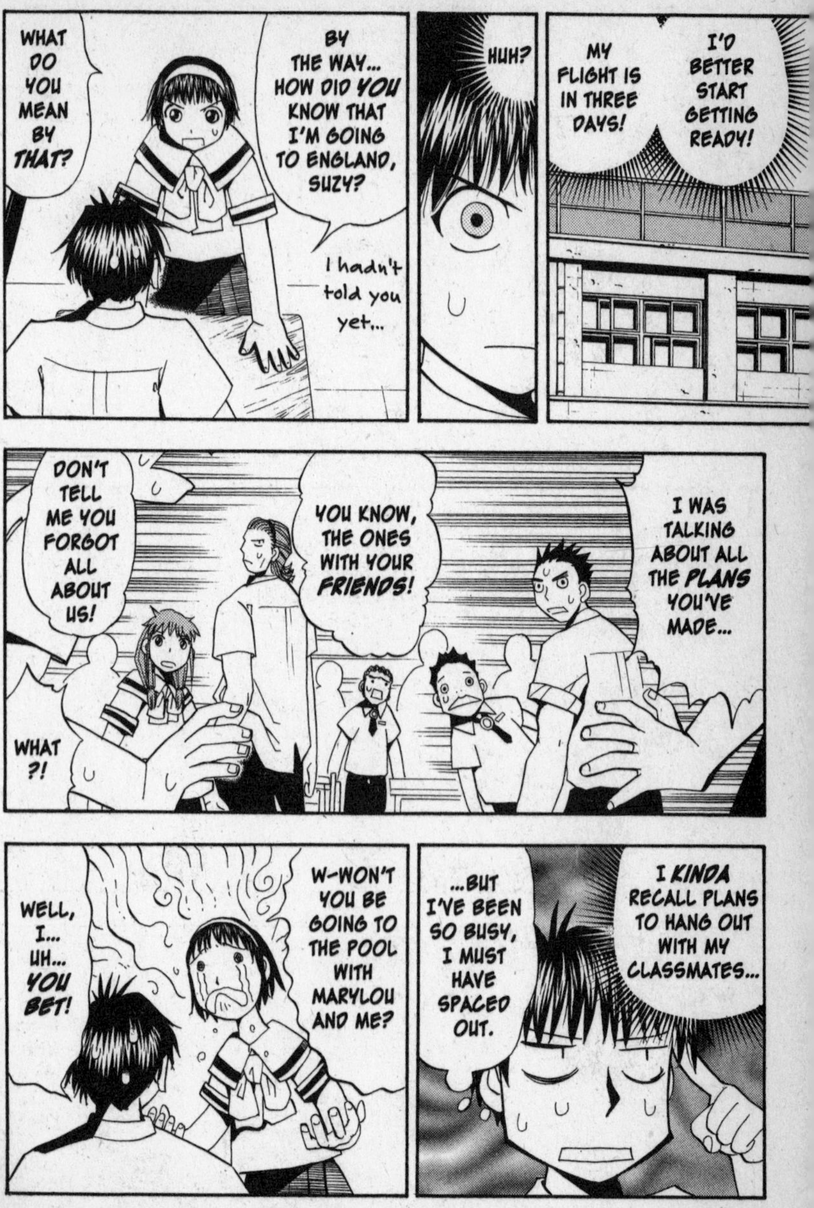
I'D BETTER START GETTING READY!
MY FLIGHT IS IN THREE DAYS!
HUH?
BY THE WAY... HOW DID YOU KNOW THAT I'M GOING TO ENGLAND, SUZY?
I hadn't told you yet...
WHAT DO YOU MEAN BY THAT?
I WAS TALKING ABOUT ALL THE PLANS YOU'VE MADE...
YOU KNOW, THE ONES WITH YOUR FRIENDS!
DON'T TELL ME YOU FORGOT ALL ABOUT US!
WHAT ?!
I KINDA RECALL PLANS TO HANG OUT WITH MY CLASSMATES...
...BUT I'VE BEEN SO BUSY, I MUST HAVE SPACED OUT.
W-WON'T YOU BE GOING TO THE POOL WITH MARYLOU AND ME?
WELL, I... UH... YOU BET!

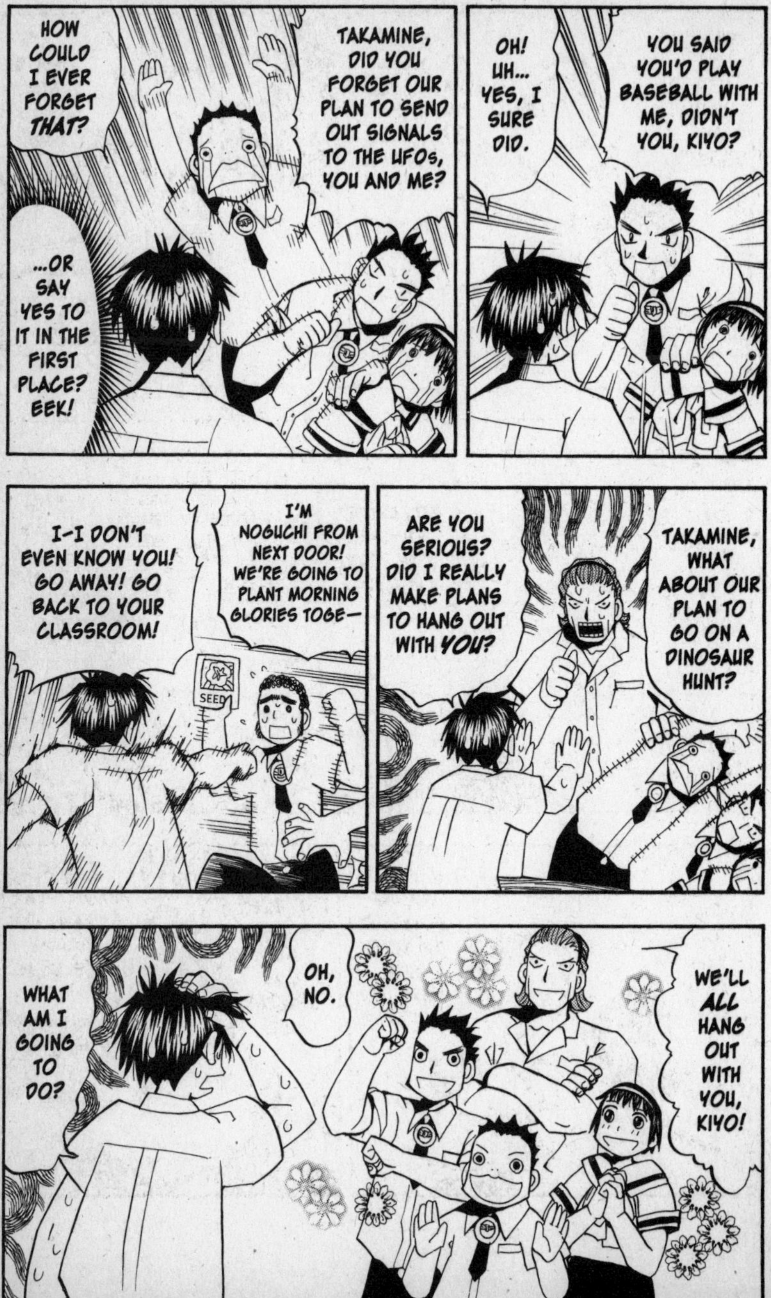
YOU SAID YOU'D PLAY BASEBALL WITH ME, DIDN'T YOU, KIYO?
OH! UH... YES, I SURE DID.
TAKAMINE, DID YOU FORGET OUR PLAN TO SEND OUT SIGNALS TO THE UFOs, YOU AND ME?
HOW COULD I EVER FORGET *THAT?*
...OR SAY YES TO IT IN THE FIRST PLACE? EEK!
TAKAMINE, WHAT ABOUT OUR PLAN TO GO ON A DINOSAUR HUNT?
ARE YOU SERIOUS? DID I REALLY MAKE PLANS TO HANG OUT WITH *YOU?*
I'M NOGUCHI FROM NEXT DOOR! WE'RE GOING TO PLANT MORNING GLORIES TOGE—
SEED
I-I DON'T EVEN KNOW YOU! GO AWAY! GO BACK TO YOUR CLASSROOM!
WE'LL *ALL* HANG OUT WITH YOU, KIYO!
OH, NO.
WHAT AM I GOING TO DO?

Schedule

Day 3	Day 2	Day 1
	Go to the pool with Suzy and friends	8:00 AM · Play baseball with Yamanaka
		11:00 AM · Catch insects with Inoue
		1:00 PM · Fishing with Tai
		4:00 PM · Dinosaur hunting with Kane
Leave for England		6:00 PM · UFO spotting with Iwashima

...BUT IT SURE IS A TIGHT SCHEDULE.

I CAN FIT IT ALL IN...

BUT IF I CAN JUST MAKE IT TO DAY TWO...

...WHAT WITH UFOs AND A DINOSAUR HUNT!

SO, DAY ONE IS THE BUSY DAY...

IF I CAN HANDLE THIS, THEN I WON'T HAVE TO BREAK A SINGLE PROMISE.

?

HM.... WHAT ELSE CAN I DO?

...HAVE TO STAY AT HOME AGAIN?

DO I...

!

YOU WILL? WOW!

ZATCH, IF IT ALL GOES SMOOTHLY, I MIGHT TAKE YOU TO THE POOL WITH ME ON DAY TWO!

YOU CAN HELP ME OUT!

14

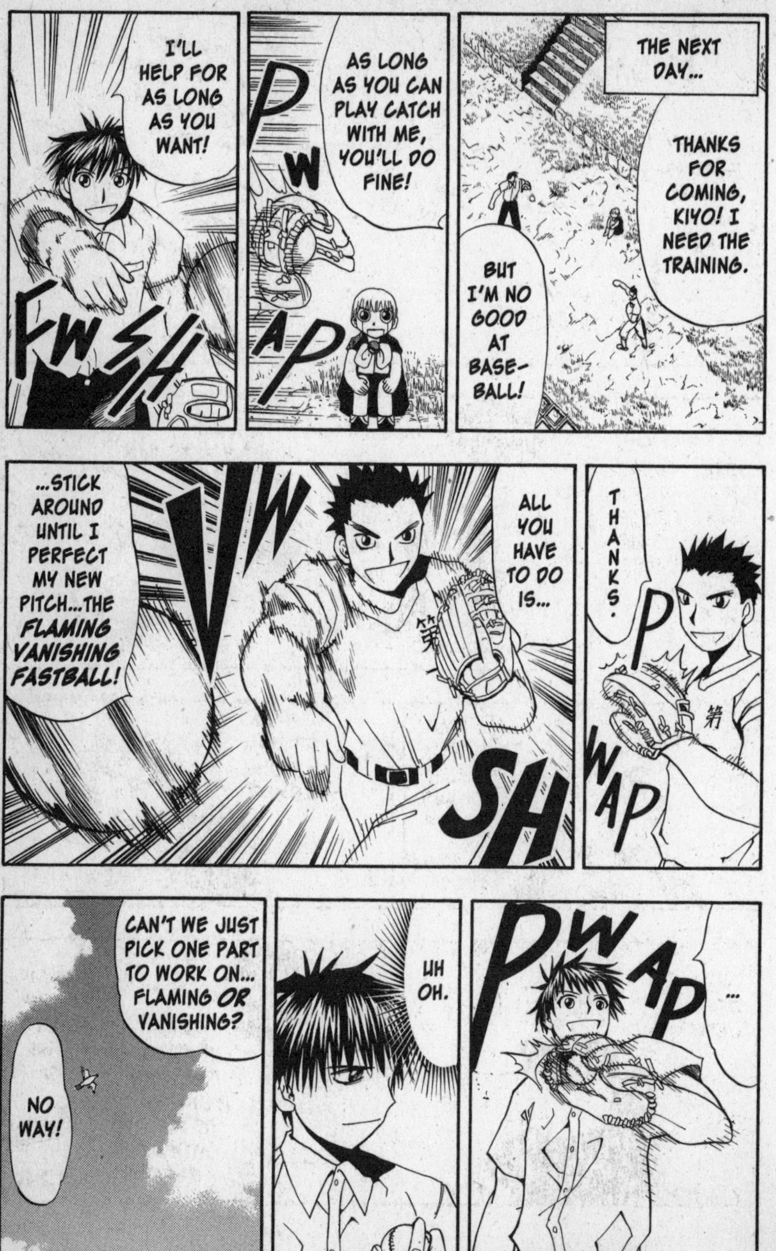
THE NEXT DAY...
THANKS FOR COMING, KIYO! I NEED THE TRAINING.
BUT I'M NO GOOD AT BASE-BALL!
AS LONG AS YOU CAN PLAY CATCH WITH ME, YOU'LL DO FINE!
PWAP
I'LL HELP FOR AS LONG AS YOU WANT!
FWSH
THANKS.
PWAP
ALL YOU HAVE TO DO IS...
...STICK AROUND UNTIL I PERFECT MY NEW PITCH...THE *FLAMING VANISHING FASTBALL!*
VWSH
PWAP
...
UH OH.
CAN'T WE JUST PICK ONE PART TO WORK ON... FLAMING *OR* VANISHING?
NO WAY!

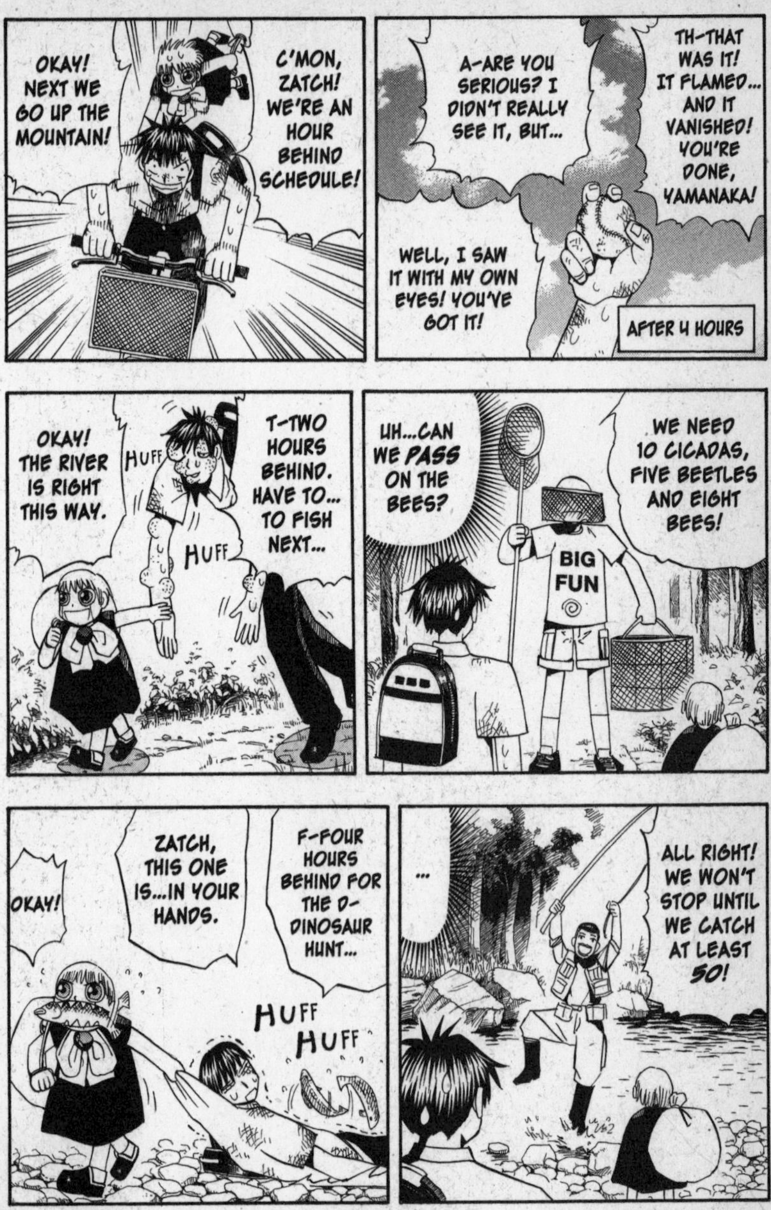
TH-THAT WAS IT! IT FLAMED... AND IT VANISHED! YOU'RE DONE, YAMANAKA!
A-ARE YOU SERIOUS? I DIDN'T REALLY SEE IT, BUT...
WELL, I SAW IT WITH MY OWN EYES! YOU'VE GOT IT!
AFTER 4 HOURS
C'MON, ZATCH! WE'RE AN HOUR BEHIND SCHEDULE!
OKAY! NEXT WE GO UP THE MOUNTAIN!
WE NEED 10 CICADAS, FIVE BEETLES AND EIGHT BEES!
BIG FUN
UH...CAN WE *PASS* ON THE BEES?
T-TWO HOURS BEHIND. HAVE TO... TO FISH NEXT...
HUFF
OKAY! THE RIVER IS RIGHT THIS WAY.
HUFF
ALL RIGHT! WE WON'T STOP UNTIL WE CATCH AT LEAST *50*!
...
F-FOUR HOURS BEHIND FOR THE D-DINOSAUR HUNT...
ZATCH, THIS ONE IS...IN YOUR HANDS.
HUFF HUFF
OKAY!

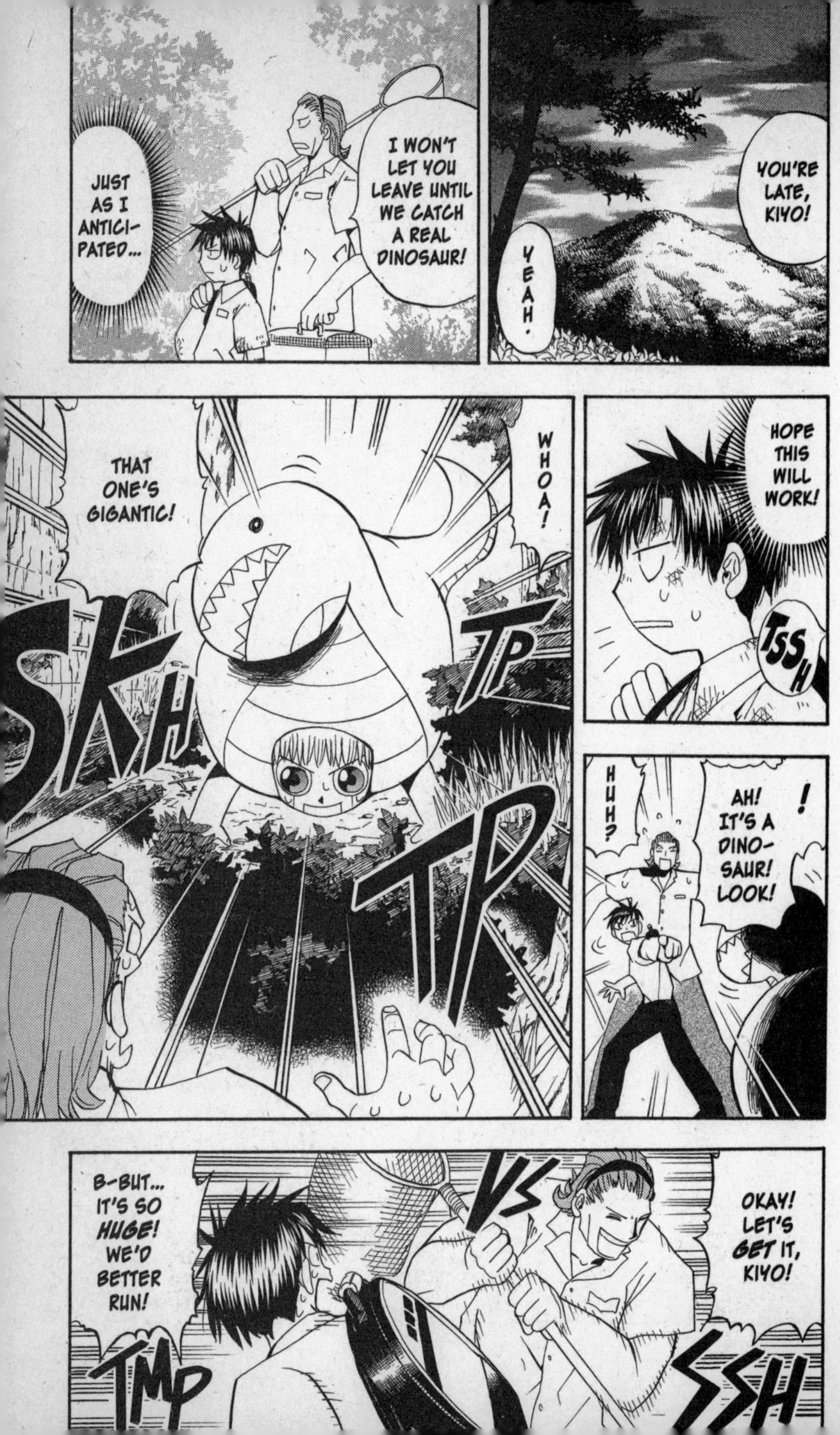
YOU'RE LATE, KIYO!
YEAH.
I WON'T LET YOU LEAVE UNTIL WE CATCH A REAL DINOSAUR!
JUST AS I ANTICIPATED...
HOPE THIS WILL WORK!
TSSH
AH! IT'S A DINOSAUR! LOOK!
!
HUH?
WHOA!
TP
TP
SKSH
THAT ONE'S GIGANTIC!
OKAY! LET'S GET IT, KIYO!
SSH
VS
B-BUT... IT'S SO HUGE! WE'D BETTER RUN!
TMP

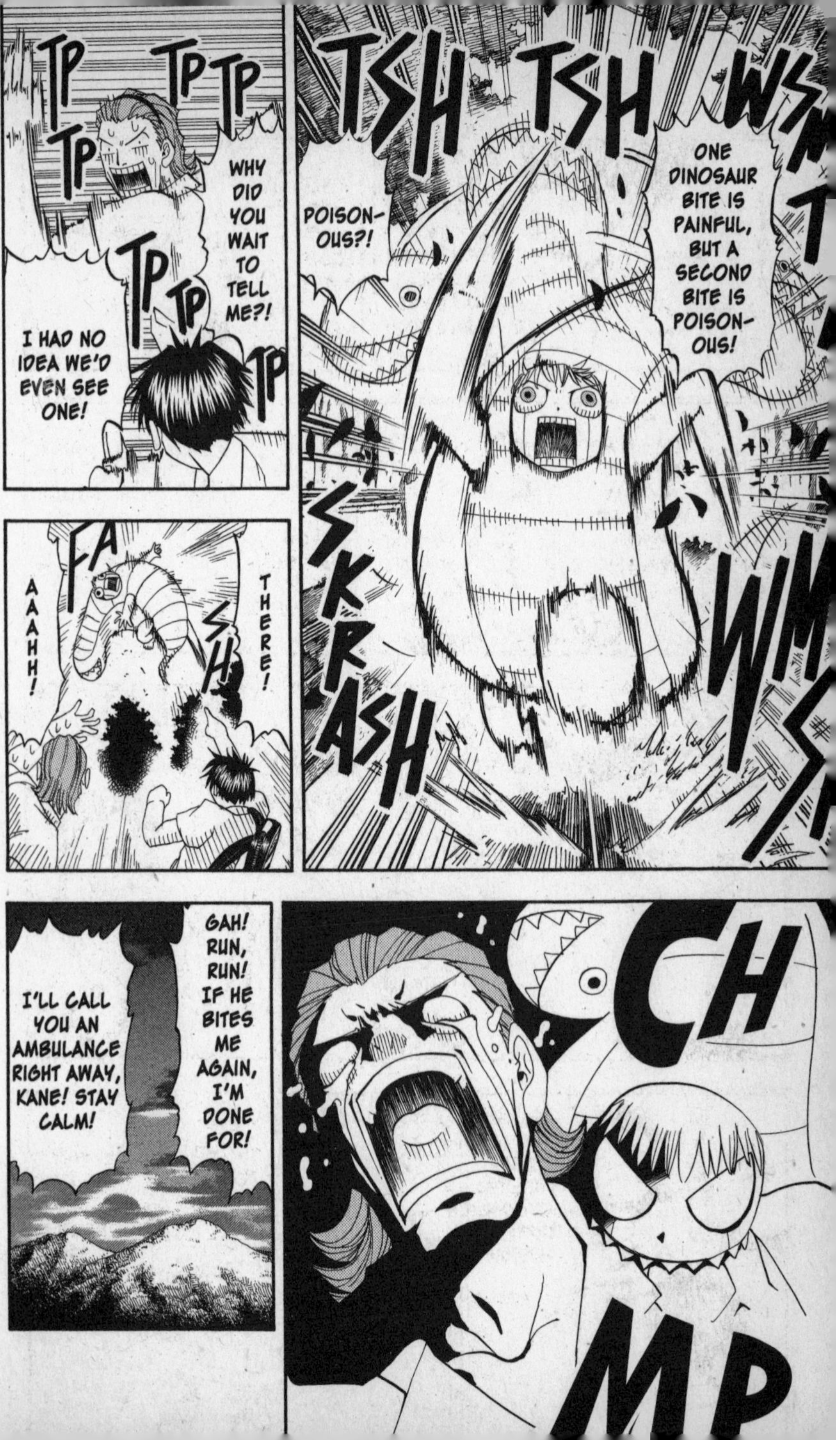
TSH TSH
ONE DINOSAUR BITE IS PAINFUL, BUT A SECOND BITE IS POISON-OUS!
POISON-OUS?!
SKRASH
TP TP TP TP TP TP TP
WHY DID YOU WAIT TO TELL ME?!
I HAD NO IDEA WE'D EVEN SEE ONE!
FA
SH
THERE!
AAAAHH!
CH
MP
GAH! RUN, RUN! IF HE BITES ME AGAIN, I'M DONE FOR!
I'LL CALL YOU AN AMBULANCE RIGHT AWAY, KANE! STAY CALM!

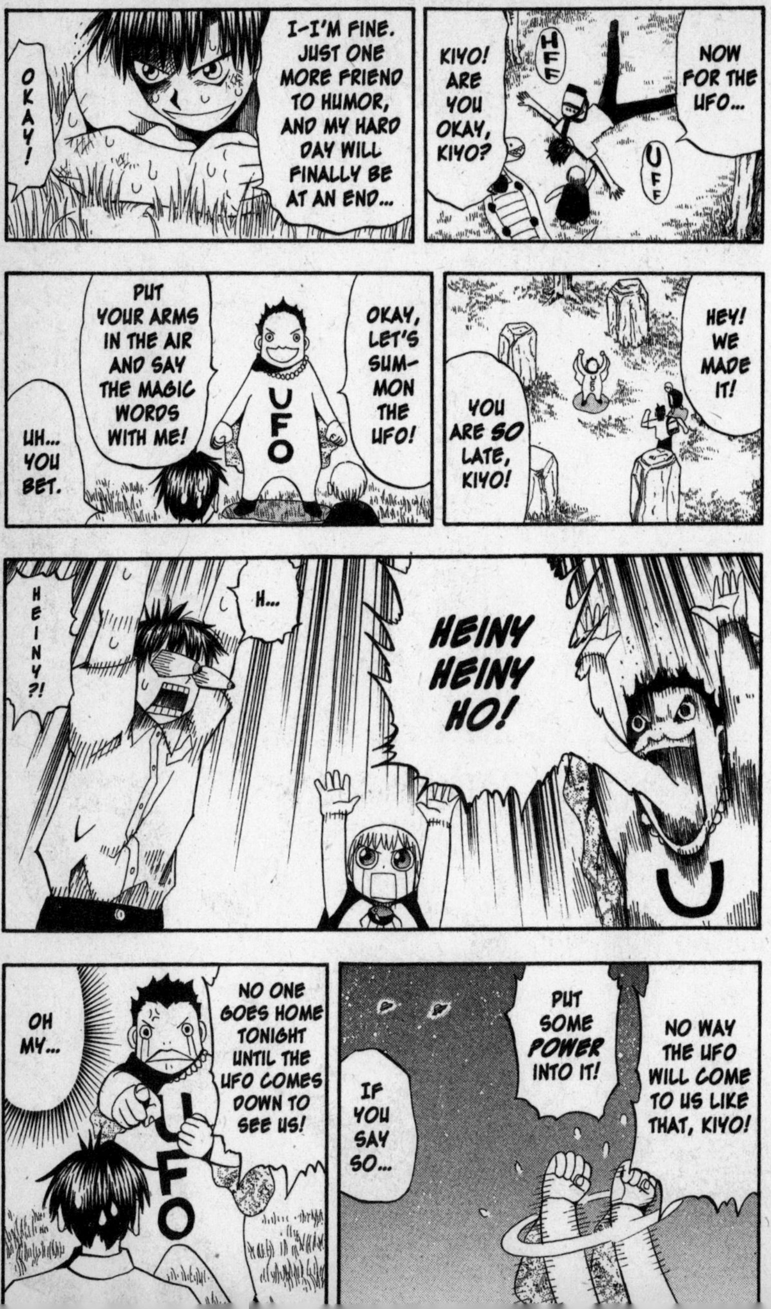
NOW FOR THE UFO...
HFF
KIYO! ARE YOU OKAY, KIYO?
UFF
I-I'M FINE. JUST ONE MORE FRIEND TO HUMOR, AND MY HARD DAY WILL FINALLY BE AT AN END...
OKAY!
HEY! WE MADE IT!
YOU ARE SO LATE, KIYO!
OKAY, LET'S SUMMON THE UFO!
PUT YOUR ARMS IN THE AIR AND SAY THE MAGIC WORDS WITH ME!
UH... YOU BET.
HEINY HEINY HO!
H...
HEINY?!
NO WAY THE UFO WILL COME TO US LIKE THAT, KIYO!
PUT SOME POWER INTO IT!
IF YOU SAY SO...
NO ONE GOES HOME TONIGHT UNTIL THE UFO COMES DOWN TO SEE US!
OH MY...

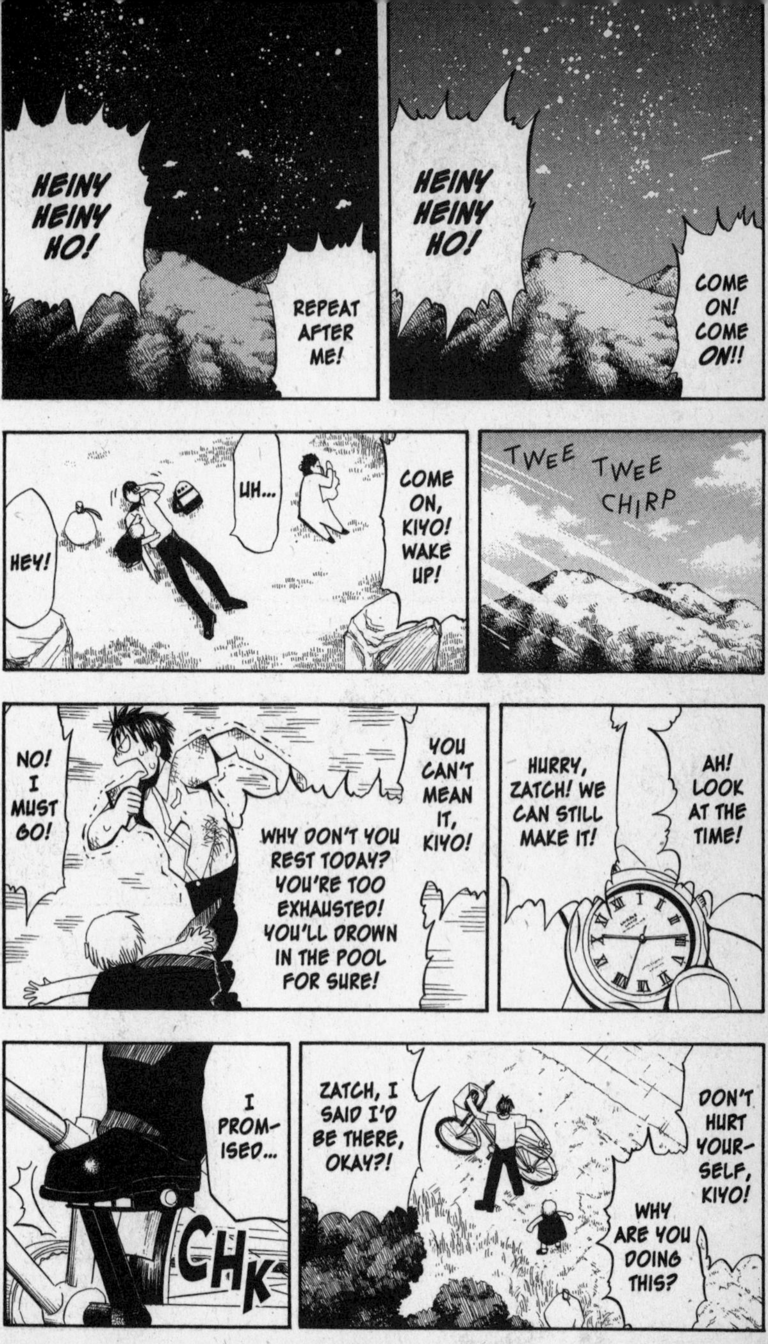
HEINY HEINY HO!
COME ON! COME ON!!
HEINY HEINY HO!
REPEAT AFTER ME!
TWEE TWEE CHIRP
COME ON, KIYO! WAKE UP!
UH...
HEY!
AH! LOOK AT THE TIME!
HURRY, ZATCH! WE CAN STILL MAKE IT!
YOU CAN'T MEAN IT, KIYO!
WHY DON'T YOU REST TODAY? YOU'RE TOO EXHAUSTED! YOU'LL DROWN IN THE POOL FOR SURE!
NO! I MUST GO!
DON'T HURT YOURSELF, KIYO!
WHY ARE YOU DOING THIS?
ZATCH, I SAID I'D BE THERE, OKAY?!
I PROMISED...
CHK

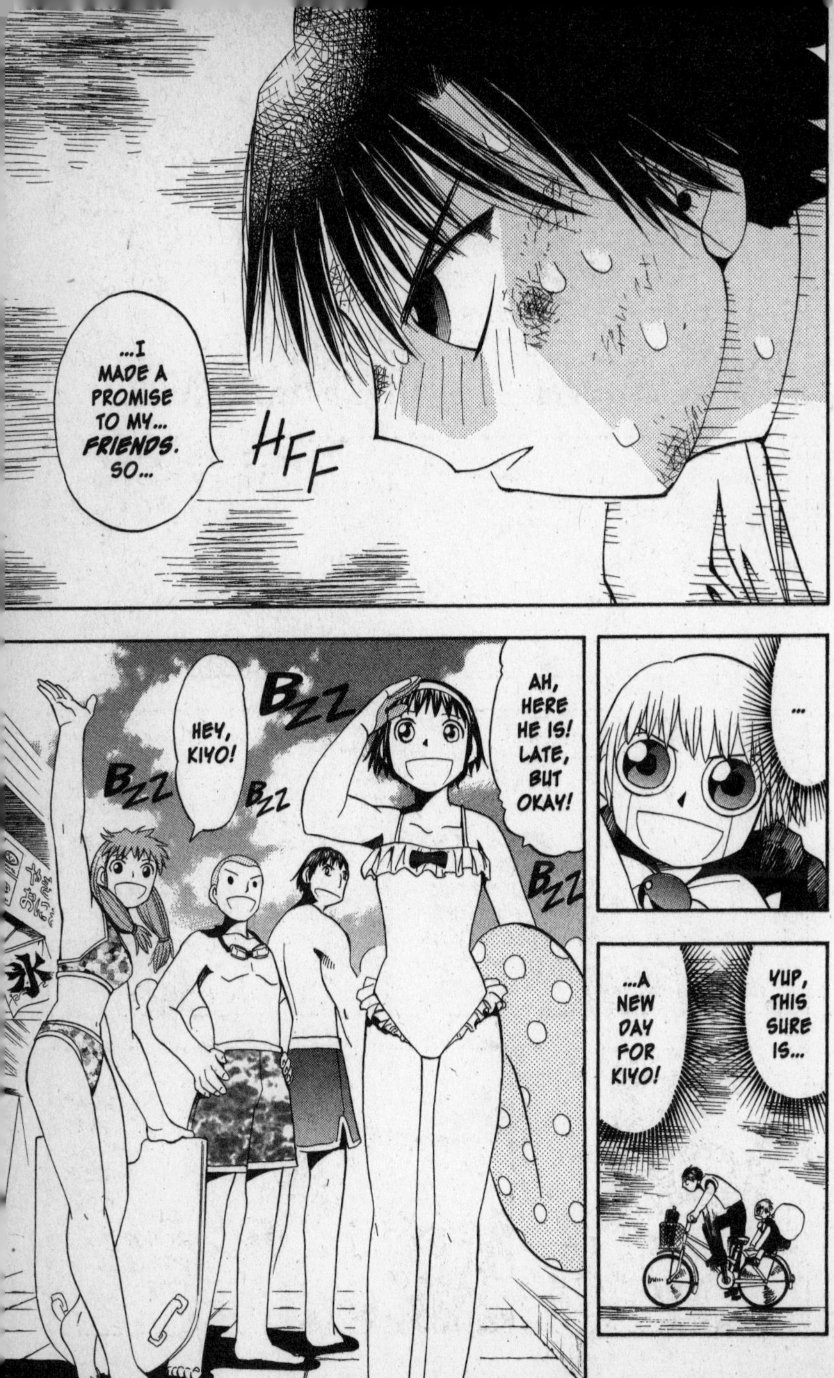
...I MADE A PROMISE TO MY... FRIENDS. SO...
HFF
...
YUP, THIS SURE IS...
...A NEW DAY FOR KIYO!
AH, HERE HE IS! LATE, BUT OKAY!
BZZ
HEY, KIYO!
BZZ
BZZ
BZZ

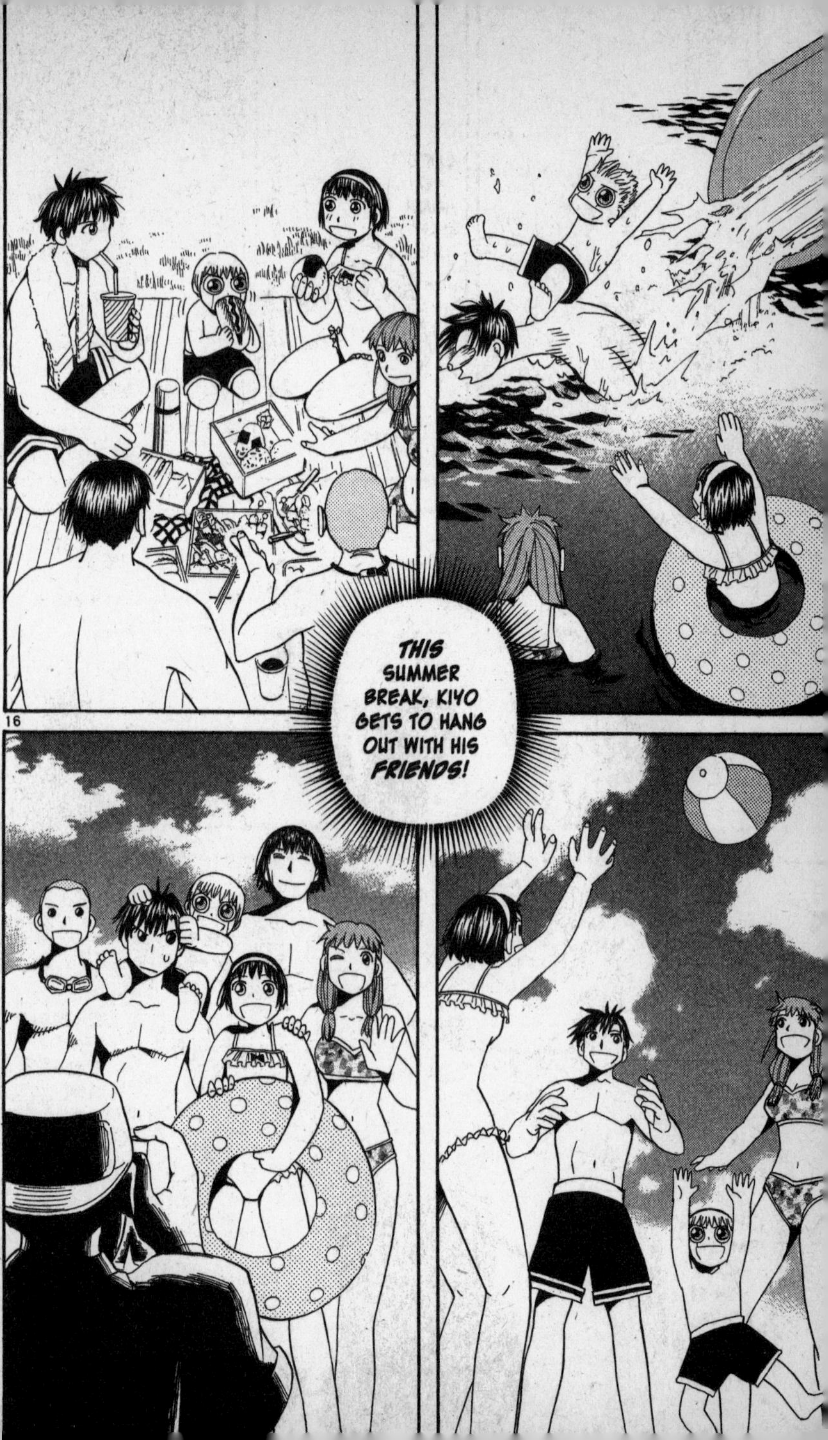
THIS SUMMER BREAK, KIYO GETS TO HANG OUT WITH HIS FRIENDS!

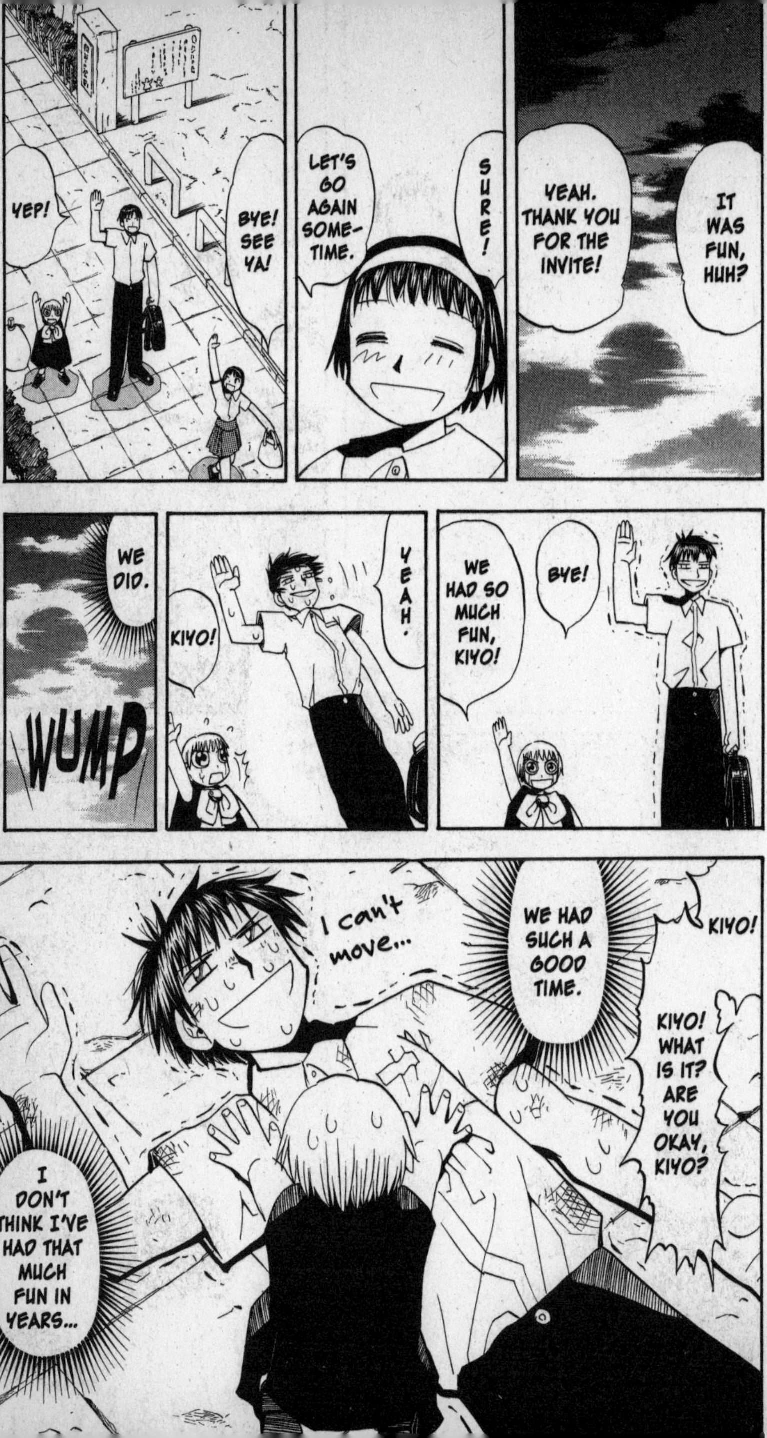
IT WAS FUN, HUH?
YEAH. THANK YOU FOR THE INVITE!
SURE!
LET'S GO AGAIN SOMETIME.
BYE! SEE YA!
YEP!
BYE!
WE HAD SO MUCH FUN, KIYO!
YEAH.
KIYO!
WE DID.
WUMP
KIYO!
WE HAD SUCH A GOOD TIME.
I can't move...
KIYO! WHAT IS IT? ARE YOU OKAY, KIYO?
I DON'T THINK I'VE HAD THAT MUCH FUN IN YEARS...

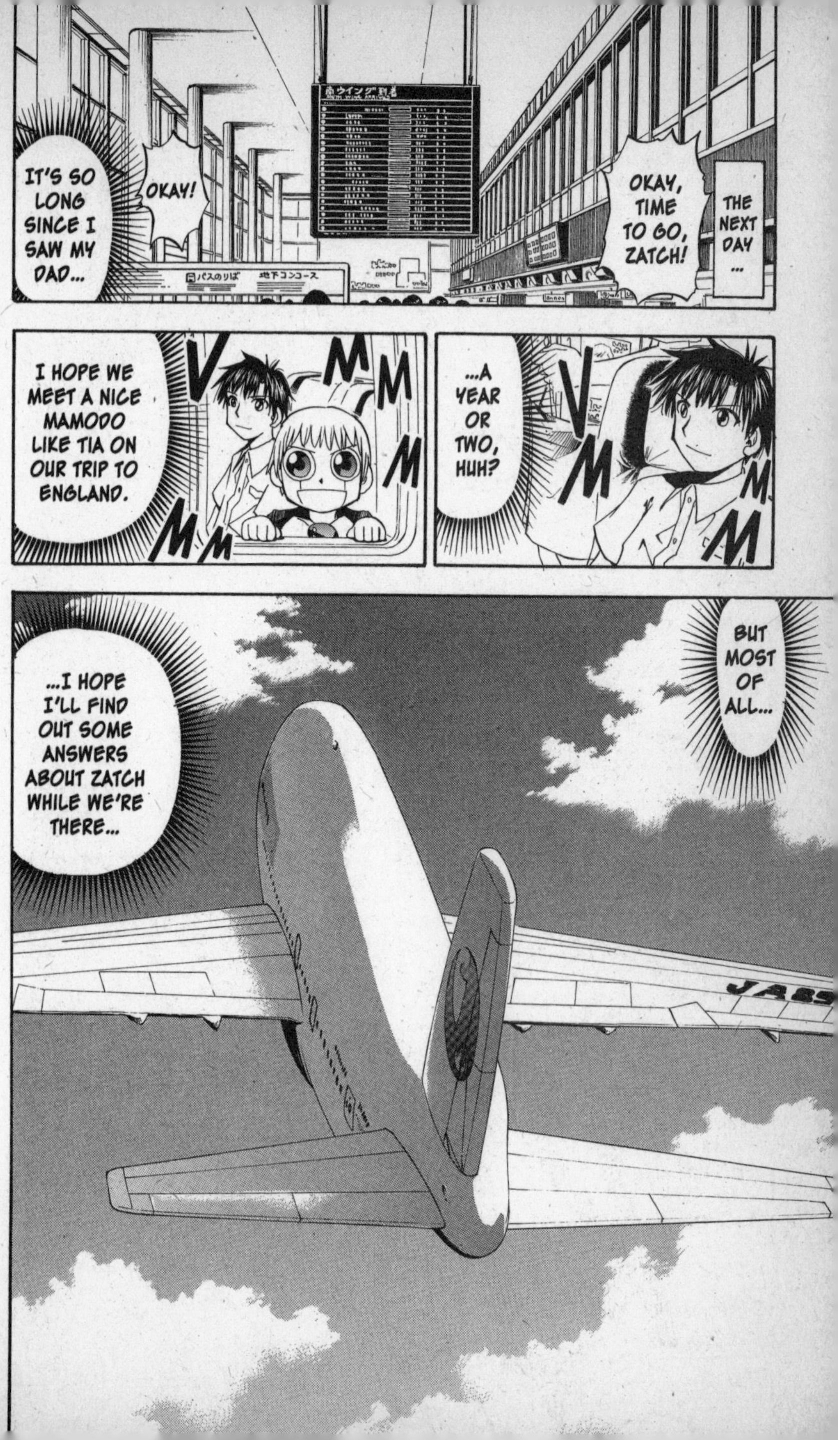
THE NEXT DAY...
OKAY, TIME TO GO, ZATCH!
OKAY!
IT'S SO LONG SINCE I SAW MY DAD...
バスのりば
地下コンコース
...A YEAR OR TWO, HUH?
I HOPE WE MEET A NICE MAMODO LIKE TIA ON OUR TRIP TO ENGLAND.
BUT MOST OF ALL...
...I HOPE I'LL FIND OUT SOME ANSWERS ABOUT ZATCH WHILE WE'RE THERE...

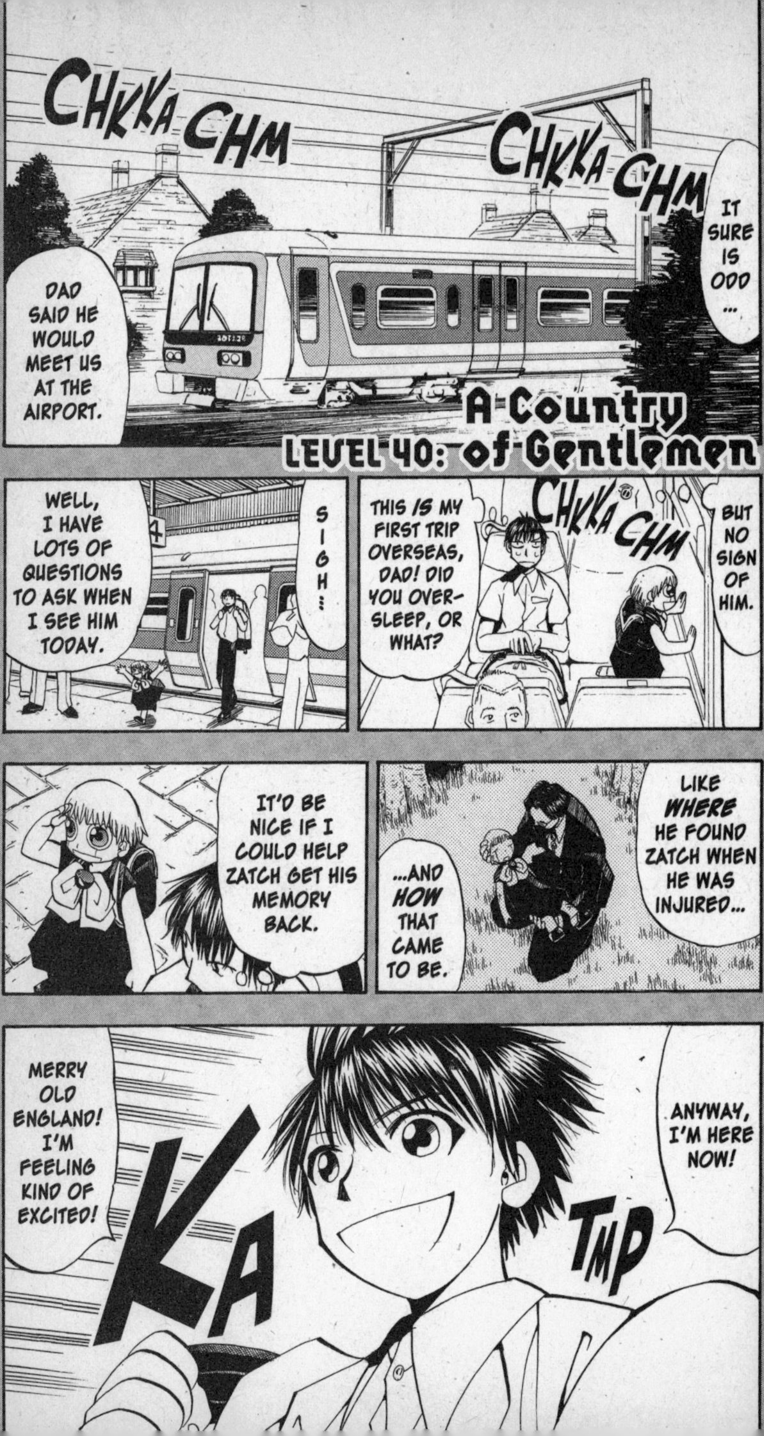
CHKKA CHM
CHKKA CHM
IT SURE IS ODD...
DAD SAID HE WOULD MEET US AT THE AIRPORT.
LEVEL 40: A Country of Gentlemen
CHKKA CHM
BUT NO SIGN OF HIM.
THIS *IS* MY FIRST TRIP OVERSEAS, DAD! DID YOU OVER-SLEEP, OR WHAT?
SIGH...
WELL, I HAVE LOTS OF QUESTIONS TO ASK WHEN I SEE HIM TODAY.
LIKE *WHERE* HE FOUND ZATCH WHEN HE WAS INJURED...
...AND *HOW* THAT CAME TO BE.
IT'D BE NICE IF I COULD HELP ZATCH GET HIS MEMORY BACK.
ANYWAY, I'M HERE NOW!
MERRY OLD ENGLAND! I'M FEELING KIND OF EXCITED!
KA
TMP

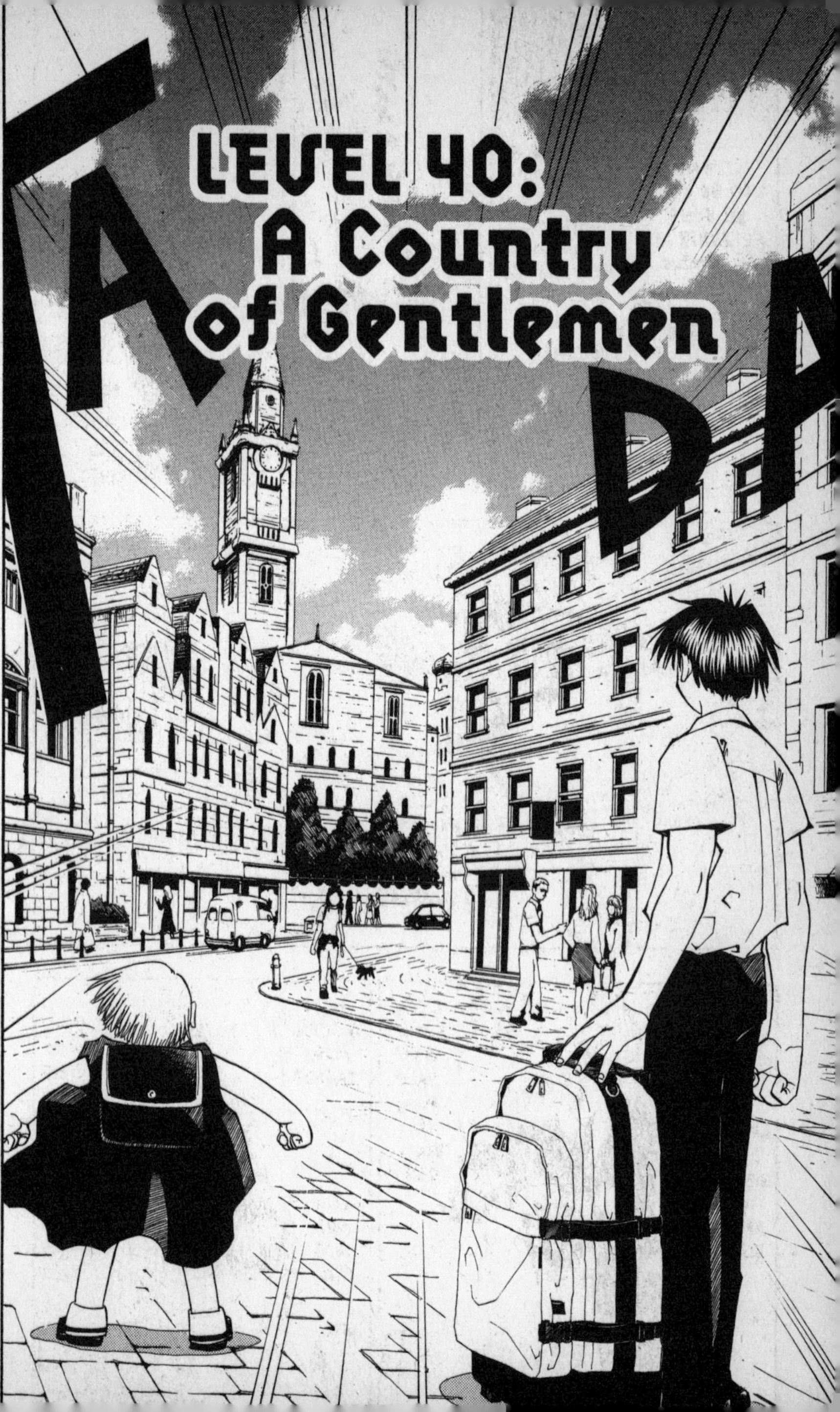
TA
DA
LEVEL 40:
A Country
of Gentlemen

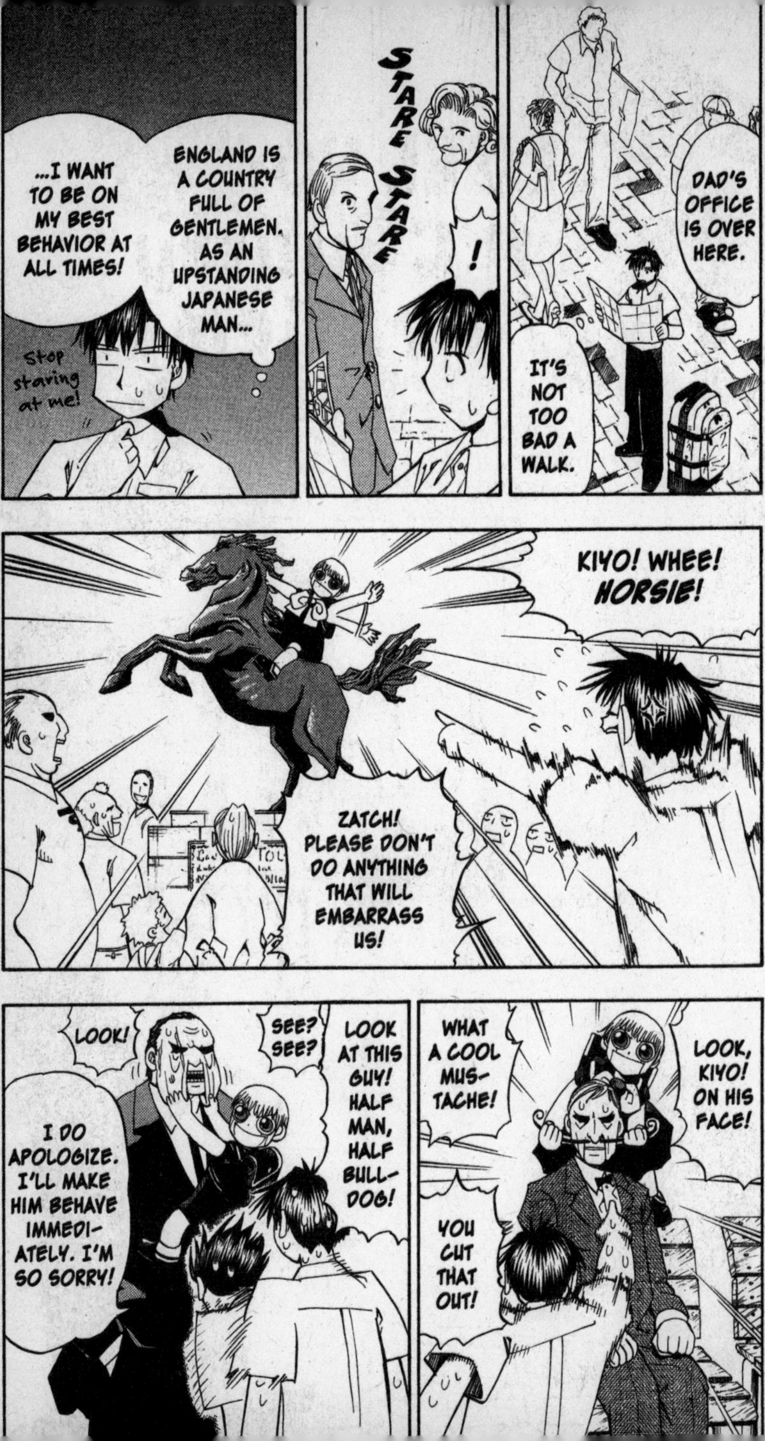
DAD'S OFFICE IS OVER HERE.
IT'S NOT TOO BAD A WALK.
STARE STARE
!
ENGLAND IS A COUNTRY FULL OF GENTLEMEN. AS AN UPSTANDING JAPANESE MAN...
...I WANT TO BE ON MY BEST BEHAVIOR AT ALL TIMES!
Stop staring at me!
KIYO! WHEE! HORSIE!
ZATCH! PLEASE DON'T DO ANYTHING THAT WILL EMBARRASS US!
LOOK, KIYO! ON HIS FACE!
WHAT A COOL MUS-TACHE!
YOU CUT THAT OUT!
LOOK AT THIS GUY! HALF MAN, HALF BULL-DOG!
SEE? SEE?
LOOK!
I DO APOLOGIZE. I'LL MAKE HIM BEHAVE IMMEDI-ATELY. I'M SO SORRY!

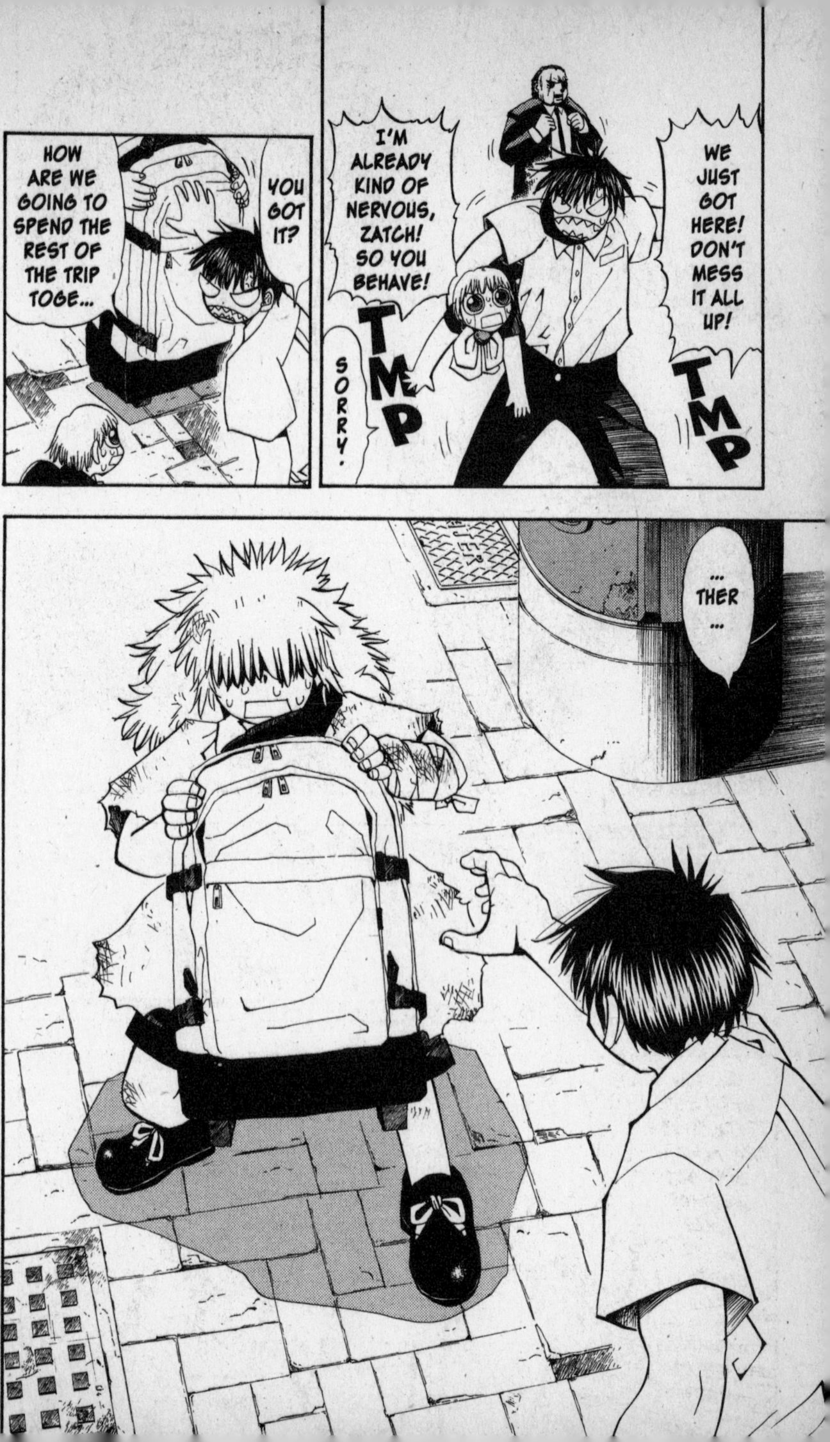
WE JUST GOT HERE! DON'T MESS IT ALL UP!
TMP
I'M ALREADY KIND OF NERVOUS, ZATCH! SO YOU BEHAVE!
TMP
SORRY.
YOU GOT IT?
HOW ARE WE GOING TO SPEND THE REST OF THE TRIP TOGE...
...THER...

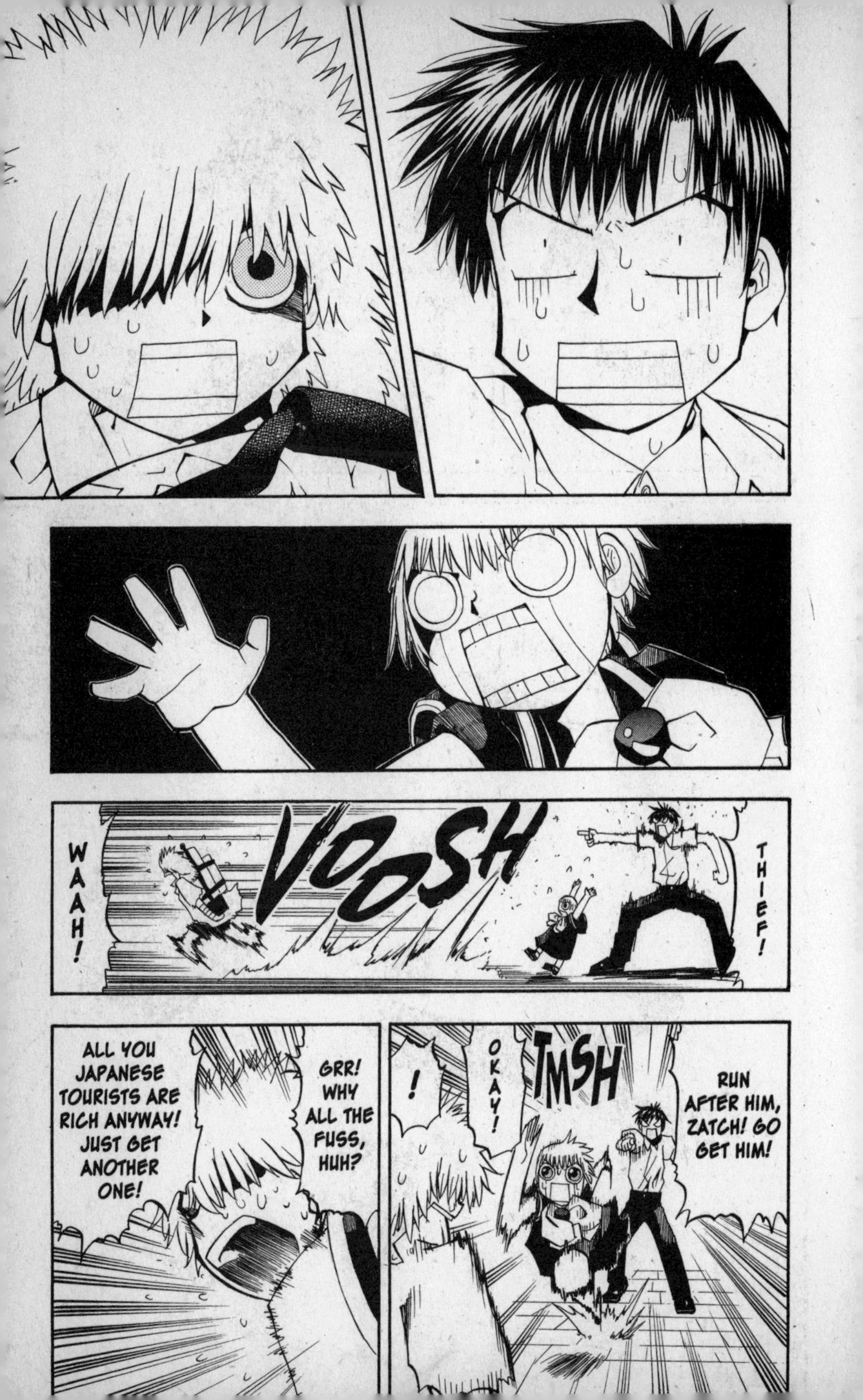
THIEF!
VOOSH
WAAH!
RUN AFTER HIM, ZATCH! GO GET HIM!
TMSH
OKAY!
!
GRR! WHY ALL THE FUSS, HUH?
ALL YOU JAPANESE TOURISTS ARE RICH ANYWAY! JUST GET ANOTHER ONE!

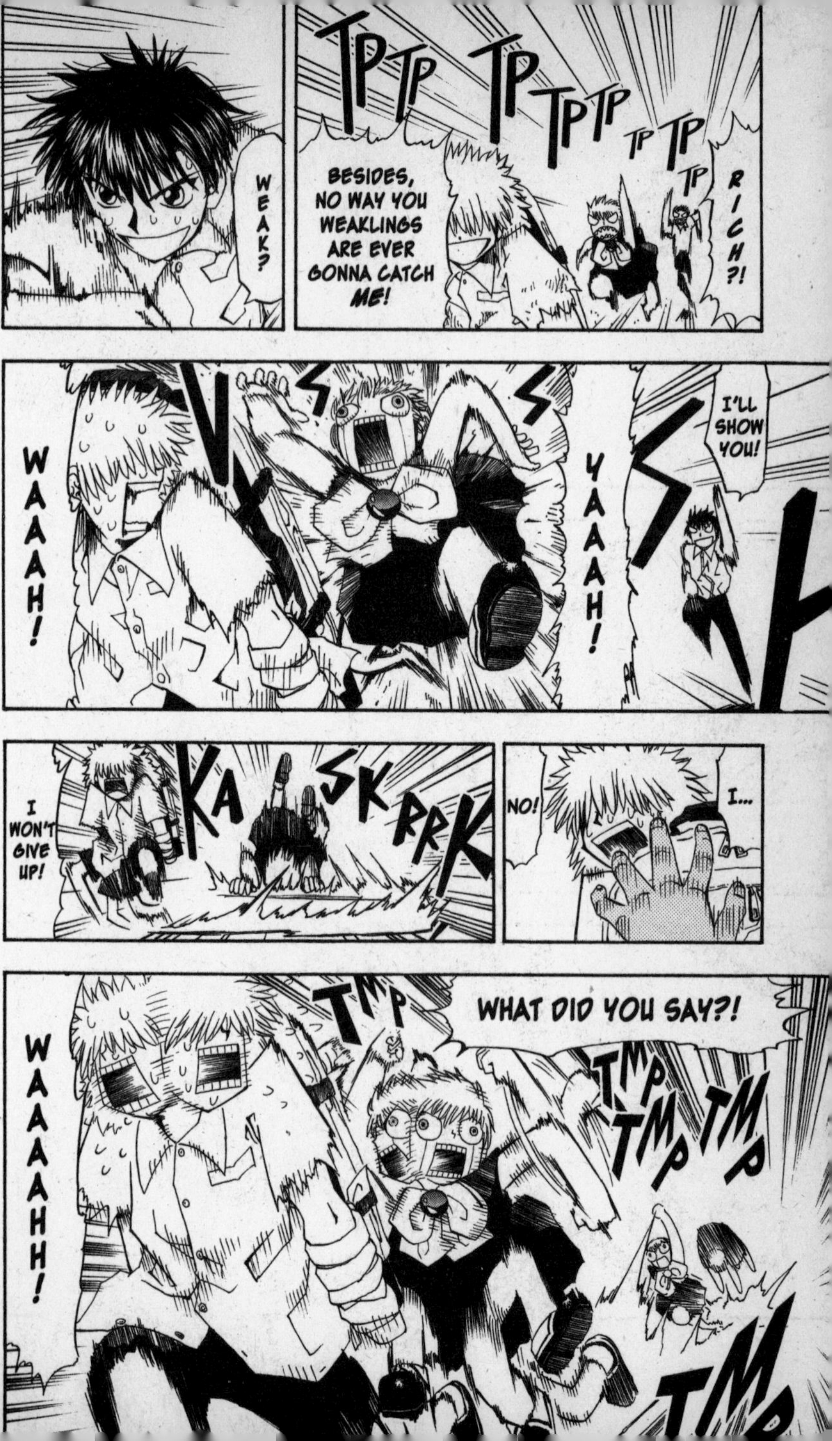
TPTP TP TPTP TP TP TP
RICH?!
BESIDES, NO WAY YOU WEAKLINGS ARE EVER GONNA CATCH ME!
WEAK?
I'LL SHOW YOU!
YAAAAH!
WAAAAH!
I...
NO!
KA SKRRK
I WON'T GIVE UP!
WHAT DID YOU SAY?!
TMP TMP TMP TMP TMP
WAAAAAHH!

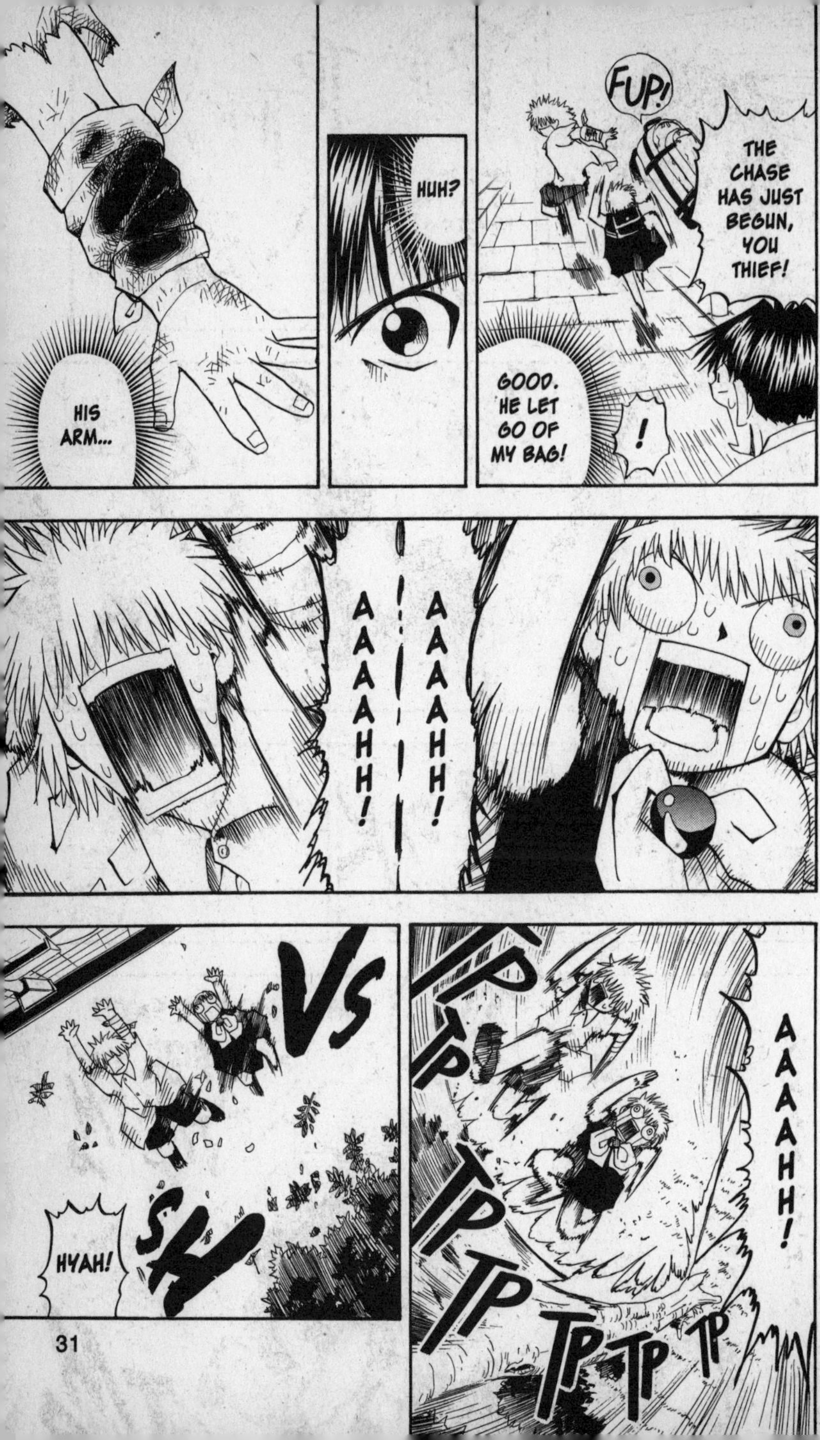
FUP!
THE CHASE HAS JUST BEGUN, YOU THIEF!
GOOD. HE LET GO OF MY BAG!
!
HUH?
HIS ARM...
AAAAAHH!
AAAAAHH!
TP TP TP TP TP TP TP TP
AAAAAHH!
VS
SH
HYAH!

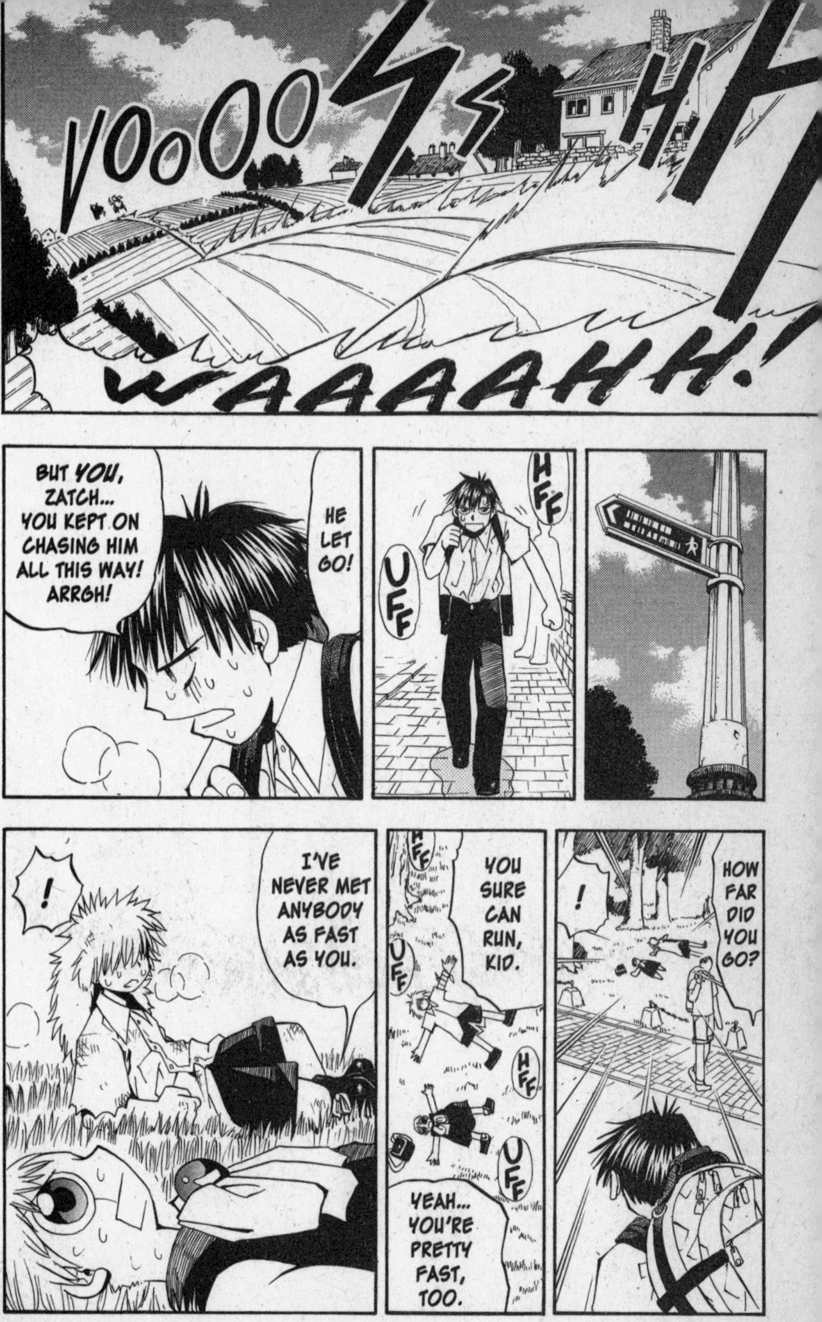
VOOOOSSHH!
WAAAAAHH!
HFF
UFF
HE LET GO!
BUT YOU, ZATCH... YOU KEPT ON CHASING HIM ALL THIS WAY! ARRGH!
!
HOW FAR DID YOU GO?
HFF
UFF
YOU SURE CAN RUN, KID.
HFF
UFF
YEAH... YOU'RE PRETTY FAST, TOO.
!
I'VE NEVER MET ANYBODY AS FAST AS YOU.

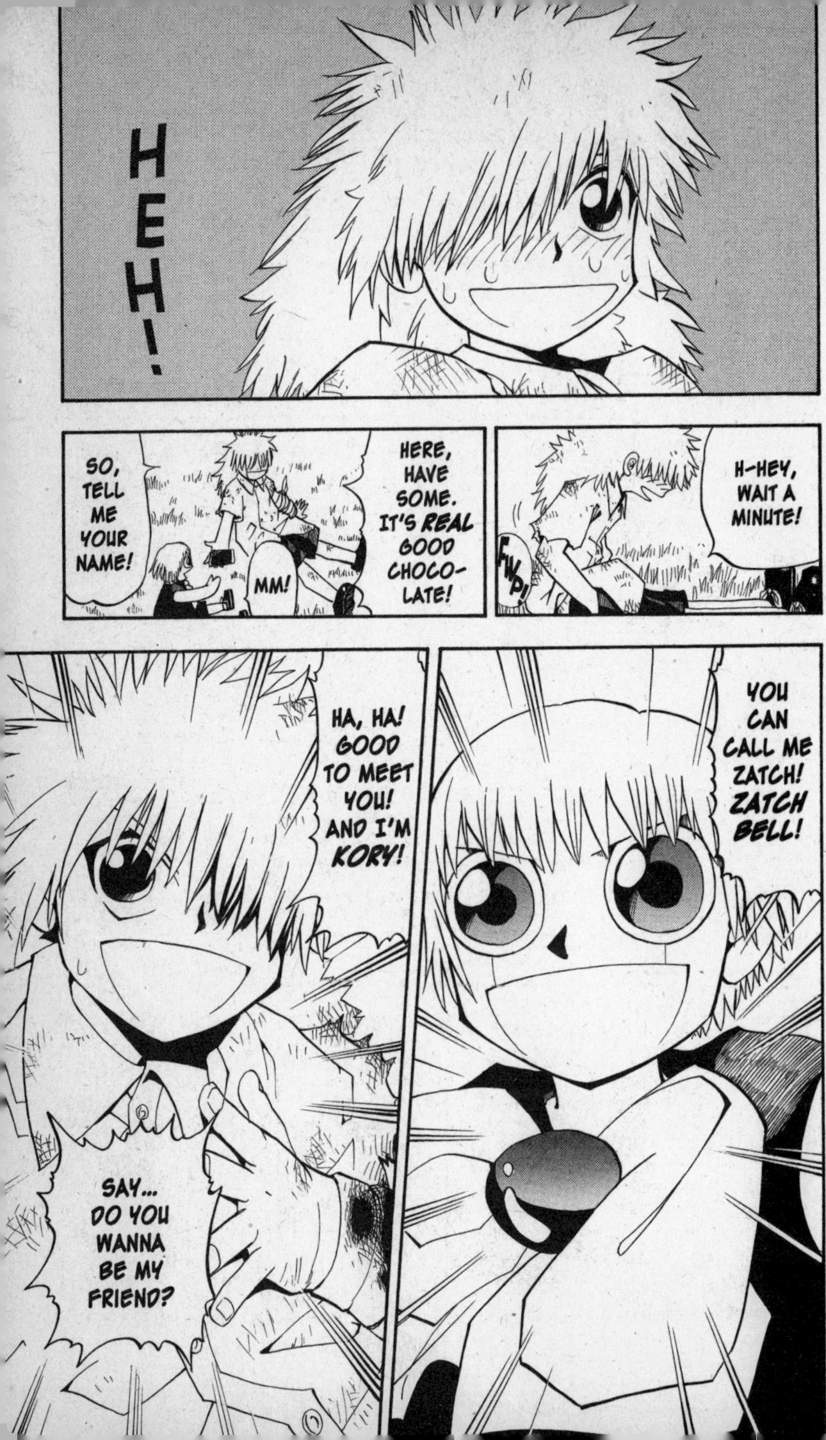
HEH!
H-HEY, WAIT A MINUTE!
FWP!
HERE, HAVE SOME. IT'S REAL GOOD CHOCOLATE!
MM!
SO, TELL ME YOUR NAME!
YOU CAN CALL ME ZATCH! ZATCH BELL!
HA, HA! GOOD TO MEET YOU! AND I'M KORY!
SAY... DO YOU WANNA BE MY FRIEND?

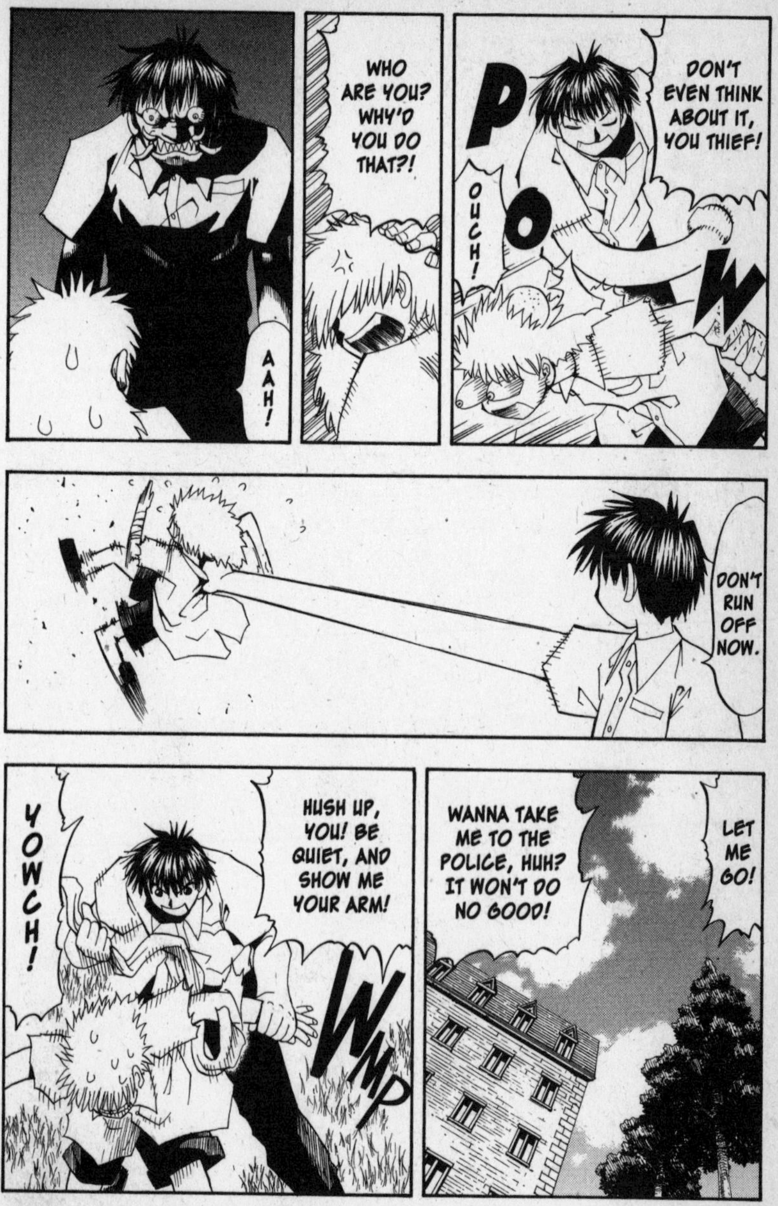
DON'T EVEN THINK ABOUT IT, YOU THIEF!
POW
OUCH!
WHO ARE YOU? WHY'D YOU DO THAT?!
AAH!
DON'T RUN OFF NOW.
LET ME GO!
WANNA TAKE ME TO THE POLICE, HUH? IT WON'T DO NO GOOD!
HUSH UP, YOU! BE QUIET, AND SHOW ME YOUR ARM!
WMP
YOWCH!

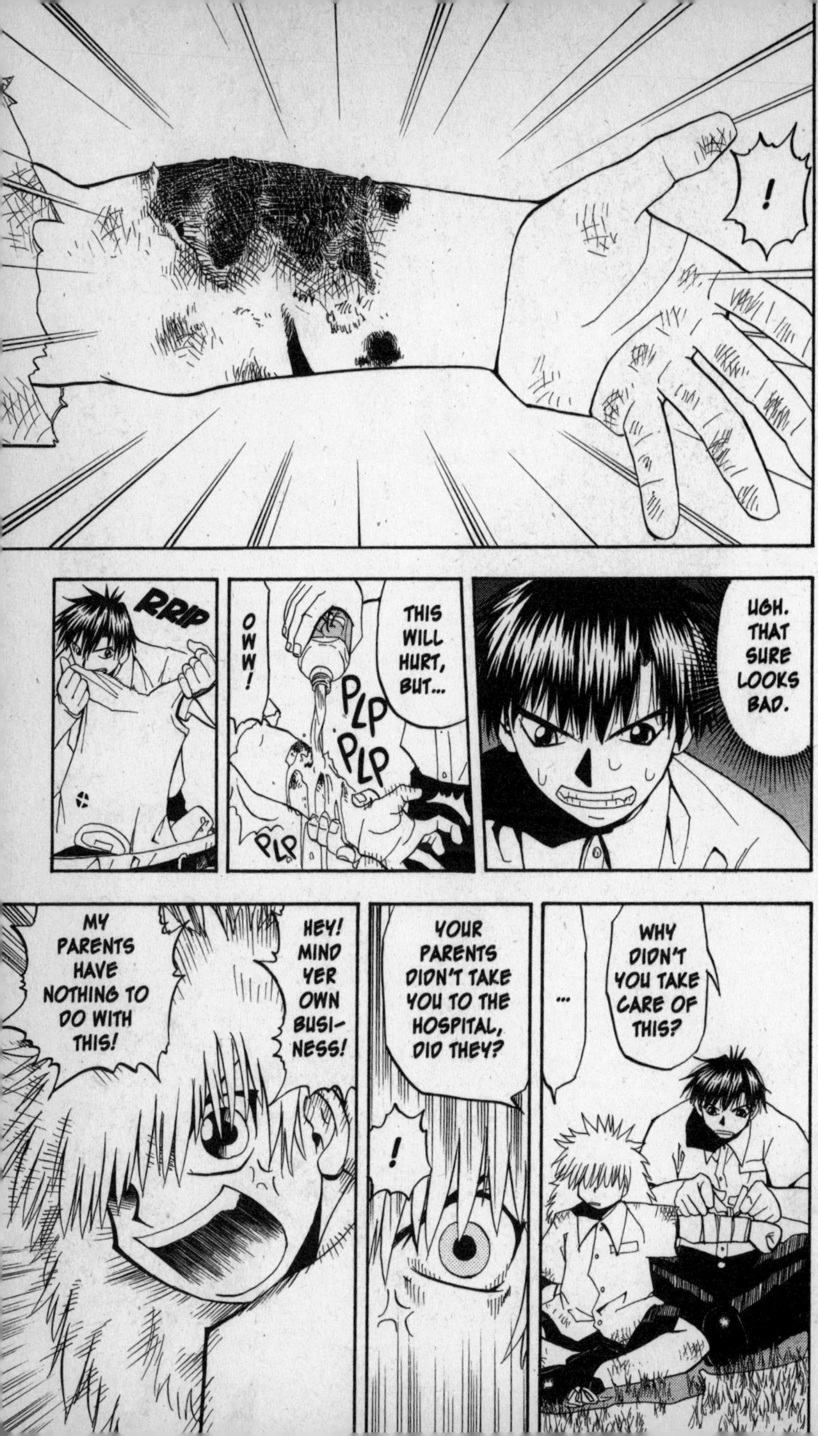
!
UGH. THAT SURE LOOKS BAD.
THIS WILL HURT, BUT...
OWW!
PLP PLP
PLP
RRIP
WHY DIDN'T YOU TAKE CARE OF THIS?
...
YOUR PARENTS DIDN'T TAKE YOU TO THE HOSPITAL, DID THEY?
!
HEY! MIND YER OWN BUSI-NESS!
MY PARENTS HAVE NOTHING TO DO WITH THIS!

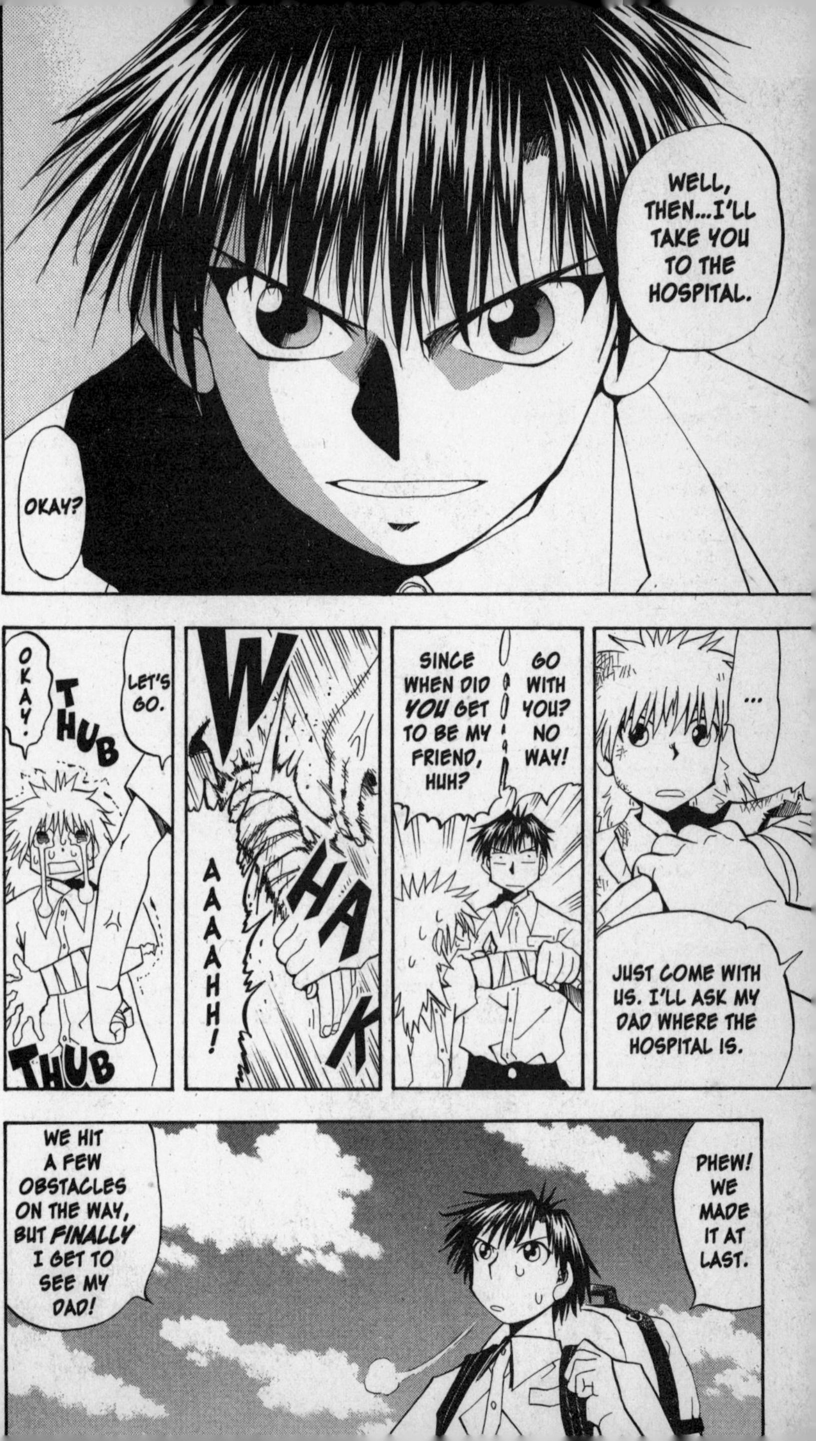
WELL, THEN...I'LL TAKE YOU TO THE HOSPITAL.
OKAY?
...
JUST COME WITH US. I'LL ASK MY DAD WHERE THE HOSPITAL IS.
GO WITH YOU? NO WAY!
SINCE WHEN DID *YOU* GET TO BE MY FRIEND, HUH?
WHAK
AAAAAHH!
LET'S GO.
OKAY!
THUB
THUB
PHEW! WE MADE IT AT LAST.
WE HIT A FEW OBSTACLES ON THE WAY, BUT *FINALLY* I GET TO SEE MY DAD!

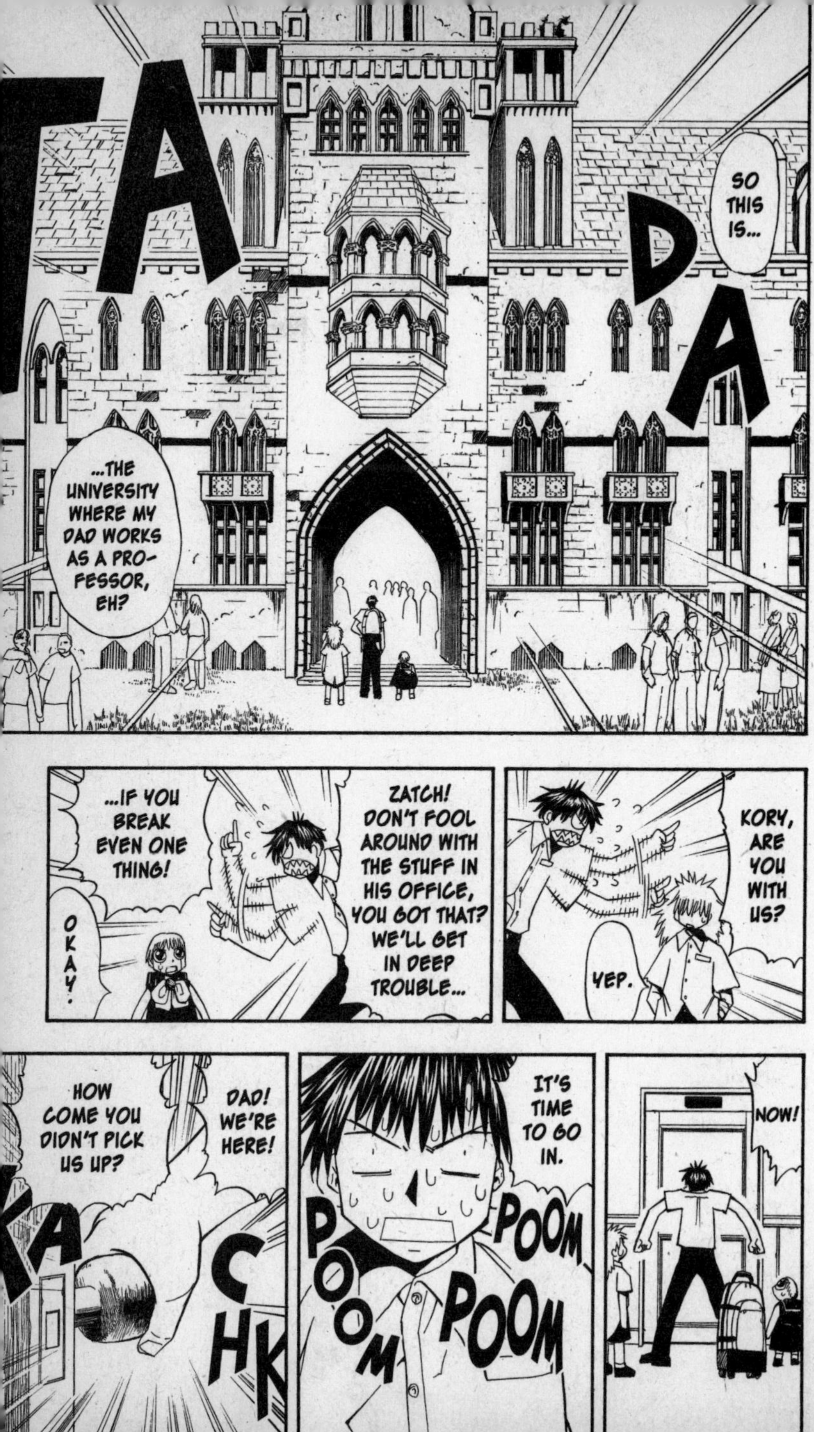
SO THIS IS...
TA DA
...THE UNIVERSITY WHERE MY DAD WORKS AS A PRO-FESSOR, EH?
KORY, ARE YOU WITH US?
YEP.
ZATCH! DON'T FOOL AROUND WITH THE STUFF IN HIS OFFICE, YOU GOT THAT? WE'LL GET IN DEEP TROUBLE...
...IF YOU BREAK EVEN ONE THING!
OKAY.
NOW!
IT'S TIME TO GO IN.
POOM
POOM
POOM
POOM
DAD! WE'RE HERE!
HOW COME YOU DIDN'T PICK US UP?
KA
CHK

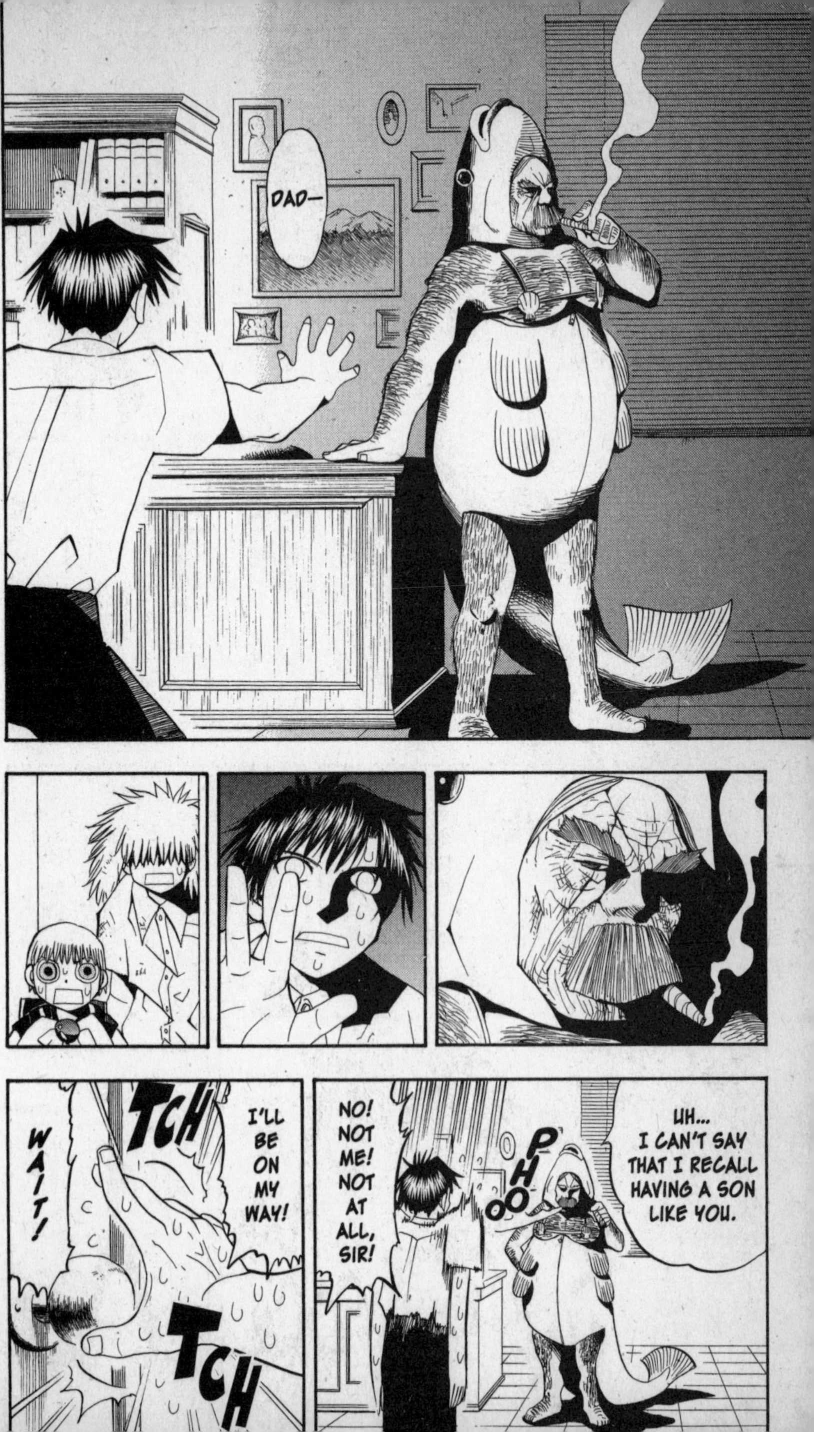
DAD—
UH... I CAN'T SAY THAT I RECALL HAVING A SON LIKE YOU.
PHOOO
NO! NOT ME! NOT AT ALL, SIR!
I'LL BE ON MY WAY!
TCH
WAIT!
TCH

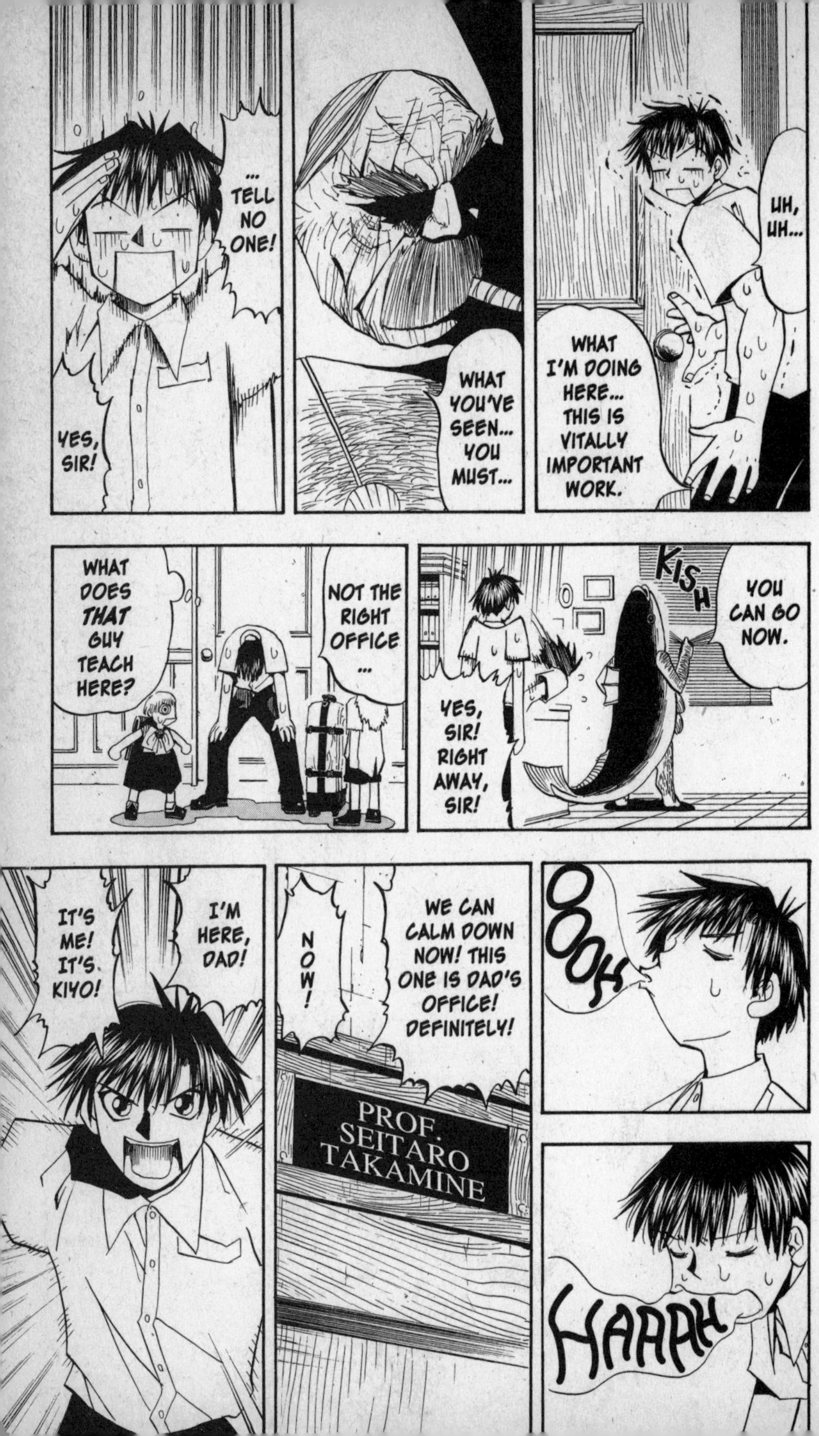
UH, UH...
WHAT I'M DOING HERE... THIS IS VITALLY IMPORTANT WORK.
WHAT YOU'VE SEEN... YOU MUST...
... TELL NO ONE!
YES, SIR!
YOU CAN GO NOW.
KISH
YES, SIR! RIGHT AWAY, SIR!
NOT THE RIGHT OFFICE ...
WHAT DOES THAT GUY TEACH HERE?
OOOH
HAAAH
WE CAN CALM DOWN NOW! THIS ONE IS DAD'S OFFICE! DEFINITELY!
NOW!
PROF. SEITARO TAKAMINE
I'M HERE, DAD!
IT'S ME! IT'S KIYO!

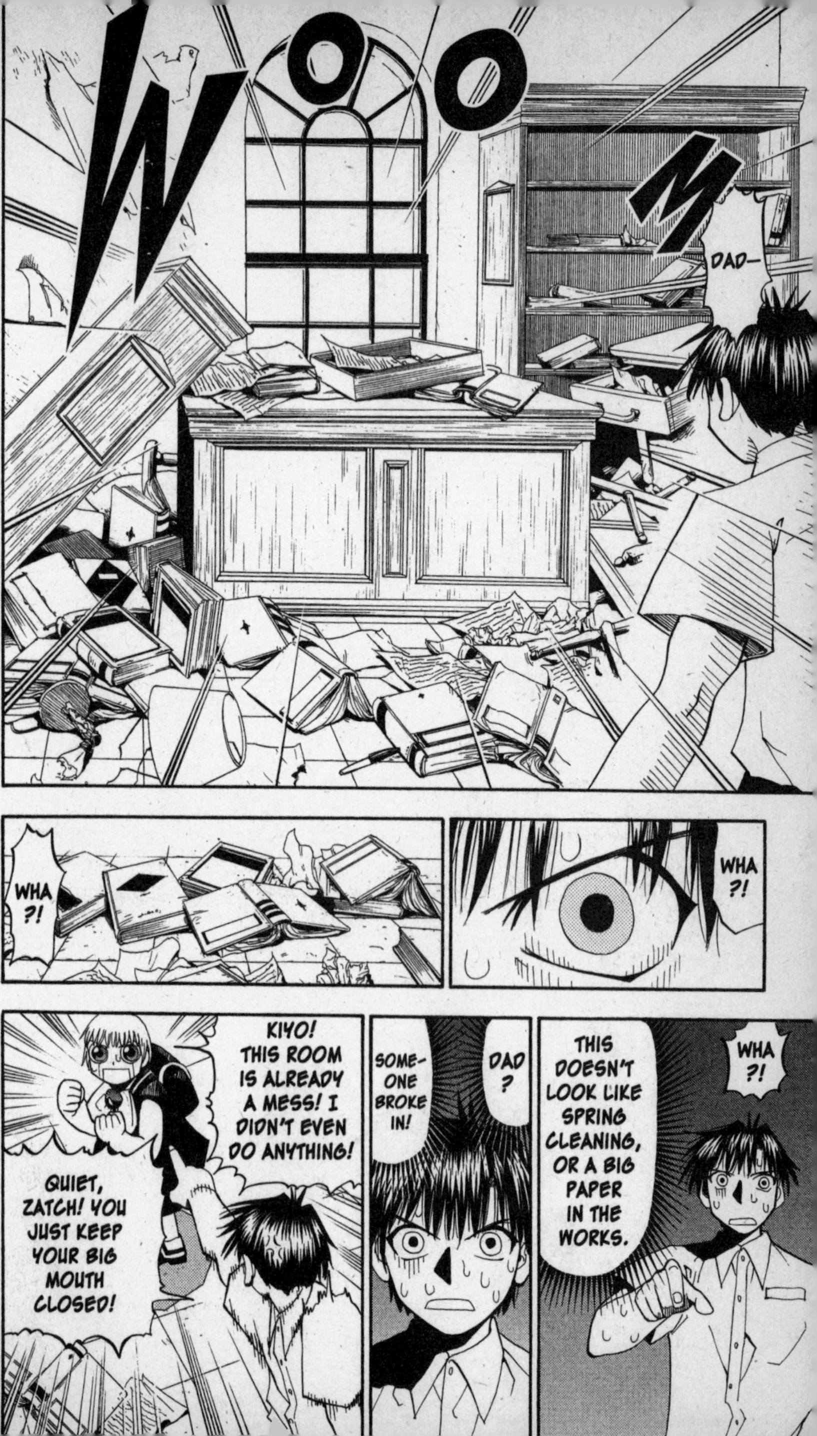
WOOOM
DAD—
WHA ?!
WHA ?!
WHA ?!
THIS DOESN'T LOOK LIKE SPRING CLEANING, OR A BIG PAPER IN THE WORKS.
DAD ?
SOME-ONE BROKE IN!
KIYO! THIS ROOM IS ALREADY A MESS! I DIDN'T EVEN DO ANYTHING!
QUIET, ZATCH! YOU JUST KEEP YOUR BIG MOUTH CLOSED!

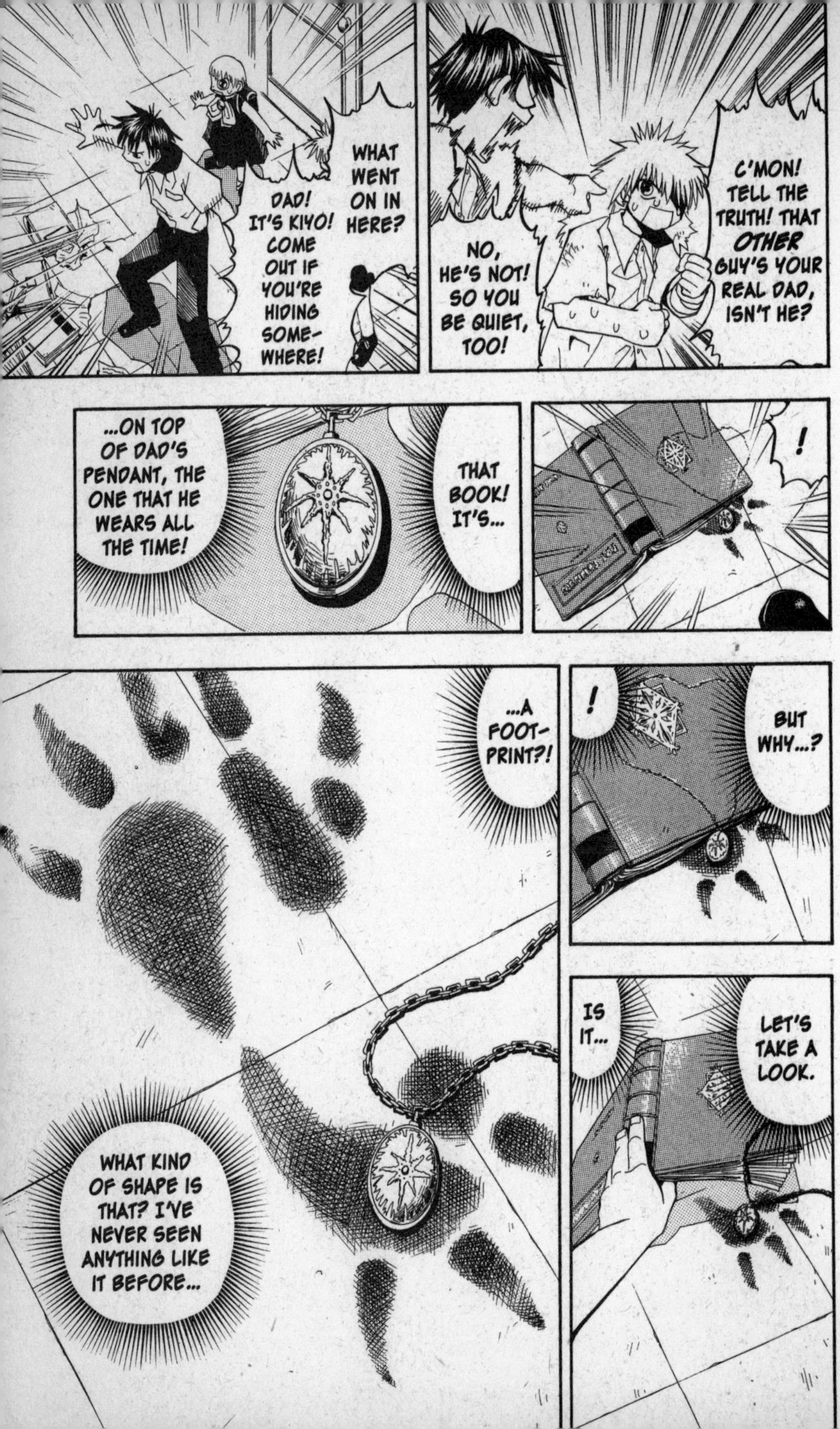
C'MON! TELL THE TRUTH! THAT OTHER GUY'S YOUR REAL DAD, ISN'T HE?
NO, HE'S NOT! SO YOU BE QUIET, TOO!
WHAT WENT ON IN HERE?
DAD! IT'S KIYO! COME OUT IF YOU'RE HIDING SOME-WHERE!
!
THAT BOOK! IT'S...
...ON TOP OF DAD'S PENDANT, THE ONE THAT HE WEARS ALL THE TIME!
BUT WHY...?
!
LET'S TAKE A LOOK.
IS IT...
...A FOOT-PRINT?!
WHAT KIND OF SHAPE IS THAT? I'VE NEVER SEEN ANYTHING LIKE IT BEFORE...

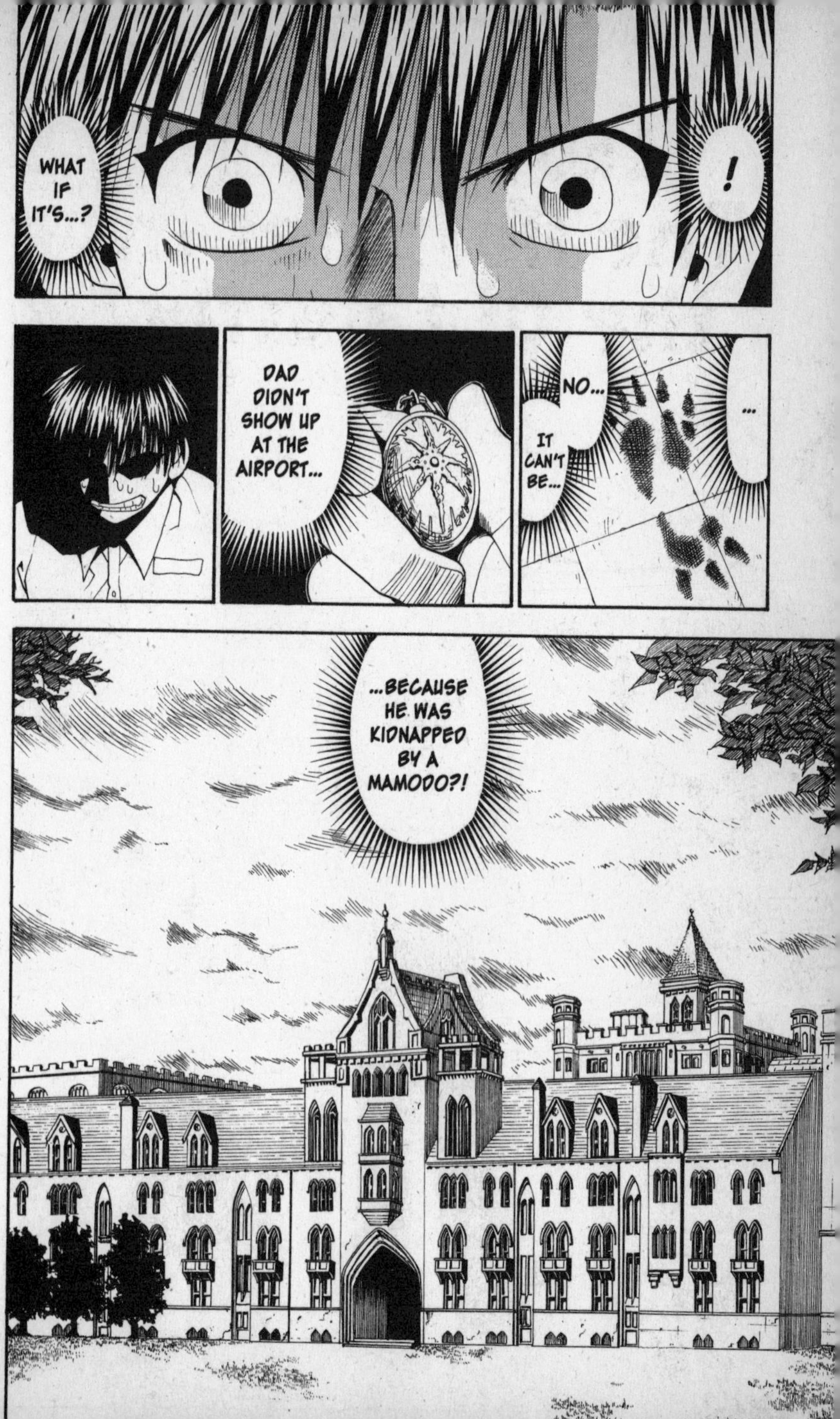
!
WHAT IF IT'S...?
...
NO...
IT CAN'T BE...
DAD DIDN'T SHOW UP AT THE AIRPORT...
...BECAUSE HE WAS KIDNAPPED BY A MAMODO?!

LEVEL 41: The Monster in the Old Castle

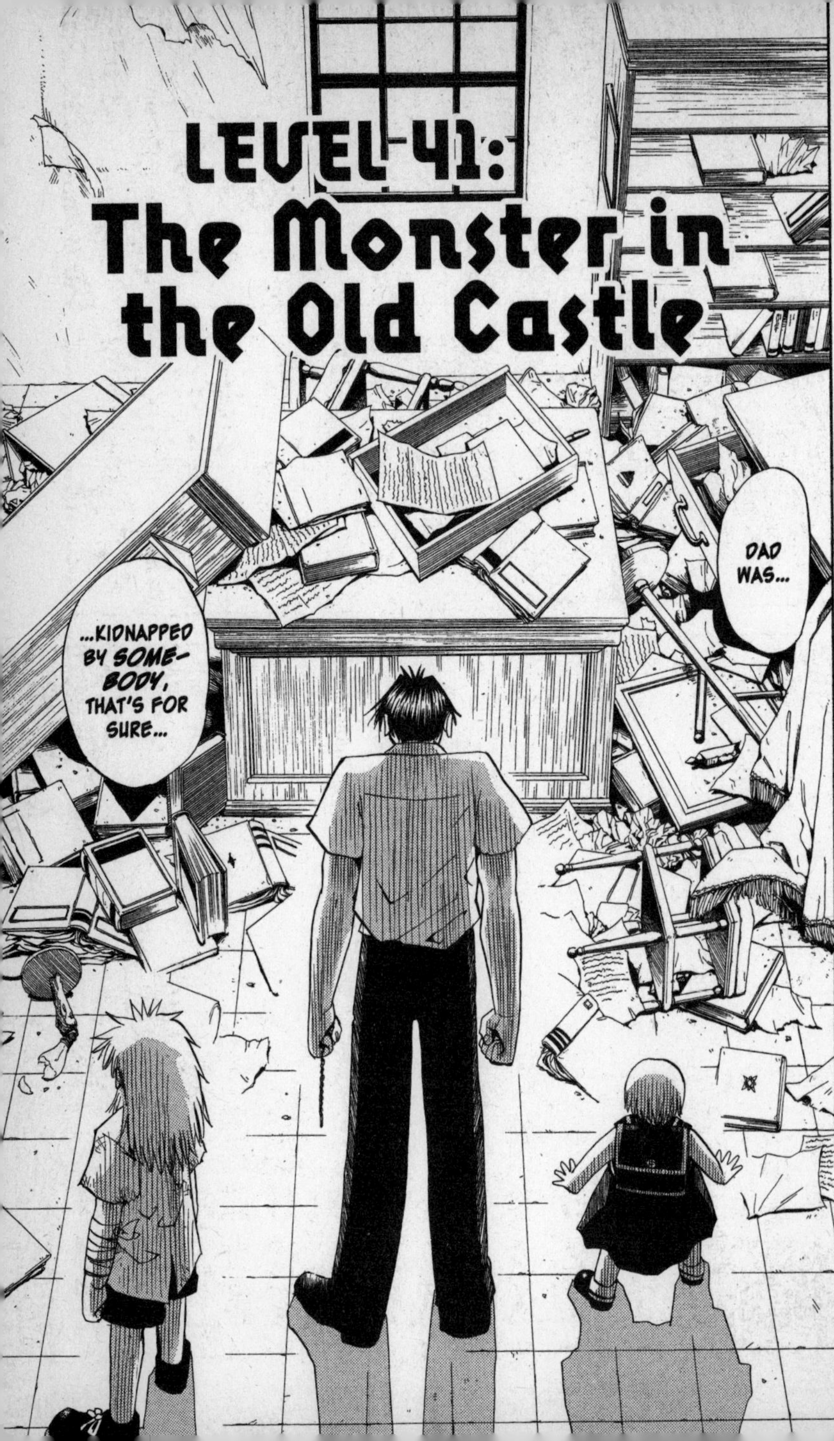
DAD WAS...
...KIDNAPPED BY SOME-BODY, THAT'S FOR SURE...

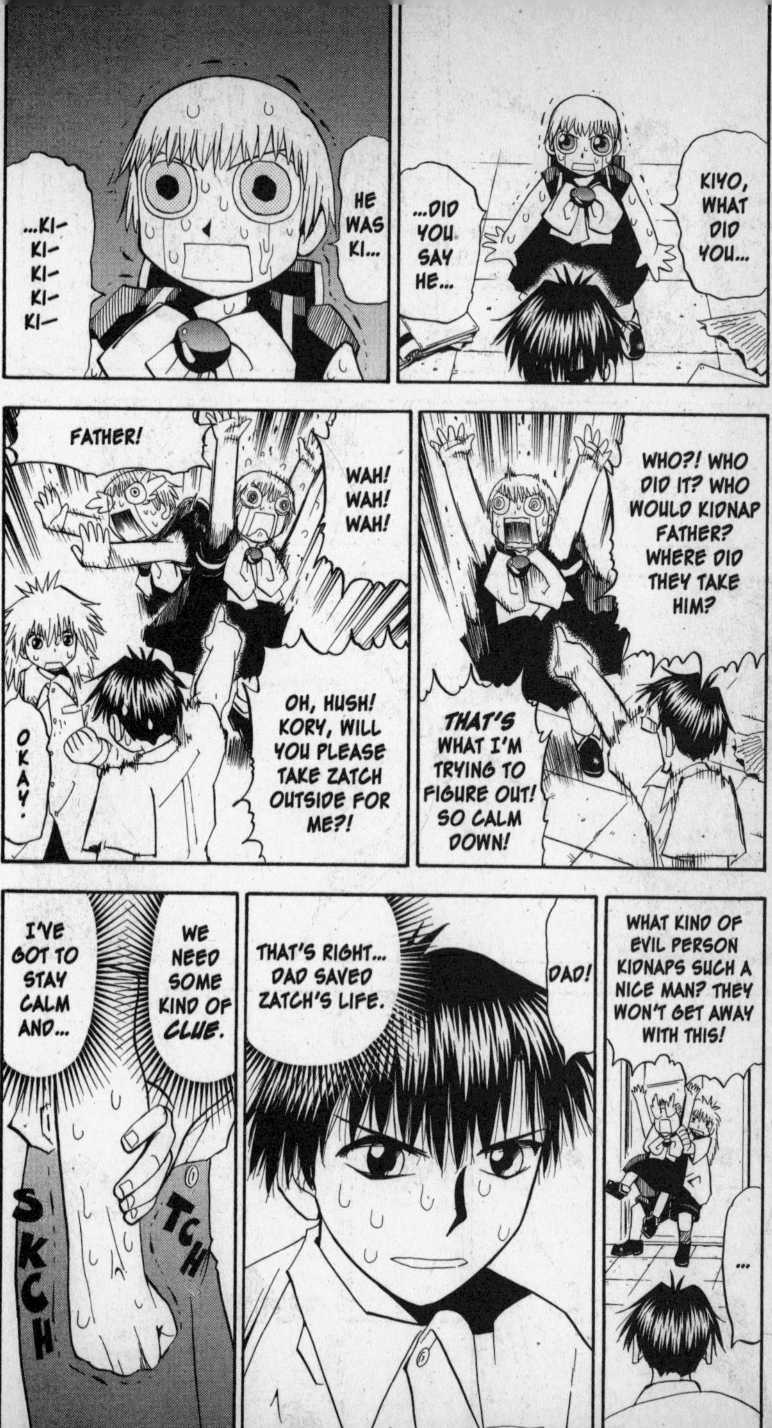
KIYO, WHAT DID YOU...
...DID YOU SAY HE...
HE WAS KI...
...KI- KI- KI- KI- KI-
WHO?! WHO DID IT? WHO WOULD KIDNAP FATHER? WHERE DID THEY TAKE HIM?
THAT'S WHAT I'M TRYING TO FIGURE OUT! SO CALM DOWN!
WAH! WAH! WAH!
FATHER!
OH, HUSH! KORY, WILL YOU PLEASE TAKE ZATCH OUTSIDE FOR ME?!
OKAY.
WHAT KIND OF EVIL PERSON KIDNAPS SUCH A NICE MAN? THEY WON'T GET AWAY WITH THIS!
...
DAD!
THAT'S RIGHT... DAD SAVED ZATCH'S LIFE.
WE NEED SOME KIND OF CLUE.
I'VE GOT TO STAY CALM AND...
TCH
SKCH

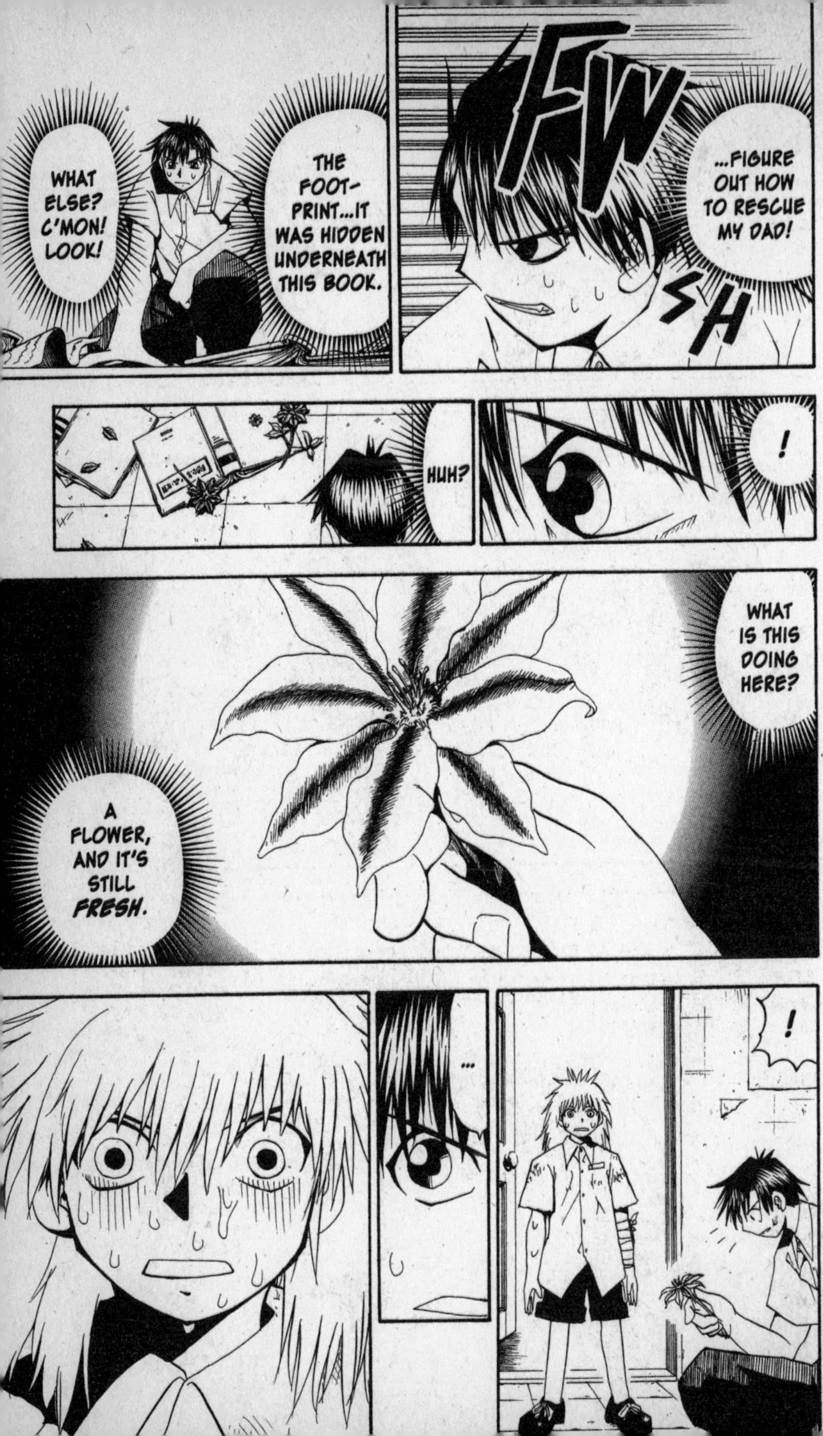
FWSH
...FIGURE OUT HOW TO RESCUE MY DAD!
THE FOOT-PRINT...IT WAS HIDDEN UNDERNEATH THIS BOOK.
WHAT ELSE? C'MON! LOOK!
!
HUH?
WHAT IS THIS DOING HERE?
A FLOWER, AND IT'S STILL FRESH.
!
...

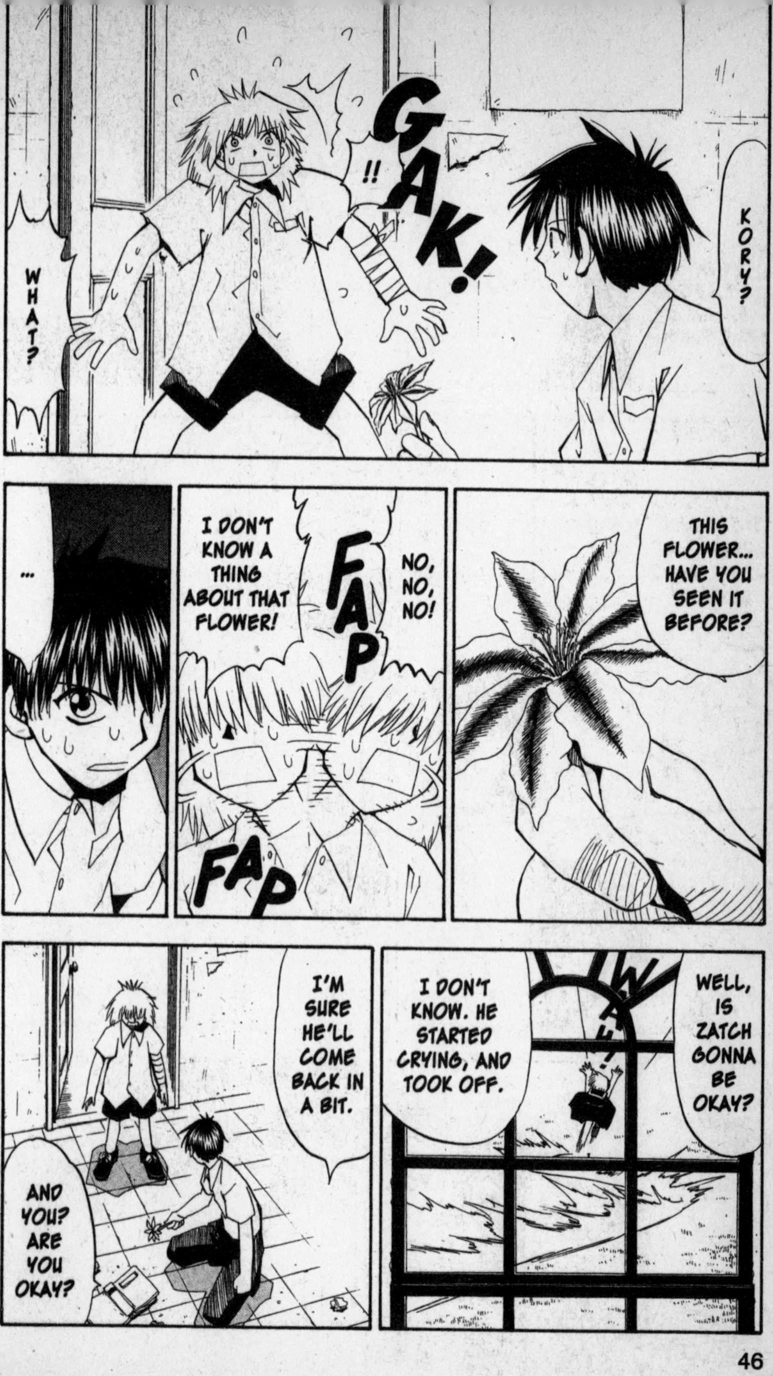
KORY?
GAK!
!!
WHAT?
THIS FLOWER... HAVE YOU SEEN IT BEFORE?
NO, NO, NO!
FAP
I DON'T KNOW A THING ABOUT THAT FLOWER!
FAP
...
WELL, IS ZATCH GONNA BE OKAY?
I DON'T KNOW. HE STARTED CRYING, AND TOOK OFF.
I'M SURE HE'LL COME BACK IN A BIT.
AND YOU? ARE YOU OKAY?

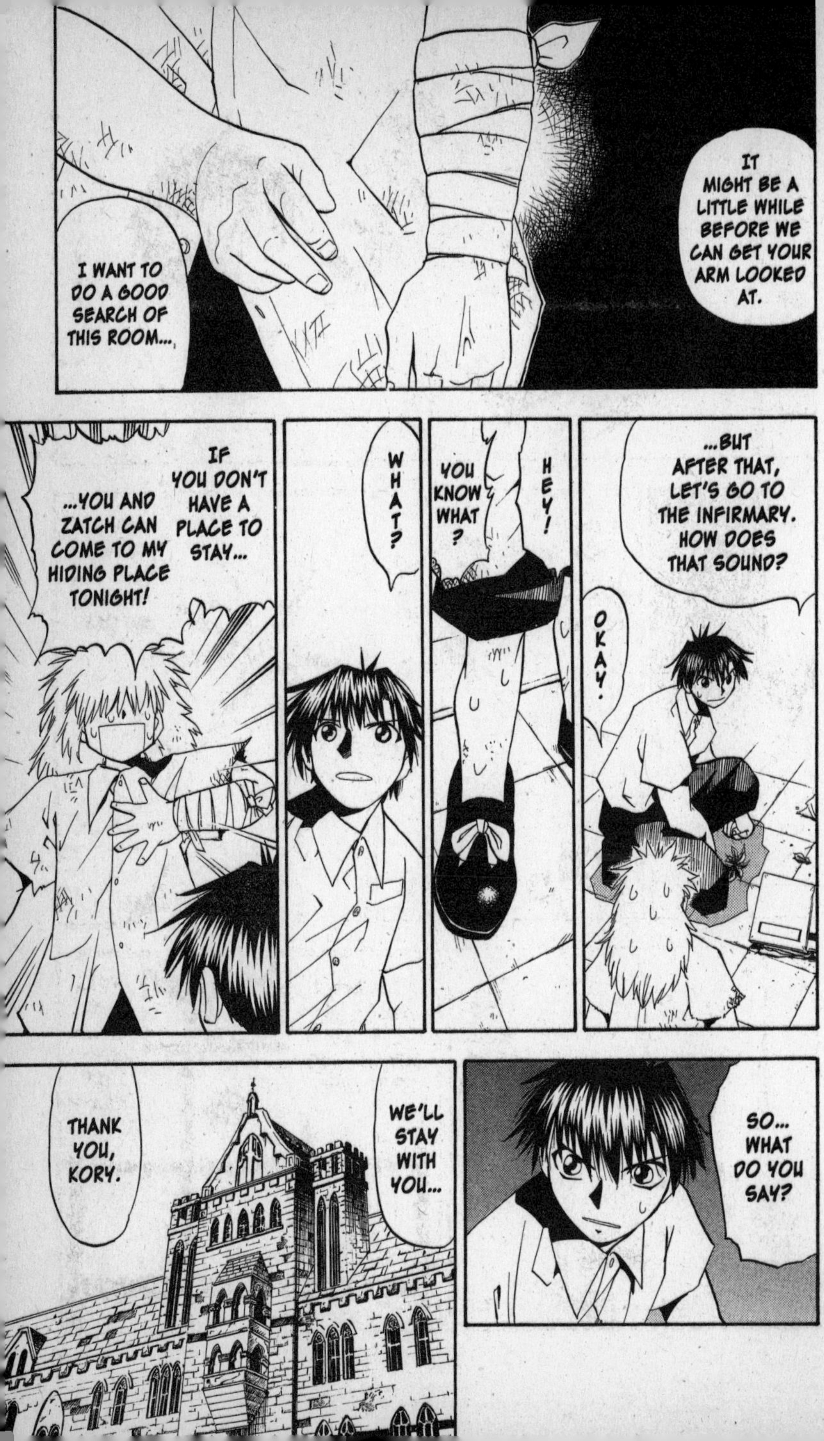
IT MIGHT BE A LITTLE WHILE BEFORE WE CAN GET YOUR ARM LOOKED AT.
I WANT TO DO A GOOD SEARCH OF THIS ROOM...
...BUT AFTER THAT, LET'S GO TO THE INFIRMARY. HOW DOES THAT SOUND?
OKAY.
HEY!
YOU KNOW WHAT?
WHAT?
IF YOU DON'T HAVE A PLACE TO STAY...
...YOU AND ZATCH CAN COME TO MY HIDING PLACE TONIGHT!
SO... WHAT DO YOU SAY?
WE'LL STAY WITH YOU...
THANK YOU, KORY.

HEY NOW, ZATCH! DON'T CRY AND EAT AT THE SAME TIME!

OH, YEAH! HEY, I KNOW!

OKAY... SNIFF!

WAAAHH!

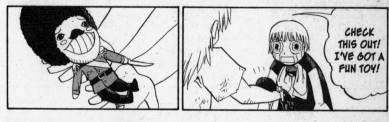

CHECK THIS OUT! I'VE GOT A FUN TOY!

...

ZATCH.

WAAAHH!

WAAHH!

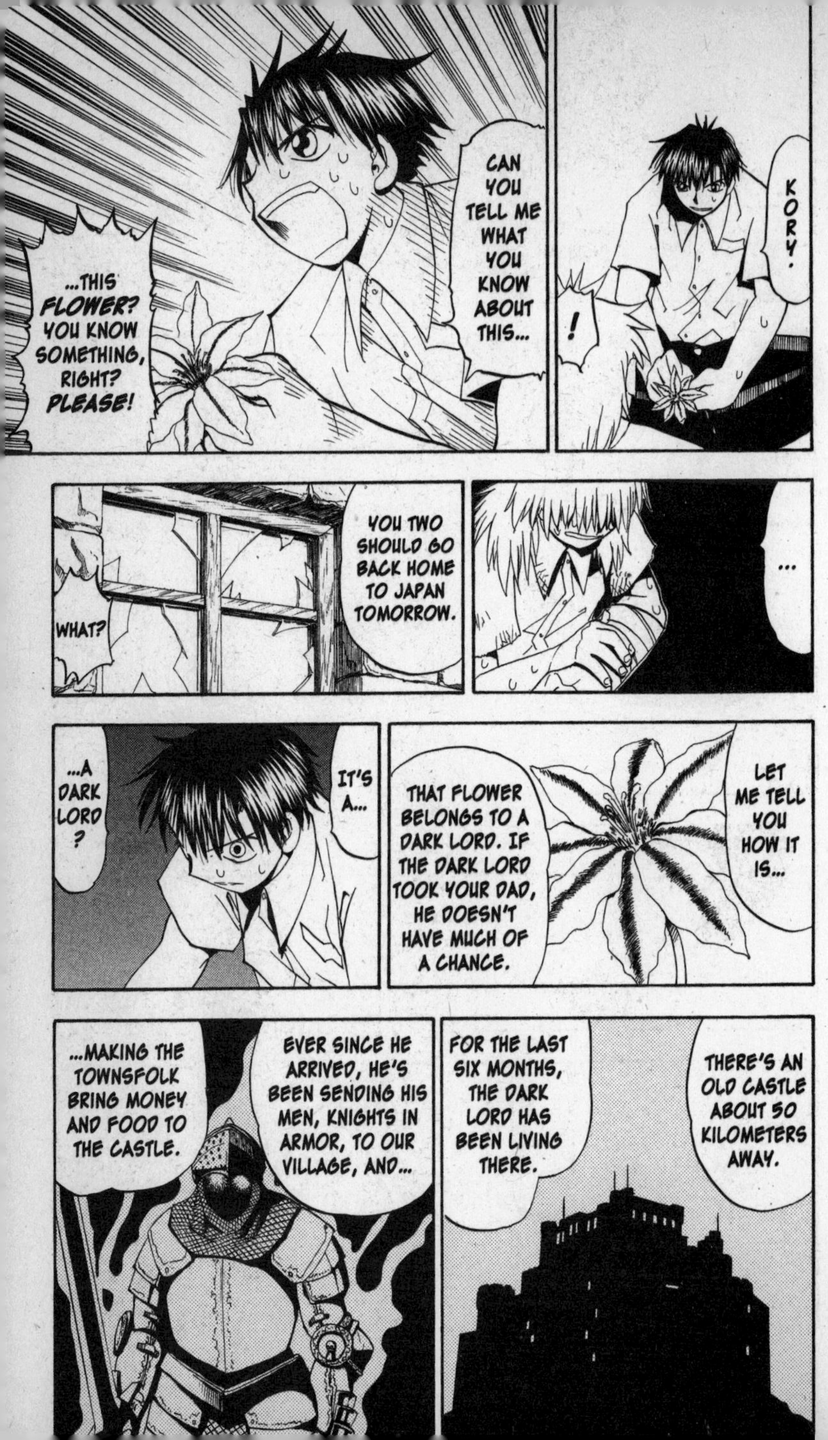
KORY.
!
CAN YOU TELL ME WHAT YOU KNOW ABOUT THIS...
...THIS FLOWER? YOU KNOW SOMETHING, RIGHT? PLEASE!
...
YOU TWO SHOULD GO BACK HOME TO JAPAN TOMORROW.
WHAT?
LET ME TELL YOU HOW IT IS...
THAT FLOWER BELONGS TO A DARK LORD. IF THE DARK LORD TOOK YOUR DAD, HE DOESN'T HAVE MUCH OF A CHANCE.
IT'S A...
...A DARK LORD?
THERE'S AN OLD CASTLE ABOUT 50 KILOMETERS AWAY.
FOR THE LAST SIX MONTHS, THE DARK LORD HAS BEEN LIVING THERE.
EVER SINCE HE ARRIVED, HE'S BEEN SENDING HIS MEN, KNIGHTS IN ARMOR, TO OUR VILLAGE, AND...
...MAKING THE TOWNSFOLK BRING MONEY AND FOOD TO THE CASTLE.

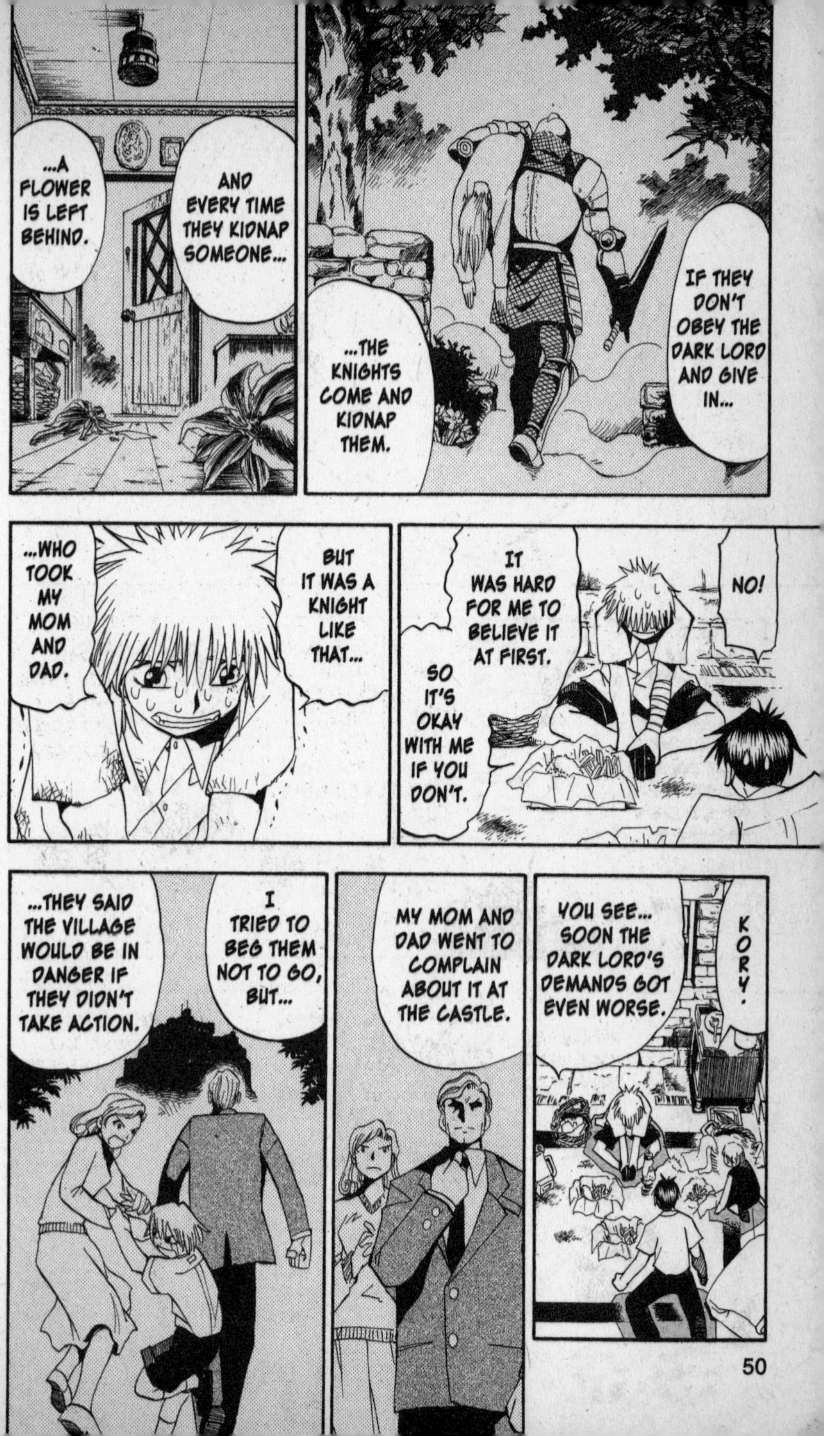
IF THEY DON'T OBEY THE DARK LORD AND GIVE IN...
...THE KNIGHTS COME AND KIDNAP THEM.
AND EVERY TIME THEY KIDNAP SOMEONE...
...A FLOWER IS LEFT BEHIND.
NO!
IT WAS HARD FOR ME TO BELIEVE IT AT FIRST.
SO IT'S OKAY WITH ME IF YOU DON'T.
BUT IT WAS A KNIGHT LIKE THAT...
...WHO TOOK MY MOM AND DAD.
KORY.
YOU SEE... SOON THE DARK LORD'S DEMANDS GOT EVEN WORSE.
MY MOM AND DAD WENT TO COMPLAIN ABOUT IT AT THE CASTLE.
I TRIED TO BEG THEM NOT TO GO, BUT...
...THEY SAID THE VILLAGE WOULD BE IN DANGER IF THEY DIDN'T TAKE ACTION.

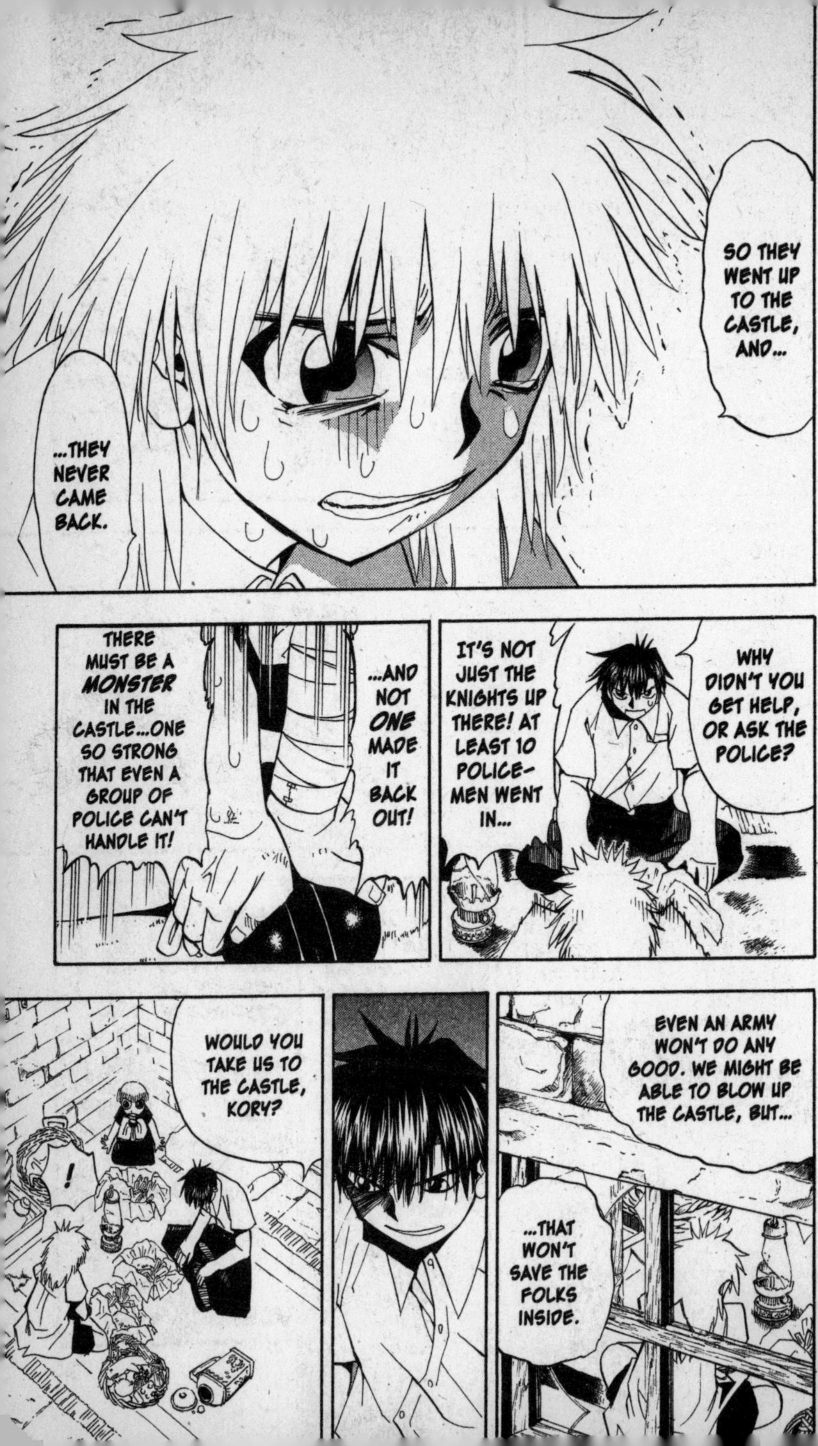
SO THEY WENT UP TO THE CASTLE, AND...
...THEY NEVER CAME BACK.
WHY DIDN'T YOU GET HELP, OR ASK THE POLICE?
IT'S NOT JUST THE KNIGHTS UP THERE! AT LEAST 10 POLICEMEN WENT IN...
...AND NOT ONE MADE IT BACK OUT!
THERE MUST BE A MONSTER IN THE CASTLE...ONE SO STRONG THAT EVEN A GROUP OF POLICE CAN'T HANDLE IT!
EVEN AN ARMY WON'T DO ANY GOOD. WE MIGHT BE ABLE TO BLOW UP THE CASTLE, BUT...
...THAT WON'T SAVE THE FOLKS INSIDE.
WOULD YOU TAKE US TO THE CASTLE, KORY?
!

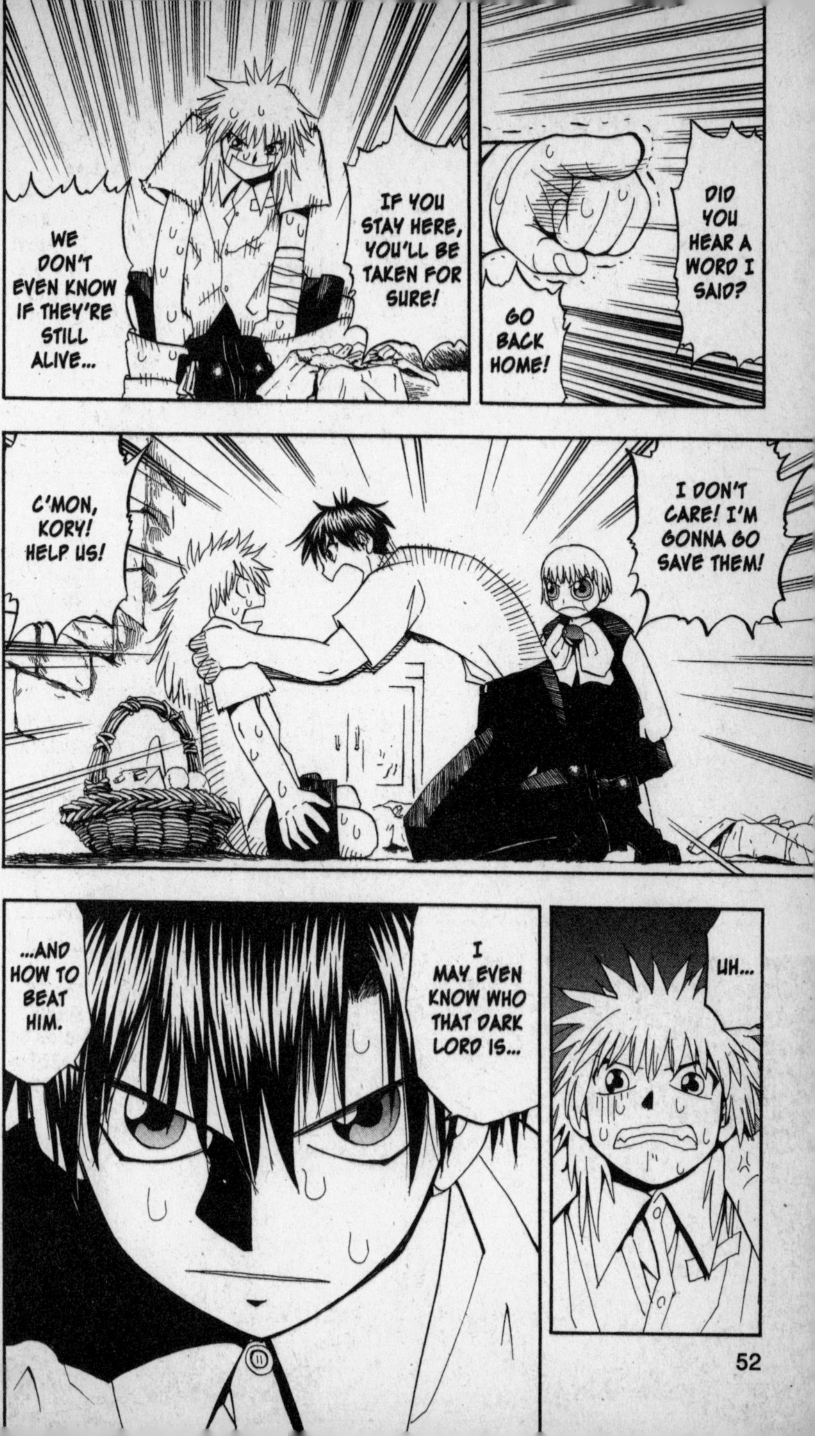
DID YOU HEAR A WORD I SAID?
GO BACK HOME!
IF YOU STAY HERE, YOU'LL BE TAKEN FOR SURE!
WE DON'T EVEN KNOW IF THEY'RE STILL ALIVE...
I DON'T CARE! I'M GONNA GO SAVE THEM!
C'MON, KORY! HELP US!
UH...
I MAY EVEN KNOW WHO THAT DARK LORD IS...
...AND HOW TO BEAT HIM.

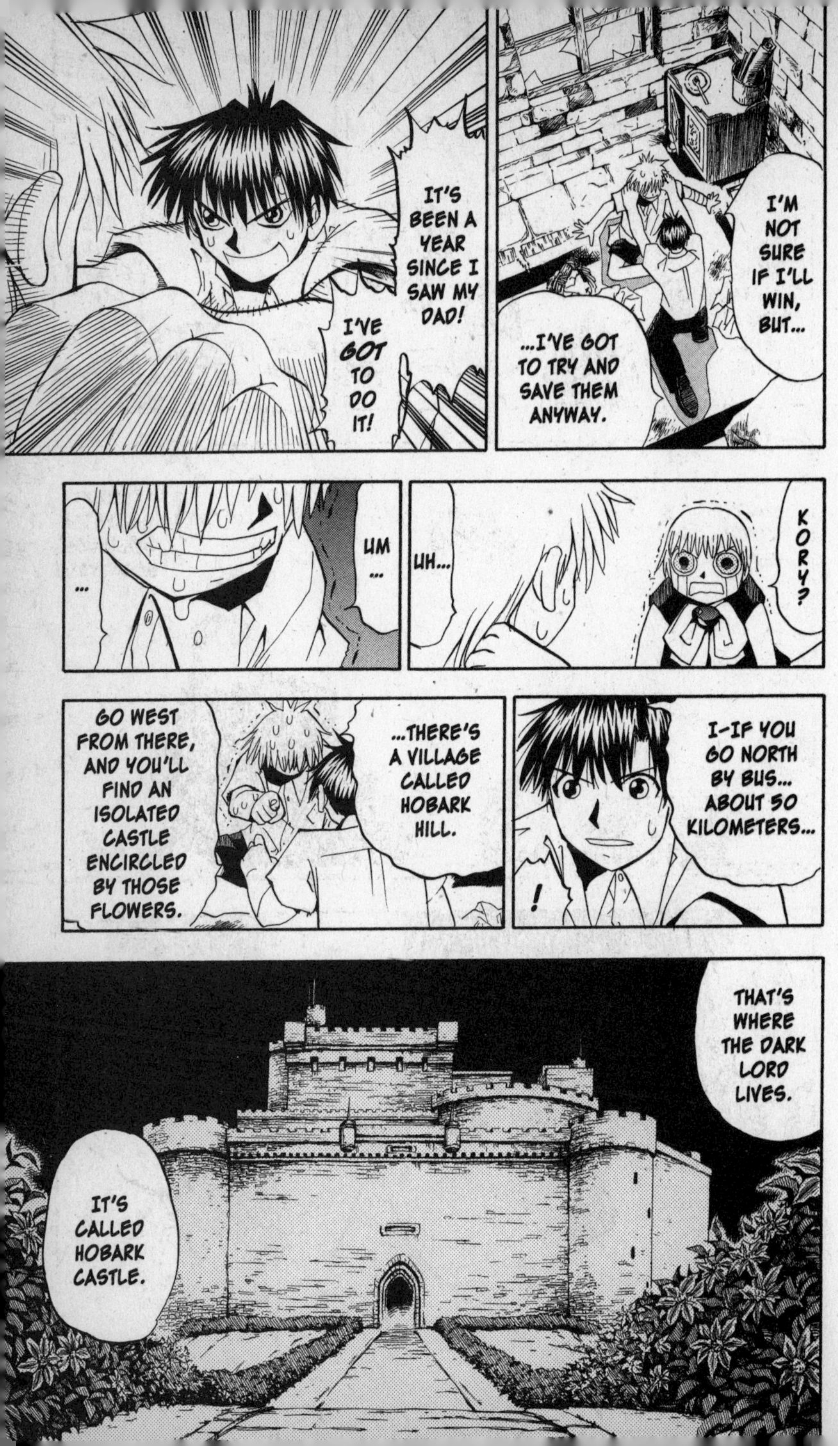
I'M NOT SURE IF I'LL WIN, BUT...
...I'VE GOT TO TRY AND SAVE THEM ANYWAY.
IT'S BEEN A YEAR SINCE I SAW MY DAD!
I'VE GOT TO DO IT!
KORY?
UH...
UM ...
...
I-IF YOU GO NORTH BY BUS... ABOUT 50 KILOMETERS...
!
...THERE'S A VILLAGE CALLED HOBARK HILL.
GO WEST FROM THERE, AND YOU'LL FIND AN ISOLATED CASTLE ENCIRCLED BY THOSE FLOWERS.
THAT'S WHERE THE DARK LORD LIVES.
IT'S CALLED HOBARK CASTLE.

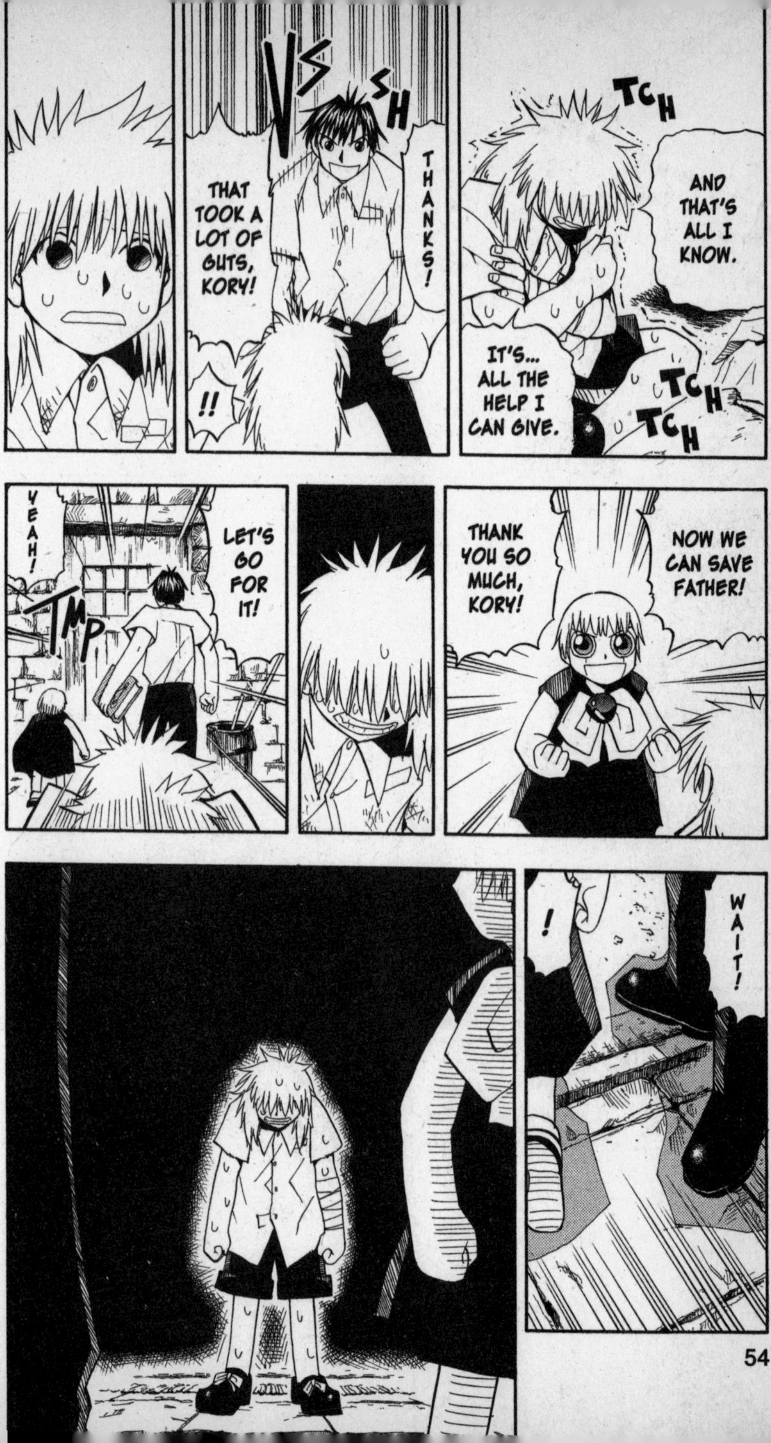
TCH
AND THAT'S ALL I KNOW.
IT'S... ALL THE HELP I CAN GIVE.
TCH
TCH
VSSH
THANKS!
THAT TOOK A LOT OF GUTS, KORY!
!!
NOW WE CAN SAVE FATHER!
THANK YOU SO MUCH, KORY!
LET'S GO FOR IT!
YEAH!
TMP
WAIT!
!

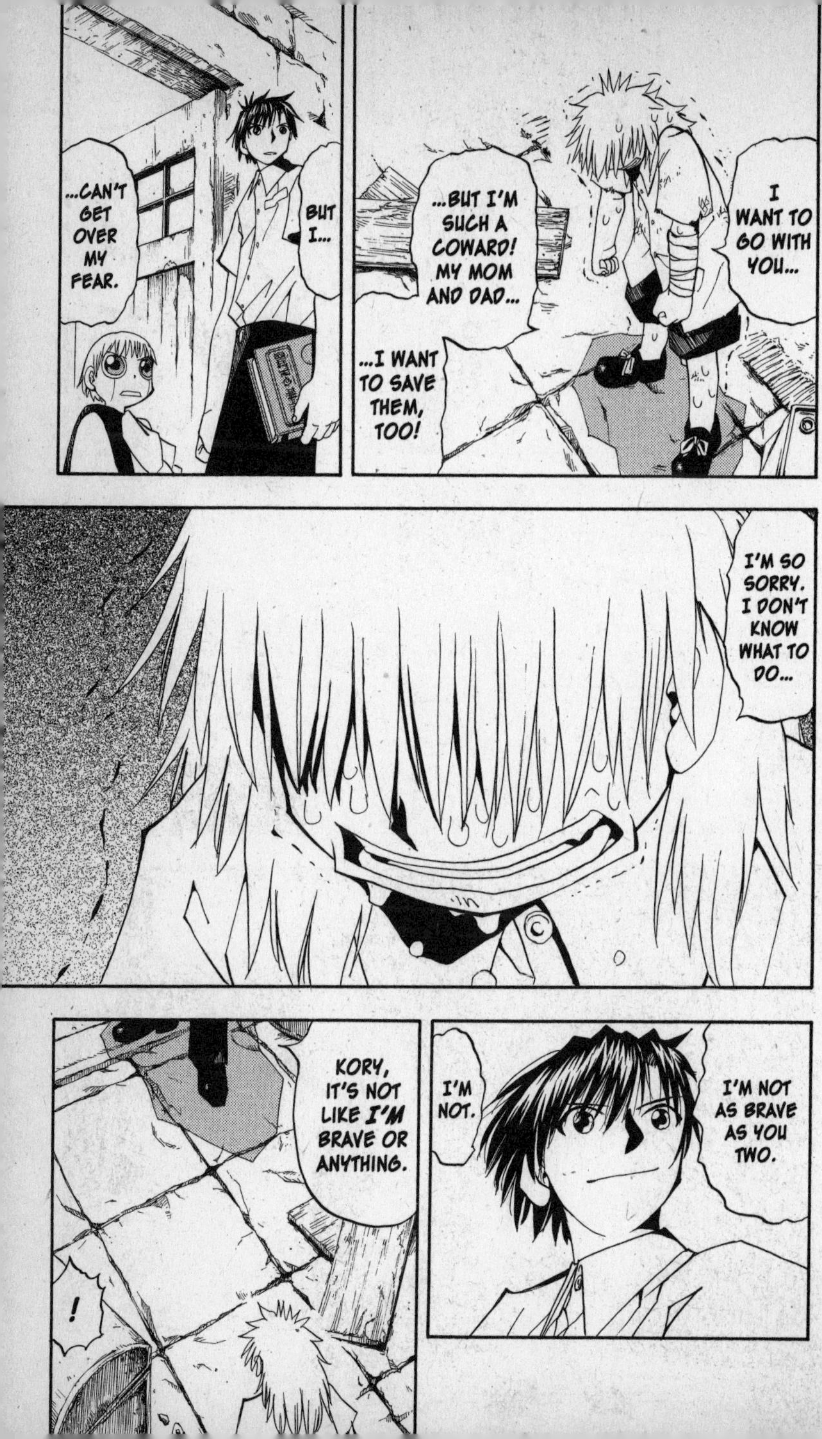
I WANT TO GO WITH YOU...
...BUT I'M SUCH A COWARD! MY MOM AND DAD...
...I WANT TO SAVE THEM, TOO!
BUT I...
...CAN'T GET OVER MY FEAR.
I'M SO SORRY. I DON'T KNOW WHAT TO DO...
I'M NOT AS BRAVE AS YOU TWO.
I'M NOT.
KORY, IT'S NOT LIKE *I'M* BRAVE OR ANYTHING.
!

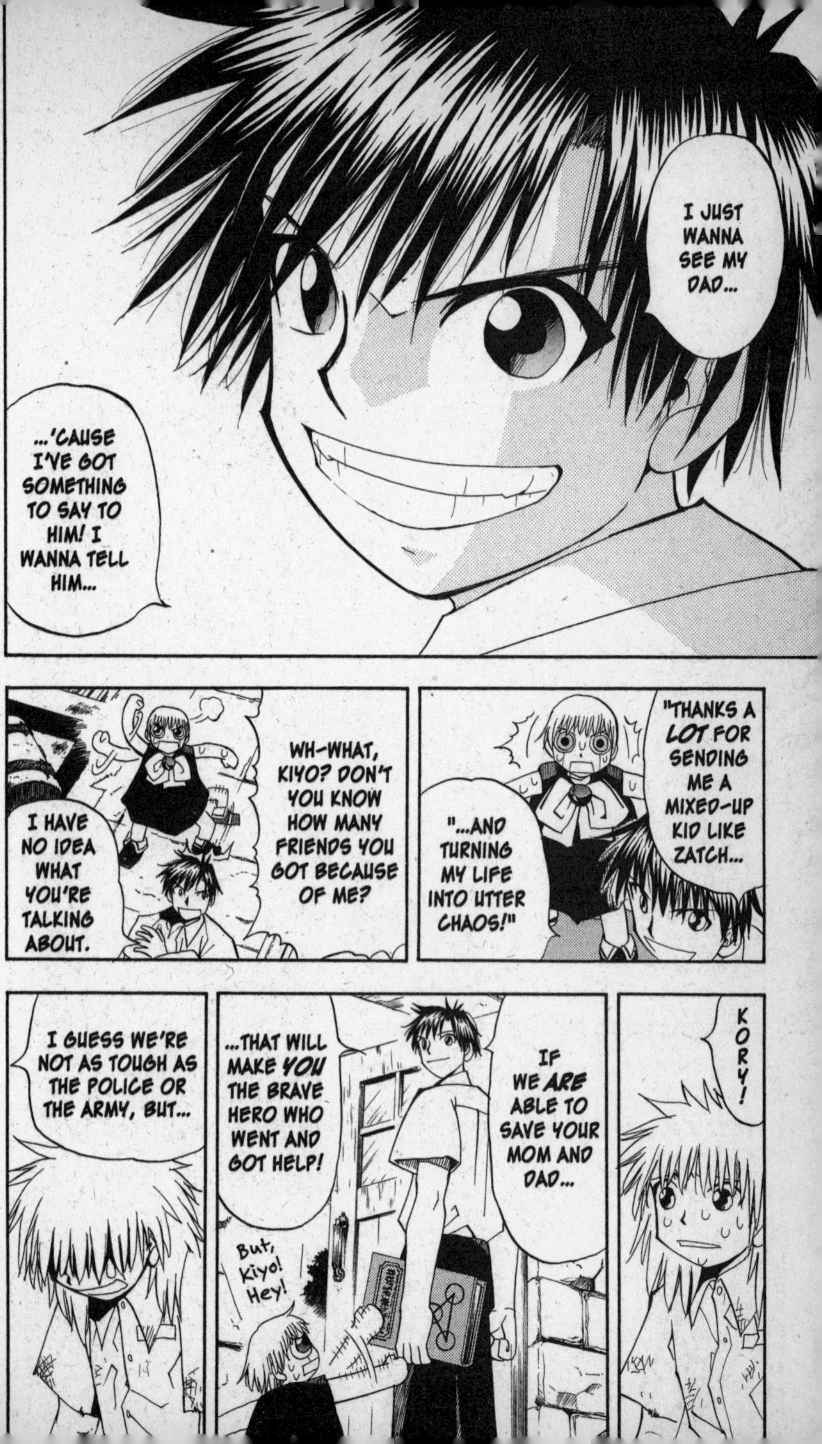
I JUST WANNA SEE MY DAD...
...'CAUSE I'VE GOT SOMETHING TO SAY TO HIM! I WANNA TELL HIM...
"THANKS A LOT FOR SENDING ME A MIXED-UP KID LIKE ZATCH...
"...AND TURNING MY LIFE INTO UTTER CHAOS!"
WH-WHAT, KIYO? DON'T YOU KNOW HOW MANY FRIENDS YOU GOT BECAUSE OF ME?
I HAVE NO IDEA WHAT YOU'RE TALKING ABOUT.
KORY!
IF WE ARE ABLE TO SAVE YOUR MOM AND DAD...
...THAT WILL MAKE YOU THE BRAVE HERO WHO WENT AND GOT HELP!
But, Kiyo! Hey!
I GUESS WE'RE NOT AS TOUGH AS THE POLICE OR THE ARMY, BUT...

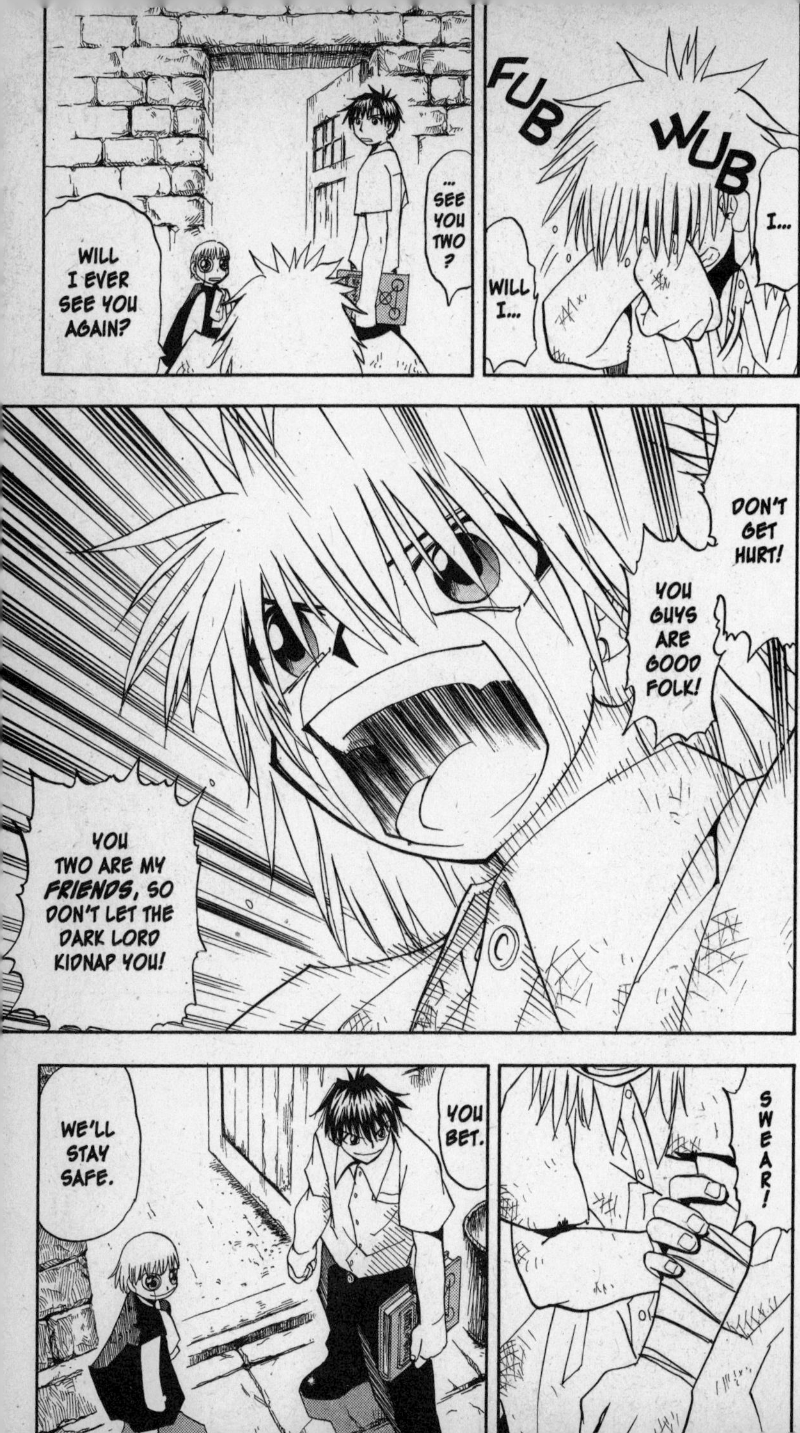
FUB
WUB
I...
WILL I...
...SEE YOU TWO?
WILL I EVER SEE YOU AGAIN?
DON'T GET HURT!
YOU GUYS ARE GOOD FOLK!
YOU TWO ARE MY *FRIENDS*, SO DON'T LET THE DARK LORD KIDNAP YOU!
SWEAR!
YOU BET.
WE'LL STAY SAFE.

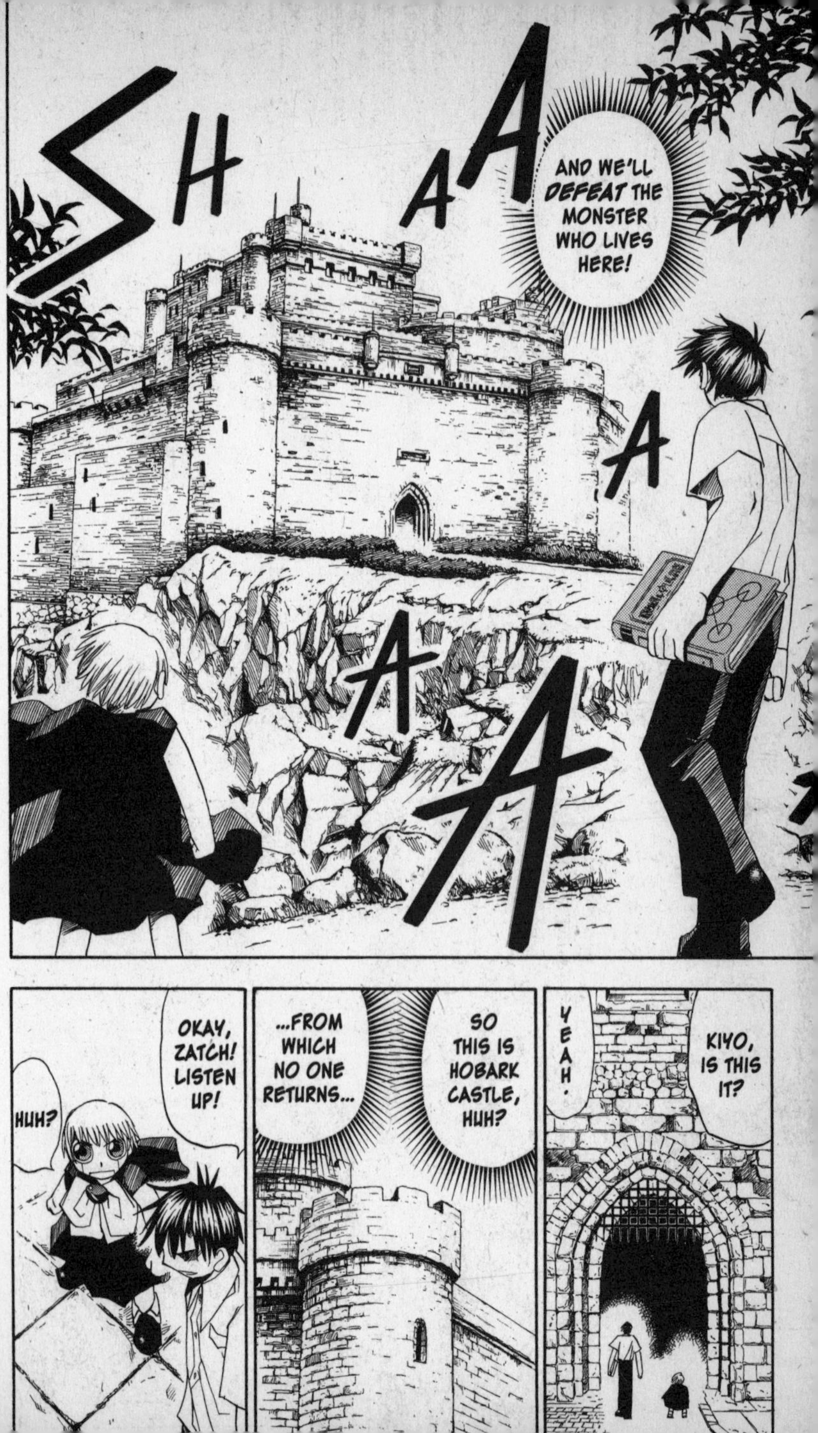
SHAAAAA
AND WE'LL DEFEAT THE MONSTER WHO LIVES HERE!
KIYO, IS THIS IT?
YEAH.
SO THIS IS HOBARK CASTLE, HUH?
...FROM WHICH NO ONE RETURNS...
OKAY, ZATCH! LISTEN UP!
HUH?

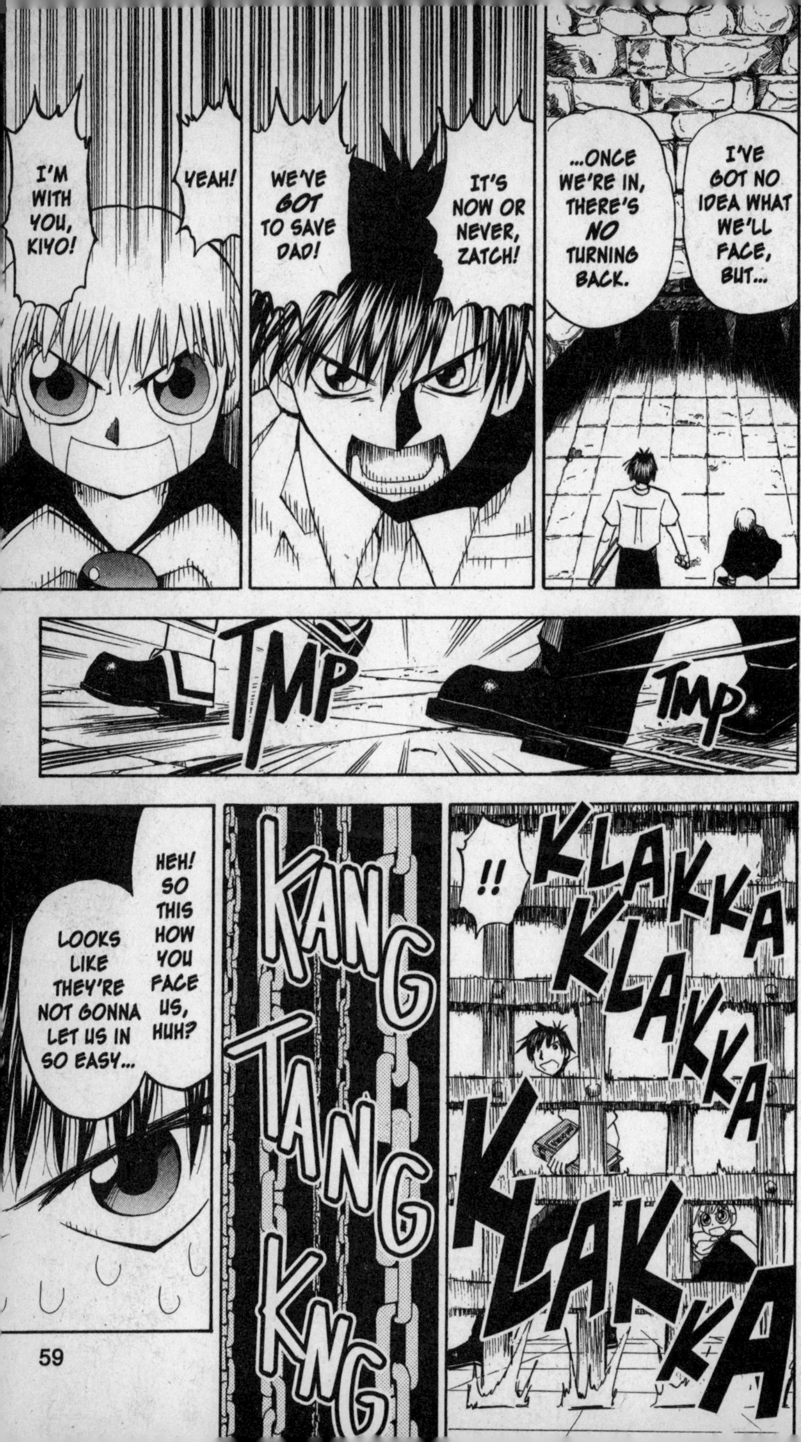
I'VE GOT NO IDEA WHAT WE'LL FACE, BUT...
...ONCE WE'RE IN, THERE'S NO TURNING BACK.
IT'S NOW OR NEVER, ZATCH!
WE'VE GOT TO SAVE DAD!
YEAH!
I'M WITH YOU, KIYO!
TMP
TMP
KLAKKA KLAKKA KLAKKA
!!
KANG TANG KNG
HEH! SO THIS HOW YOU FACE US, HUH?
LOOKS LIKE THEY'RE NOT GONNA LET US IN SO EASY...

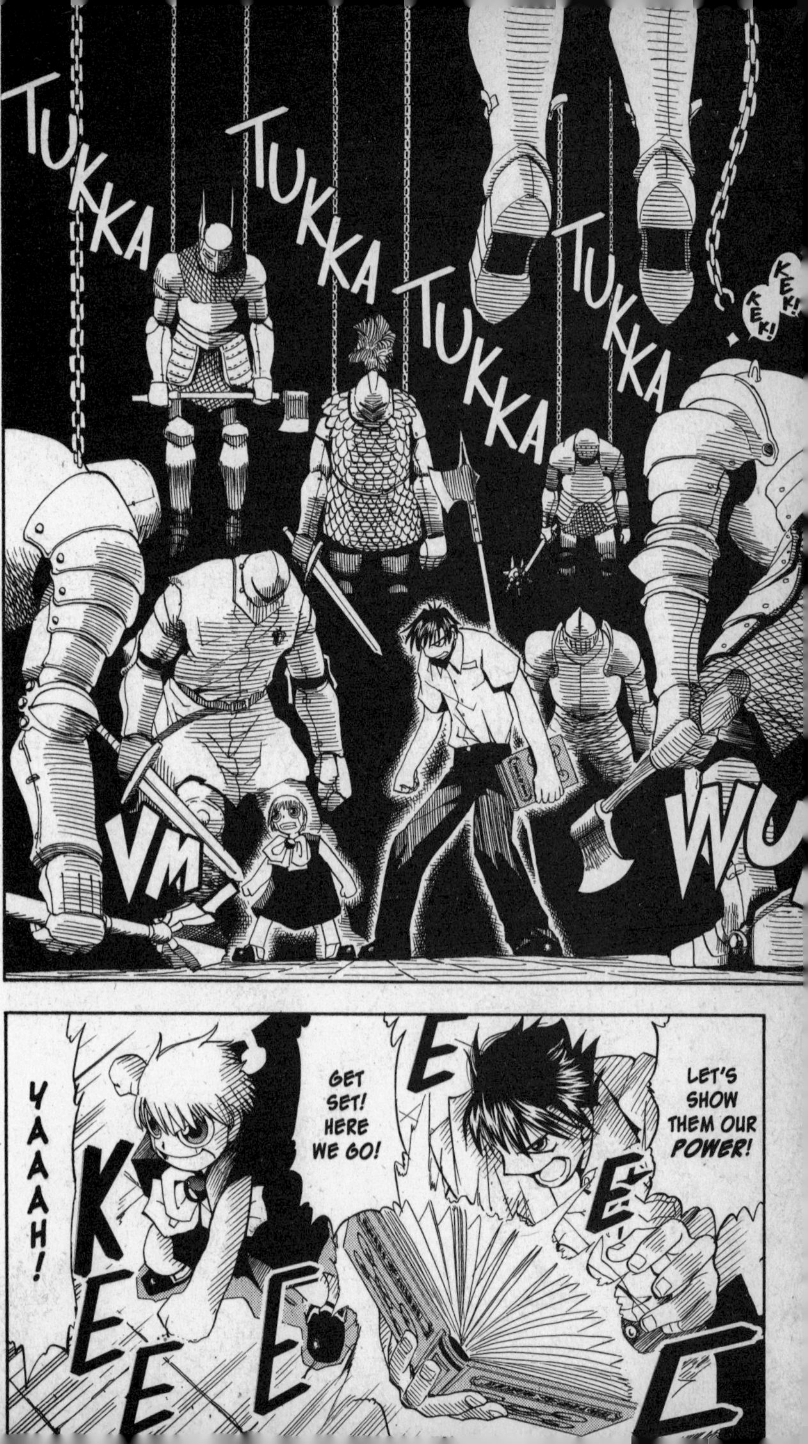
KEK! KEK!
TUKKA
TUKKA
TUKKA
TUKKA
WU
VM
LET'S SHOW THEM OUR POWER!
GET SET! HERE WE GO!
YAAAH!
KEEE

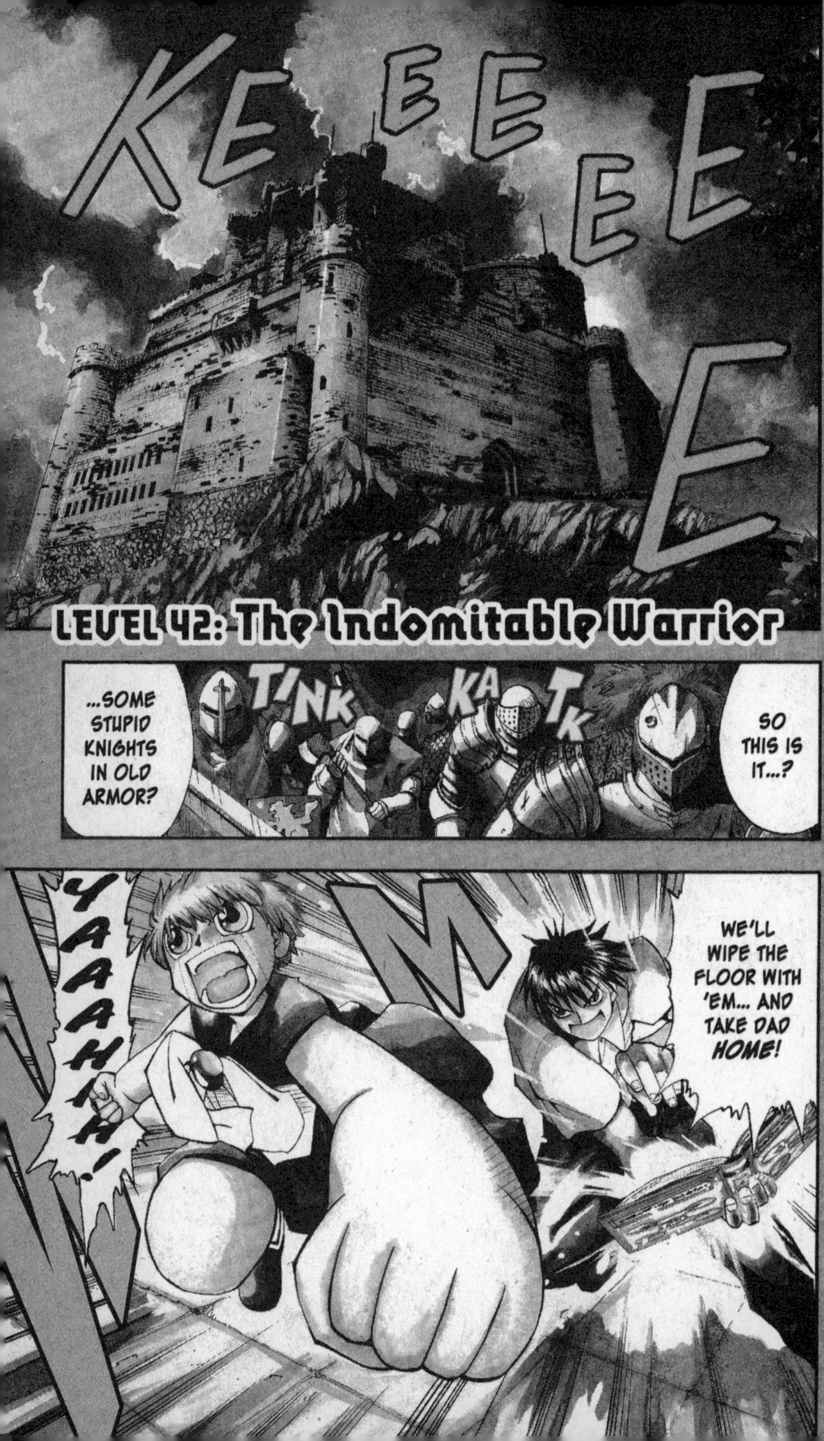
KEEEEEE
LEVEL 42: The Indomitable Warrior
SO THIS IS IT...?
TINK
KA
TK
...SOME STUPID KNIGHTS IN OLD ARMOR?
WE'LL WIPE THE FLOOR WITH 'EM... AND TAKE DAD HOME!
M
YAAAAHHH!

LEVEL 42: The Indomitable Warrior

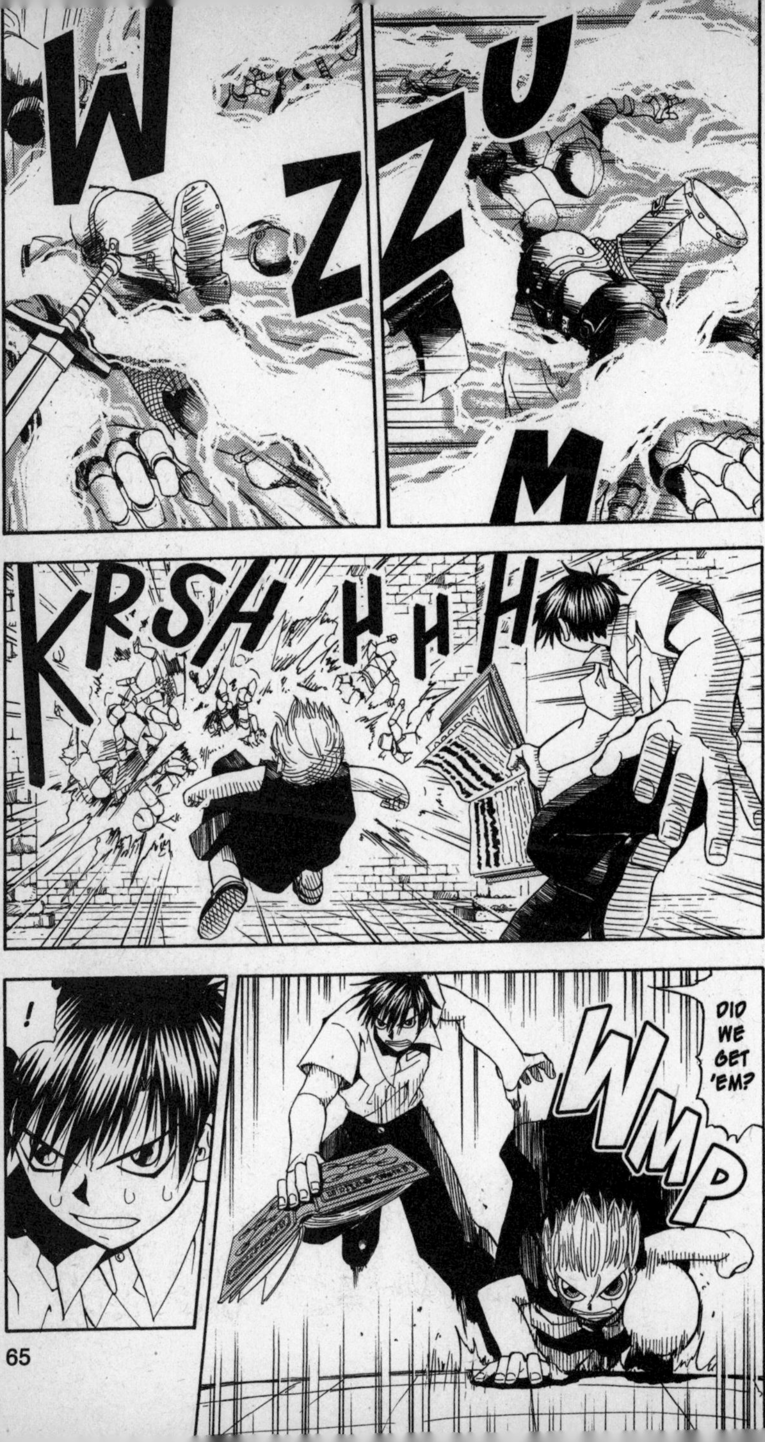
WZZUM
KRSHHHH
DID WE GET 'EM?
WMP
!

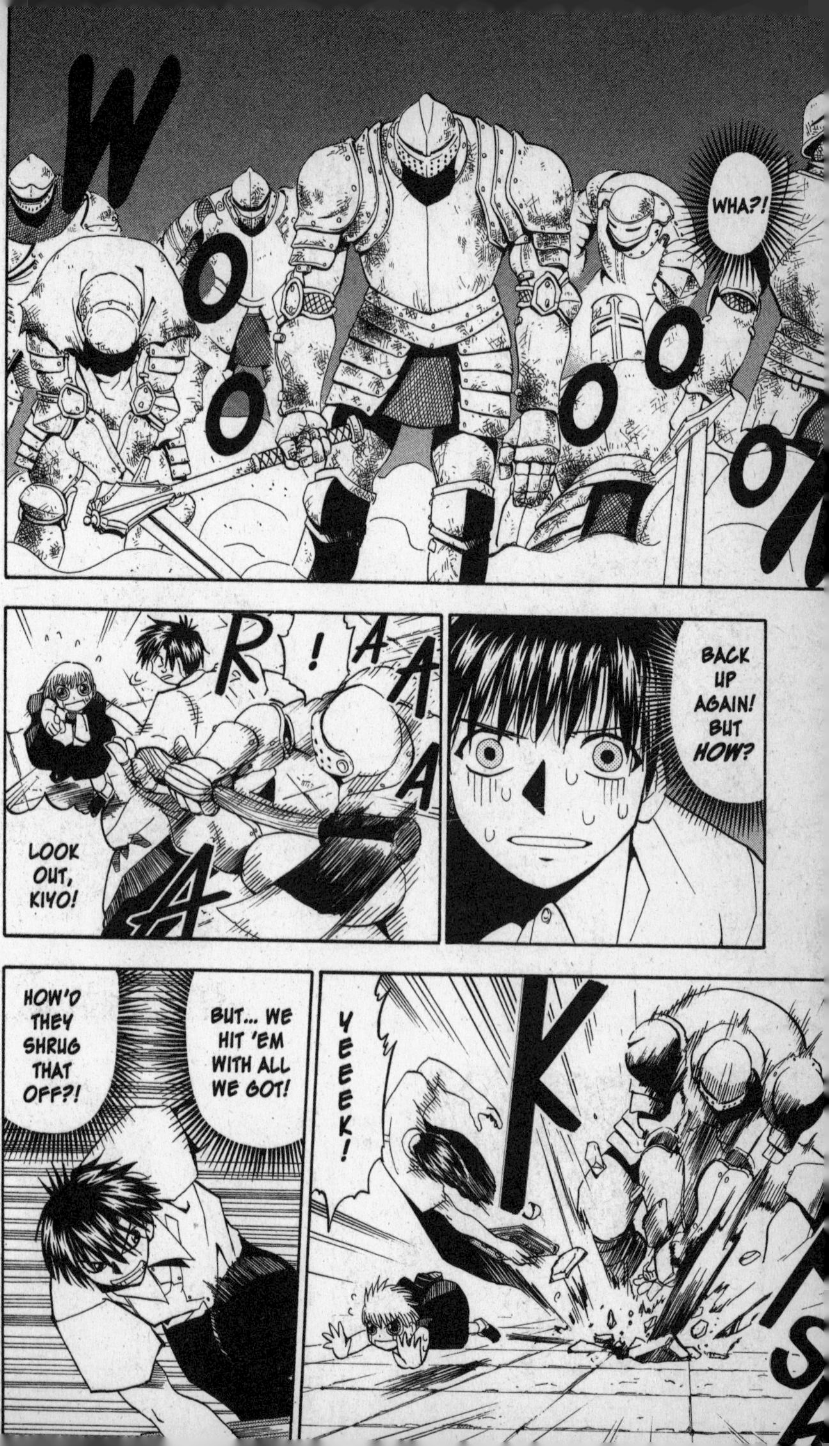
WHA?!
WOOOOOOO
BACK UP AGAIN! BUT HOW?
RAAAAA!
LOOK OUT, KIYO!
YEEEK!
BUT... WE HIT 'EM WITH ALL WE GOT!
HOW'D THEY SHRUG THAT OFF?!

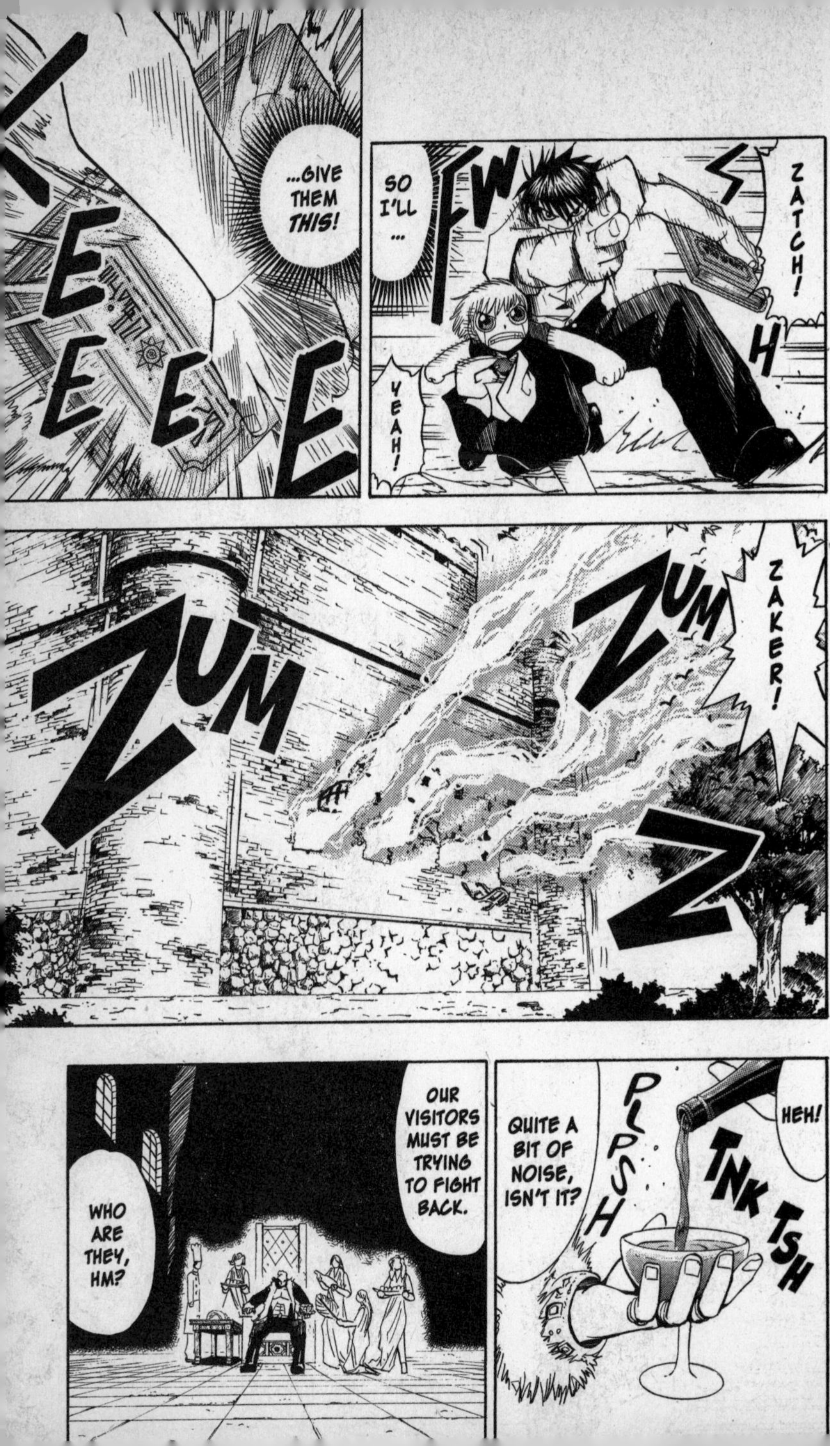
ZATCH!
FWSH
SO I'LL ...
YEAH!
...GIVE THEM THIS!
EEEE
ZAKER!
ZUM
ZUM
Z
HEH!
TNK TSH
PLPSH
QUITE A BIT OF NOISE, ISN'T IT?
OUR VISITORS MUST BE TRYING TO FIGHT BACK.
WHO ARE THEY, HM?

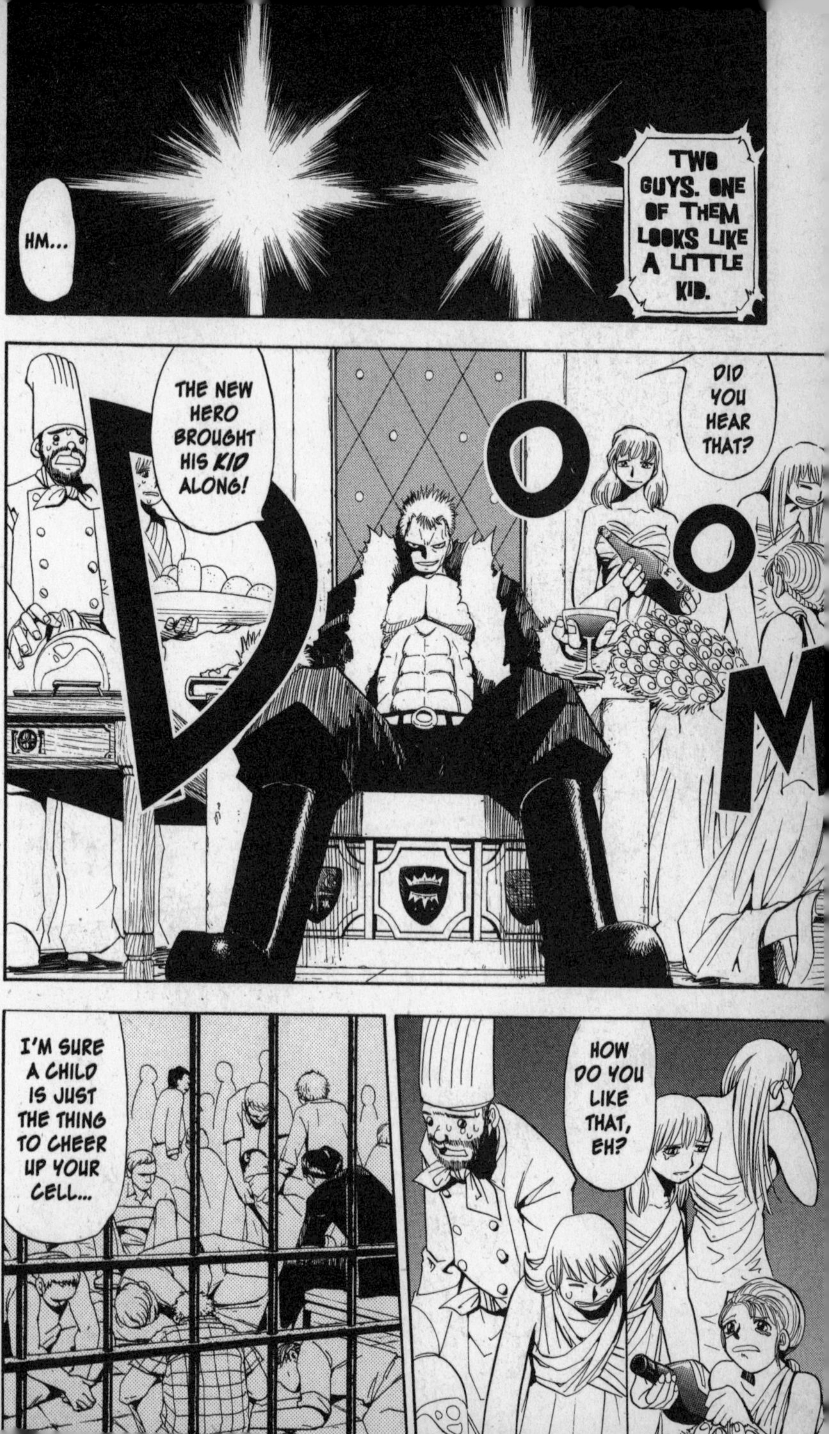
TWO GUYS. ONE OF THEM LOOKS LIKE A LITTLE KID.
HM...
DID YOU HEAR THAT?
THE NEW HERO BROUGHT HIS KID ALONG!
DOOM
HOW DO YOU LIKE THAT, EH?
I'M SURE A CHILD IS JUST THE THING TO CHEER UP YOUR CELL...

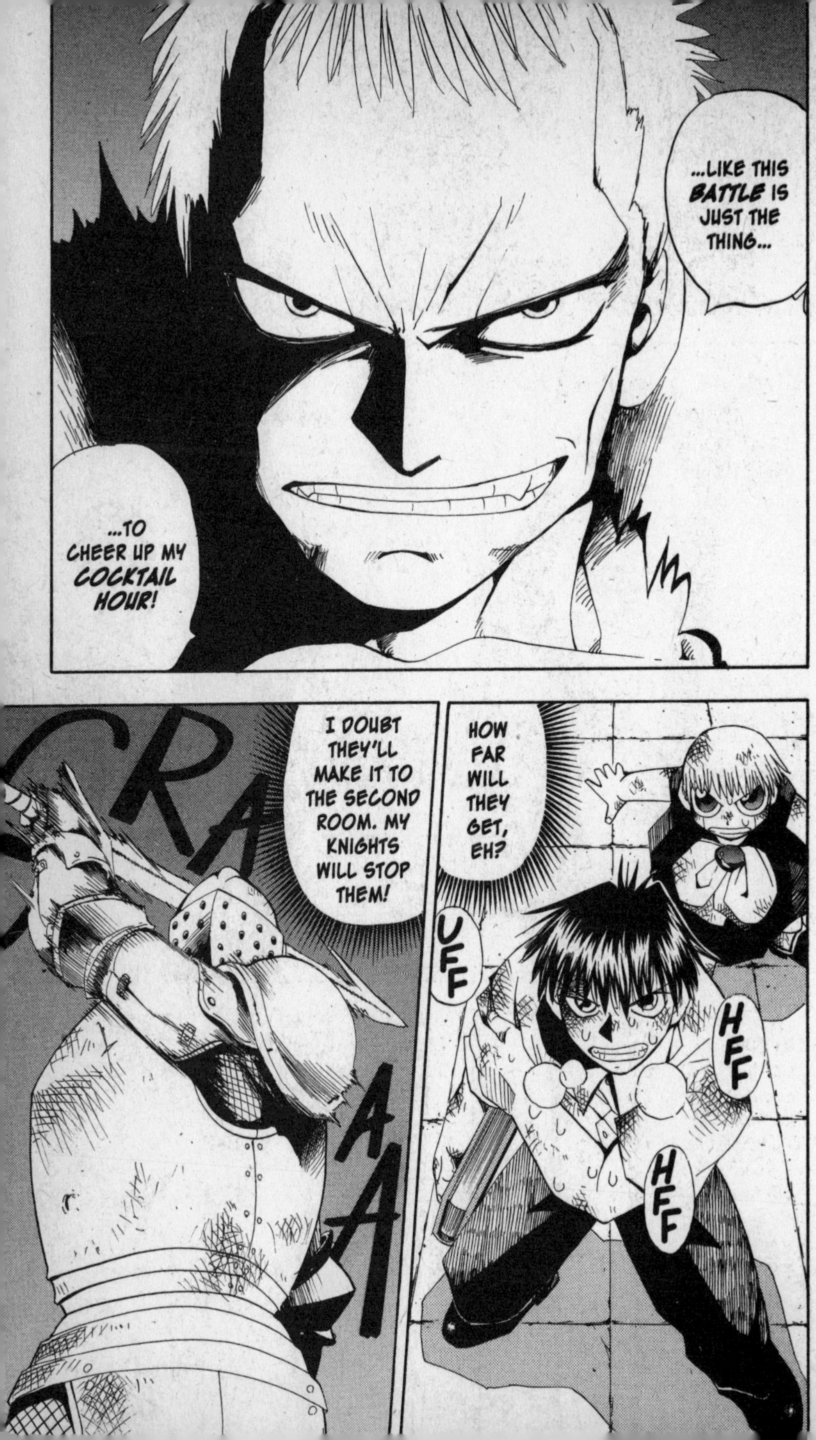
...LIKE THIS BATTLE IS JUST THE THING...
...TO CHEER UP MY COCKTAIL HOUR!
HOW FAR WILL THEY GET, EH?
UFF
HFF
HFF
I DOUBT THEY'LL MAKE IT TO THE SECOND ROOM. MY KNIGHTS WILL STOP THEM!
CRAAA

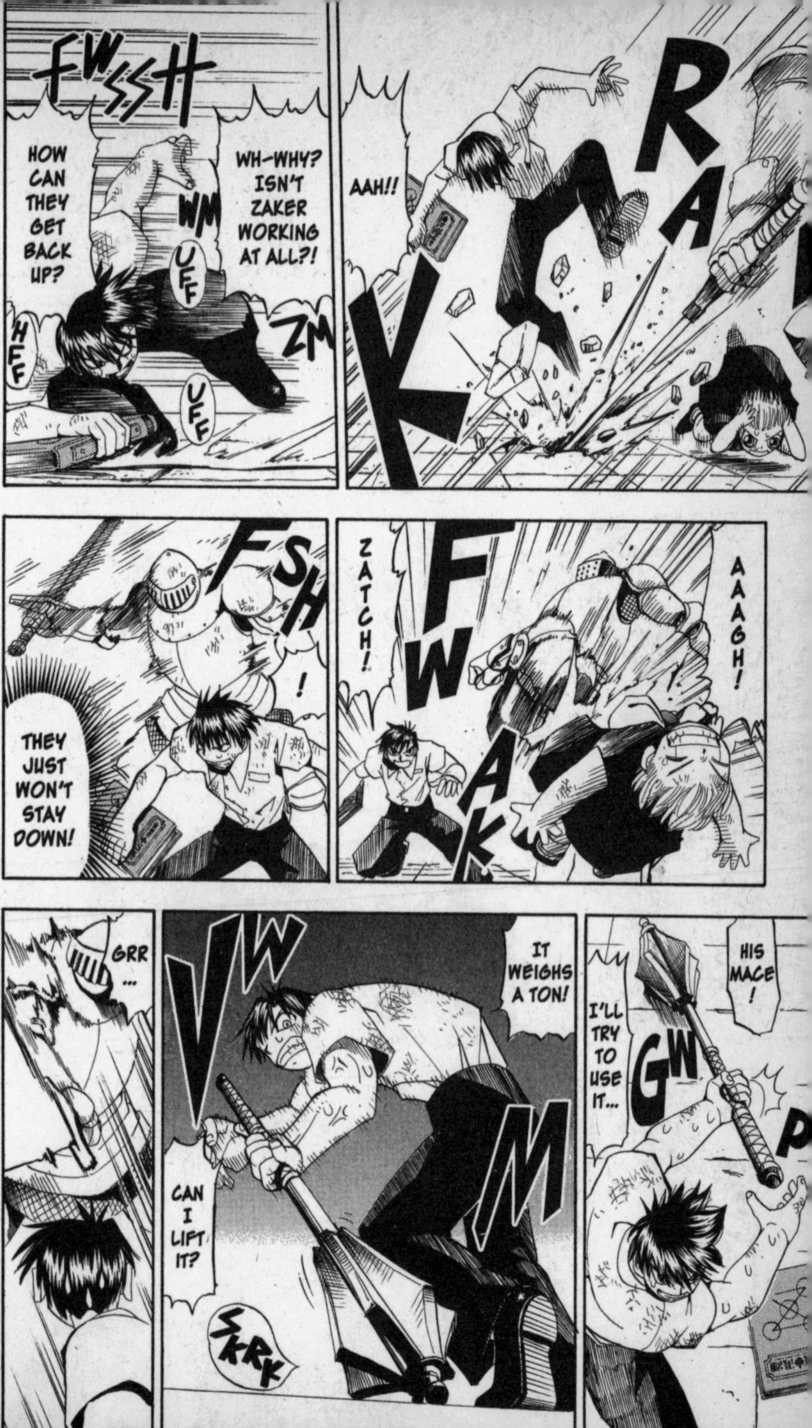
RAK
AAH!!
FWSSH
WH-WHY? ISN'T ZAKER WORKING AT ALL?!
HOW CAN THEY GET BACK UP?
WM
UFF
ZM
HFF
UFF
AAAAGH!
FWAK
ZATCH!
FSH
!
THEY JUST WON'T STAY DOWN!
HIS MACE!
I'LL TRY TO USE IT...
GW
P
IT WEIGHS A TON!
VWM
CAN I LIFT IT?
SKRK
GRR...

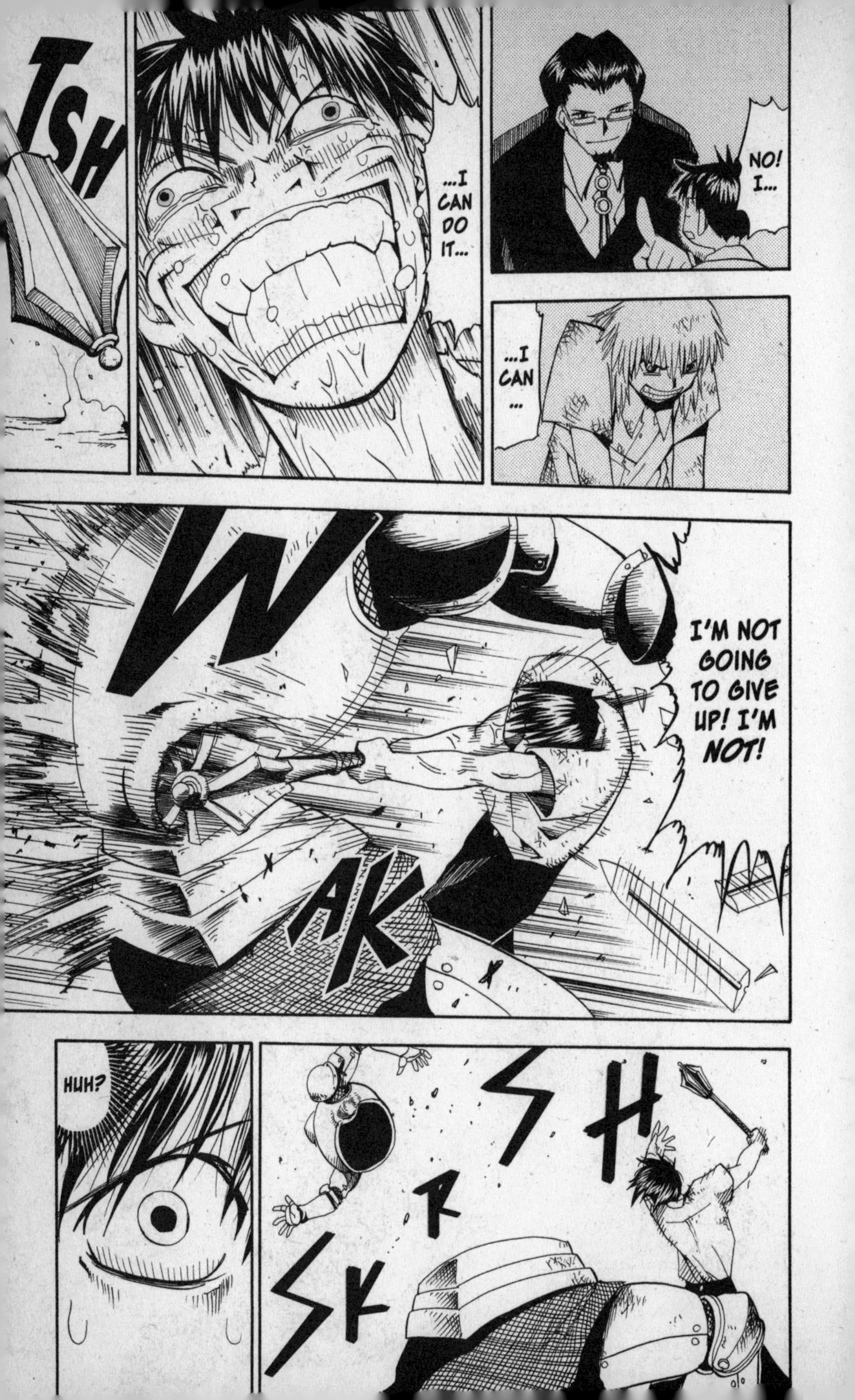
NO! I...
...I CAN ...
...I CAN DO IT...
TSH
I'M NOT GOING TO GIVE UP! I'M NOT!
W
AK
SH
R
SK
HUH?

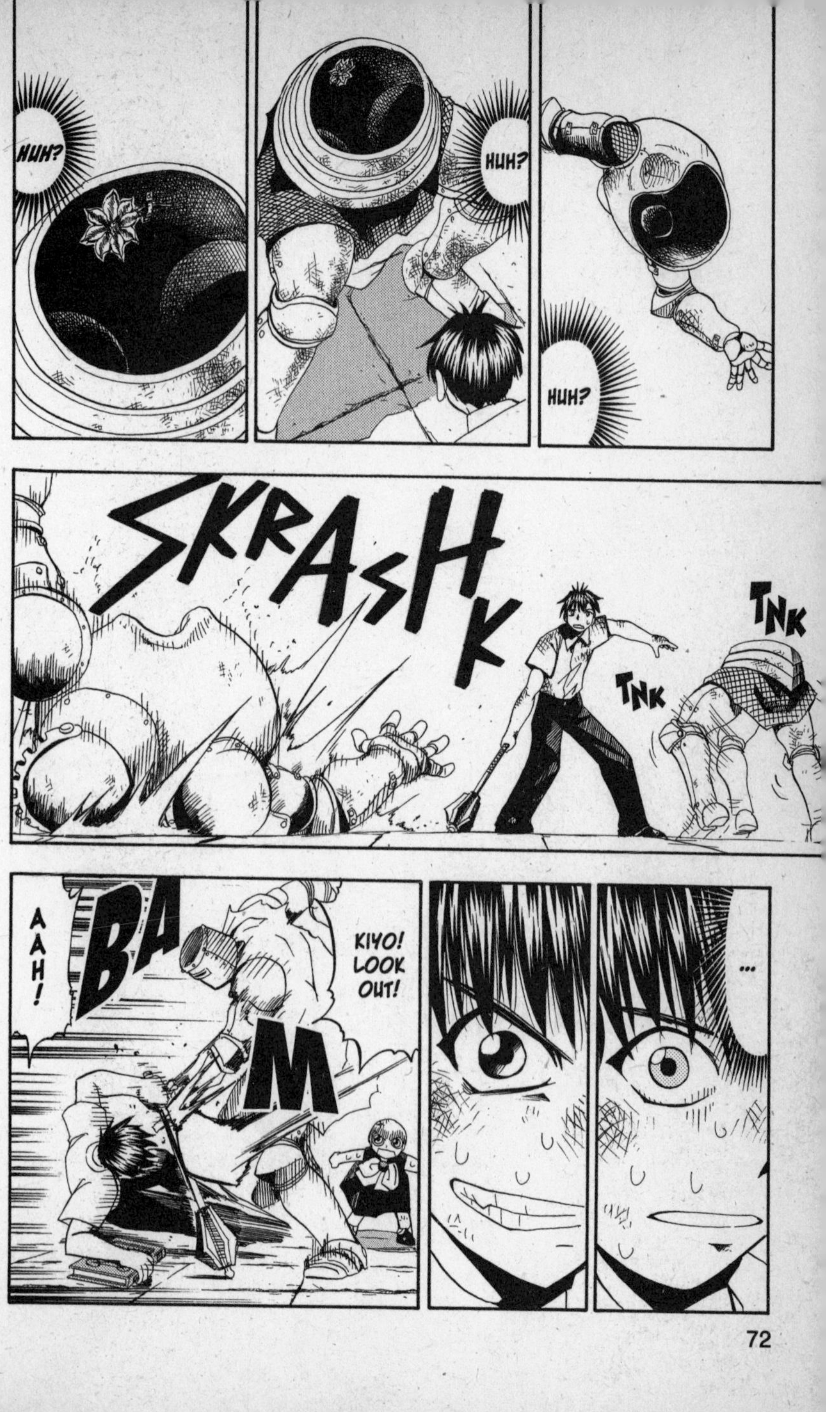
HUH?
HUH?
HUH?
SKRASHK
TNK
TNK
...
KIYO! LOOK OUT!
BAM
AAH!

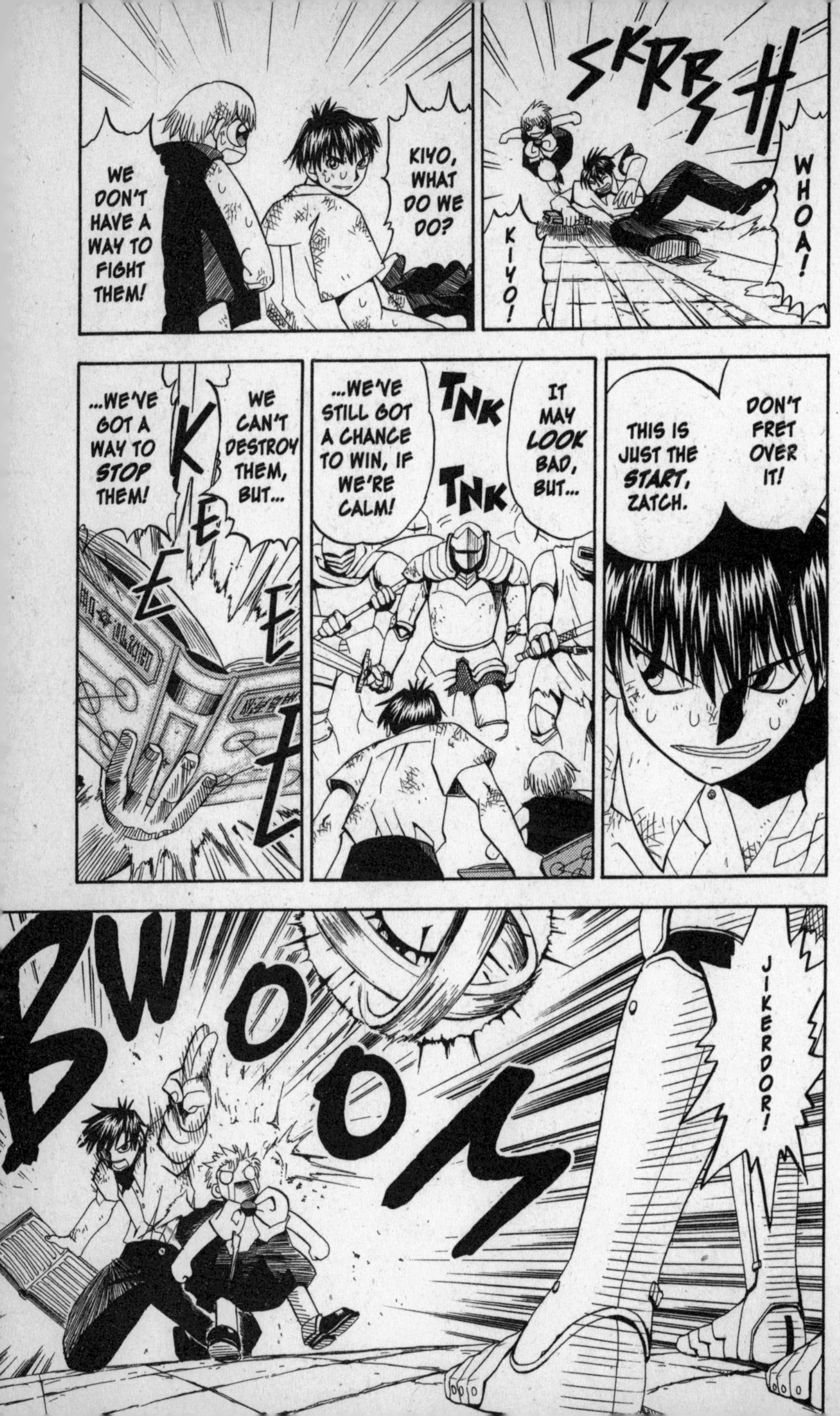
SKRRSH
WHOA!
KIYO!
KIYO, WHAT DO WE DO?
WE DON'T HAVE A WAY TO FIGHT THEM!
DON'T FRET OVER IT!
THIS IS JUST THE START, ZATCH.
IT MAY LOOK BAD, BUT...
TNK
TNK
...WE'VE STILL GOT A CHANCE TO WIN, IF WE'RE CALM!
WE CAN'T DESTROY THEM, BUT...
...WE'VE GOT A WAY TO STOP THEM!
KEEEE
JIKERDOOR!
BWOOOM

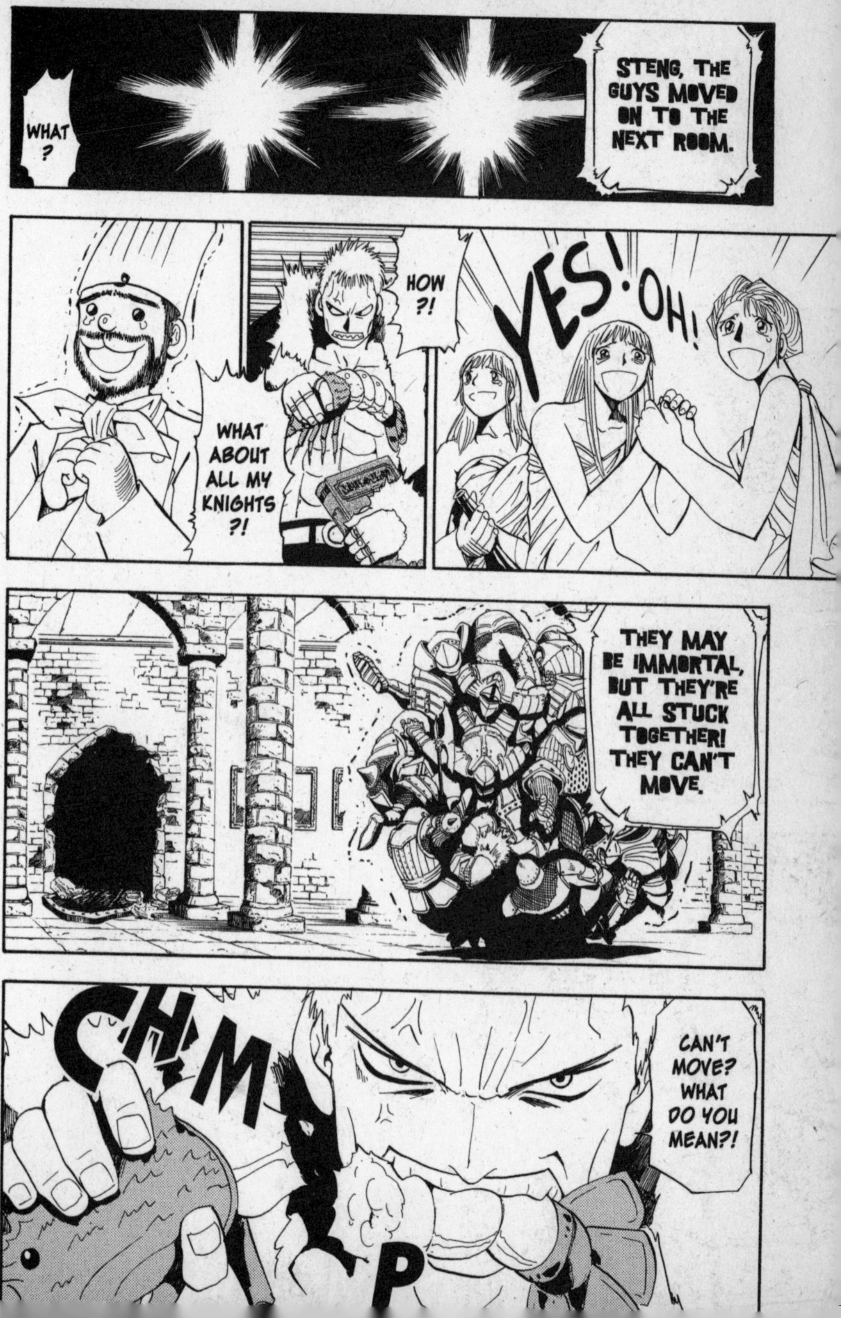
STENG, THE GUYS MOVED ON TO THE NEXT ROOM.
WHAT?
OH!
YES!
HOW?!
WHAT ABOUT ALL MY KNIGHTS?!
THEY MAY BE IMMORTAL, BUT THEY'RE ALL STUCK TOGETHER! THEY CAN'T MOVE.
CAN'T MOVE? WHAT DO YOU MEAN?!
CHOMP

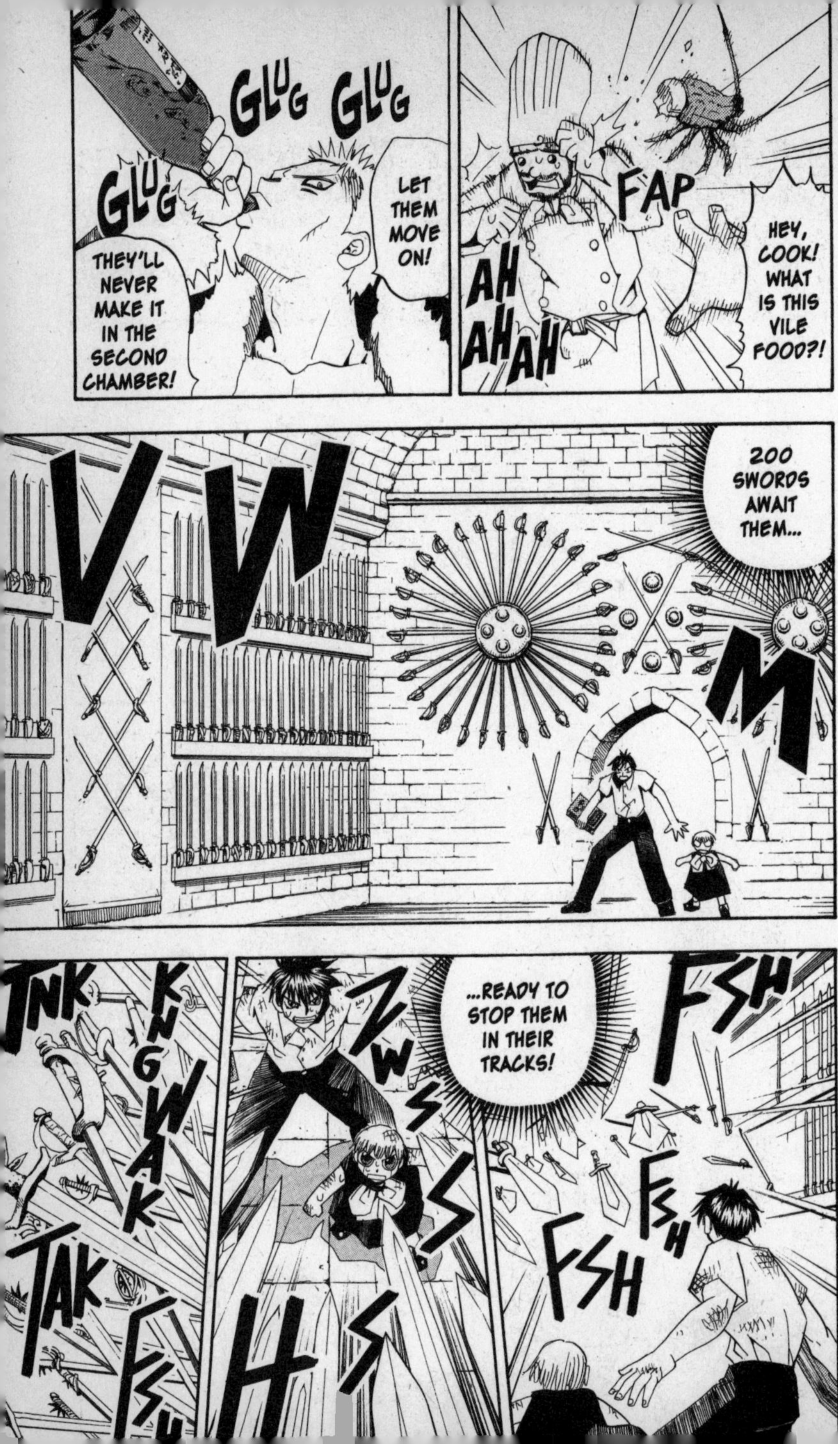
HEY, COOK! WHAT IS THIS VILE FOOD?!
FAP
AH AH AH
GLUG GLUG
LET THEM MOVE ON!
GLUG
THEY'LL NEVER MAKE IT IN THE SECOND CHAMBER!
200 SWORDS AWAIT THEM...
VWM
FSH
...READY TO STOP THEM IN THEIR TRACKS!
FSH
FSH
TNK
KNG
WAK
TAK

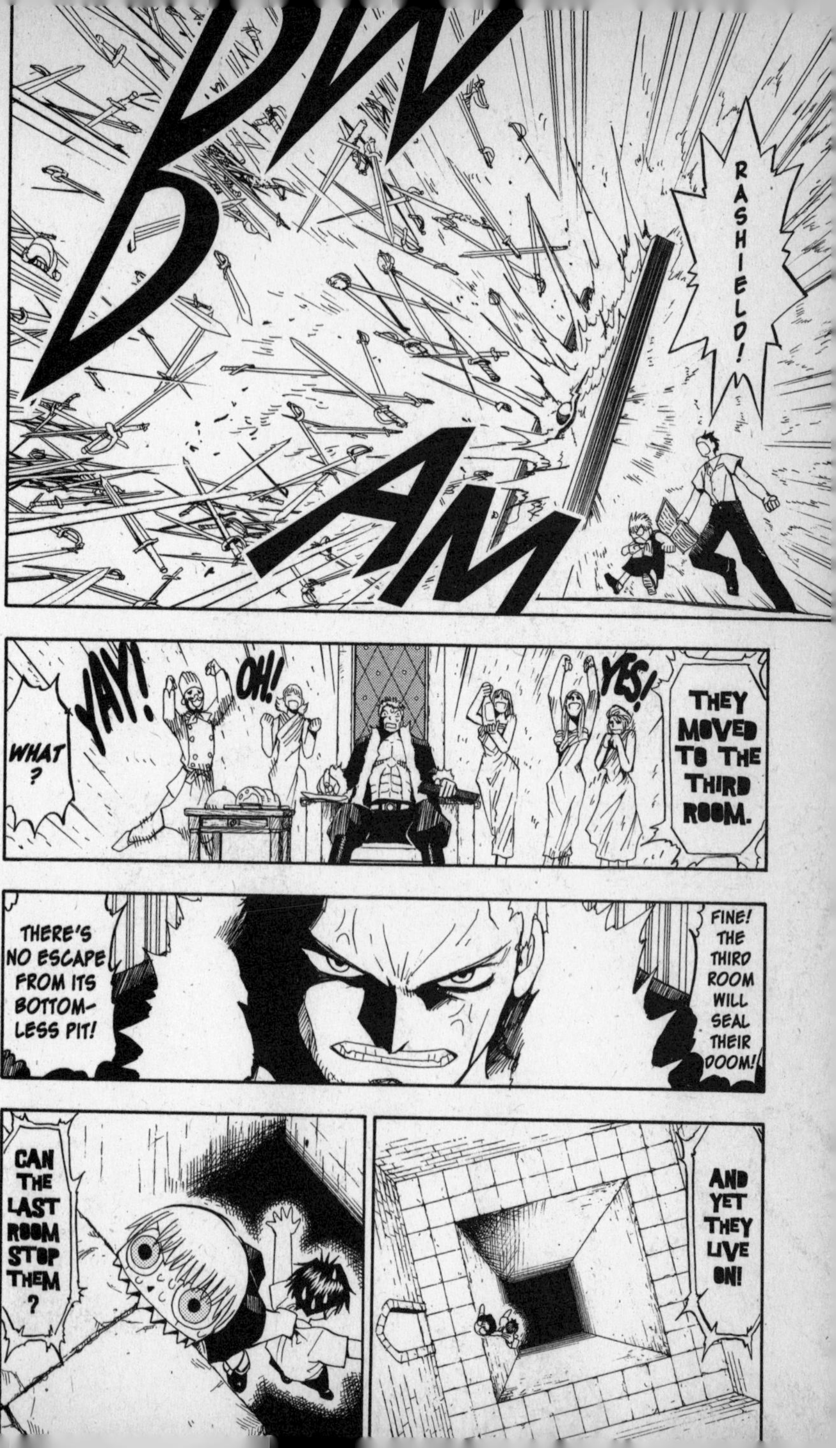
RASHIELD!
BAM
DW
THEY MOVED TO THE THIRD ROOM.
YES!
OH!
YAY!
WHAT?
FINE! THE THIRD ROOM WILL SEAL THEIR DOOM!
THERE'S NO ESCAPE FROM ITS BOTTOMLESS PIT!
AND YET THEY LIVE ON!
CAN THE LAST ROOM STOP THEM?

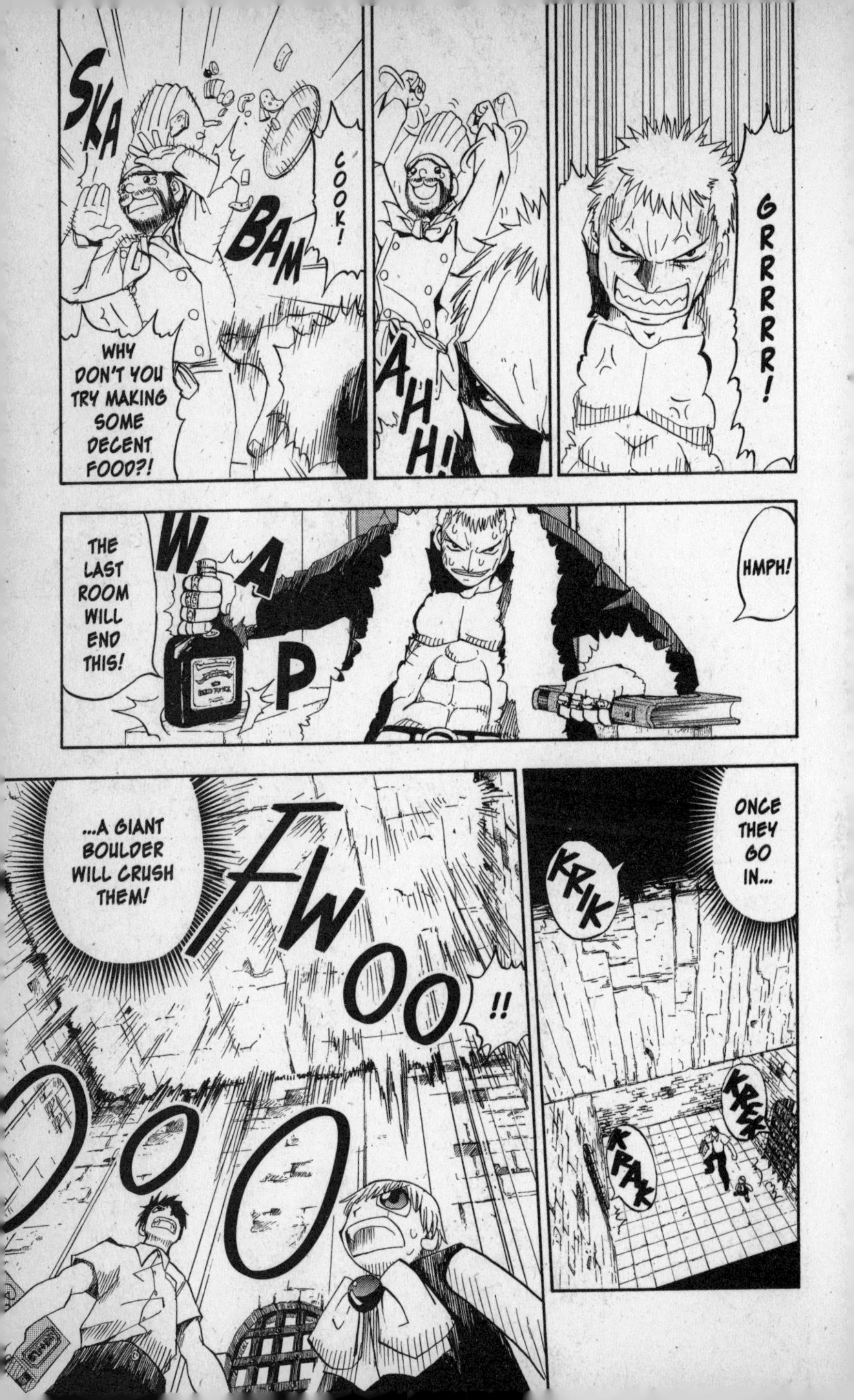
GRRRRR!
AHH!
COOK!
SKA
BAM
WHY DON'T YOU TRY MAKING SOME DECENT FOOD?!
HMPH!
THE LAST ROOM WILL END THIS!
WAP
ONCE THEY GO IN...
KRIK
KREK
KRAK
...A GIANT BOULDER WILL CRUSH THEM!
FWOOOOO!!

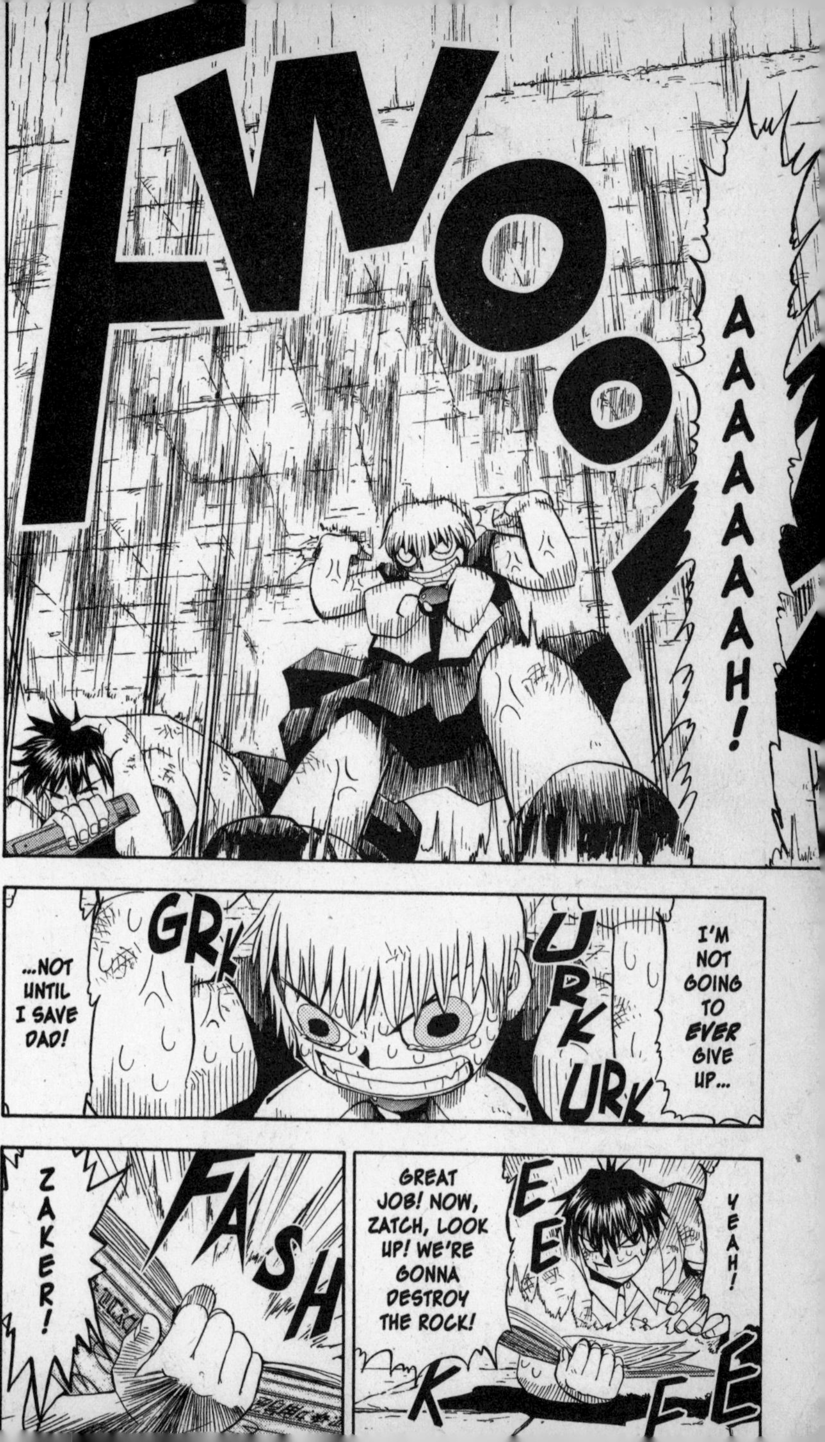
FWOOO
AAAAAAH!
I'M NOT GOING TO EVER GIVE UP...
URK URK
GRK
...NOT UNTIL I SAVE DAD!
YEAH!
EE
GREAT JOB! NOW, ZATCH, LOOK UP! WE'RE GONNA DESTROY THE ROCK!
KEE
FASH
ZAKER!

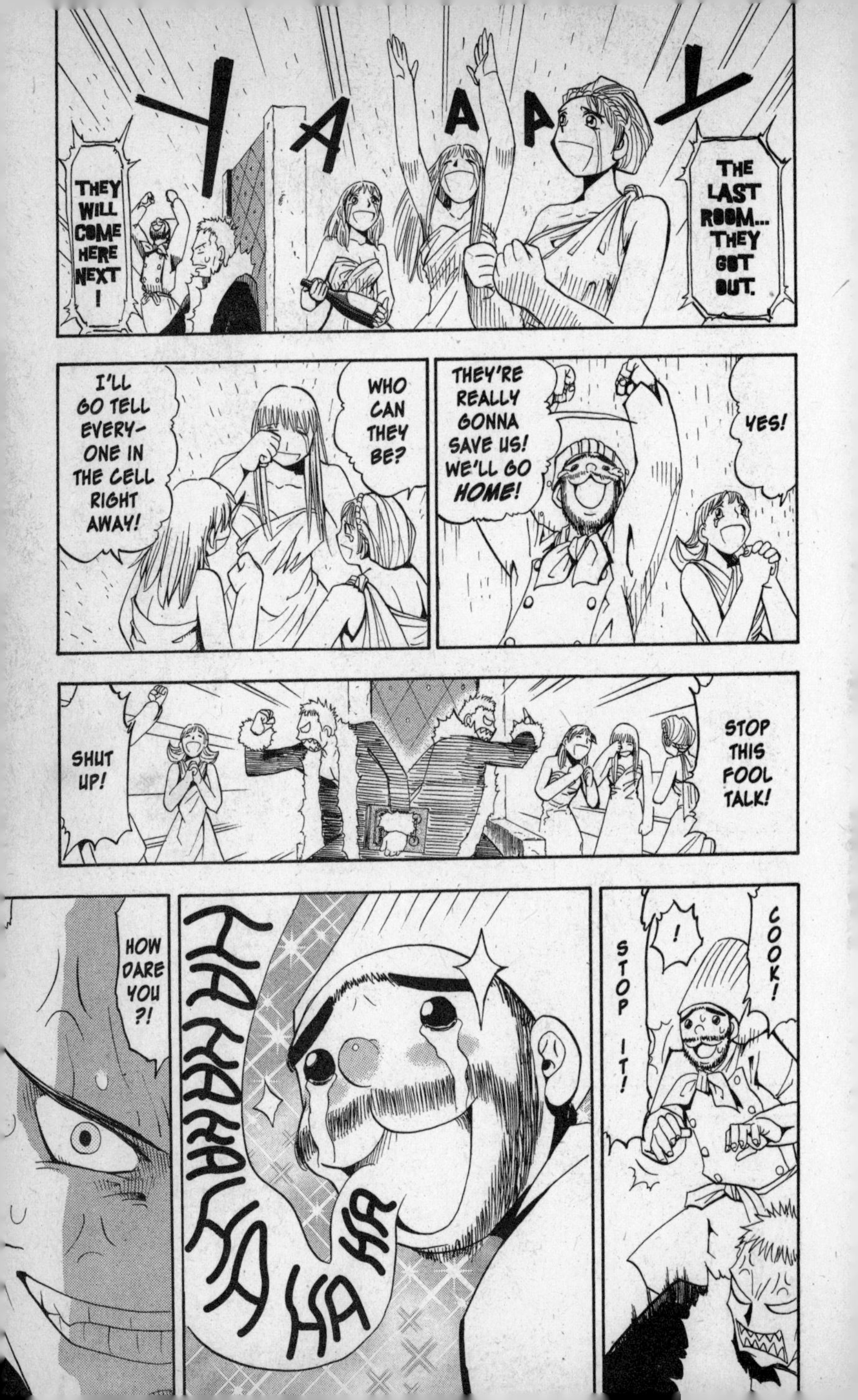

YAAAY
THE LAST ROOM... THEY GOT OUT.
THEY WILL COME HERE NEXT!
YES!
THEY'RE REALLY GONNA SAVE US! WE'LL GO HOME!
WHO CAN THEY BE?
I'LL GO TELL EVERYONE IN THE CELL RIGHT AWAY!
STOP THIS FOOL TALK!
SHUT UP!
COOK!
!
STOP IT!
HAHAHAHA HA HA
HOW DARE YOU?!

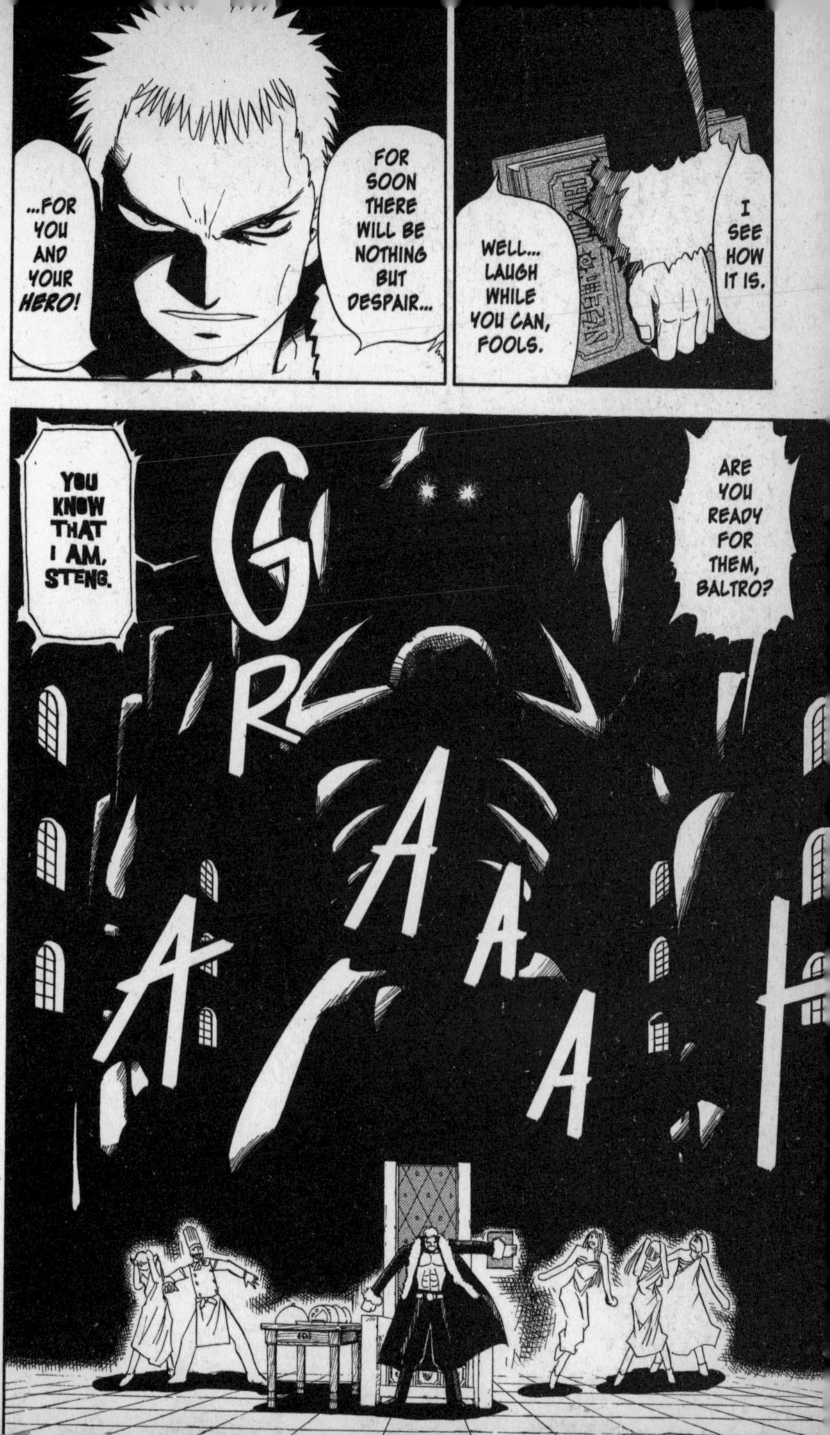
I SEE HOW IT IS.
WELL... LAUGH WHILE YOU CAN, FOOLS.
FOR SOON THERE WILL BE NOTHING BUT DESPAIR...
...FOR YOU AND YOUR HERO!
ARE YOU READY FOR THEM, BALTRO?
YOU KNOW THAT I AM, STENG.
GRAAAAA!

LEVEL 43: The Biggest Mamodo

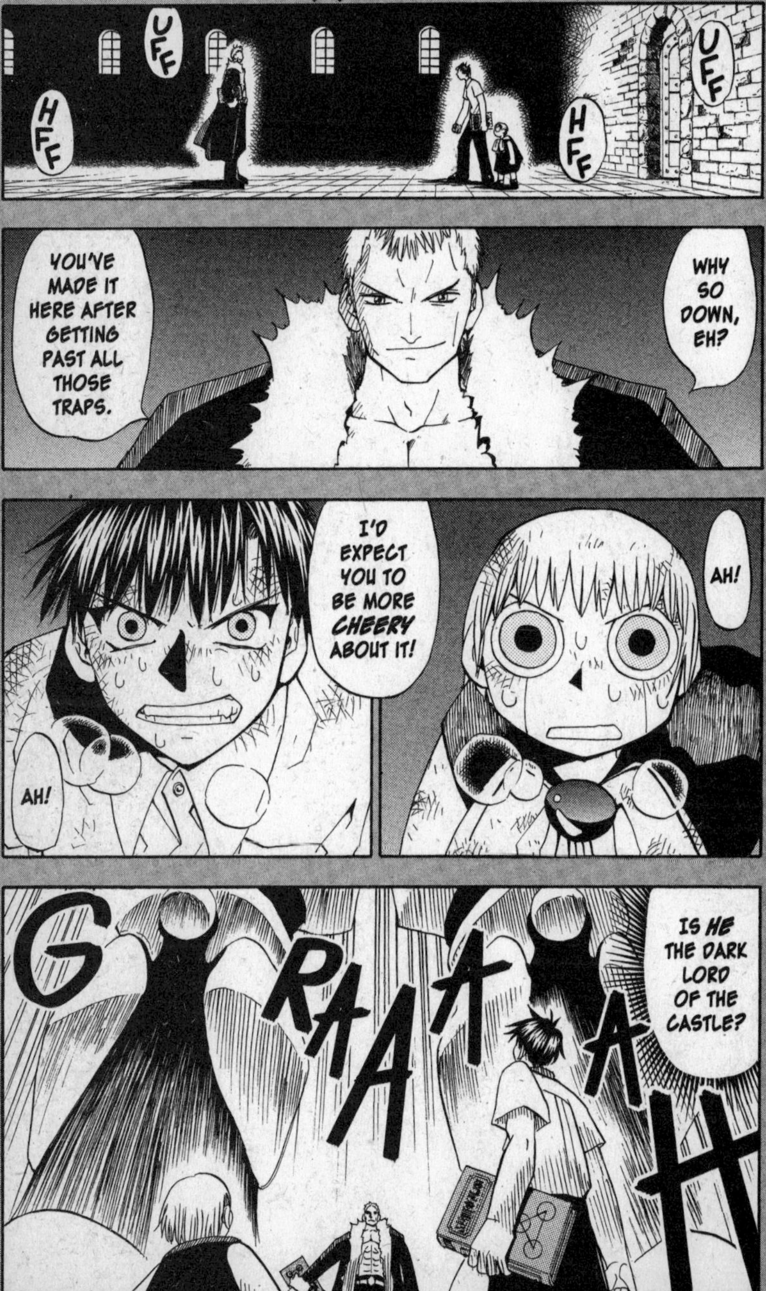
HFF
UFF
HFF
UFF
WHY SO DOWN, EH?
YOU'VE MADE IT HERE AFTER GETTING PAST ALL THOSE TRAPS.
AH!
I'D EXPECT YOU TO BE MORE CHEERY ABOUT IT!
AH!
IS HE THE DARK LORD OF THE CASTLE?
GRAAAAH

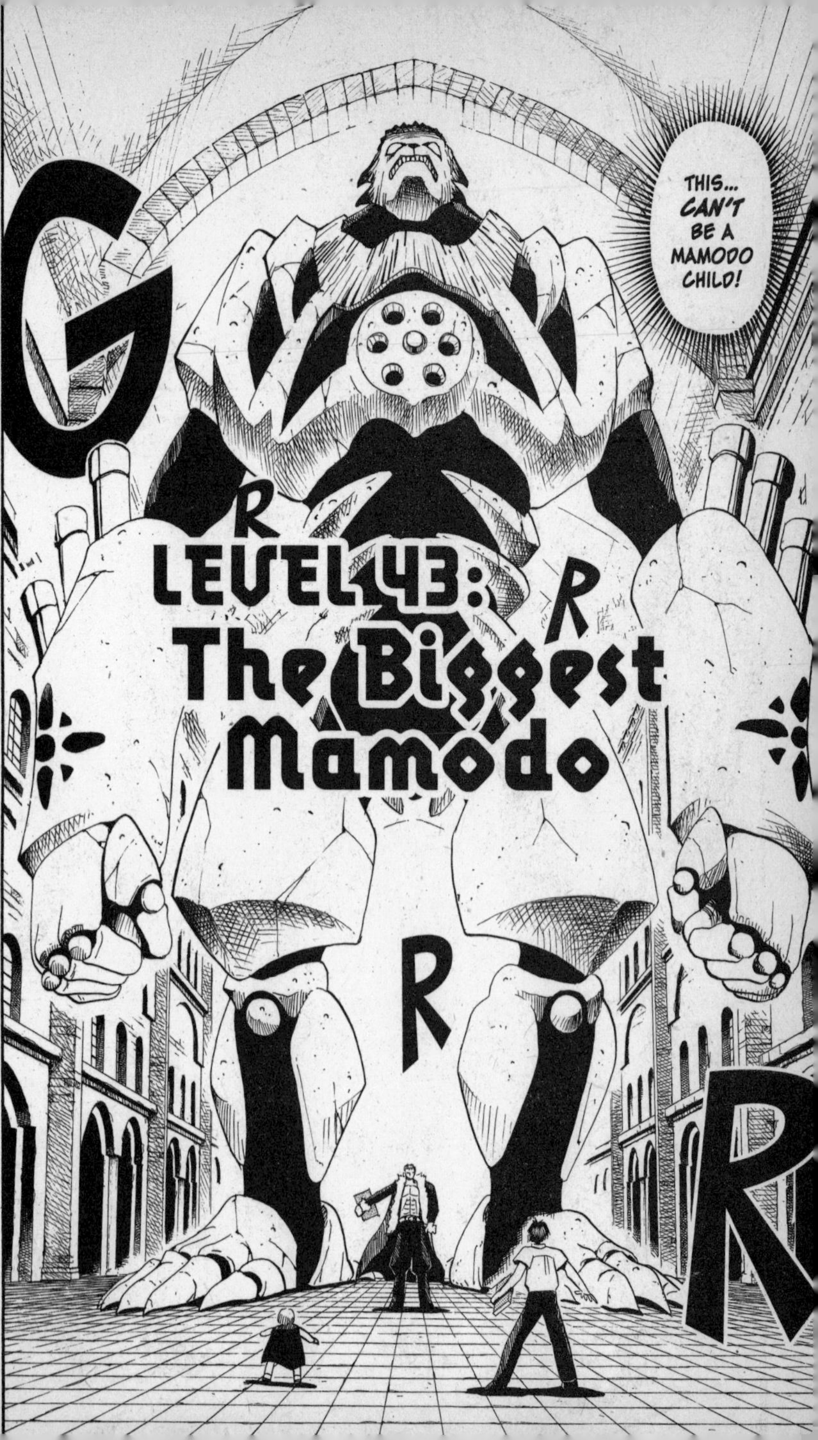
THIS... CAN'T BE A MAMODO CHILD!
GRRRR
LEVEL 43: The Biggest Mamodo

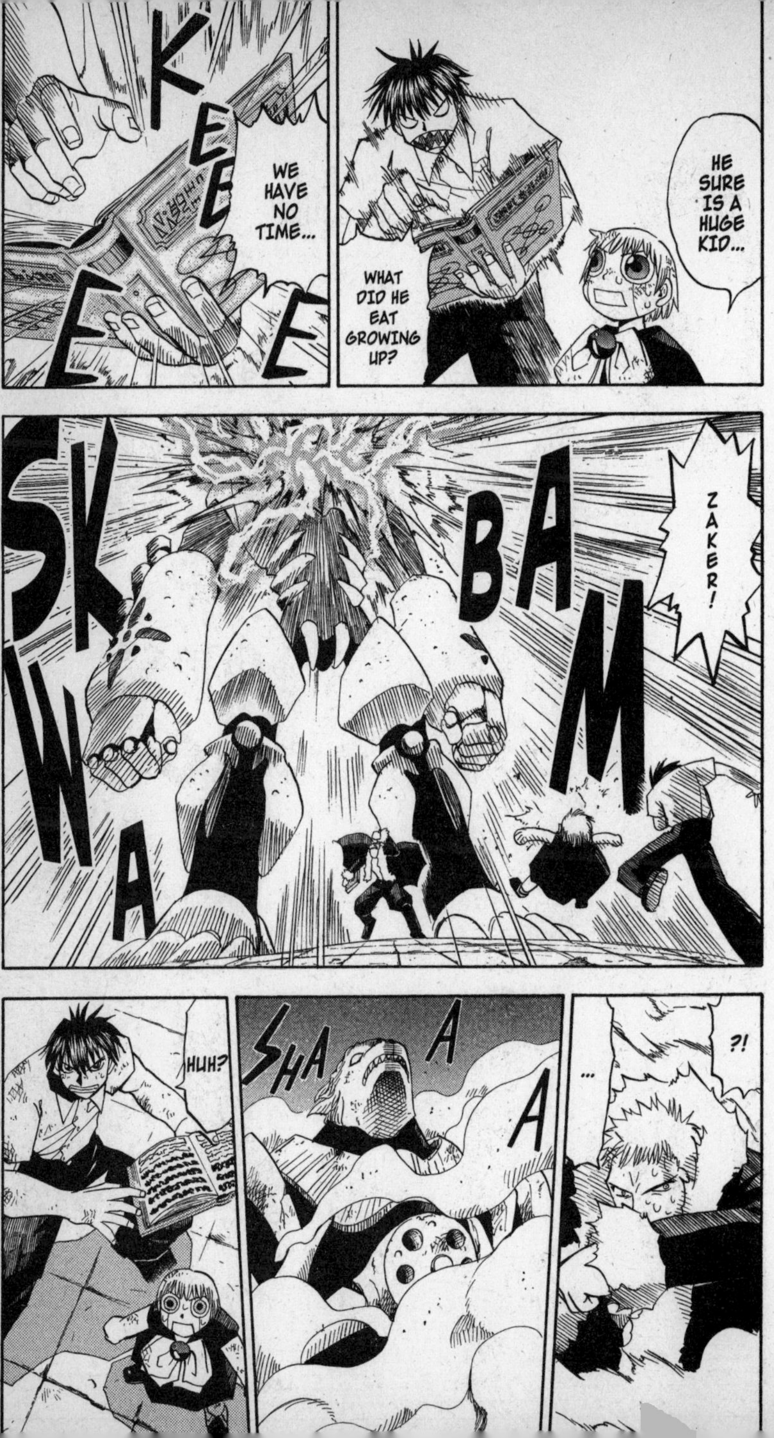

HE SURE IS A HUGE KID...
WHAT DID HE EAT GROWING UP?
WE HAVE NO TIME...
KEEEE
ZAKER!
BAM
SKWAA
?!
...
SHAAA
HUH?

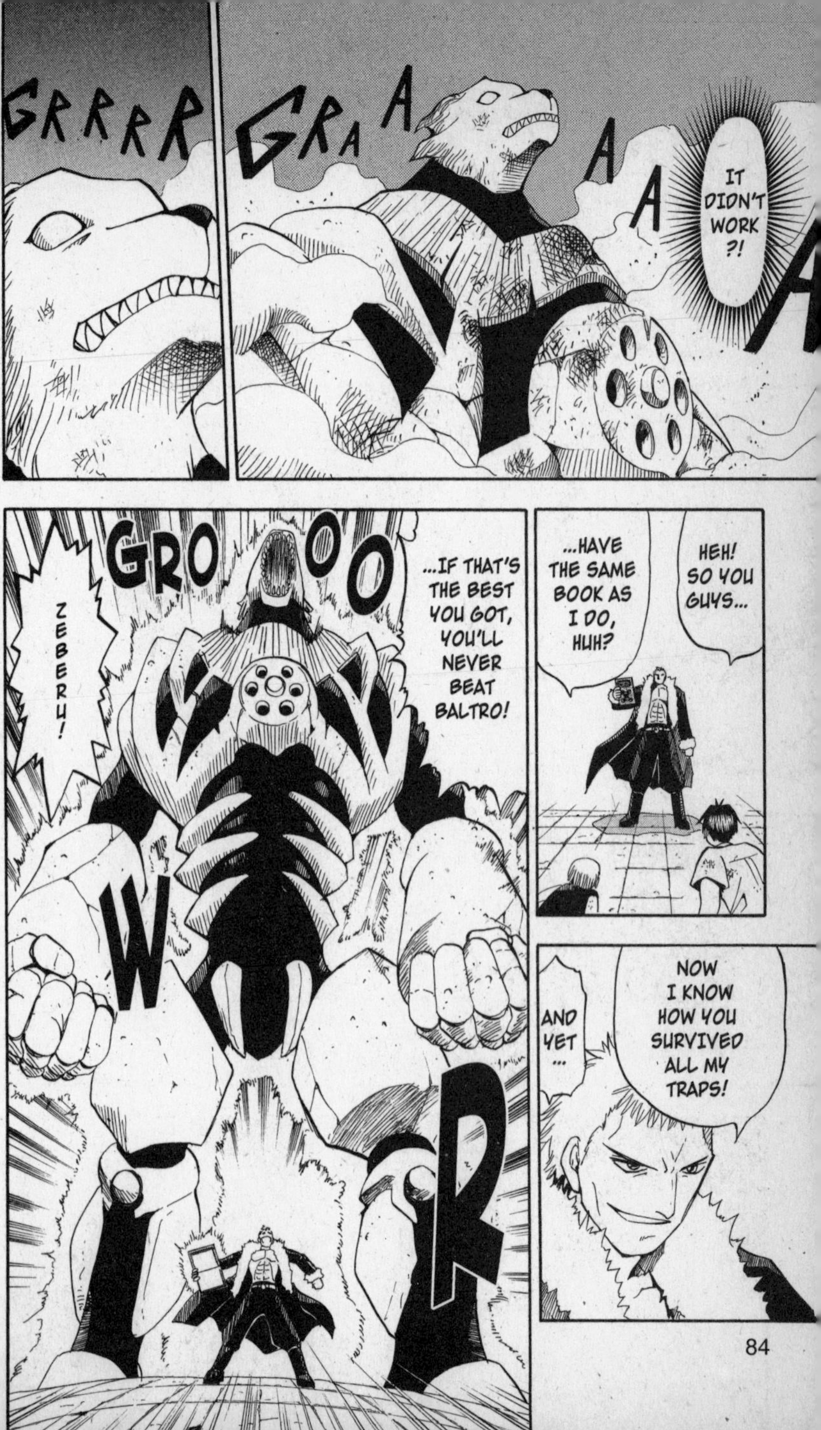
GRAAAAAA
IT DIDN'T WORK ?!
GRRRR
HEH! SO YOU GUYS...
...HAVE THE SAME BOOK AS I DO, HUH?
NOW I KNOW HOW YOU SURVIVED ALL MY TRAPS!
AND YET ...
...IF THAT'S THE BEST YOU GOT, YOU'LL NEVER BEAT BALTRO!
ZEBERU!
GROOOWR

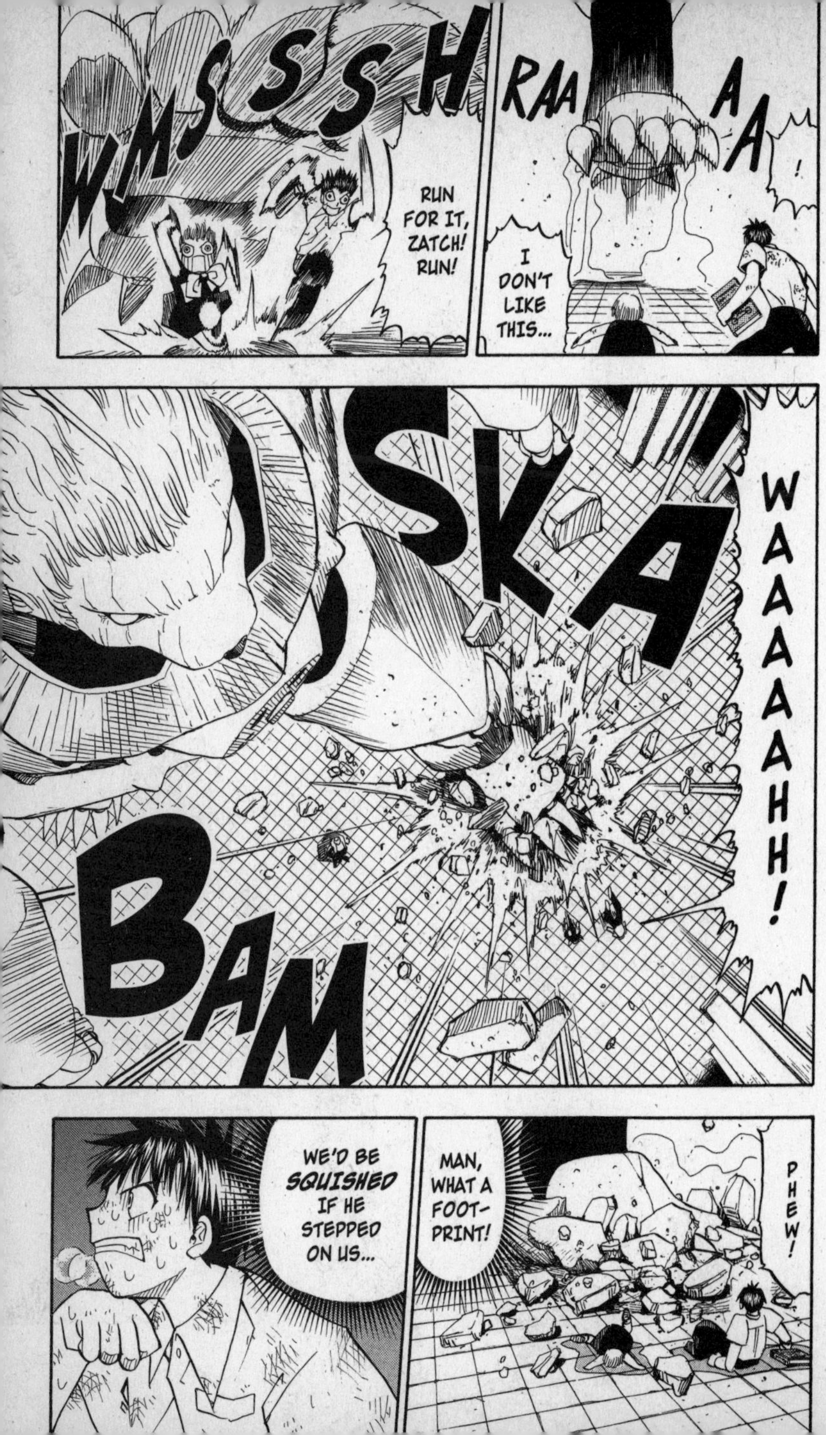
RAAAAA
!
I DON'T LIKE THIS...
WMSSSH
RUN FOR IT, ZATCH! RUN!
WAAAAAHH!
SKA
BAM
PHEW!
MAN, WHAT A FOOT-PRINT!
WE'D BE SQUISHED IF HE STEPPED ON US...

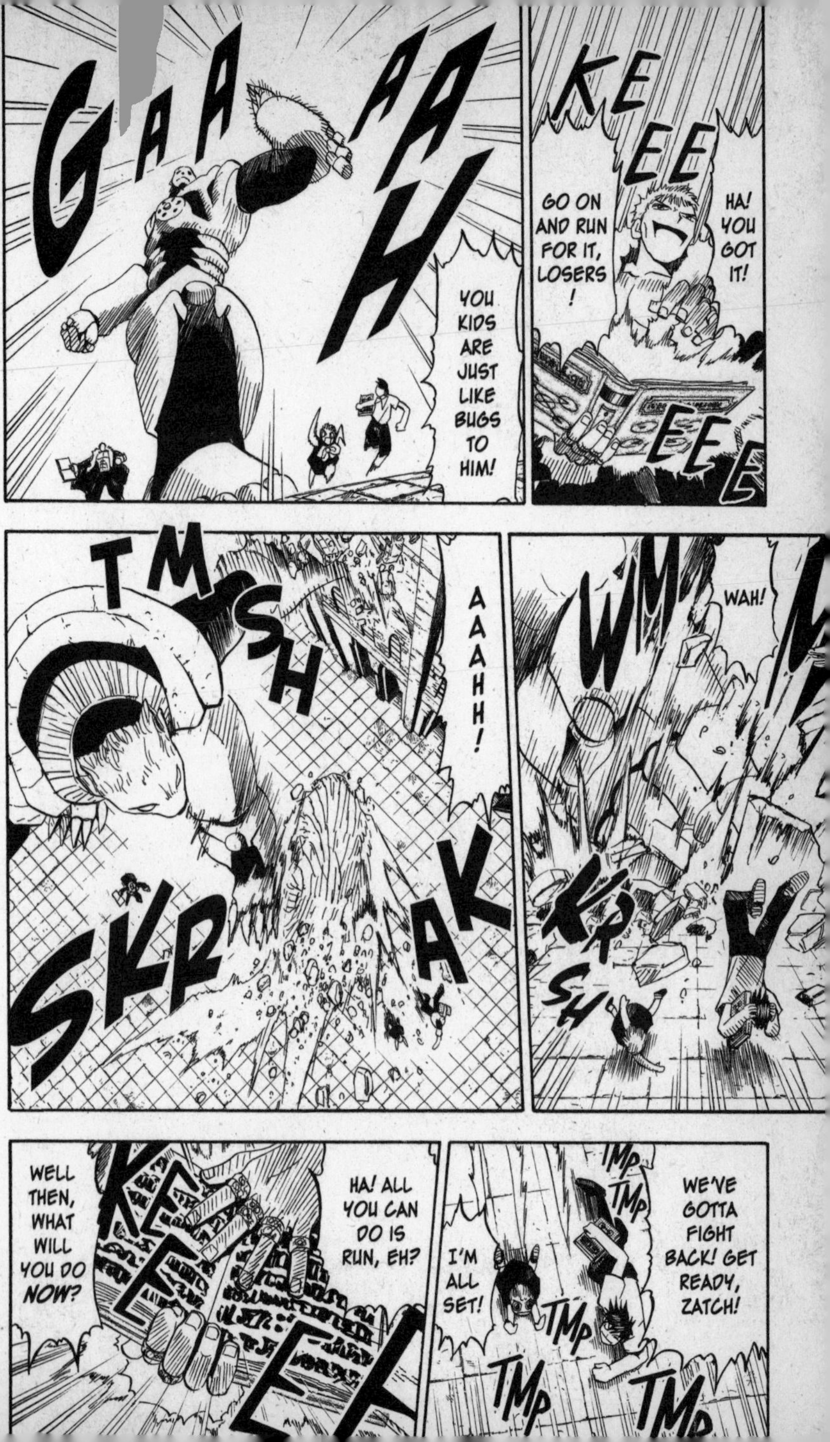
KEEEEEEE
HA! YOU GOT IT!
GO ON AND RUN FOR IT, LOSERS!
GAAAAH
YOU KIDS ARE JUST LIKE BUGS TO HIM!
WMM
WAH!
KRRSH
TMSH
AAAHH!
SKRAK
TMP TMP
WE'VE GOTTA FIGHT BACK! GET READY, ZATCH!
I'M ALL SET!
TMP
TMP
TMP
HA! ALL YOU CAN DO IS RUN, EH?
WELL THEN, WHAT WILL YOU DO NOW?

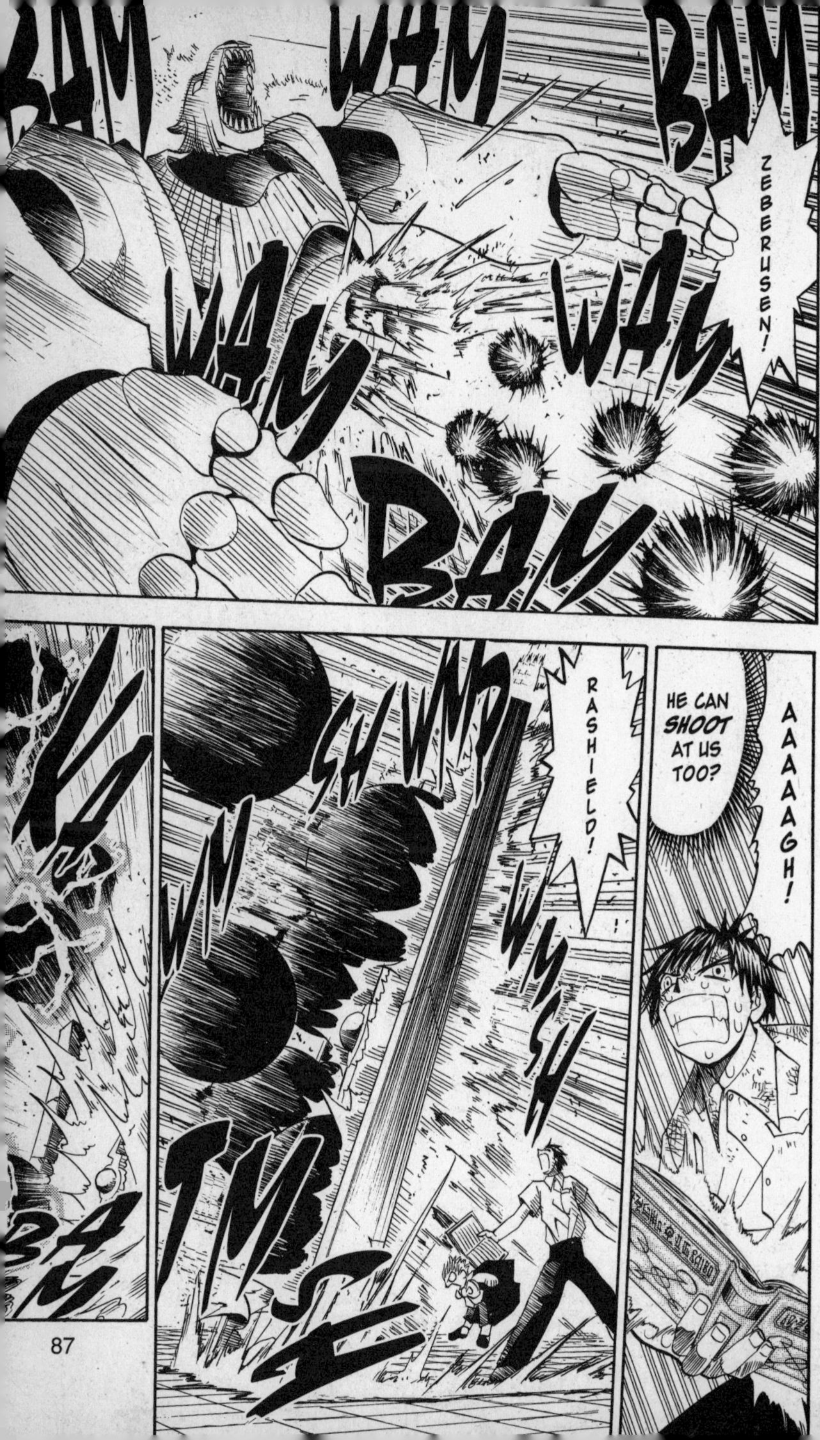
BAM
ZEBERUSEN!
WHAM
BAM
WAM
WAM
BAM
AAAAAGH!
HE CAN SHOOT AT US TOO?
RASHIELD!
BAM

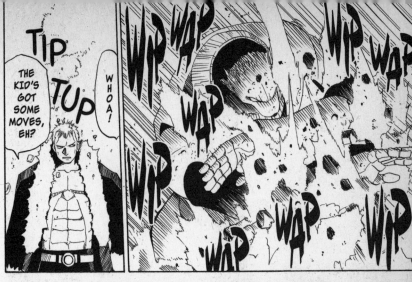

WIP WAP
WAP
WIP
WAP
WAP
WIP WAP
WIP
WHOA!
TIP
TUP
THE KID'S GOT SOME MOVES, EH?
I JUST USED OUR BEST BLOCK, AND...
...NOT A DENT IN HIM?!
FSSHHH
AGAINST BALTRO AND HIS POWER, NO ONE'S GOOD ENOUGH!
HE'S THE BEST THERE IS, NO DOUBT ABOUT IT!
AND AS LONG AS I USE HIM...
...I'LL ALWAYS BE STRONG, EVEN IF I LEAVE THIS CASTLE BEHIND!
KEEEE
I CAN GET ANYTHING I WANT! I CAN PARTY ALL THE TIME!

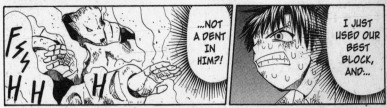

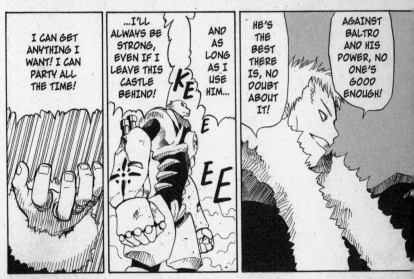

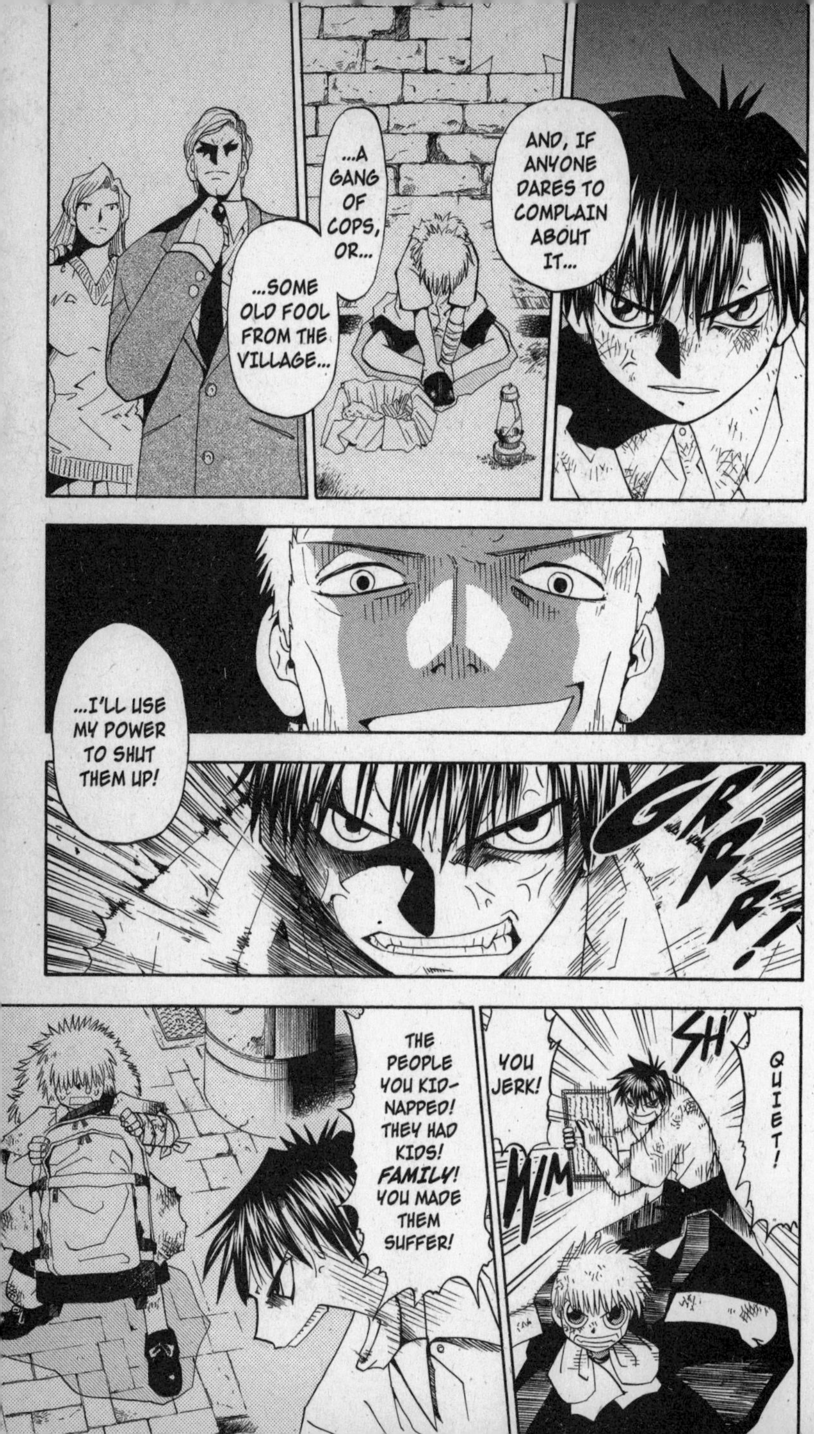
AND, IF ANYONE DARES TO COMPLAIN ABOUT IT...
...A GANG OF COPS, OR...
...SOME OLD FOOL FROM THE VILLAGE...
...I'LL USE MY POWER TO SHUT THEM UP!
GRRR!
QUIET!
SH
YOU JERK!
WM
THE PEOPLE YOU KID-NAPPED! THEY HAD KIDS! ***FAMILY!*** YOU MADE THEM SUFFER!

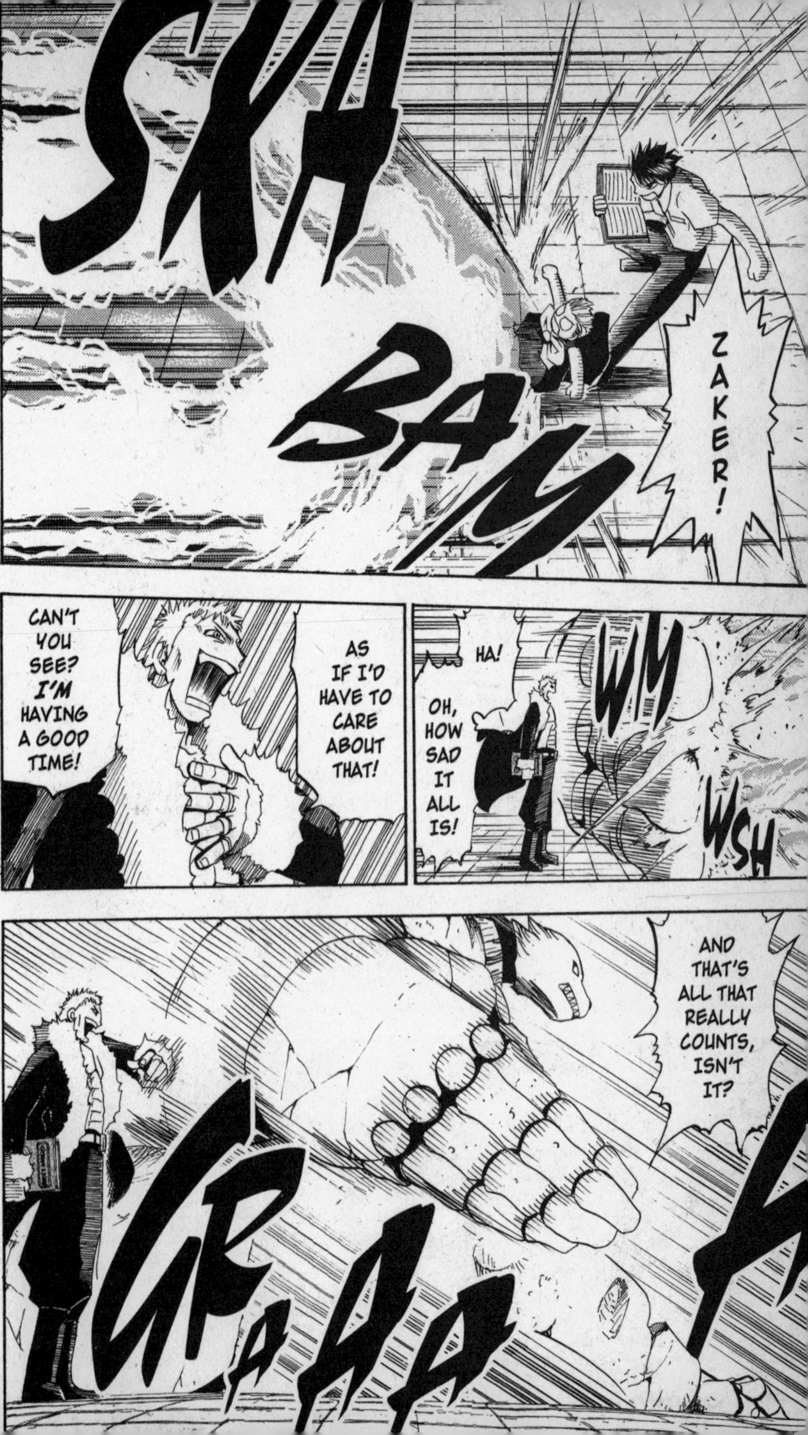
ZAKER!
SKA
BAM
HA!
OH, HOW SAD IT ALL IS!
WM
WSH
AS IF I'D HAVE TO CARE ABOUT THAT!
CAN'T YOU SEE? I'M HAVING A GOOD TIME!
AND THAT'S ALL THAT REALLY COUNTS, ISN'T IT?

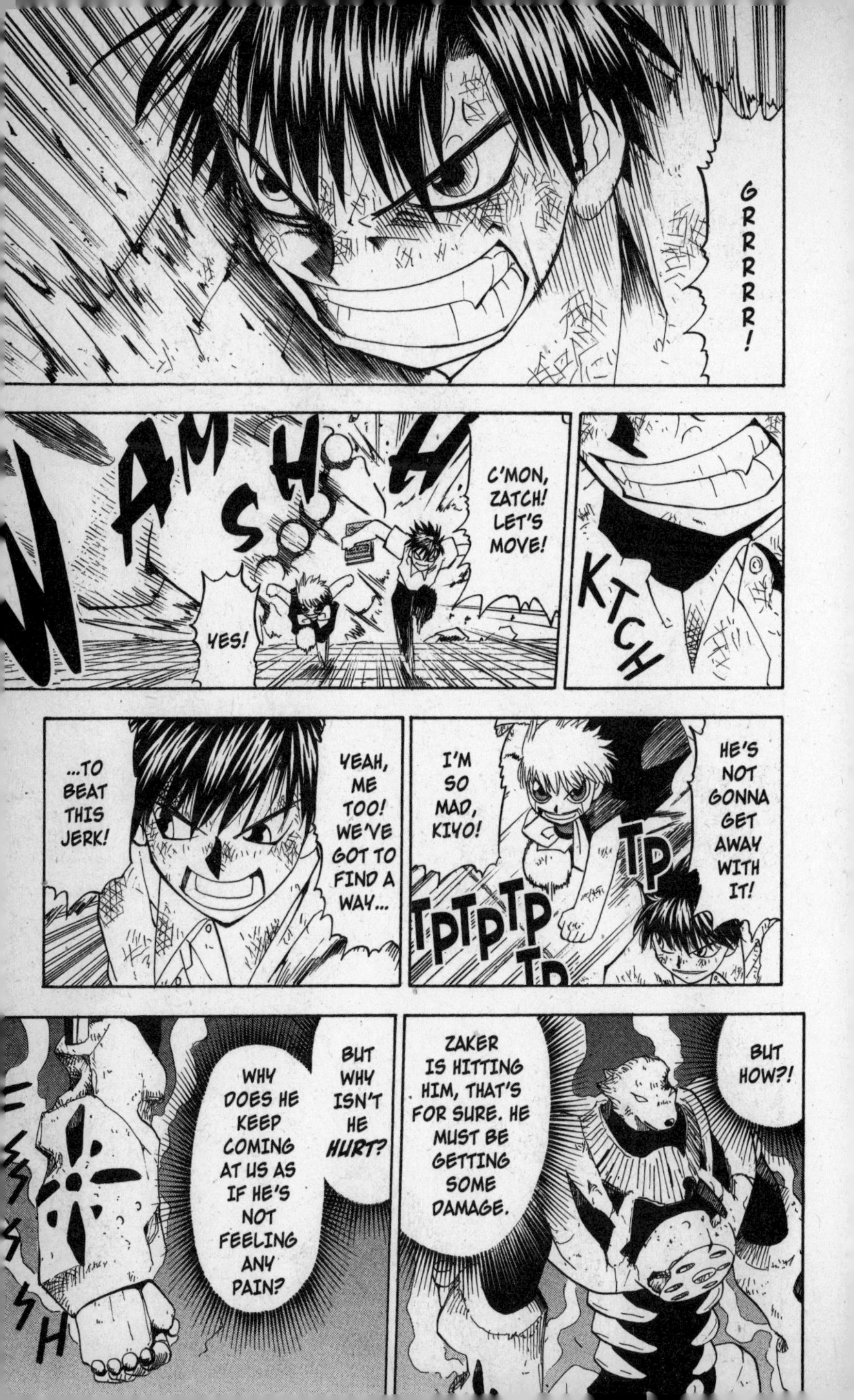
GRRRRR!
KTCH
C'MON, ZATCH! LET'S MOVE!
YES!
HE'S NOT GONNA GET AWAY WITH IT!
I'M SO MAD, KIYO!
TPTPTPTP
YEAH, ME TOO! WE'VE GOT TO FIND A WAY...
...TO BEAT THIS JERK!
BUT HOW?!
ZAKER IS HITTING HIM, THAT'S FOR SURE. HE MUST BE GETTING SOME DAMAGE.
BUT WHY ISN'T HE *HURT*?
WHY DOES HE KEEP COMING AT US AS IF HE'S NOT FEELING ANY PAIN?

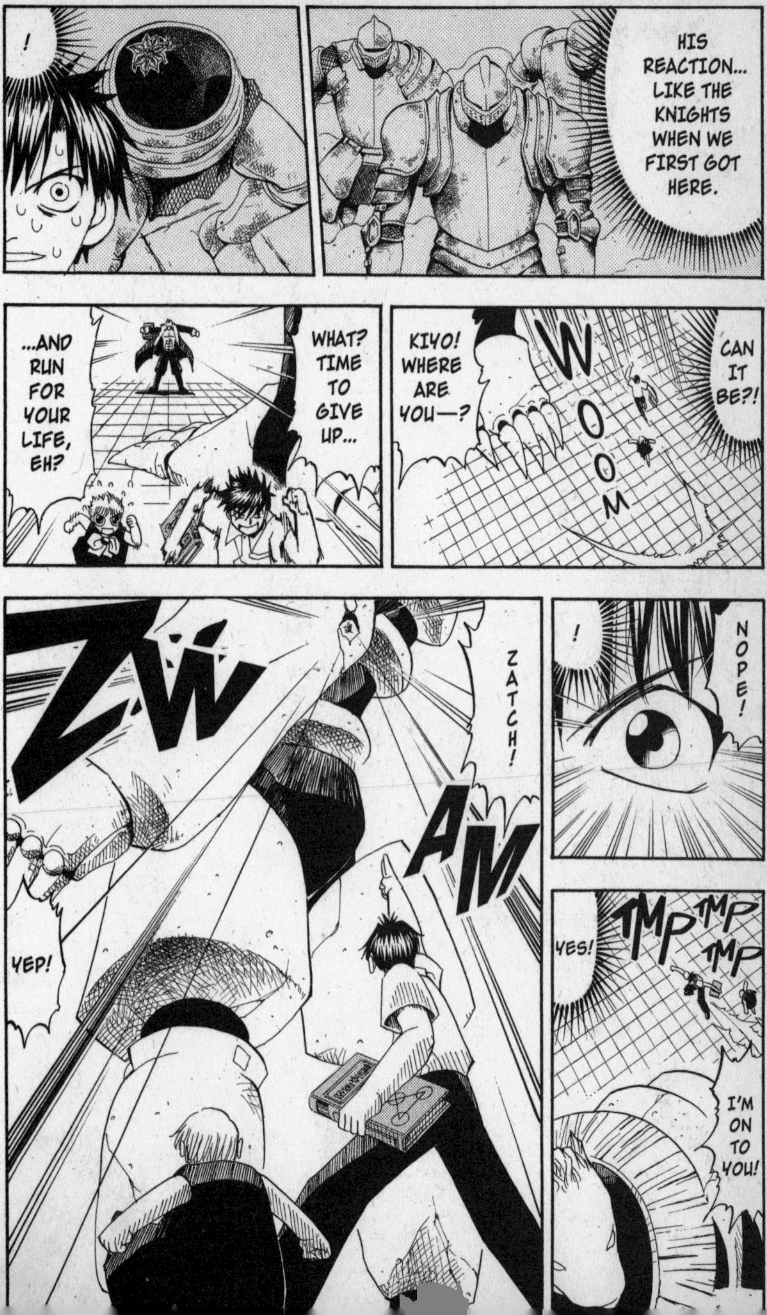
HIS REACTION... LIKE THE KNIGHTS WHEN WE FIRST GOT HERE.
!
CAN IT BE?!
WOOOOM
KIYO! WHERE ARE YOU—?
WHAT? TIME TO GIVE UP...
...AND RUN FOR YOUR LIFE, EH?
NOPE!
!
TMP TMP TMP
YES!
I'M ON TO YOU!
ZATCH!
ZWAM
YEP!

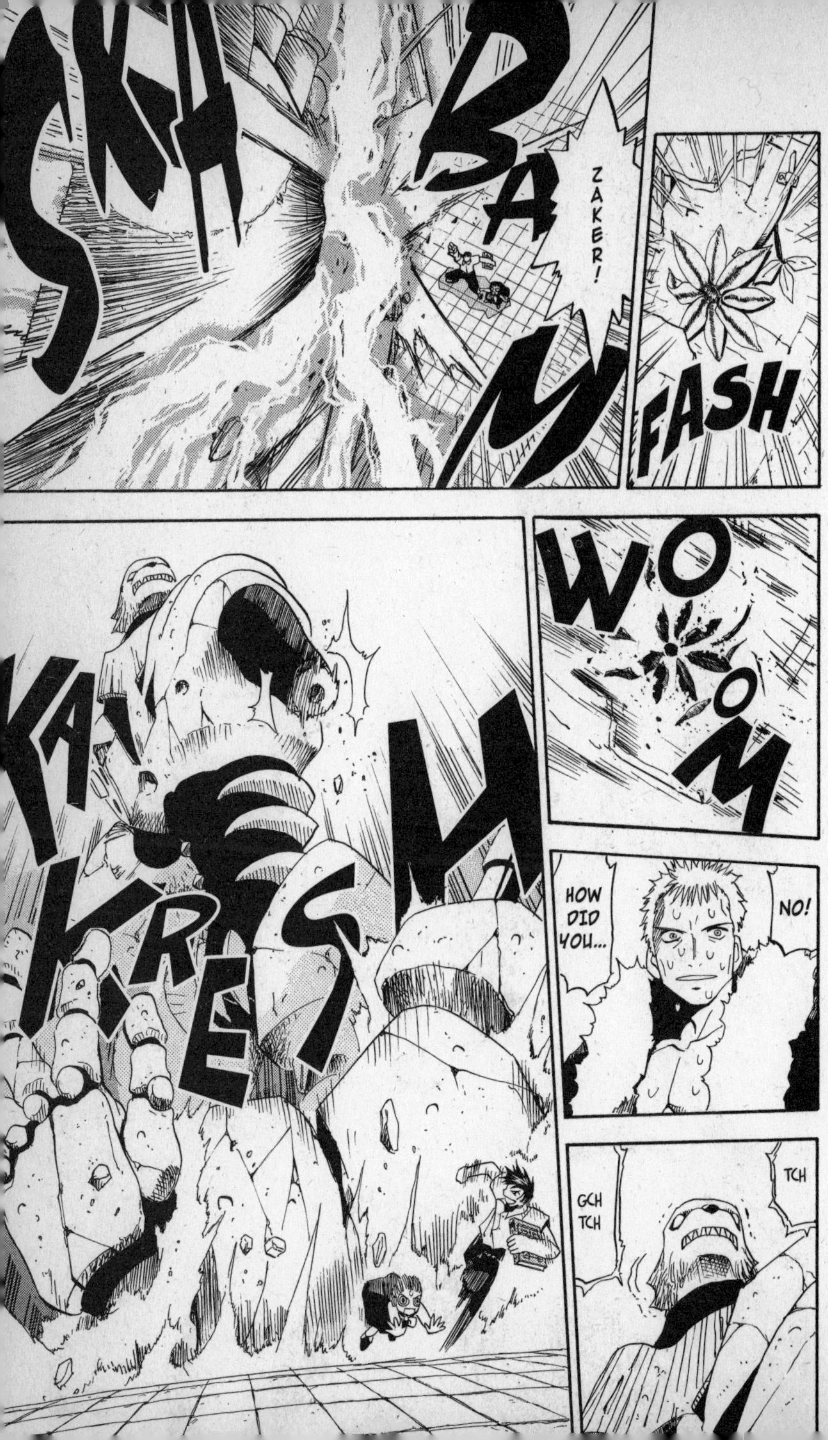
FASH
ZAKER!
BAM
WOOM
NO!
HOW DID YOU...
TCH
GCH TCH
KA
KRESH

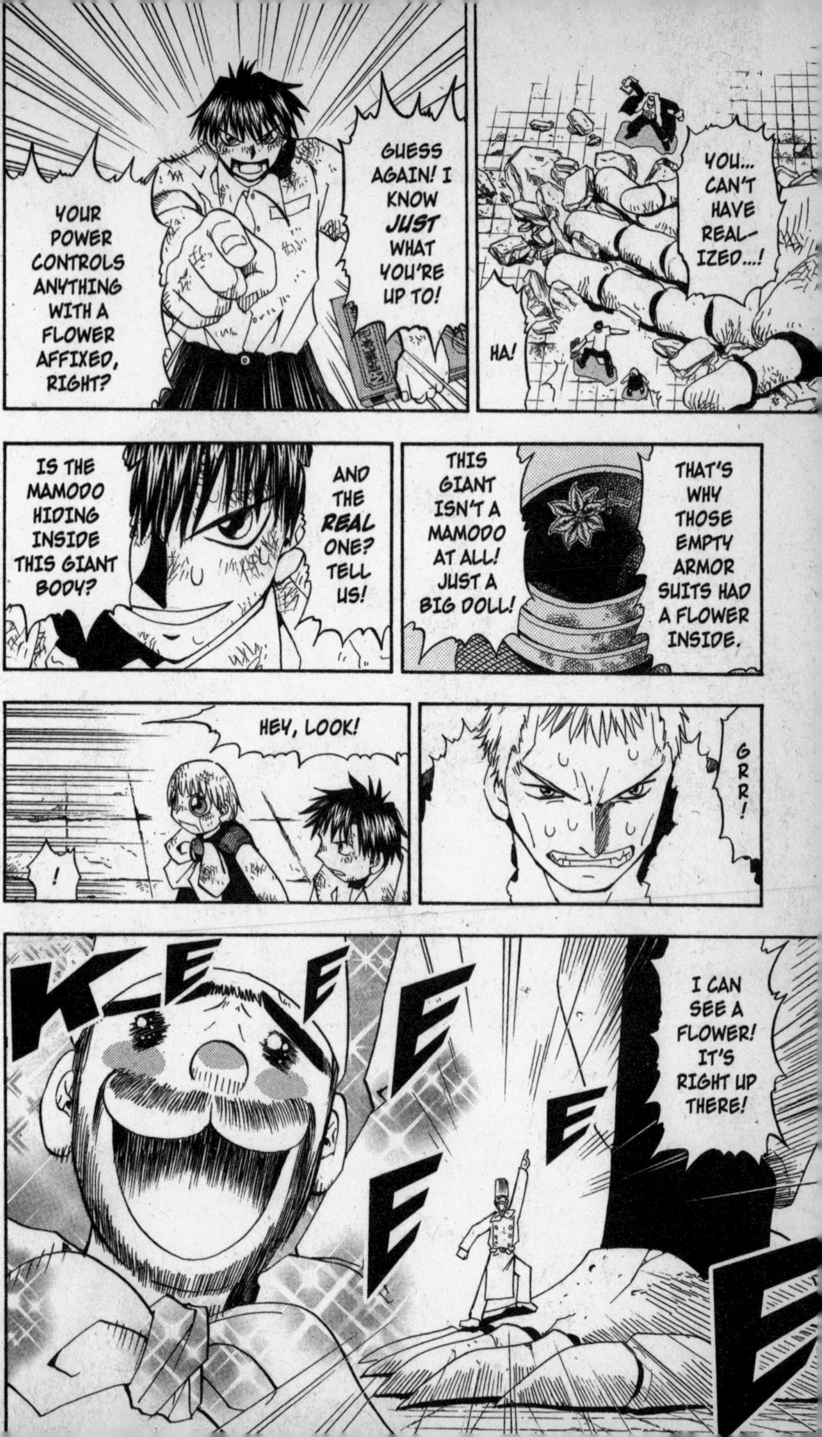
YOU... CAN'T HAVE REAL-IZED...!
HA!
GUESS AGAIN! I KNOW JUST WHAT YOU'RE UP TO!
YOUR POWER CONTROLS ANYTHING WITH A FLOWER AFFIXED, RIGHT?
THAT'S WHY THOSE EMPTY ARMOR SUITS HAD A FLOWER INSIDE.
THIS GIANT ISN'T A MAMODO AT ALL! JUST A BIG DOLL!
AND THE REAL ONE? TELL US!
IS THE MAMODO HIDING INSIDE THIS GIANT BODY?
GRR!
HEY, LOOK!
!
I CAN SEE A FLOWER! IT'S RIGHT UP THERE!
KLEEEEEEE

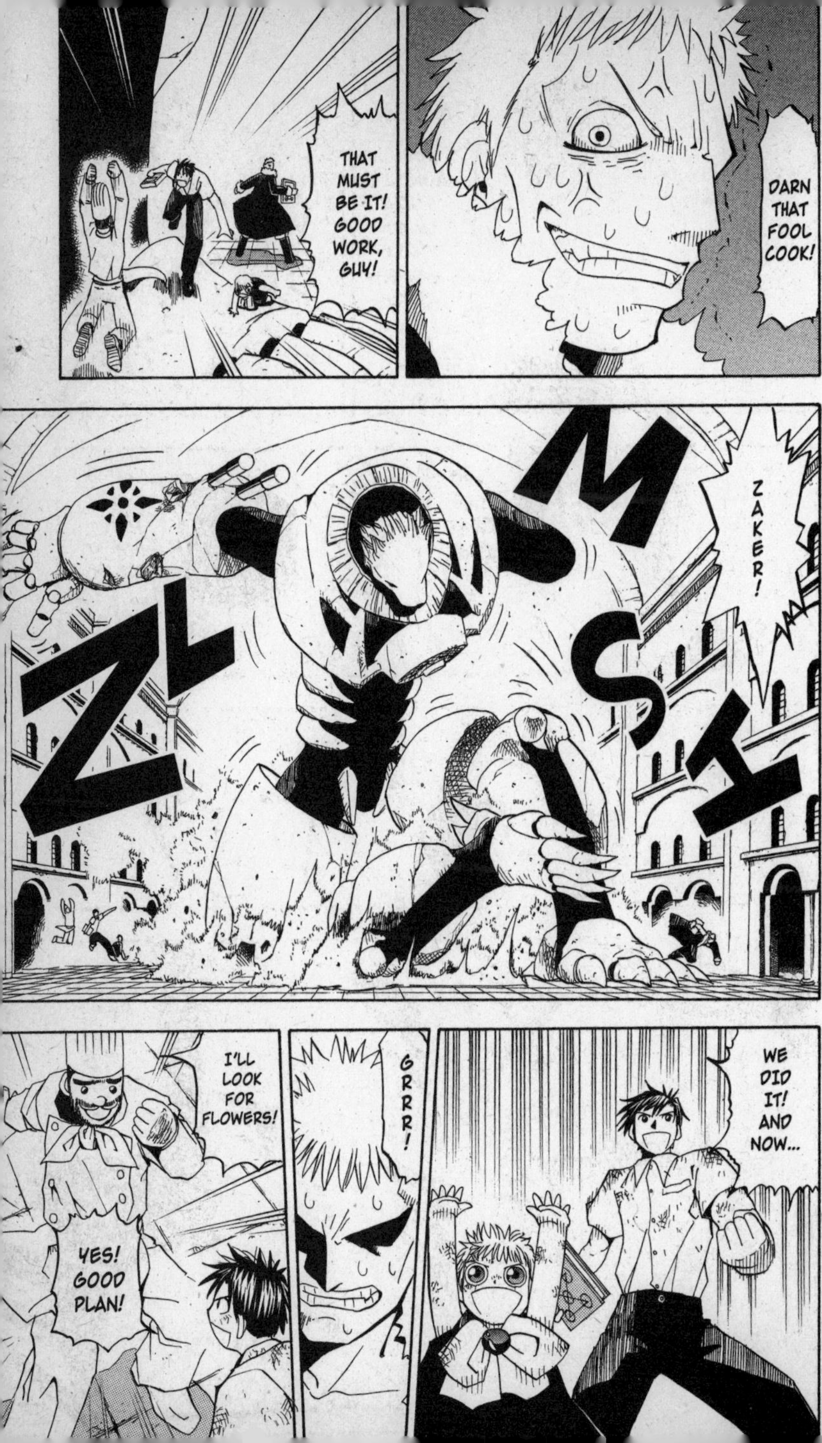
DARN THAT FOOL COOK!
THAT MUST BE IT! GOOD WORK, GUY!
ZAKER!
ZMSH
WE DID IT! AND NOW...
GRRR!
I'LL LOOK FOR FLOWERS!
YES! GOOD PLAN!

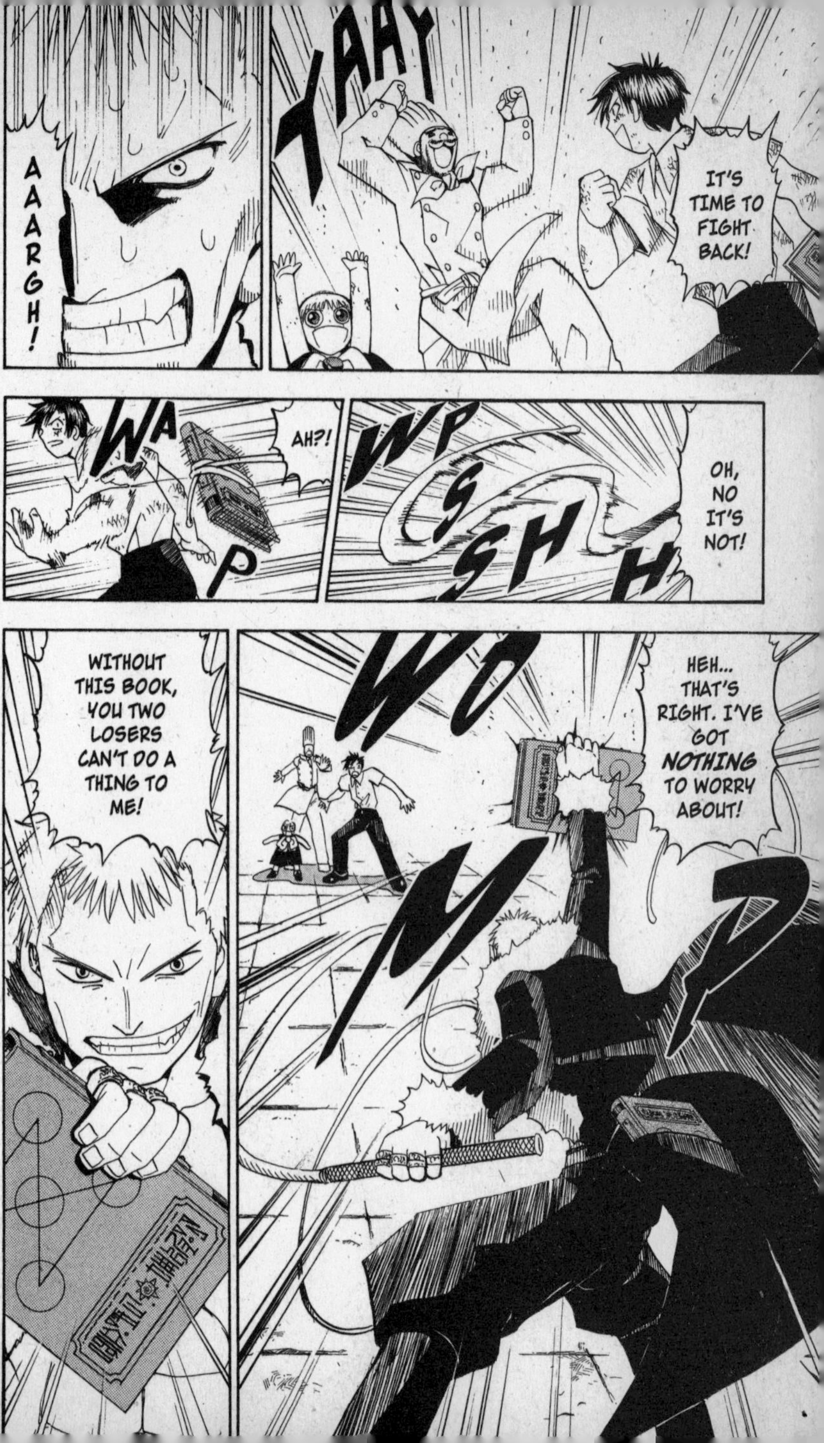
IT'S TIME TO FIGHT BACK!
YAAY
AAAARGH!
OH, NO IT'S NOT!
WPSSHH
AH?!
WAP
HEH... THAT'S RIGHT. I'VE GOT *NOTHING* TO WORRY ABOUT!
WOMP
WITHOUT THIS BOOK, YOU TWO LOSERS CAN'T DO A THING TO ME!

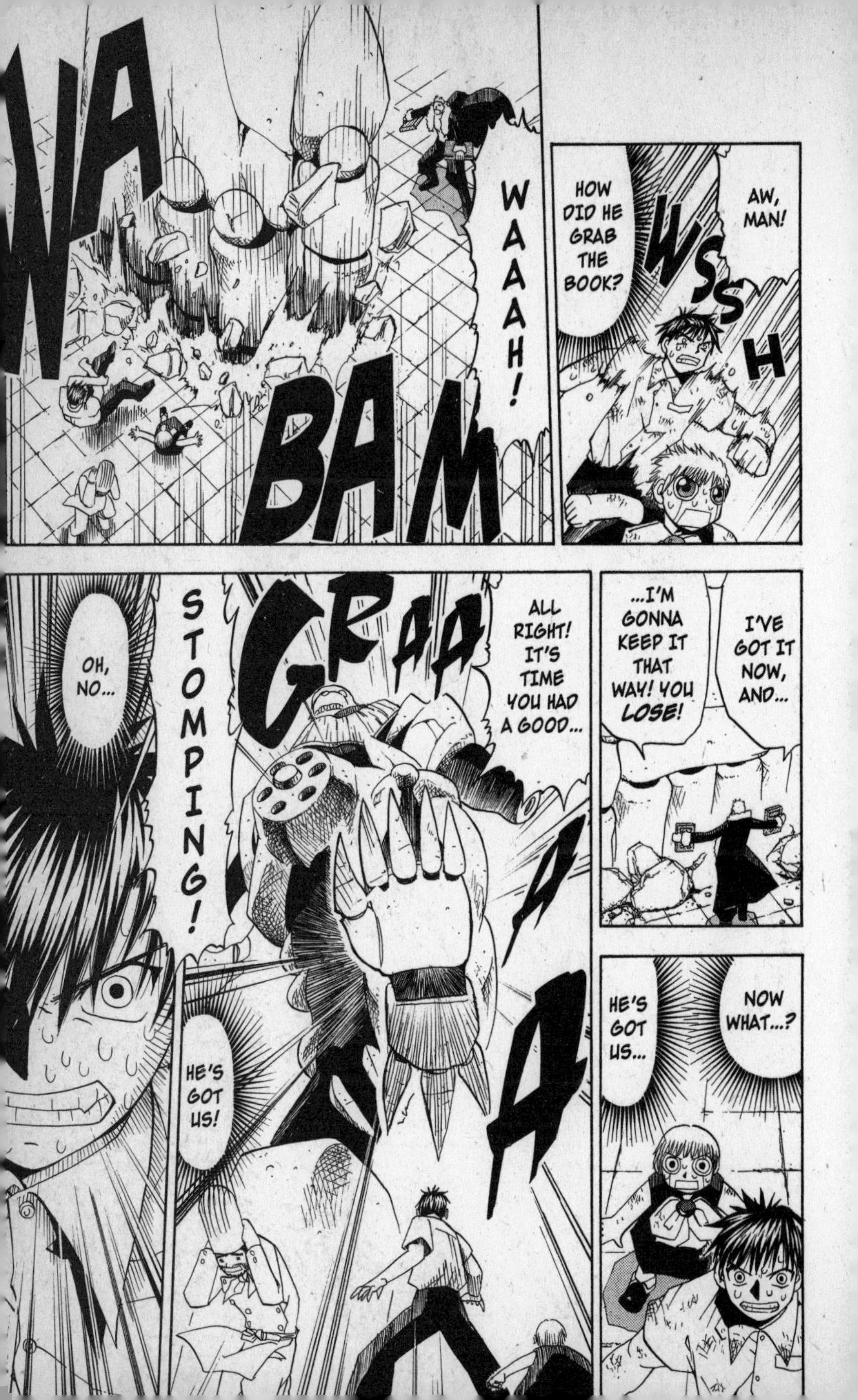
AW, MAN!
HOW DID HE GRAB THE BOOK?
WSSH
WAAAAH!
WA
BAM
I'VE GOT IT NOW, AND...
...I'M GONNA KEEP IT THAT WAY! YOU LOSE!
NOW WHAT...?
HE'S GOT US...
ALL RIGHT! IT'S TIME YOU HAD A GOOD...
GRAAAA
STOMPING!
OH, NO...
HE'S GOT US!

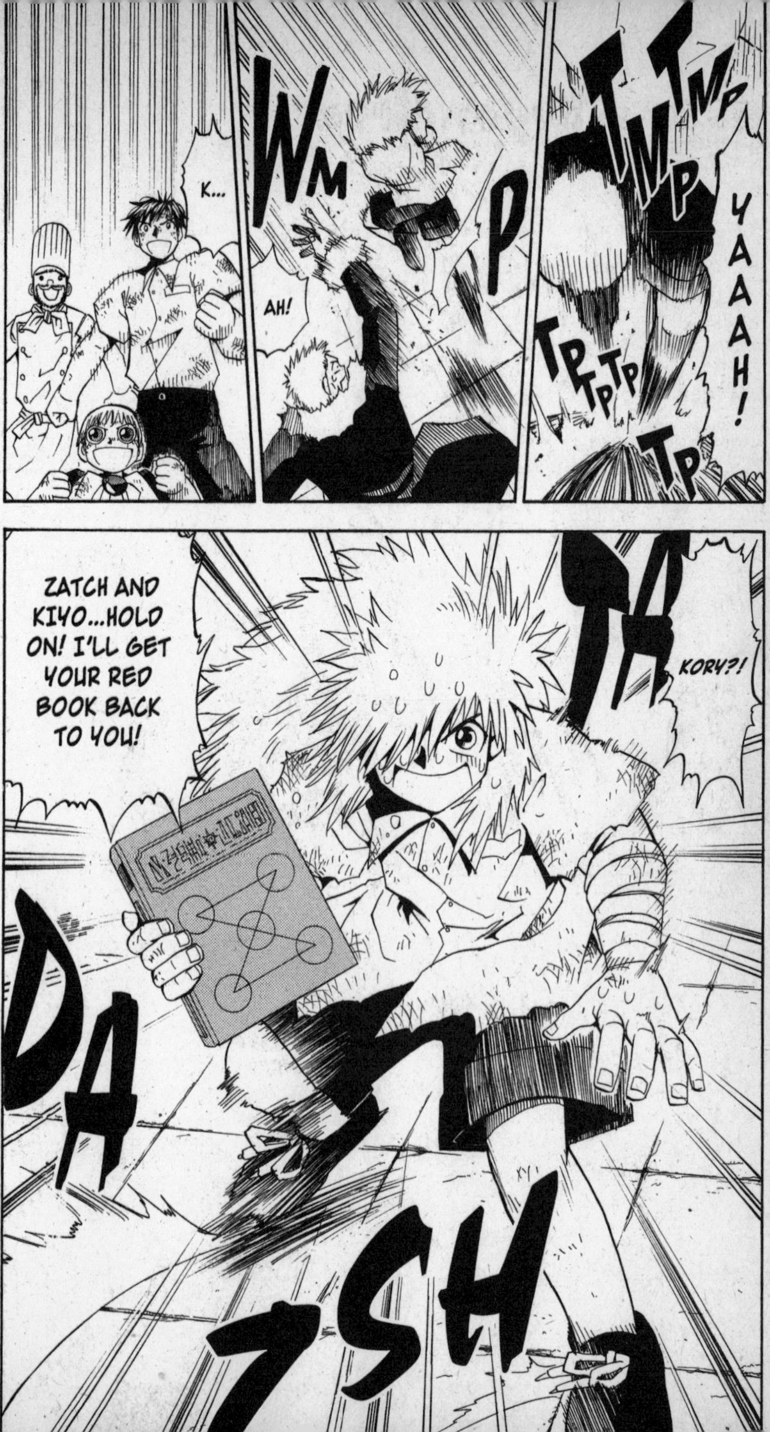
TMP TMP TMP
YAAAAH!
TPTPTP
TP
WMP
AH!
K...
TA
KORY?!
ZATCH AND KIYO...HOLD ON! I'LL GET YOUR RED BOOK BACK TO YOU!
DASH

LEVEL 44: Beyond Fear

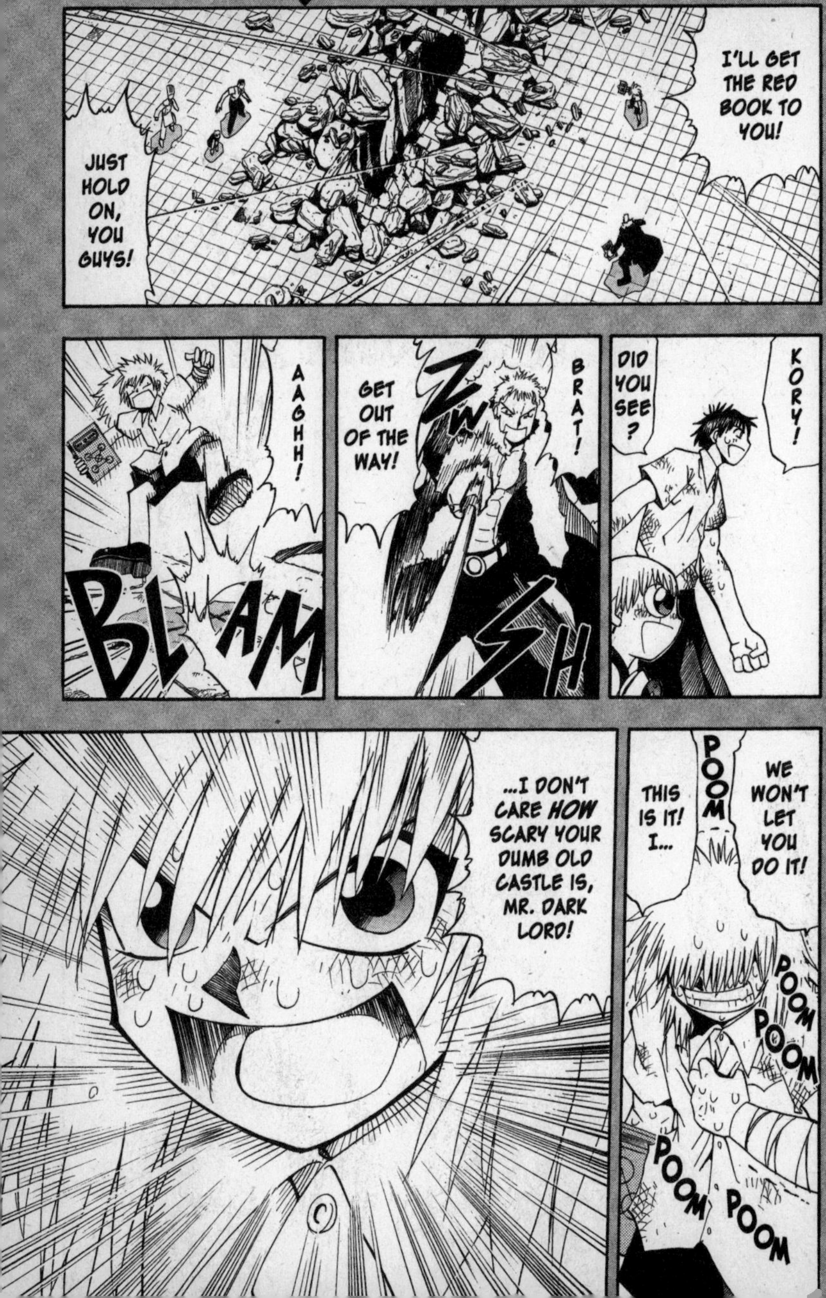
I'LL GET THE RED BOOK TO YOU!
JUST HOLD ON, YOU GUYS!
KORY!
DID YOU SEE?
BRAT!
GET OUT OF THE WAY!
ZWSH
AAGHH!
BLAM
WE WON'T LET YOU DO IT!
POOM
THIS IS IT! I...
POOM POOM POOM POOM POOM
...I DON'T CARE *HOW* SCARY YOUR DUMB OLD CASTLE IS, MR. DARK LORD!

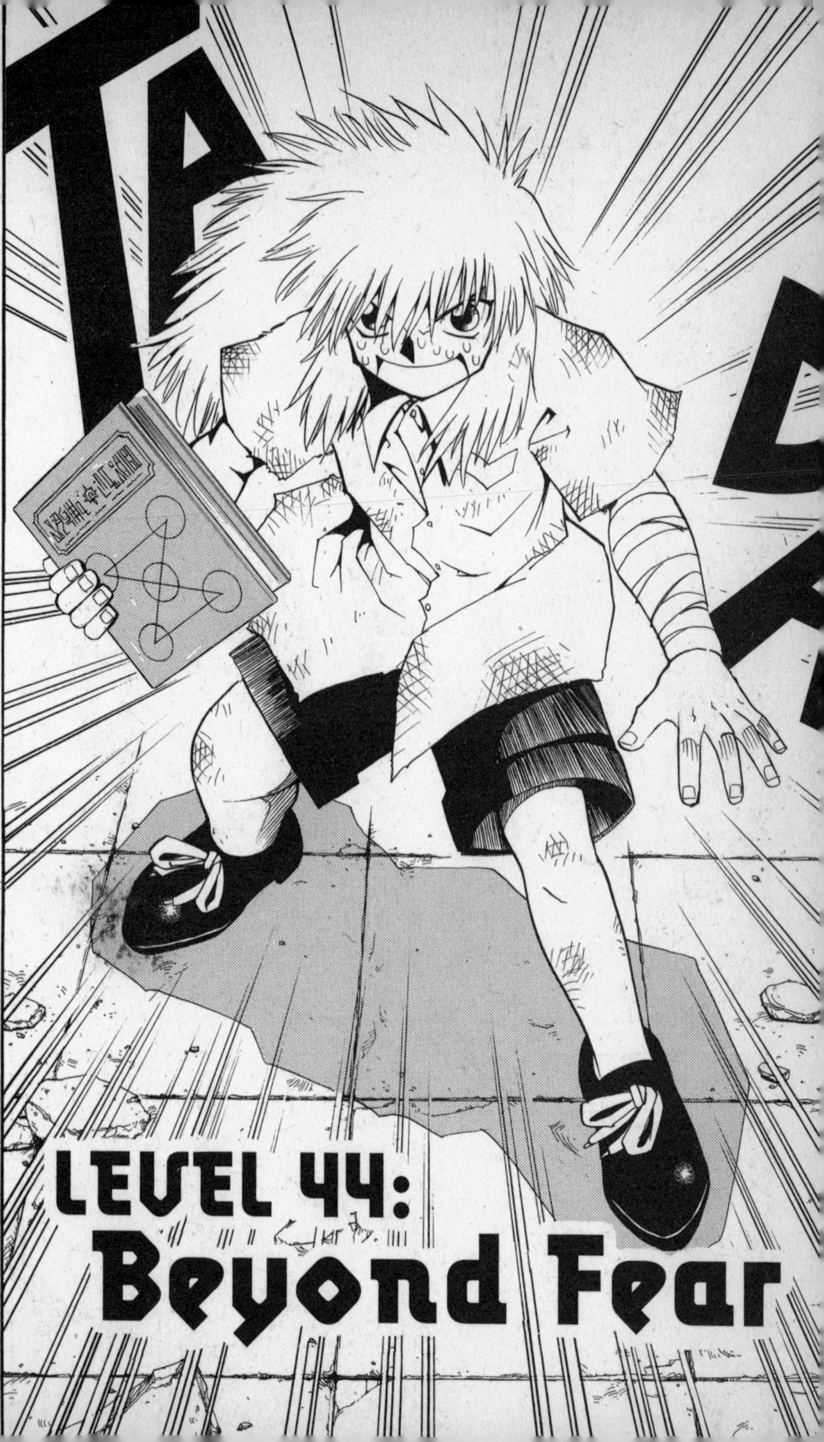
TA
LEVEL 44:
Beyond Fear

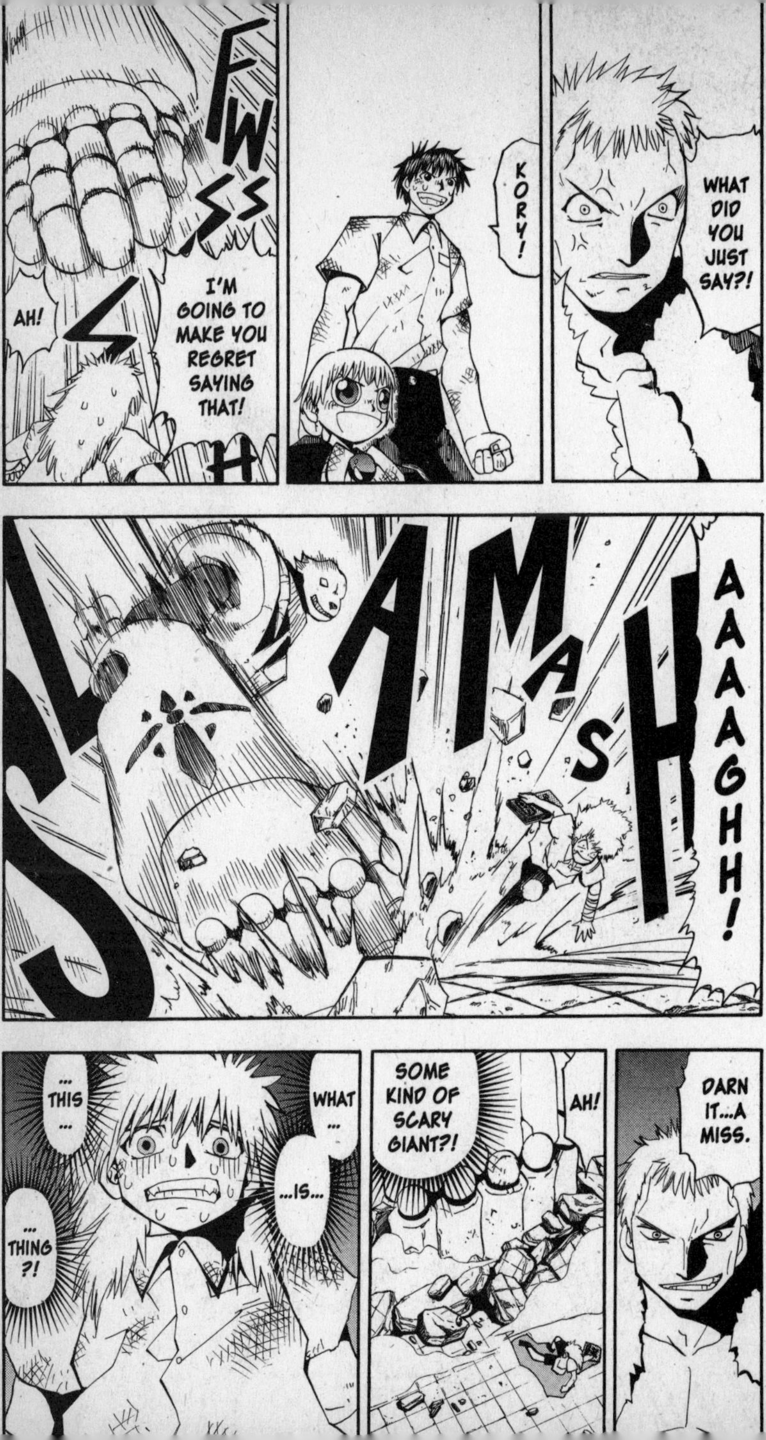

WHAT DID YOU JUST SAY?!
KORY!
FWSSSH
I'M GOING TO MAKE YOU REGRET SAYING THAT!
AH!
AAAAAGHH!
SLAMASH
DARN IT...A MISS.
AH!
SOME KIND OF SCARY GIANT?!
WHAT ...
...IS...
... THIS ...
... THING ?!

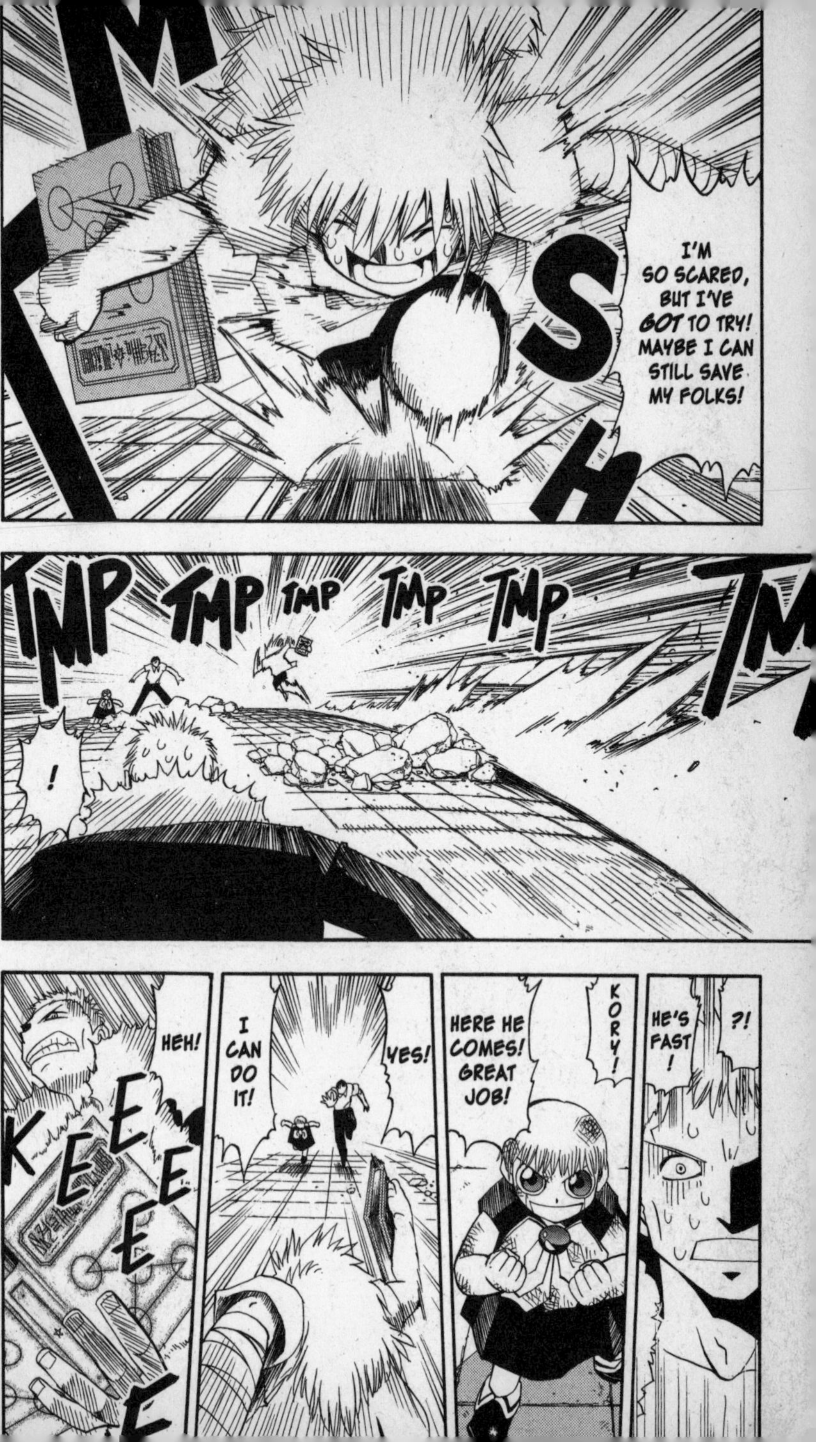
I'M SO SCARED, BUT I'VE GOT TO TRY! MAYBE I CAN STILL SAVE MY FOLKS!
TMP TMP TMP TMP TMP TMP
!
?!
HE'S FAST!
KORY!
HERE HE COMES! GREAT JOB!
YES!
I CAN DO IT!
HEH!
KEEEEE

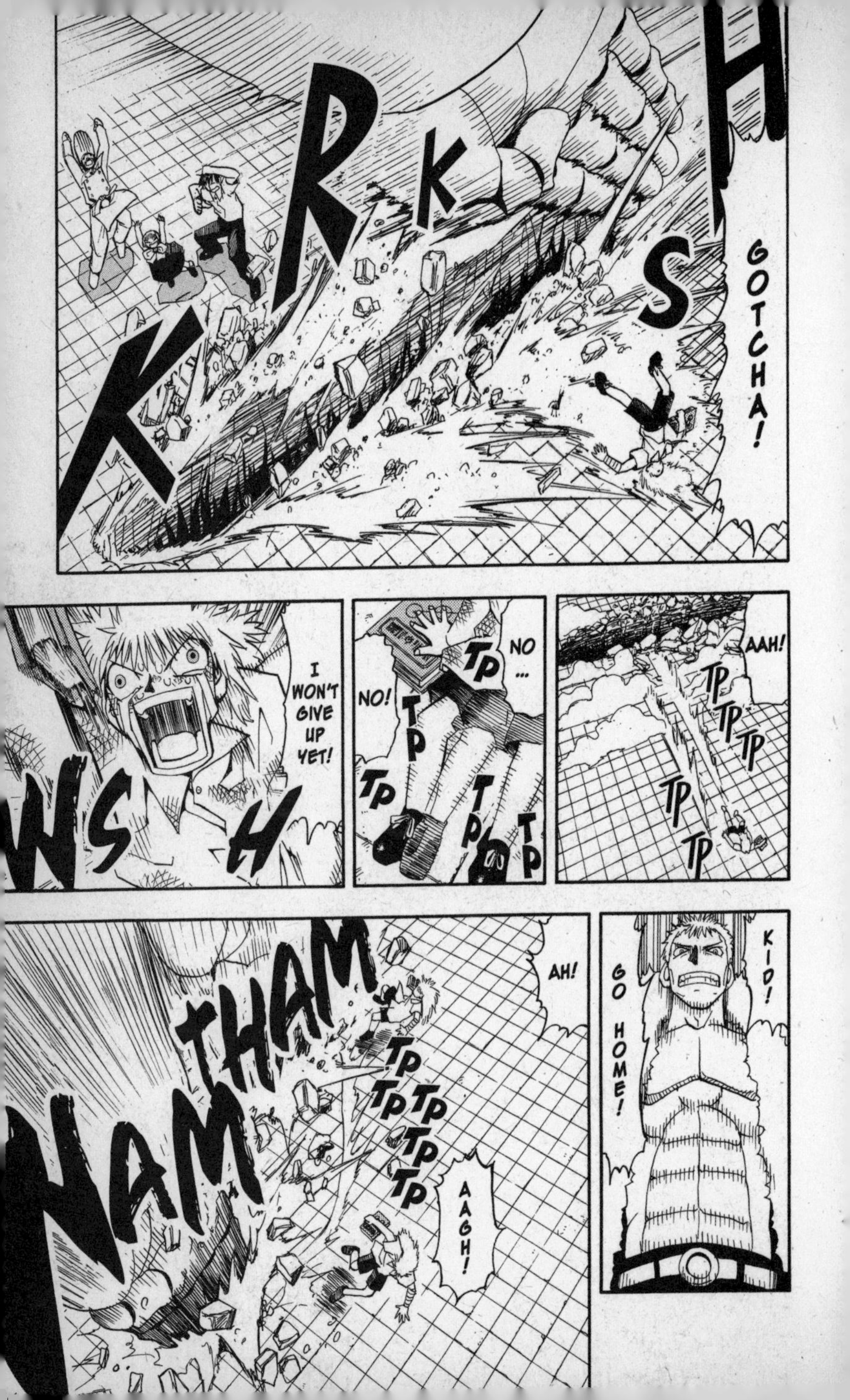
KRKSH
GOTCHA!
AAH!
TP TP TP TP TP TP
NO...
NO!
TP TP TP TP TP
I WON'T GIVE UP YET!
WSH
KID!
GO HOME!
AH!
THAM THAM HAM
TP TP TP TP TP TP
AAGH!

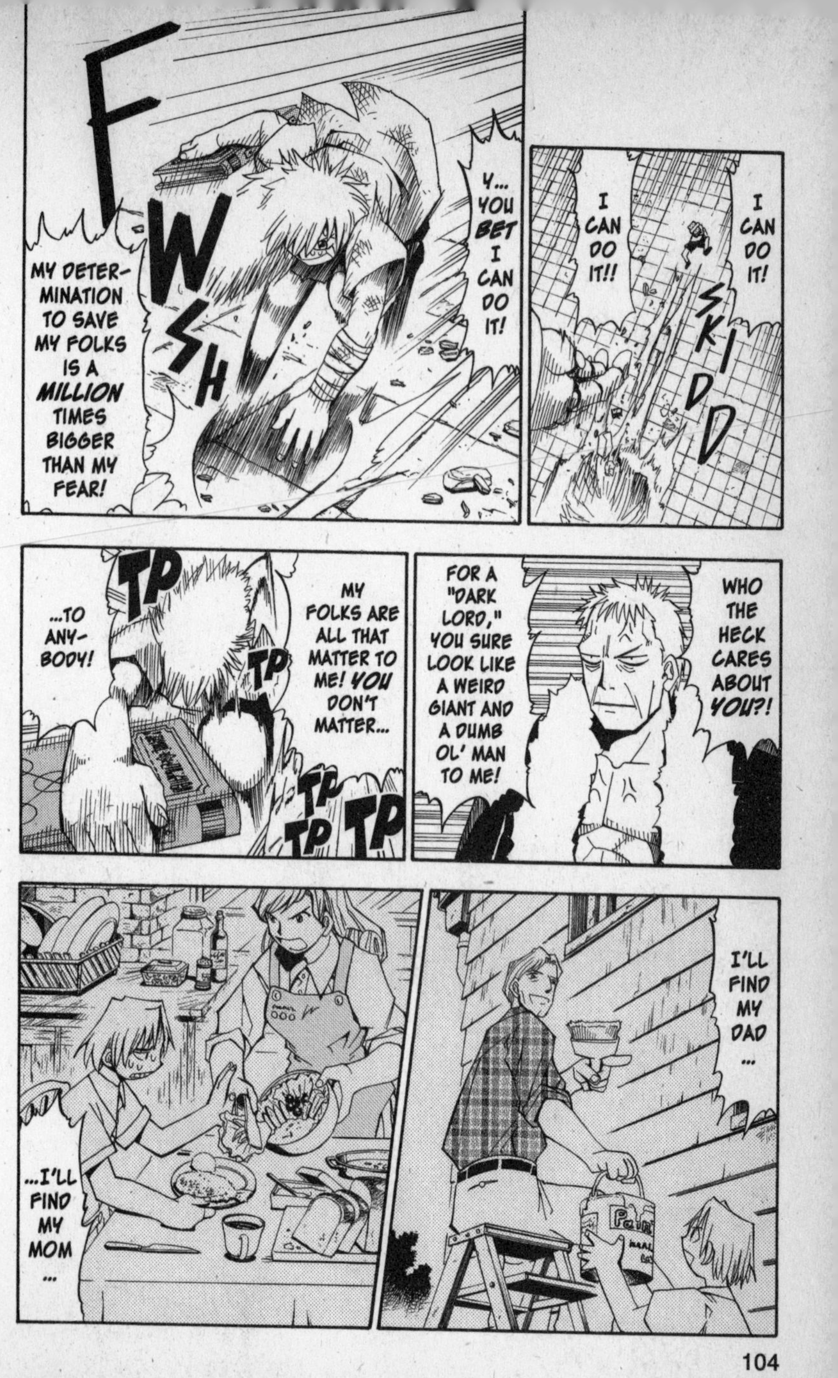
I CAN DO IT!
SKIDD
I CAN DO IT!!
Y... YOU BET I CAN DO IT!
FWSH
MY DETERMINATION TO SAVE MY FOLKS IS A MILLION TIMES BIGGER THAN MY FEAR!
WHO THE HECK CARES ABOUT YOU?!
FOR A "DARK LORD," YOU SURE LOOK LIKE A WEIRD GIANT AND A DUMB OL' MAN TO ME!
TP TP TP TP TP
MY FOLKS ARE ALL THAT MATTER TO ME! YOU DON'T MATTER...
...TO ANYBODY!
I'LL FIND MY DAD...
...I'LL FIND MY MOM...

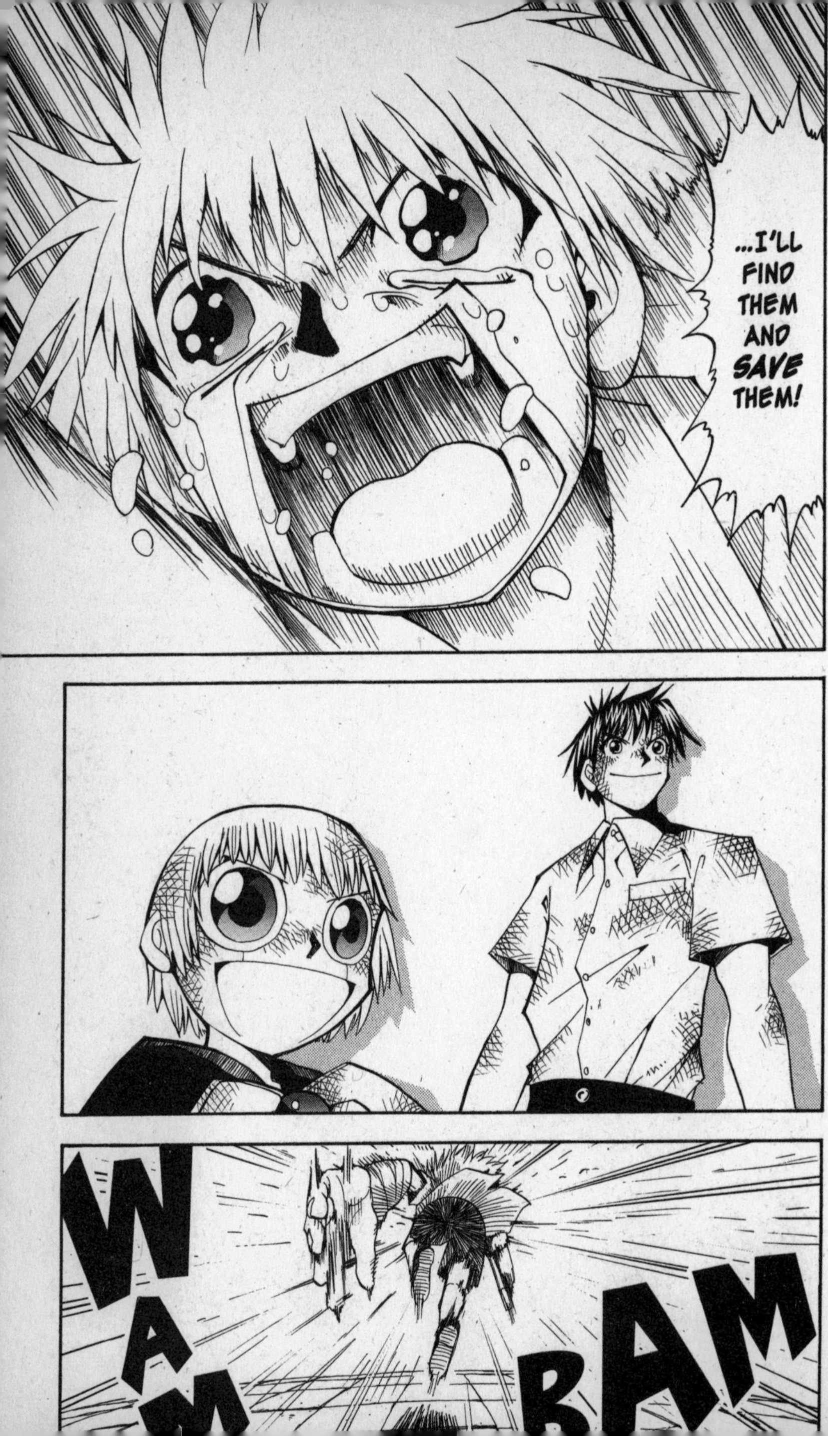
...I'LL FIND THEM AND SAVE THEM!
WAM
BAM

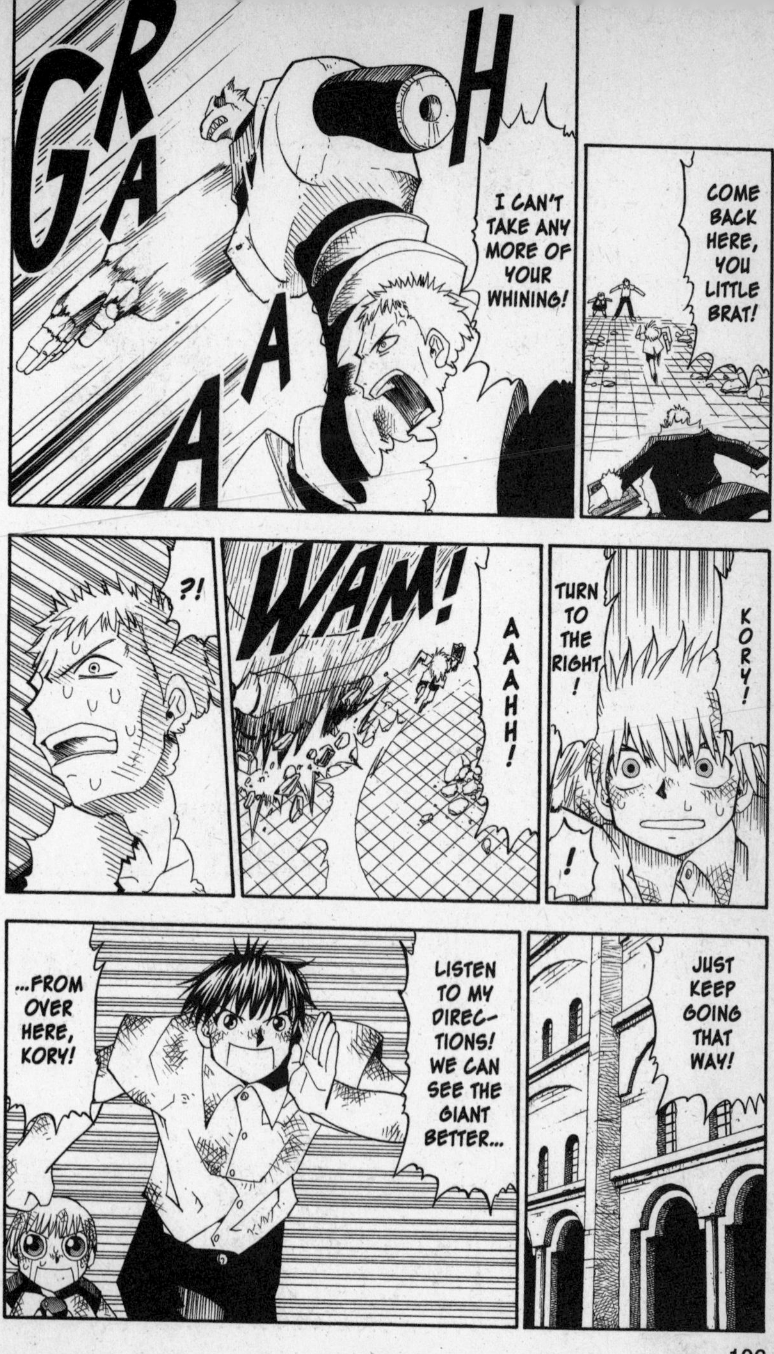
COME BACK HERE, YOU LITTLE BRAT!
I CAN'T TAKE ANY MORE OF YOUR WHINING!
GRAAAAH
KORY!
TURN TO THE RIGHT!
!
AAAAHH!
WAM!
?!
JUST KEEP GOING THAT WAY!
LISTEN TO MY DIRECTIONS! WE CAN SEE THE GIANT BETTER...
...FROM OVER HERE, KORY!

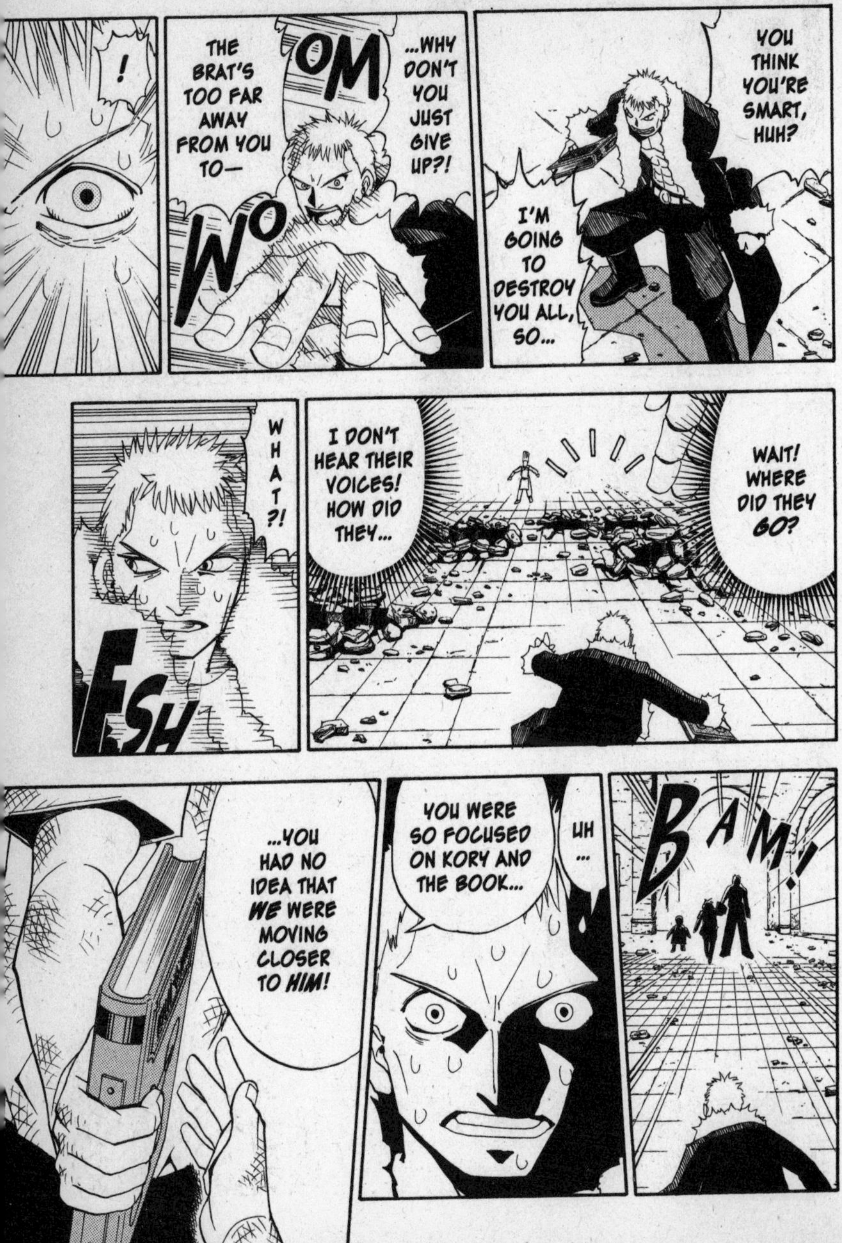
YOU THINK YOU'RE SMART, HUH?
I'M GOING TO DESTROY YOU ALL, SO...
...WHY DON'T YOU JUST GIVE UP?!
THE BRAT'S TOO FAR AWAY FROM YOU TO—
WOOM
!
WAIT! WHERE DID THEY GO?
I DON'T HEAR THEIR VOICES! HOW DID THEY...
WHAT?!
FSH
BAM!
UH ...
YOU WERE SO FOCUSED ON KORY AND THE BOOK...
...YOU HAD NO IDEA THAT WE WERE MOVING CLOSER TO HIM!

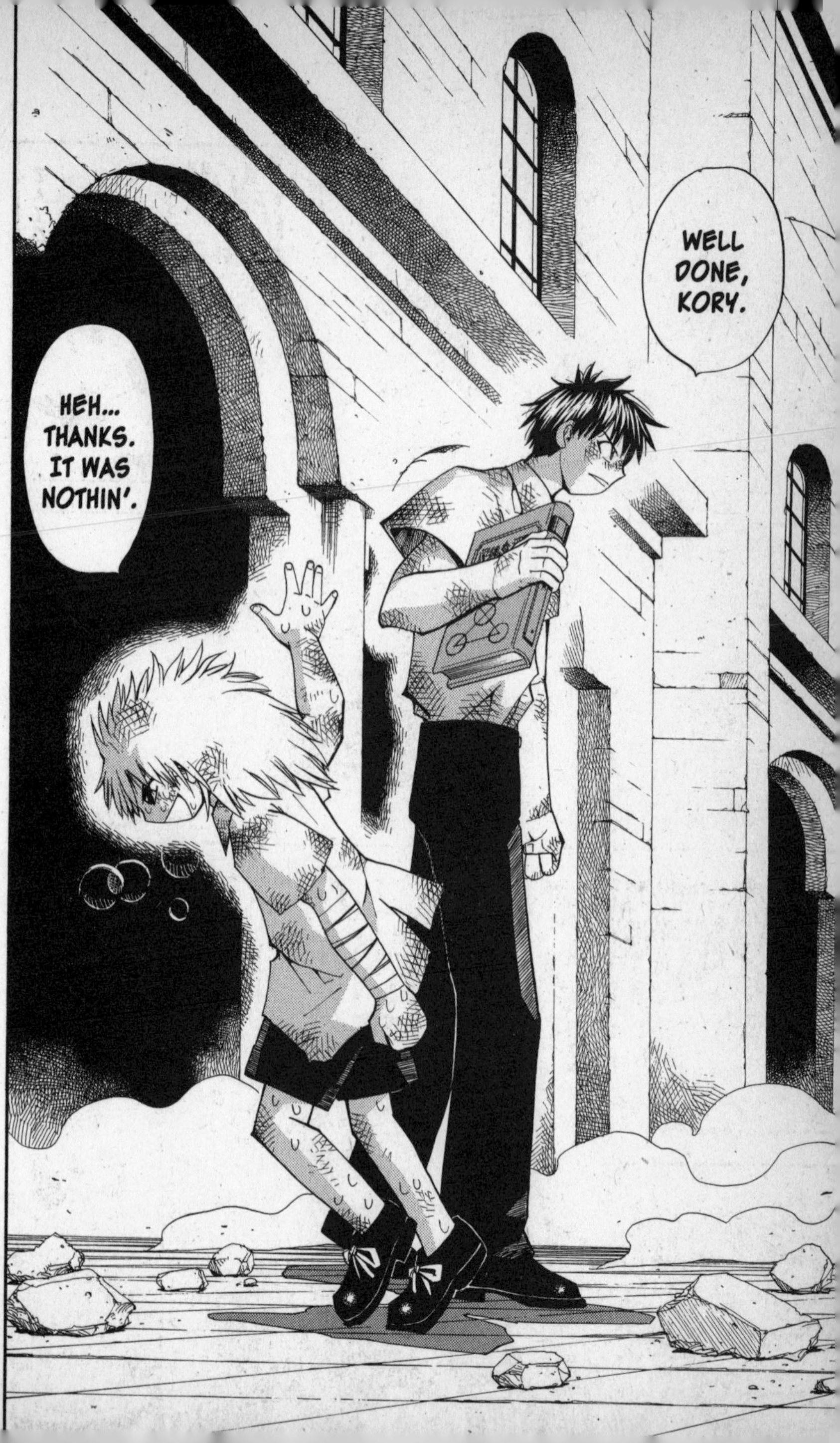
WELL DONE, KORY.
HEH... THANKS. IT WAS NOTHIN'.

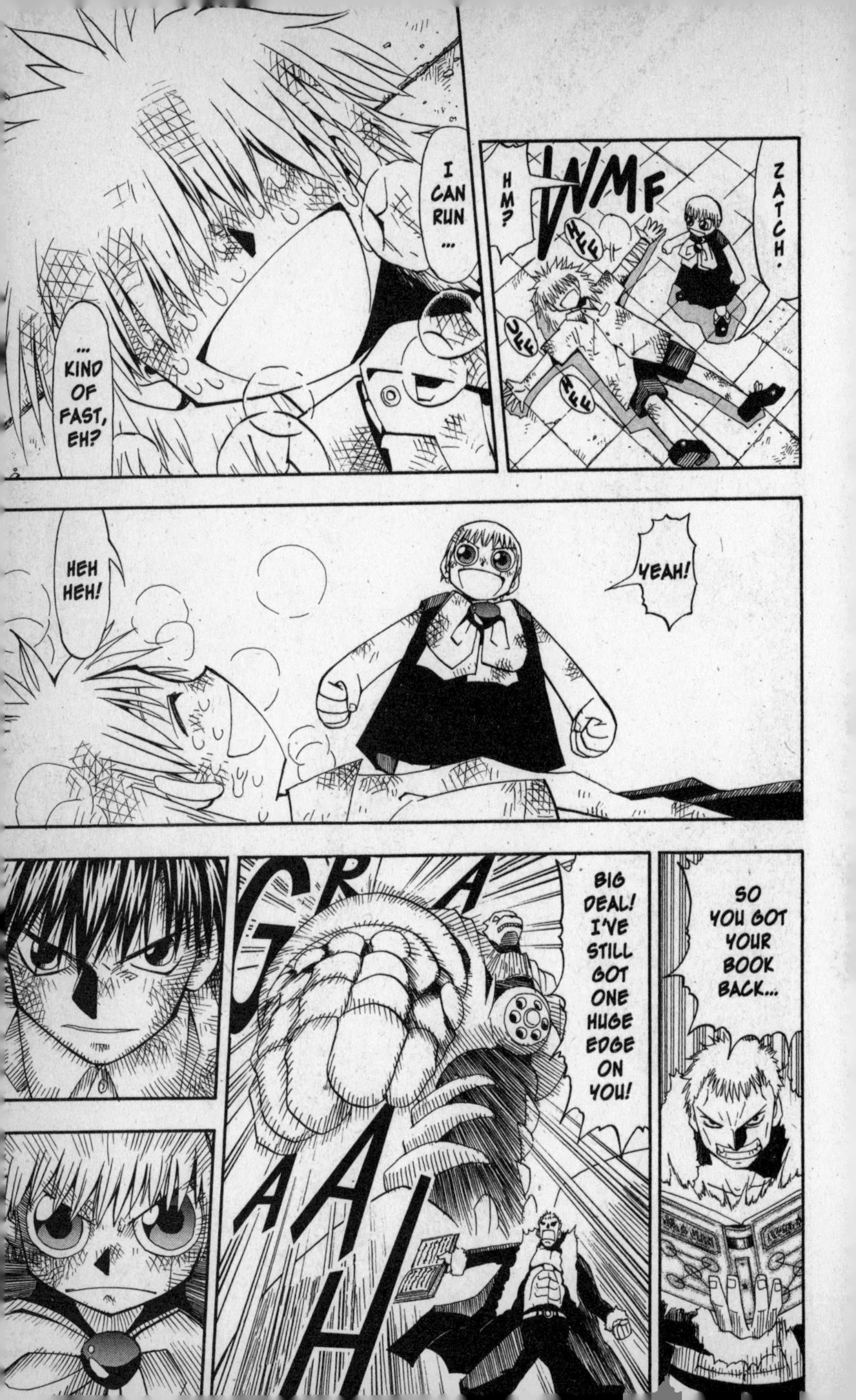
ZATCH.
WMF
HM?
HUFF
UFF
HUFF
I CAN RUN...
...KIND OF FAST, EH?
YEAH!
HEH HEH!
SO YOU GOT YOUR BOOK BACK...
BIG DEAL! I'VE STILL GOT ONE HUGE EDGE ON YOU!
GRAAAAH!

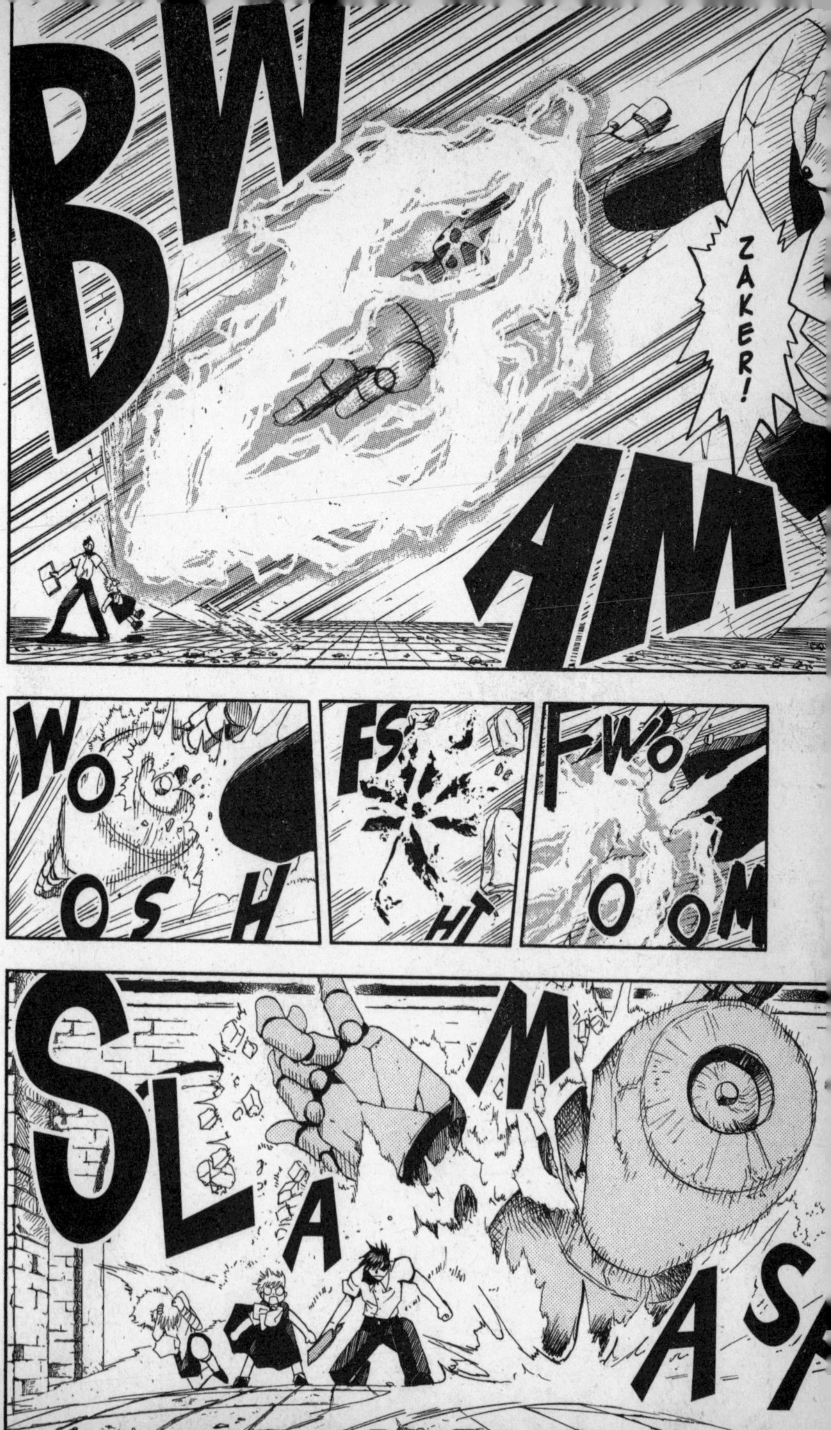
ZAKER!
BWAM
FWOOM
FSHT
WOOSH
SLAM

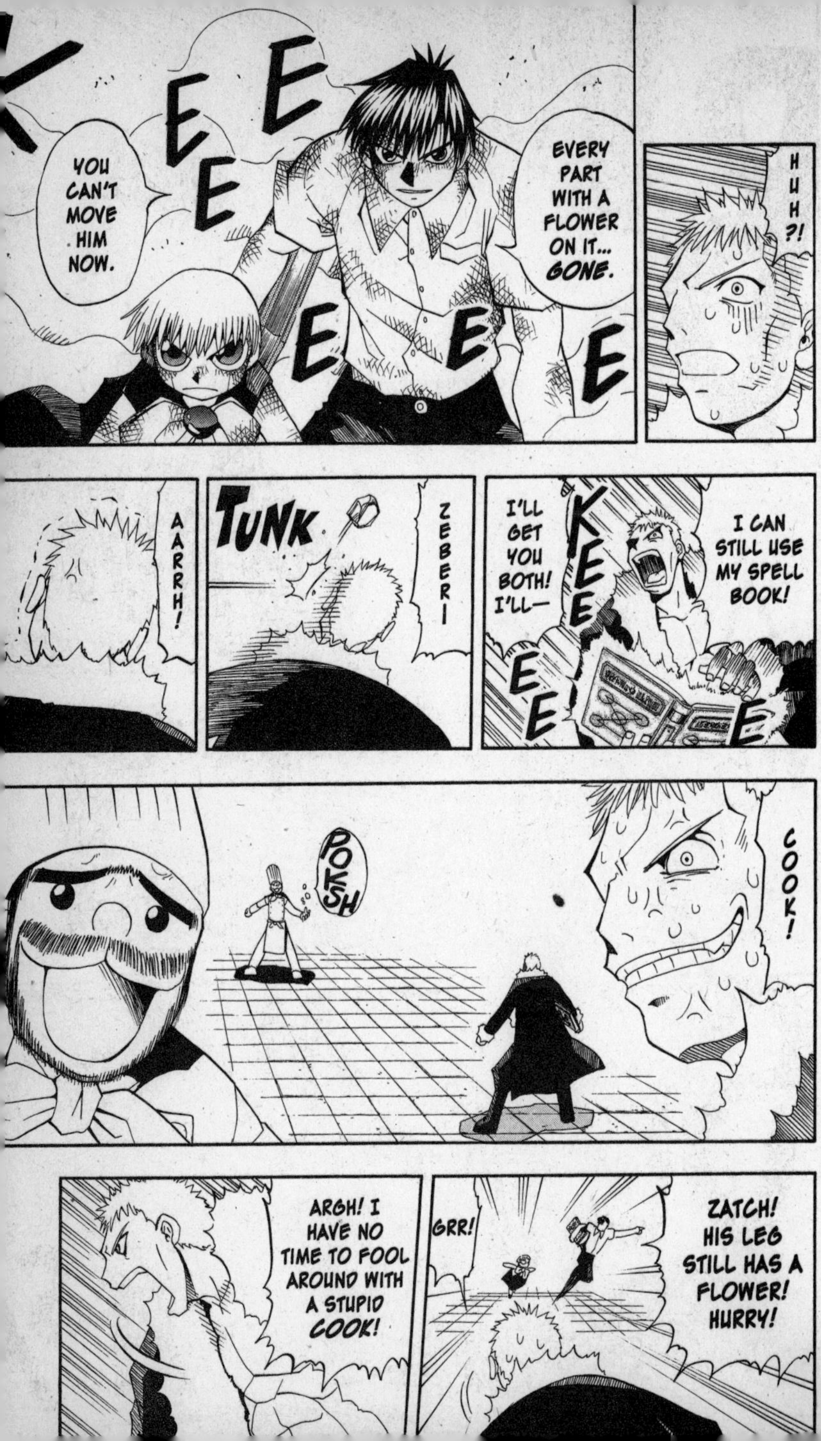
HUH?!
EVERY PART WITH A FLOWER ON IT... GONE.
YOU CAN'T MOVE HIM NOW.
KEEEEEE
I CAN STILL USE MY SPELL BOOK!
I'LL GET YOU BOTH! I'LL—
KEEEEEE
ZEBERI
TUNK
AARRH!
COOK!
POKSH
ZATCH! HIS LEG STILL HAS A FLOWER! HURRY!
GRR!
ARGH! I HAVE NO TIME TO FOOL AROUND WITH A STUPID COOK!

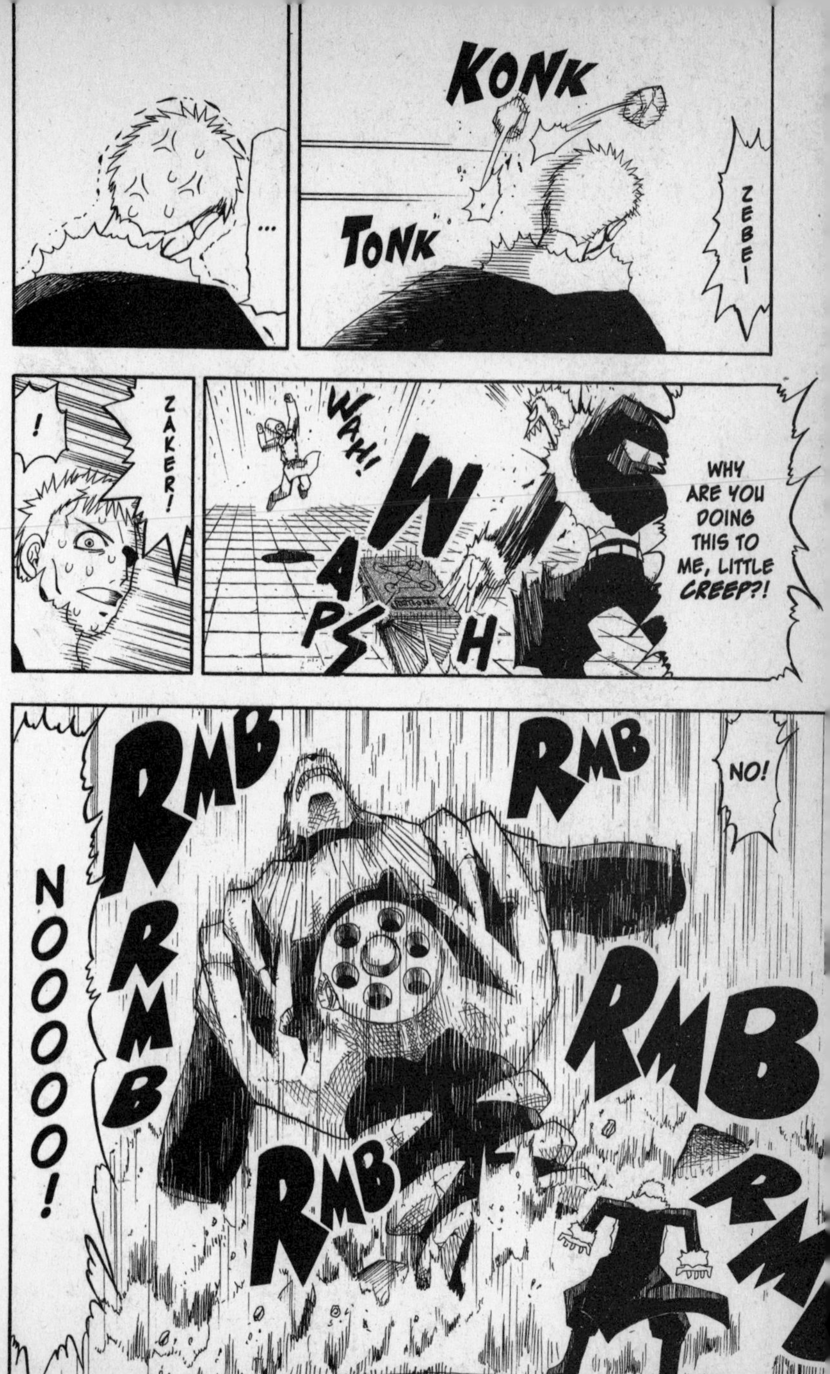
ZEBEI
KONK
TONK
...
WHY ARE YOU DOING THIS TO ME, LITTLE CREEP?!
WAH!
WAPSH
ZAKER!
!
NO!
RMB
RMB
RMB
RMB
RMB
RMB
RM
NOOOOOO!

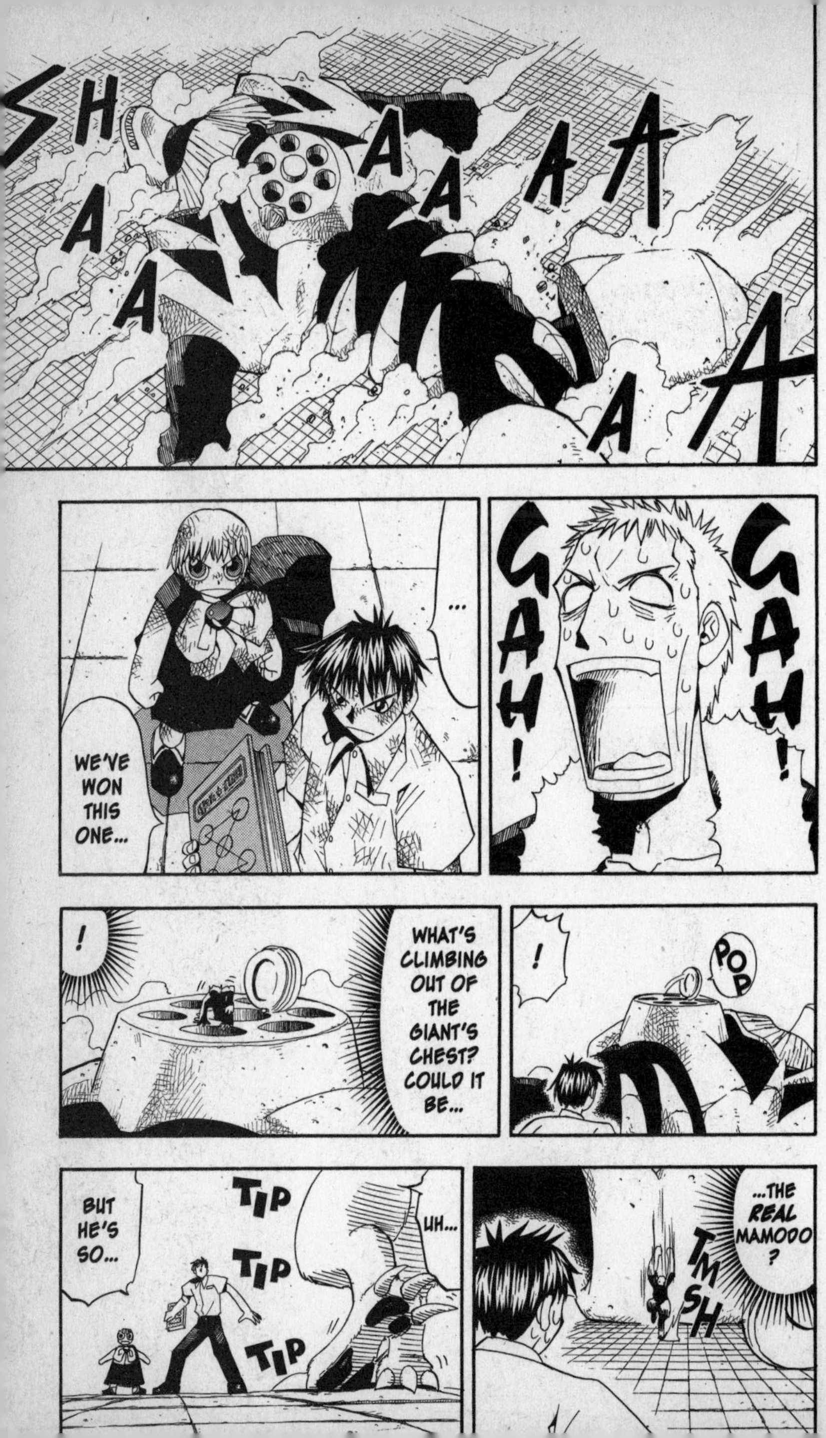
SHAAAAAAAA
GAH!
GAH!
...
WE'VE WON THIS ONE...
!
POP
WHAT'S CLIMBING OUT OF THE GIANT'S CHEST? COULD IT BE...
!
...THE REAL MAMODO?
TMSH
UH...
TIP
TIP
TIP
BUT HE'S SO...

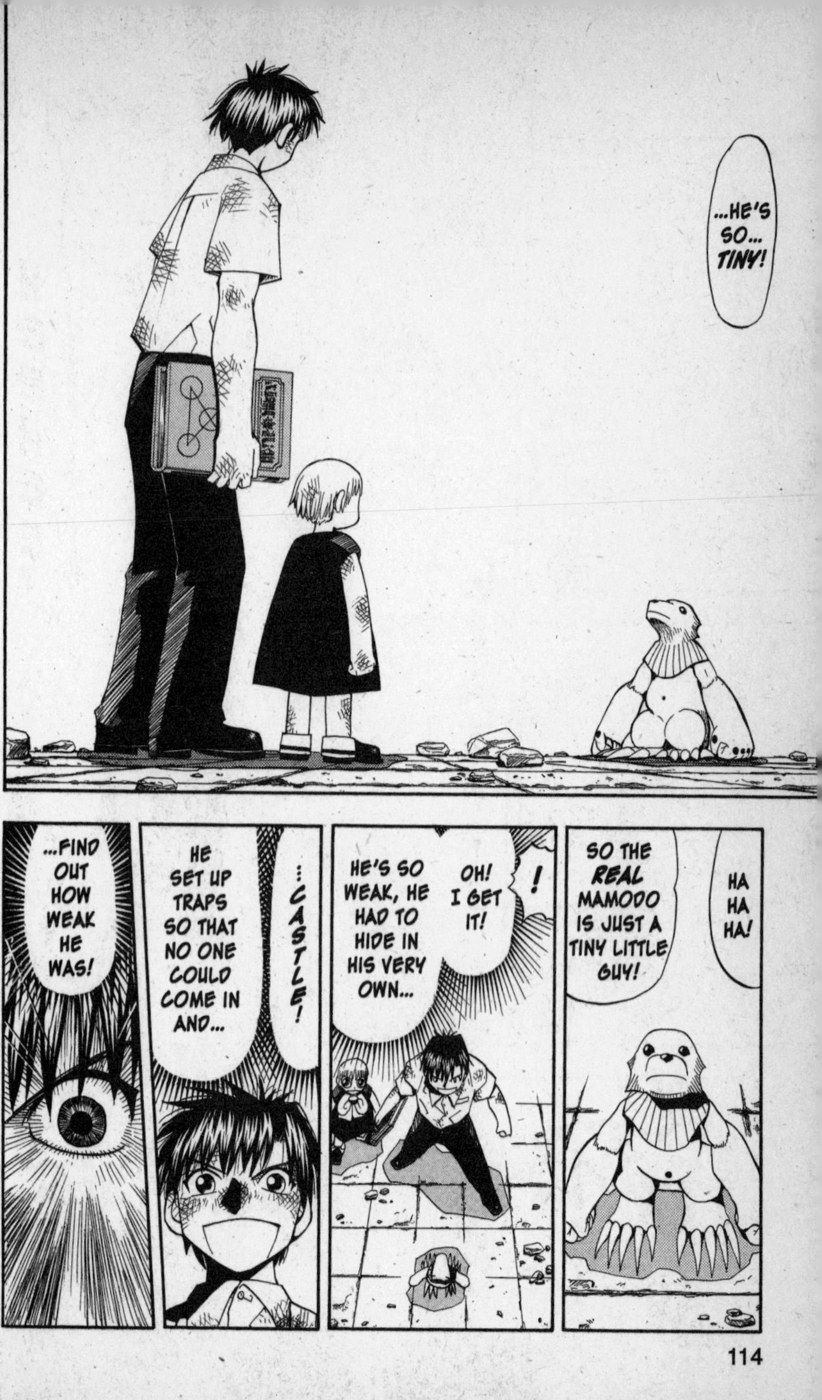
...HE'S SO... TINY!
HA HA HA!
SO THE REAL MAMODO IS JUST A TINY LITTLE GUY!
!
OH! I GET IT!
HE'S SO WEAK, HE HAD TO HIDE IN HIS VERY OWN...
...CASTLE!
HE SET UP TRAPS SO THAT NO ONE COULD COME IN AND...
...FIND OUT HOW WEAK HE WAS!

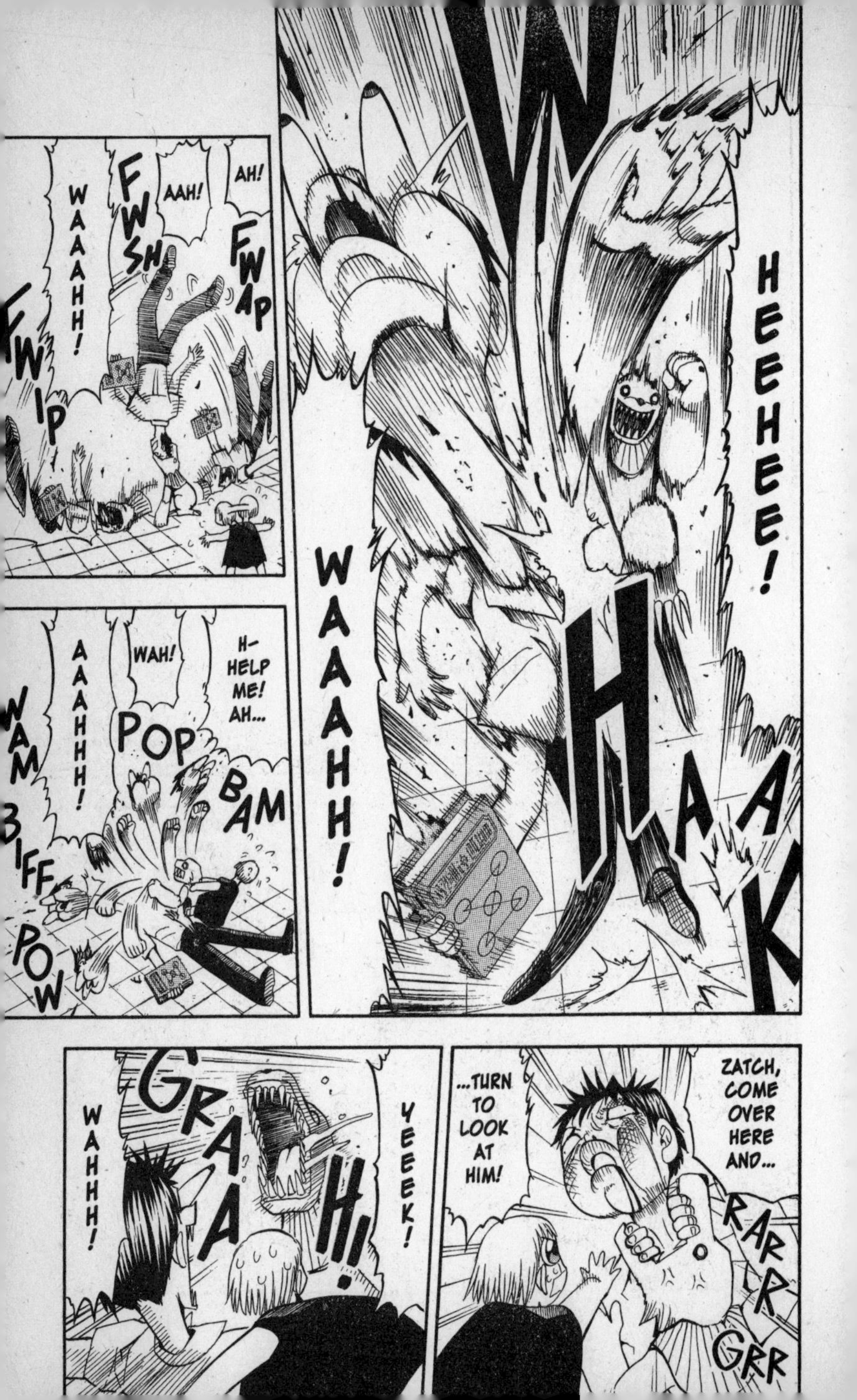
HEEHEE!
WHAAAK
WAAAAHH!
AH!
FWAP
AAH!
FWSH
WAAAAHH!
FWIP
H-HELP ME! AH...
WAH!
POP
BAM
AAAAHHH!
WAM
BIFF
POW
ZATCH, COME OVER HERE AND...
...TURN TO LOOK AT HIM!
RARR
GRR
YEEEK!
GRAAH!
WAHHH!

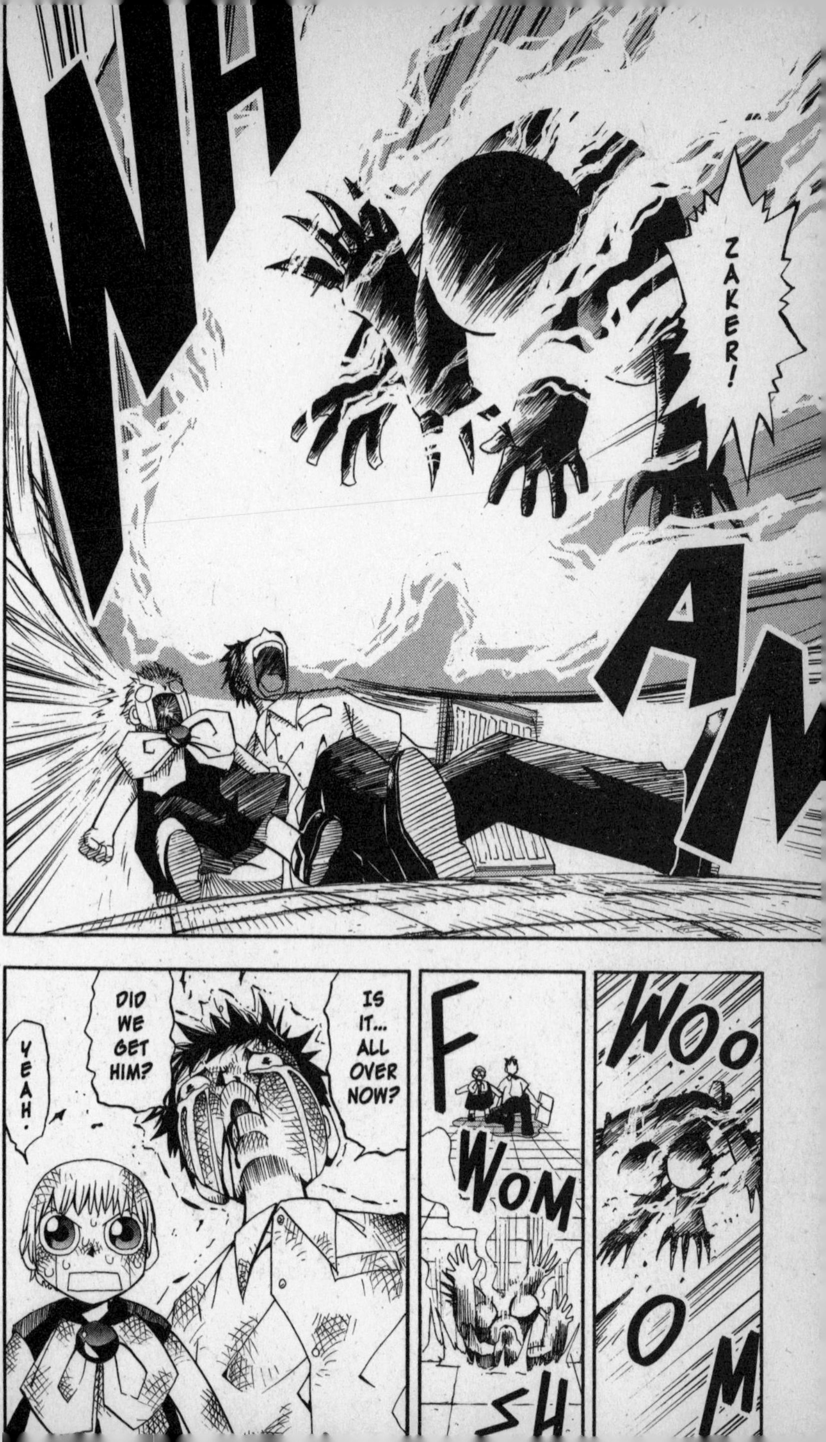
ZAKER!
WHAM
WOOOM
FWOM
SH
IS IT... ALL OVER NOW?
DID WE GET HIM?
YEAH.

LEVEL 45: Kiyo's Father

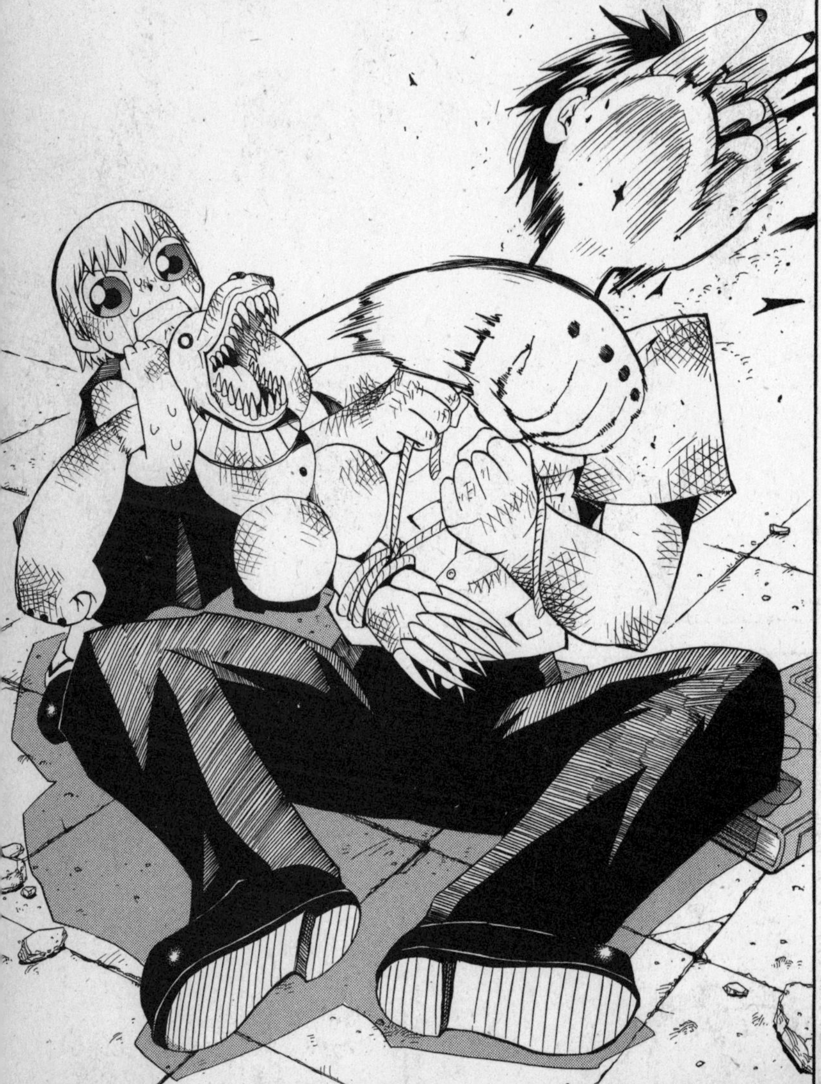

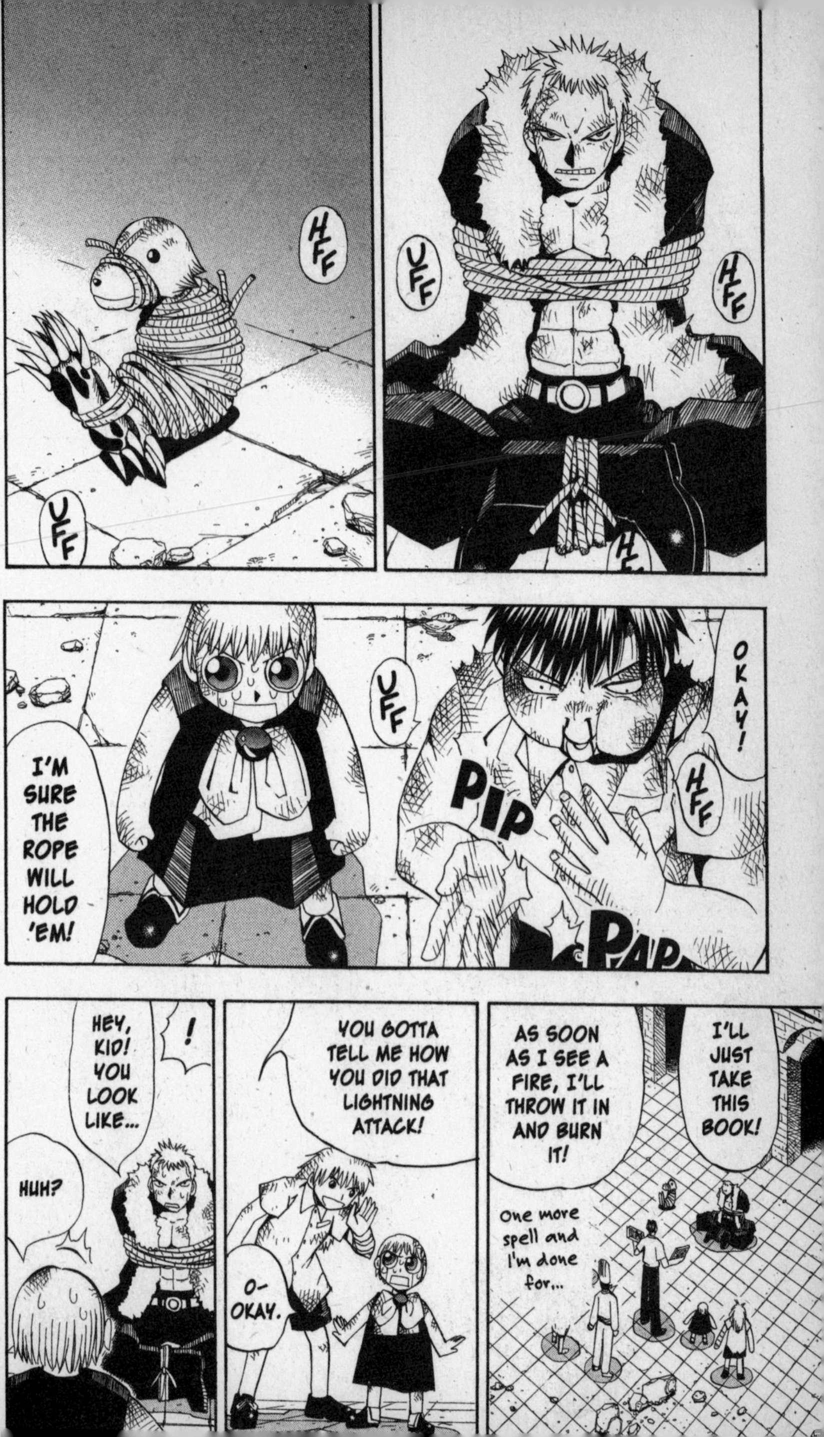
HFF
UFF
HFF
UFF
OKAY!
UFF
HFF
PIP
PAP
I'M SURE THE ROPE WILL HOLD 'EM!
I'LL JUST TAKE THIS BOOK!
AS SOON AS I SEE A FIRE, I'LL THROW IT IN AND BURN IT!
One more spell and I'm done for...
YOU GOTTA TELL ME HOW YOU DID THAT LIGHTNING ATTACK!
O-OKAY.
!
HEY, KID! YOU LOOK LIKE...
HUH?

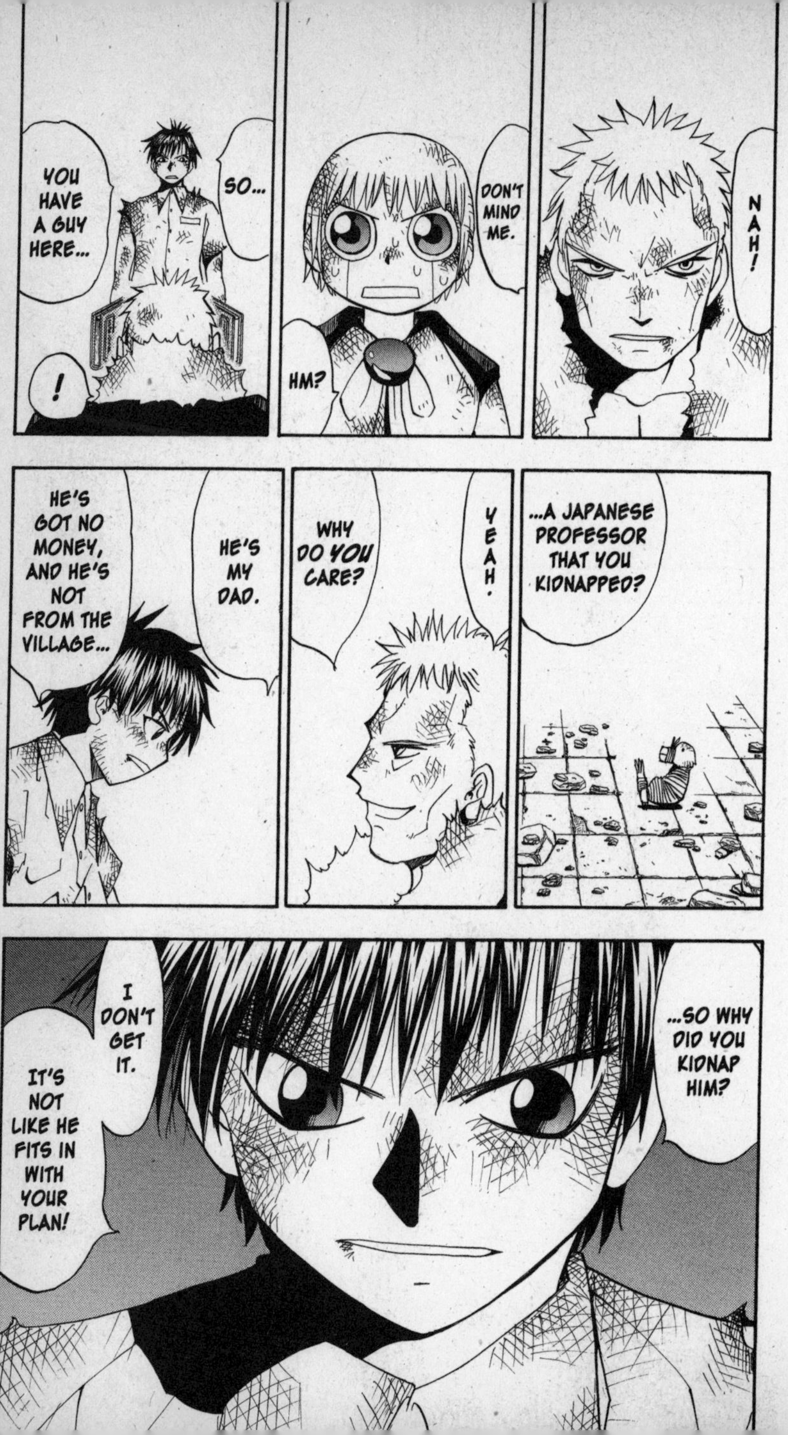
NAH!
DON'T MIND ME.
HM?
SO...
YOU HAVE A GUY HERE...
!
...A JAPANESE PROFESSOR THAT YOU KIDNAPPED?
YEAH.
WHY DO YOU CARE?
HE'S MY DAD.
HE'S GOT NO MONEY, AND HE'S NOT FROM THE VILLAGE...
...SO WHY DID YOU KIDNAP HIM?
I DON'T GET IT.
IT'S NOT LIKE HE FITS IN WITH YOUR PLAN!

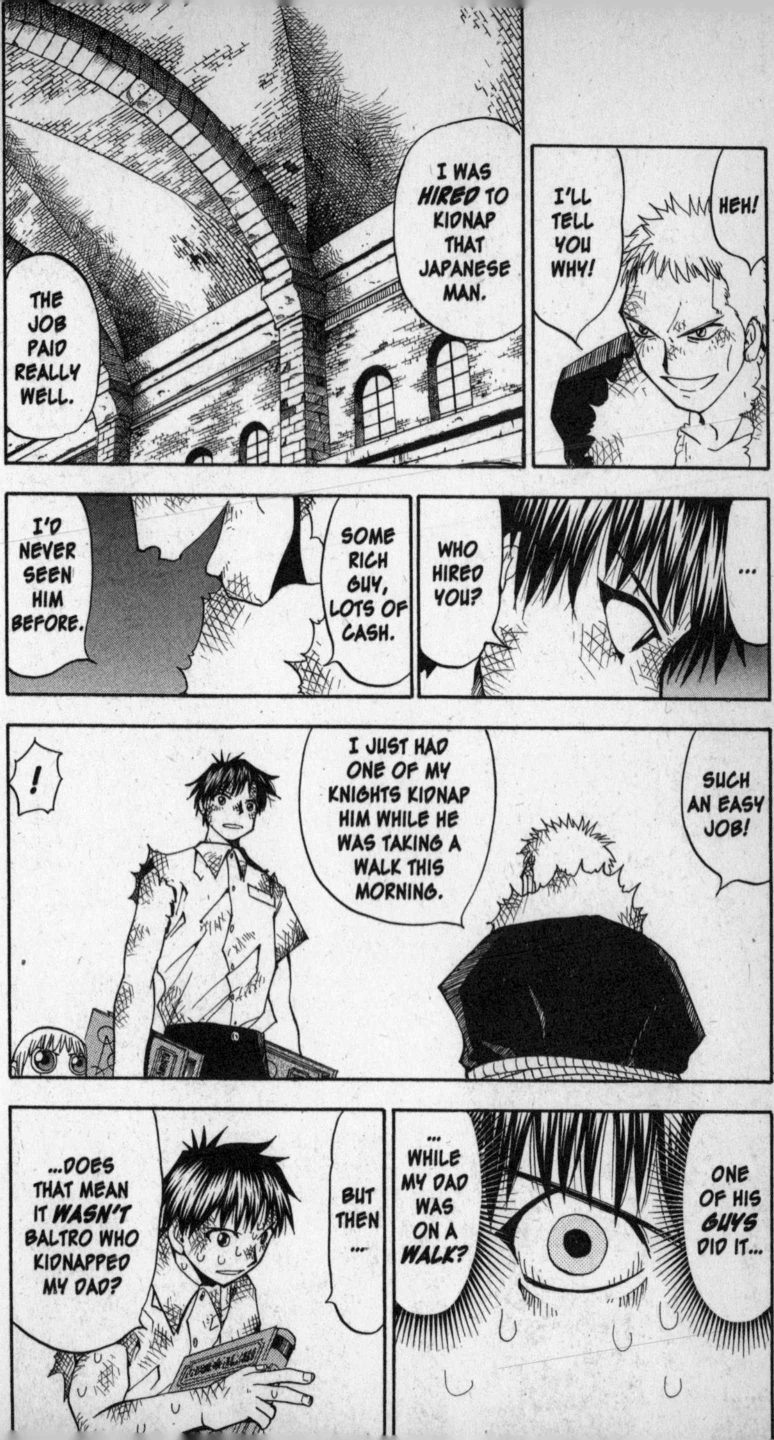
HEH!
I'LL TELL YOU WHY!
I WAS HIRED TO KIDNAP THAT JAPANESE MAN.
THE JOB PAID REALLY WELL.
...
WHO HIRED YOU?
SOME RICH GUY, LOTS OF CASH.
I'D NEVER SEEN HIM BEFORE.
SUCH AN EASY JOB!
I JUST HAD ONE OF MY KNIGHTS KIDNAP HIM WHILE HE WAS TAKING A WALK THIS MORNING.
!
ONE OF HIS GUYS DID IT...
...WHILE MY DAD WAS ON A WALK?
BUT THEN...
...DOES THAT MEAN IT WASN'T BALTRO WHO KIDNAPPED MY DAD?

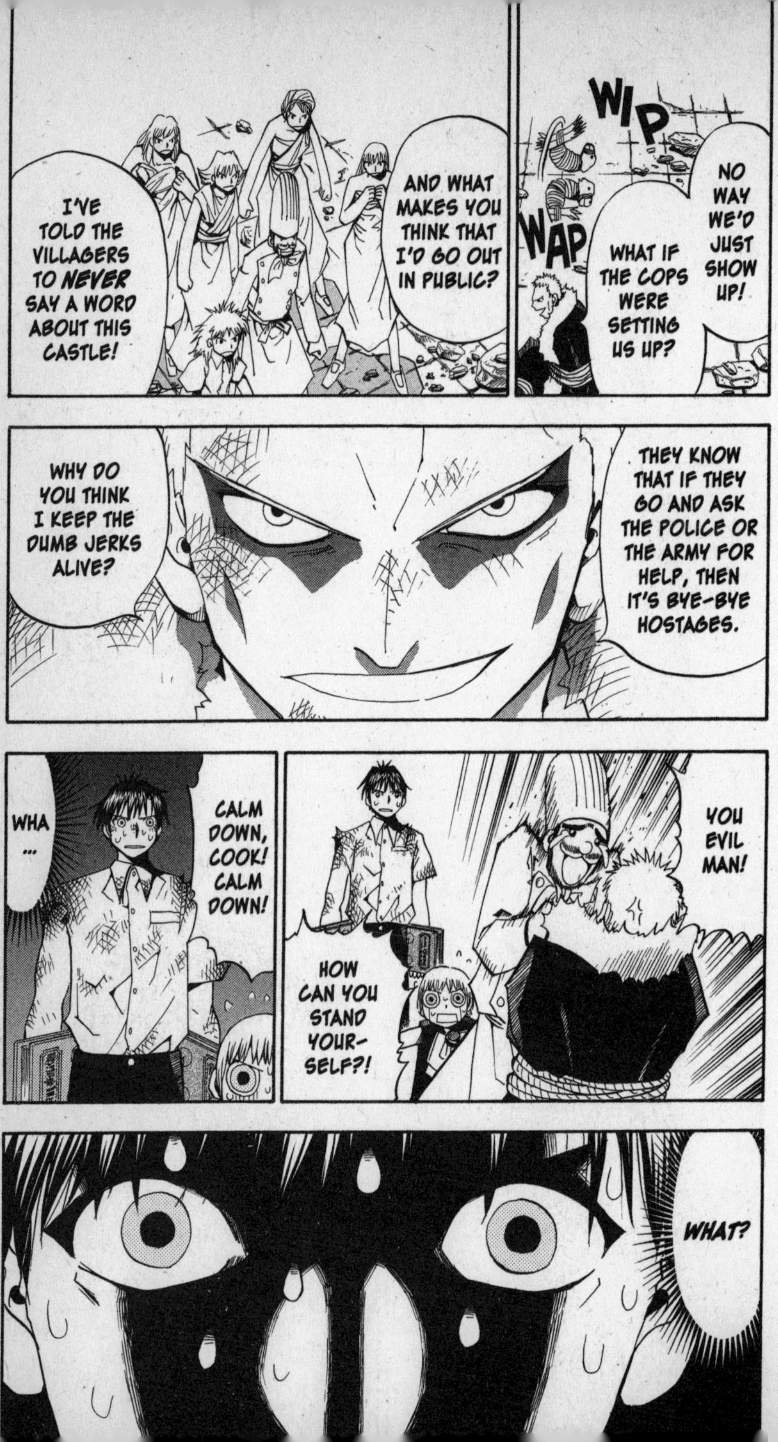
WIP
WAP
NO WAY WE'D JUST SHOW UP!
WHAT IF THE COPS WERE SETTING US UP?
AND WHAT MAKES YOU THINK THAT I'D GO OUT IN PUBLIC?
I'VE TOLD THE VILLAGERS TO ***NEVER*** SAY A WORD ABOUT THIS CASTLE!
THEY KNOW THAT IF THEY GO AND ASK THE POLICE OR THE ARMY FOR HELP, THEN IT'S BYE-BYE HOSTAGES.
WHY DO YOU THINK I KEEP THE DUMB JERKS ALIVE?
YOU EVIL MAN!
HOW CAN YOU STAND YOUR-SELF?!
CALM DOWN, COOK! CALM DOWN!
WHA...
WHAT?

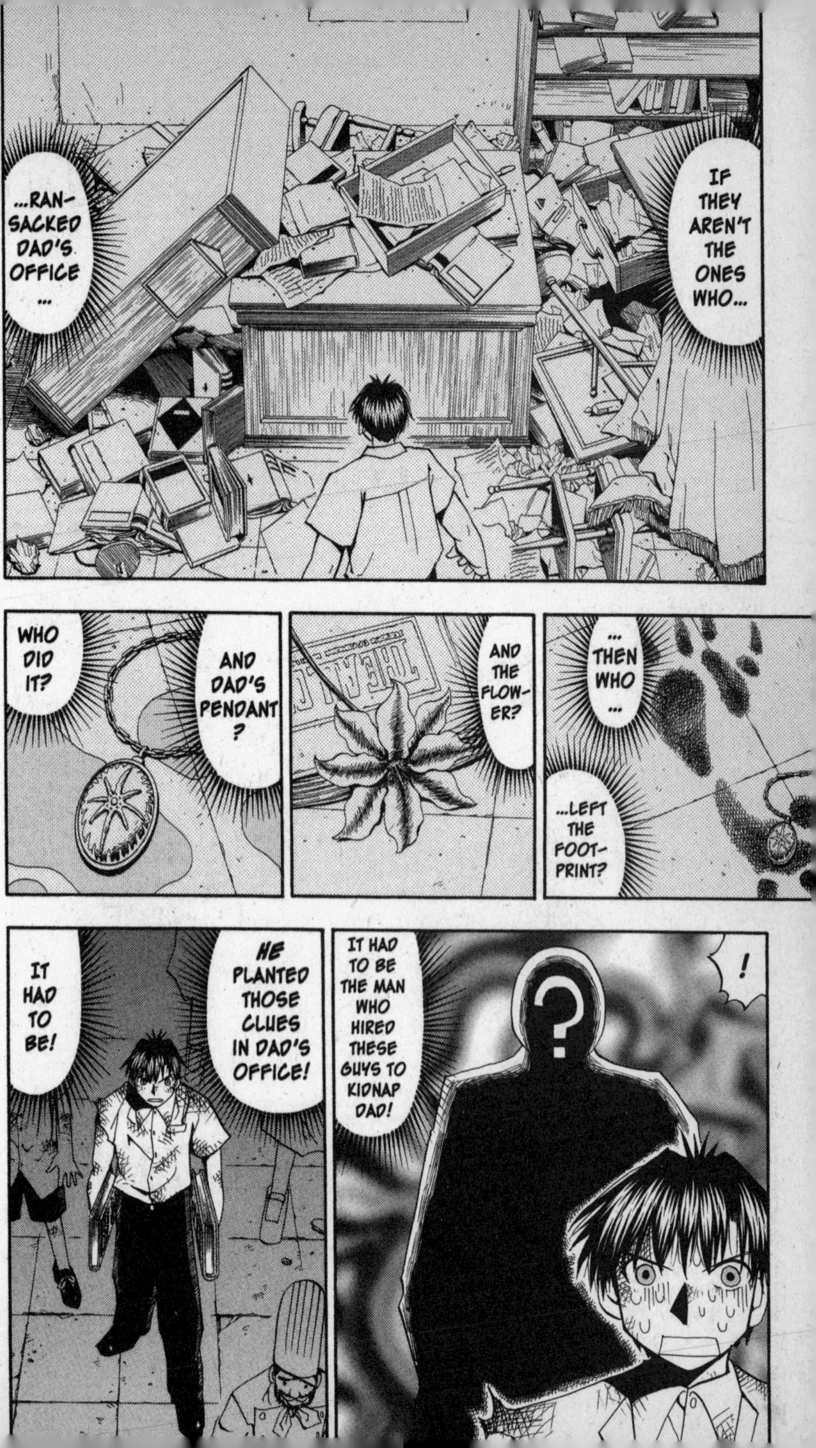
IF THEY AREN'T THE ONES WHO...
...RAN-SACKED DAD'S OFFICE ...
... THEN WHO ...
...LEFT THE FOOT-PRINT?
AND THE FLOWER?
AND DAD'S PENDANT ?
WHO DID IT?
!
IT HAD TO BE THE MAN WHO HIRED THESE GUYS TO KIDNAP DAD!
HE PLANTED THOSE CLUES IN DAD'S OFFICE!
IT HAD TO BE!

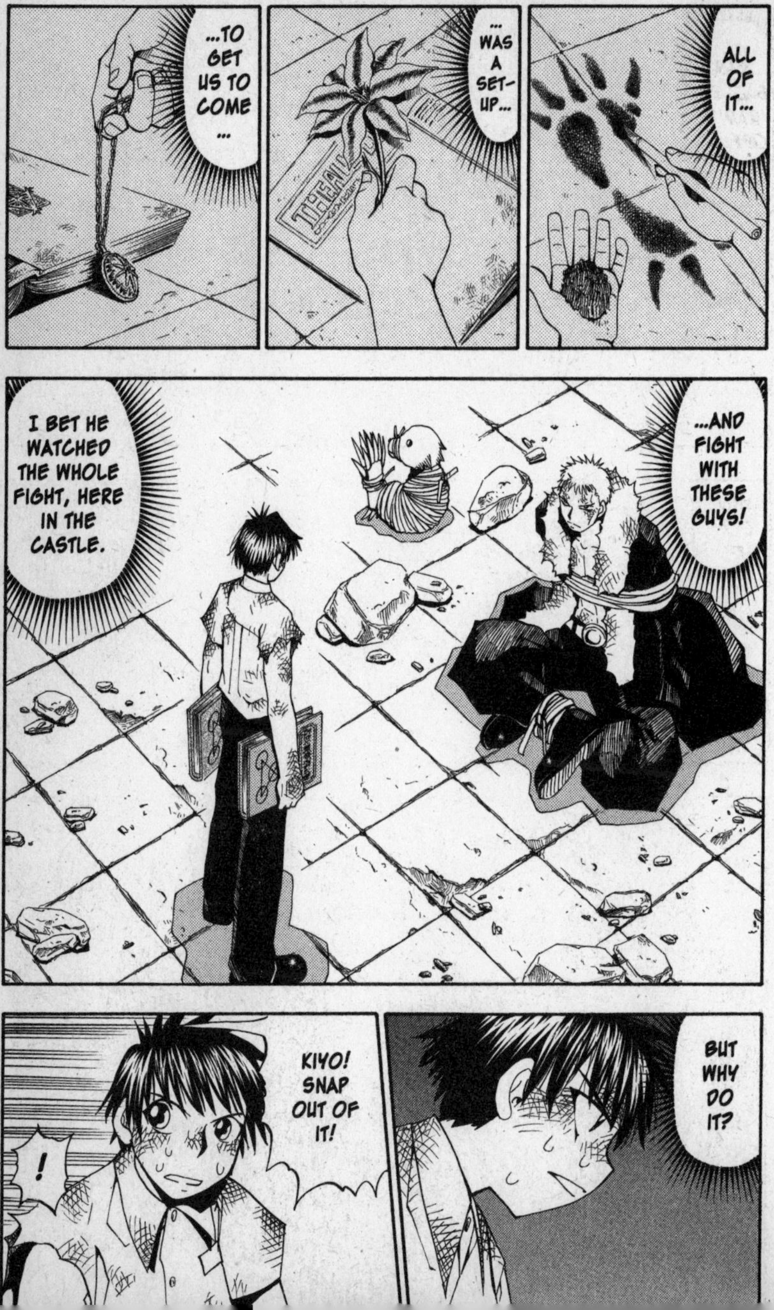
ALL OF IT...
...WAS A SET-UP...
...TO GET US TO COME ...
...AND FIGHT WITH THESE GUYS!
I BET HE WATCHED THE WHOLE FIGHT, HERE IN THE CASTLE.
BUT WHY DO IT?
KIYO! SNAP OUT OF IT!
!

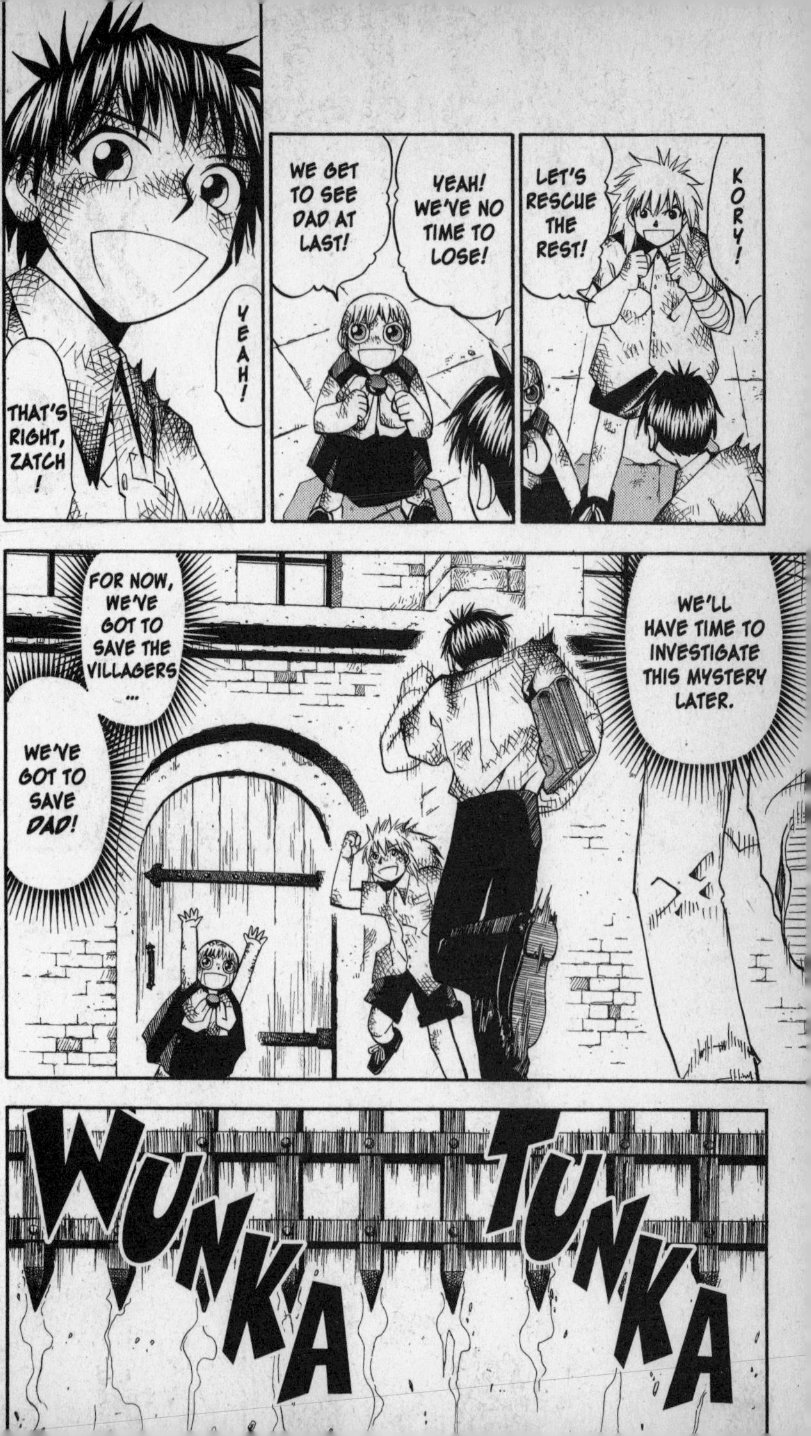
THAT'S RIGHT, ZATCH!
YEAH!
WE GET TO SEE DAD AT LAST!
YEAH! WE'VE NO TIME TO LOSE!
LET'S RESCUE THE REST!
KORY!
FOR NOW, WE'VE GOT TO SAVE THE VILLAGERS...
WE'VE GOT TO SAVE DAD!
WE'LL HAVE TIME TO INVESTIGATE THIS MYSTERY LATER.
WUNKA
TUNKA

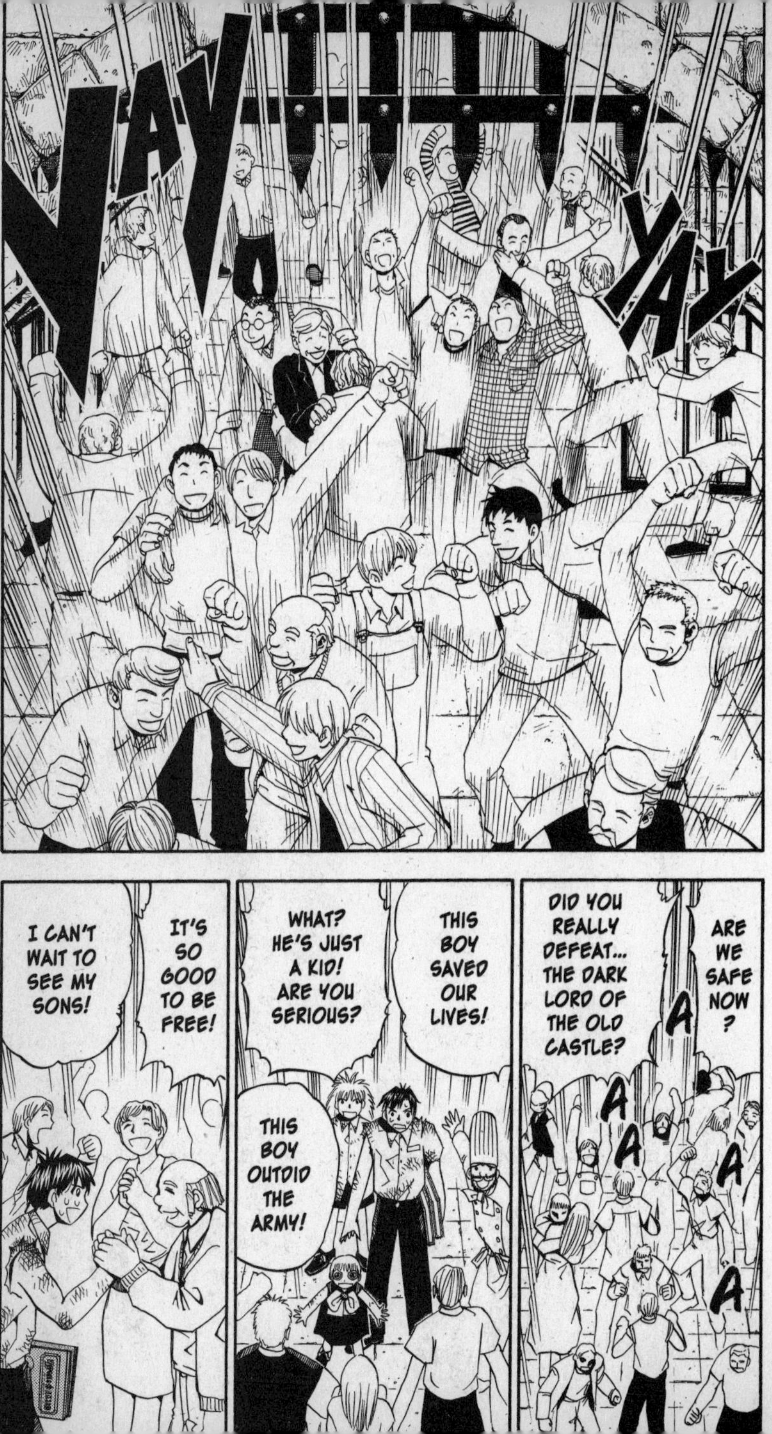
YAY
YAY
ARE WE SAFE NOW?
DID YOU REALLY DEFEAT... THE DARK LORD OF THE OLD CASTLE?
AAAAAA
THIS BOY SAVED OUR LIVES!
WHAT? HE'S JUST A KID! ARE YOU SERIOUS?
THIS BOY OUTDID THE ARMY!
IT'S SO GOOD TO BE FREE!
I CAN'T WAIT TO SEE MY SONS!

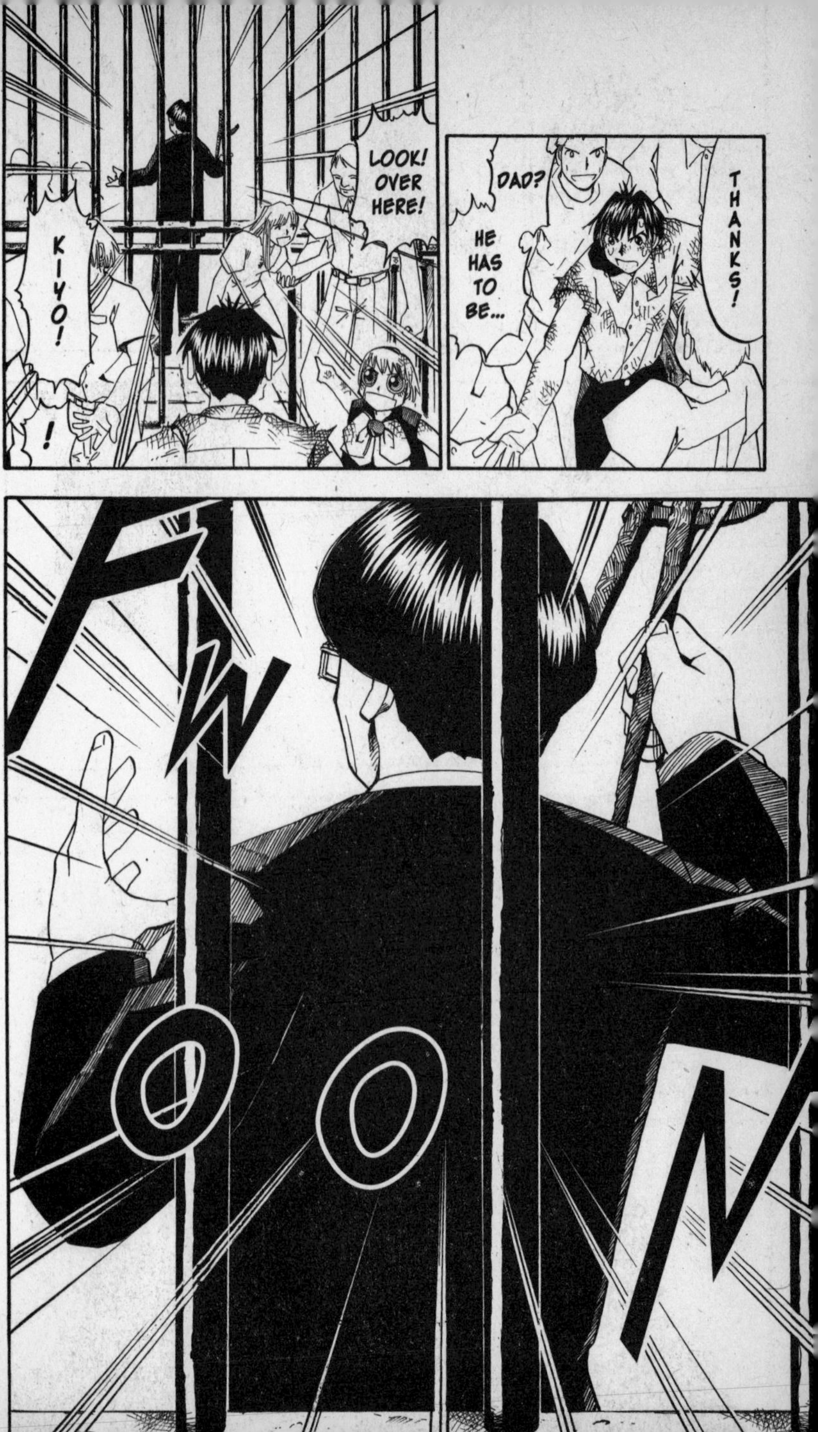
THANKS!
DAD?
HE HAS TO BE...
LOOK! OVER HERE!
KIYO!
!
FWOOM

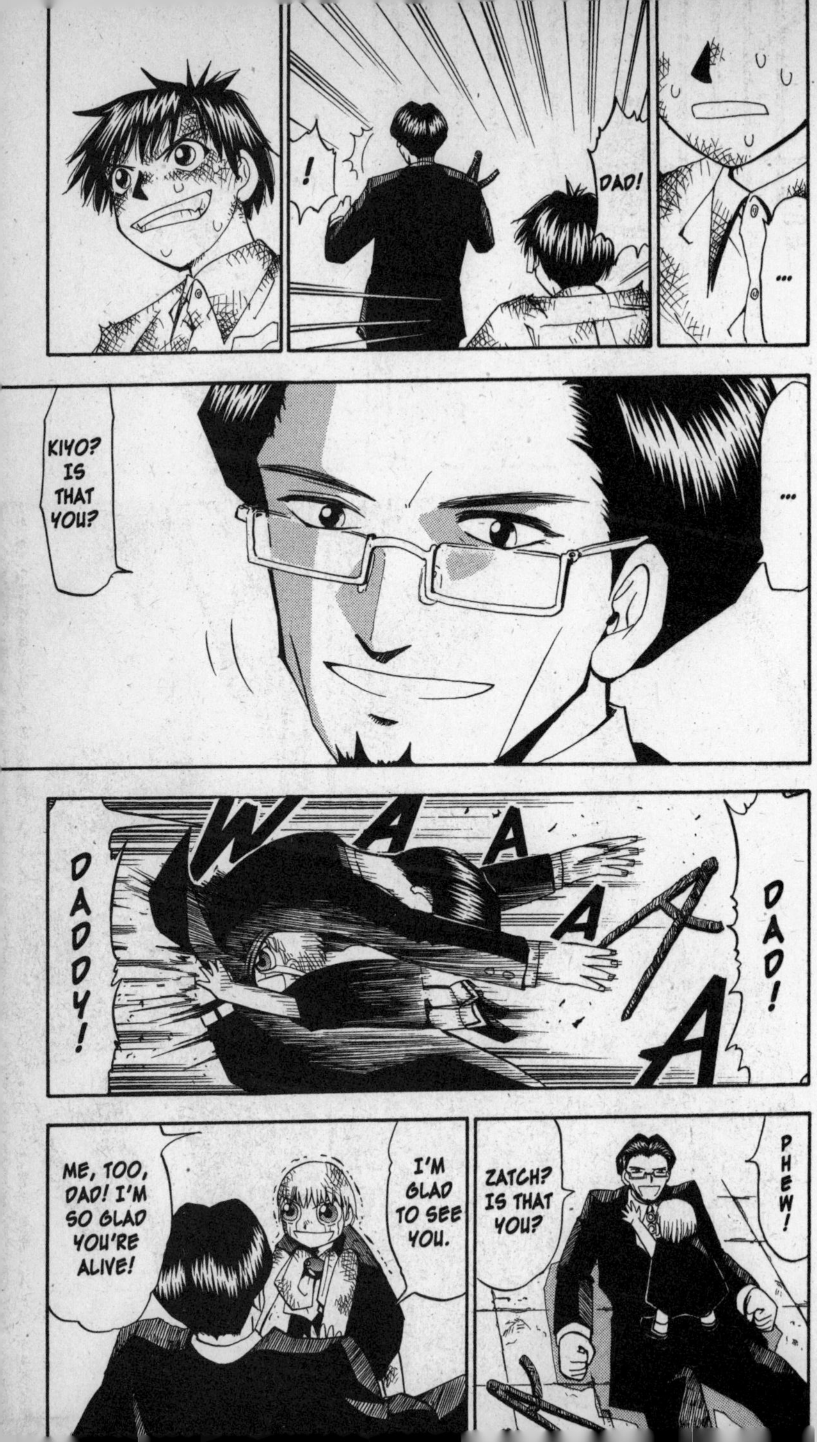
...
DAD!
!
...
KIYO? IS THAT YOU?
DAD!
WAAAAAA
DADDY!
PHEW!
ZATCH? IS THAT YOU?
I'M GLAD TO SEE YOU.
ME, TOO, DAD! I'M SO GLAD YOU'RE ALIVE!

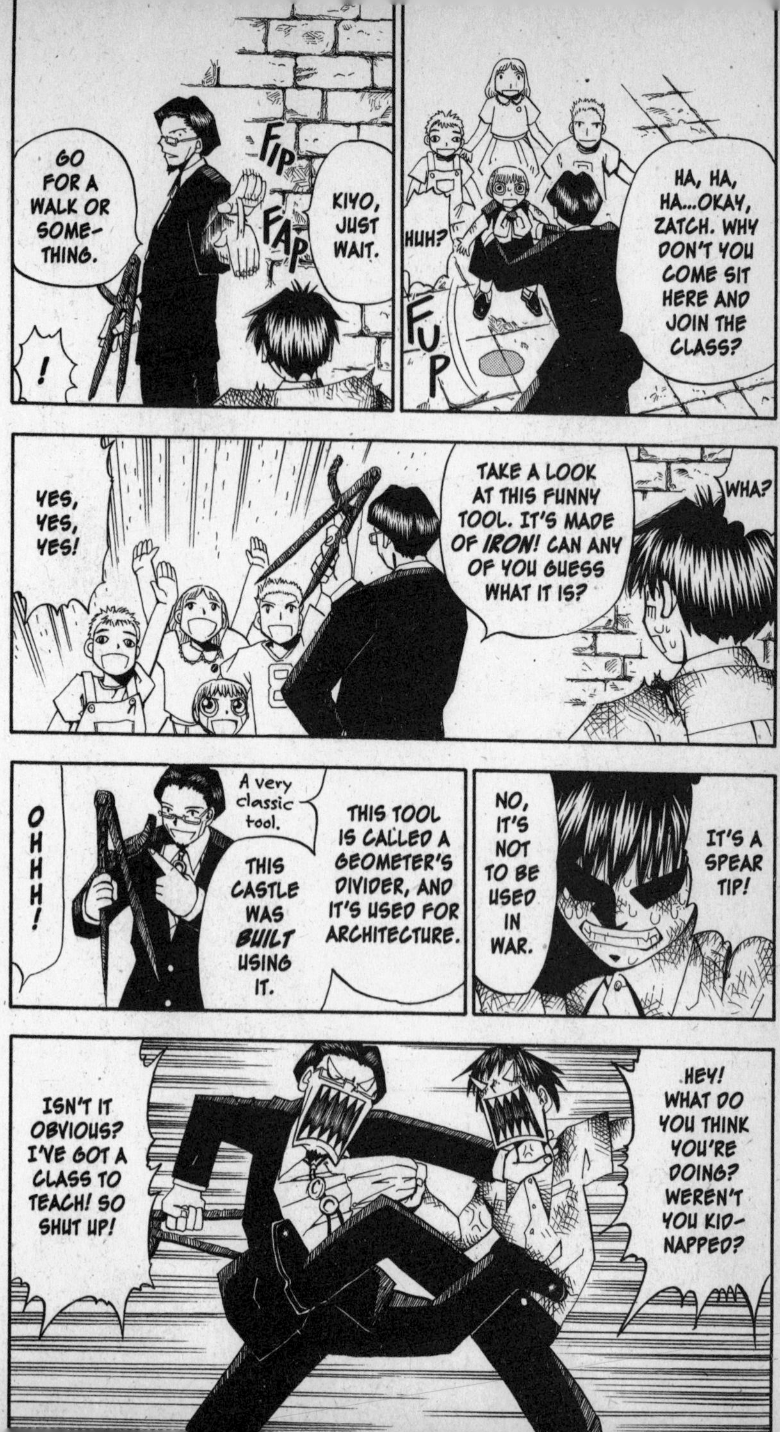
HA, HA, HA...OKAY, ZATCH. WHY DON'T YOU COME SIT HERE AND JOIN THE CLASS?
HUH?
FUP
KIYO, JUST WAIT.
FIP FAP
GO FOR A WALK OR SOME-THING.
!
WHA?
TAKE A LOOK AT THIS FUNNY TOOL. IT'S MADE OF IRON! CAN ANY OF YOU GUESS WHAT IT IS?
YES, YES, YES!
IT'S A SPEAR TIP!
NO, IT'S NOT TO BE USED IN WAR.
THIS TOOL IS CALLED A GEOMETER'S DIVIDER, AND IT'S USED FOR ARCHITECTURE.
A very classic tool.
THIS CASTLE WAS BUILT USING IT.
OHHHH!
HEY! WHAT DO YOU THINK YOU'RE DOING? WEREN'T YOU KID-NAPPED?
ISN'T IT OBVIOUS? I'VE GOT A CLASS TO TEACH! SO SHUT UP!

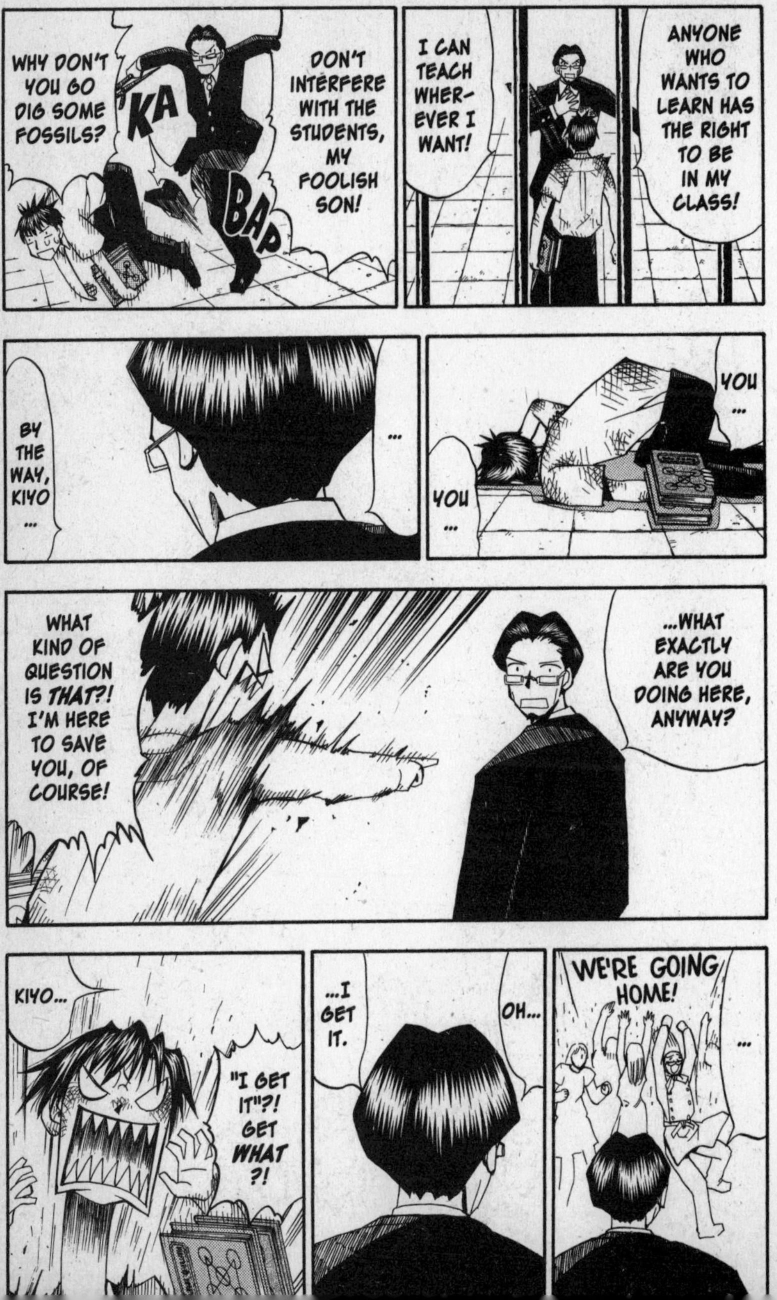
ANYONE WHO WANTS TO LEARN HAS THE RIGHT TO BE IN MY CLASS!
I CAN TEACH WHEREVER I WANT!
DON'T INTERFERE WITH THE STUDENTS, MY FOOLISH SON!
KA
BAP
WHY DON'T YOU GO DIG SOME FOSSILS?
YOU ...
YOU ...
...
BY THE WAY, KIYO ...
...WHAT EXACTLY ARE YOU DOING HERE, ANYWAY?
WHAT KIND OF QUESTION IS *THAT*?! I'M HERE TO SAVE YOU, OF COURSE!
WE'RE GOING HOME!
...
OH...
...I GET IT.
KIYO...
"I GET IT"?! GET *WHAT*?!

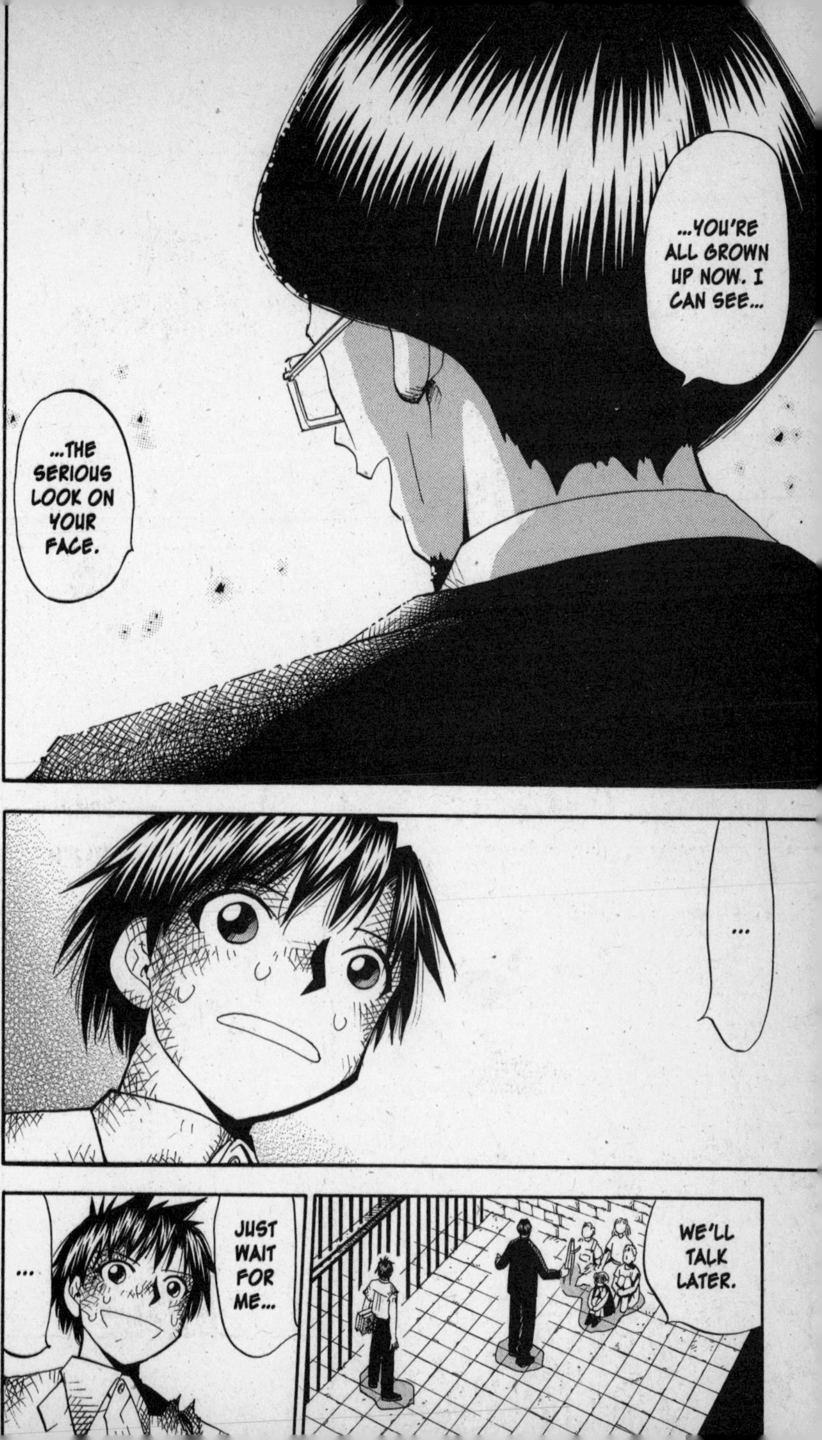
...YOU'RE ALL GROWN UP NOW. I CAN SEE...
...THE SERIOUS LOOK ON YOUR FACE.
...
WE'LL TALK LATER.
JUST WAIT FOR ME...
...

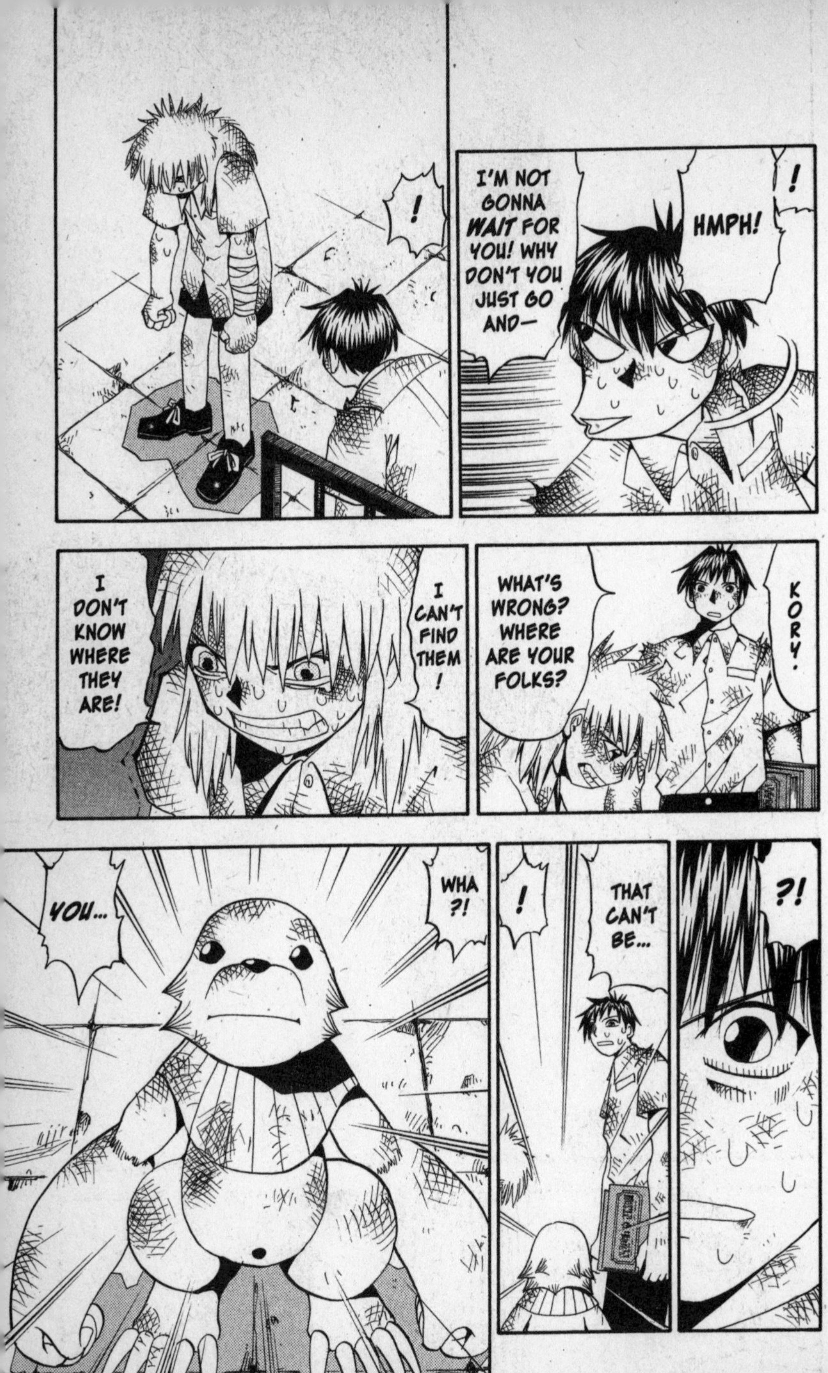
!
HMPH!
I'M NOT GONNA WAIT FOR YOU! WHY DON'T YOU JUST GO AND—
!
KORY.
WHAT'S WRONG? WHERE ARE YOUR FOLKS?
I CAN'T FIND THEM!
I DON'T KNOW WHERE THEY ARE!
?!
THAT CAN'T BE...
!
WHA ?!
YOU...

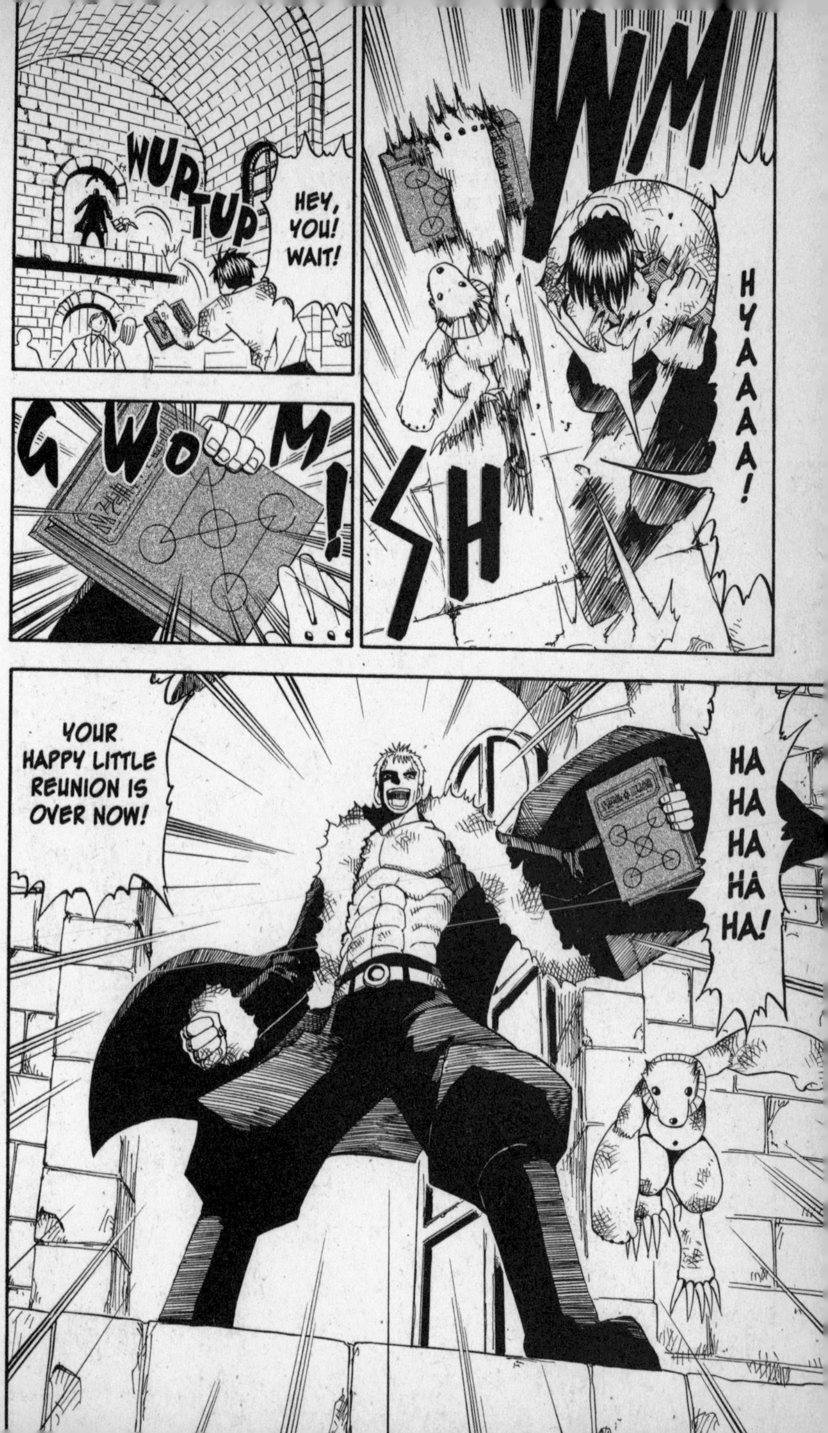
WM
HYAAAA!
SH
WUPTUP
HEY, YOU! WAIT!
GWOM!
HA HA HA HA HA!
YOUR HAPPY LITTLE REUNION IS OVER NOW!

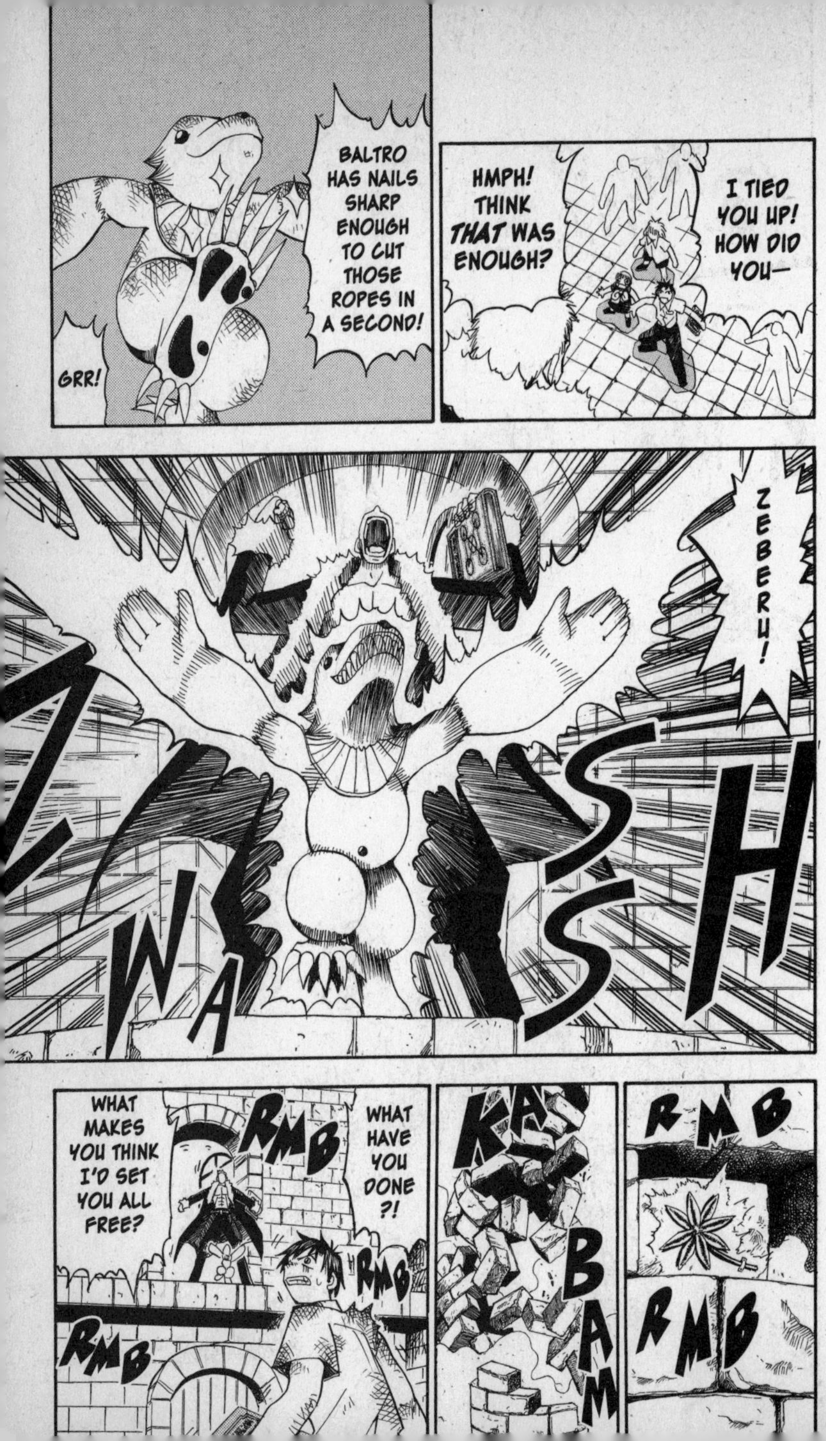
I TIED YOU UP! HOW DID YOU—
HMPH! THINK *THAT* WAS ENOUGH?
BALTRO HAS NAILS SHARP ENOUGH TO CUT THOSE ROPES IN A SECOND!
GRR!
ZEBERU!
WASSH
RMB
RMB
KA-
BAM
RMB
WHAT HAVE YOU DONE ?!
WHAT MAKES YOU THINK I'D SET YOU ALL FREE?
RMB
RMB

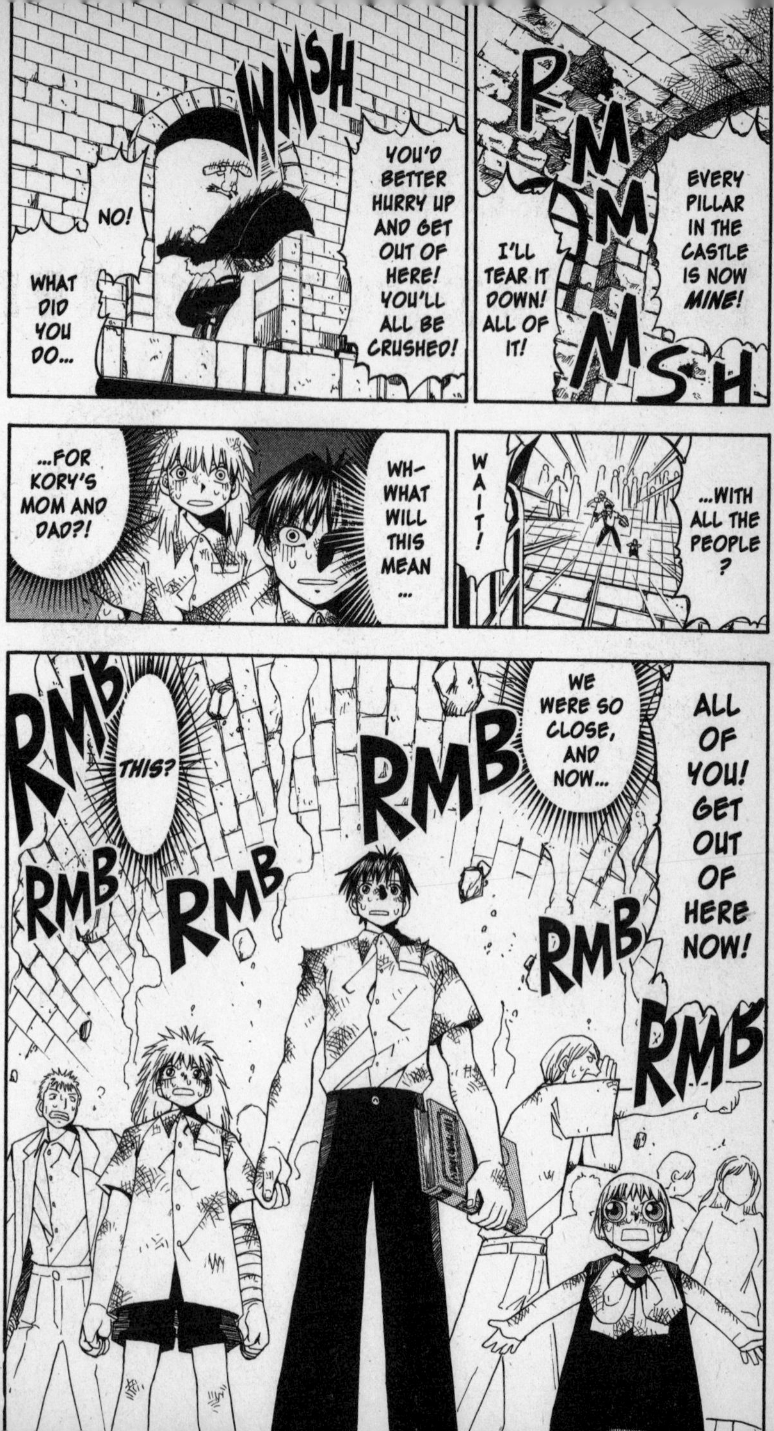
EVERY PILLAR IN THE CASTLE IS NOW MINE!
RMMMMSH
I'LL TEAR IT DOWN! ALL OF IT!
YOU'D BETTER HURRY UP AND GET OUT OF HERE! YOU'LL ALL BE CRUSHED!
WMSH
NO!
WHAT DID YOU DO...
...WITH ALL THE PEOPLE?
WAIT!
WH-WHAT WILL THIS MEAN...
...FOR KORY'S MOM AND DAD?!
ALL OF YOU! GET OUT OF HERE NOW!
WE WERE SO CLOSE, AND NOW...
RMB
THIS?
RMB
RMB
RMB
RMB
RMB
RMB

LEVEL 46: The Puppet Master

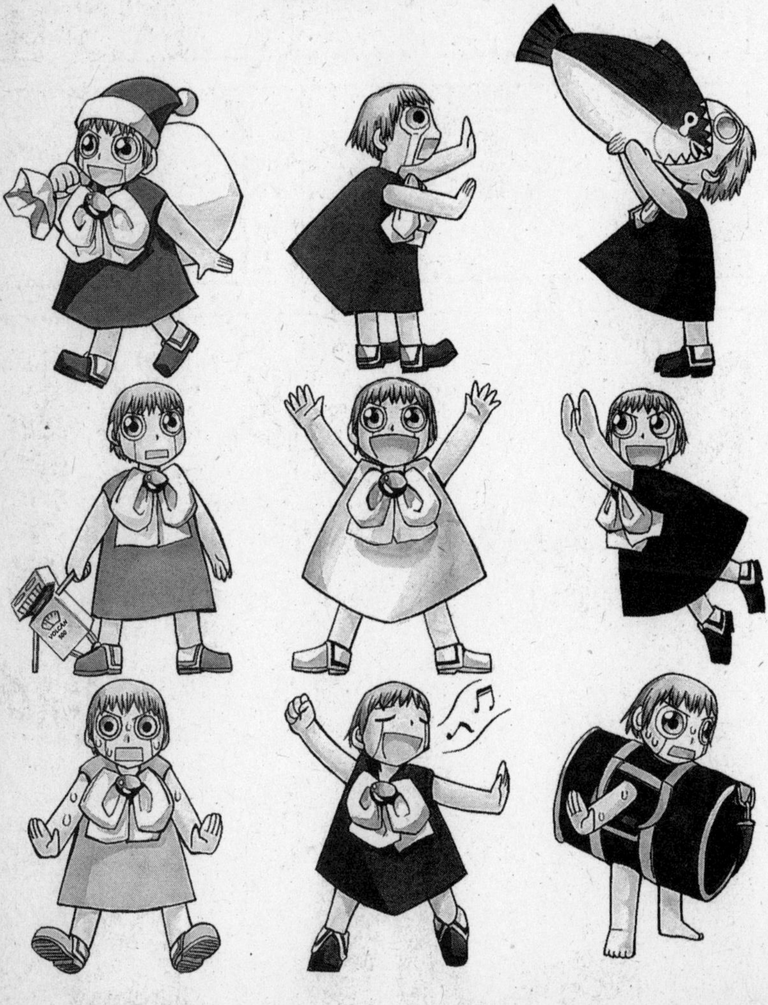

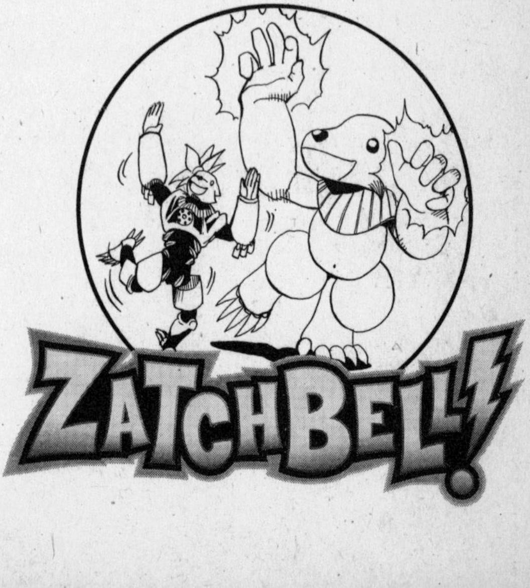
ZATCH BELL!

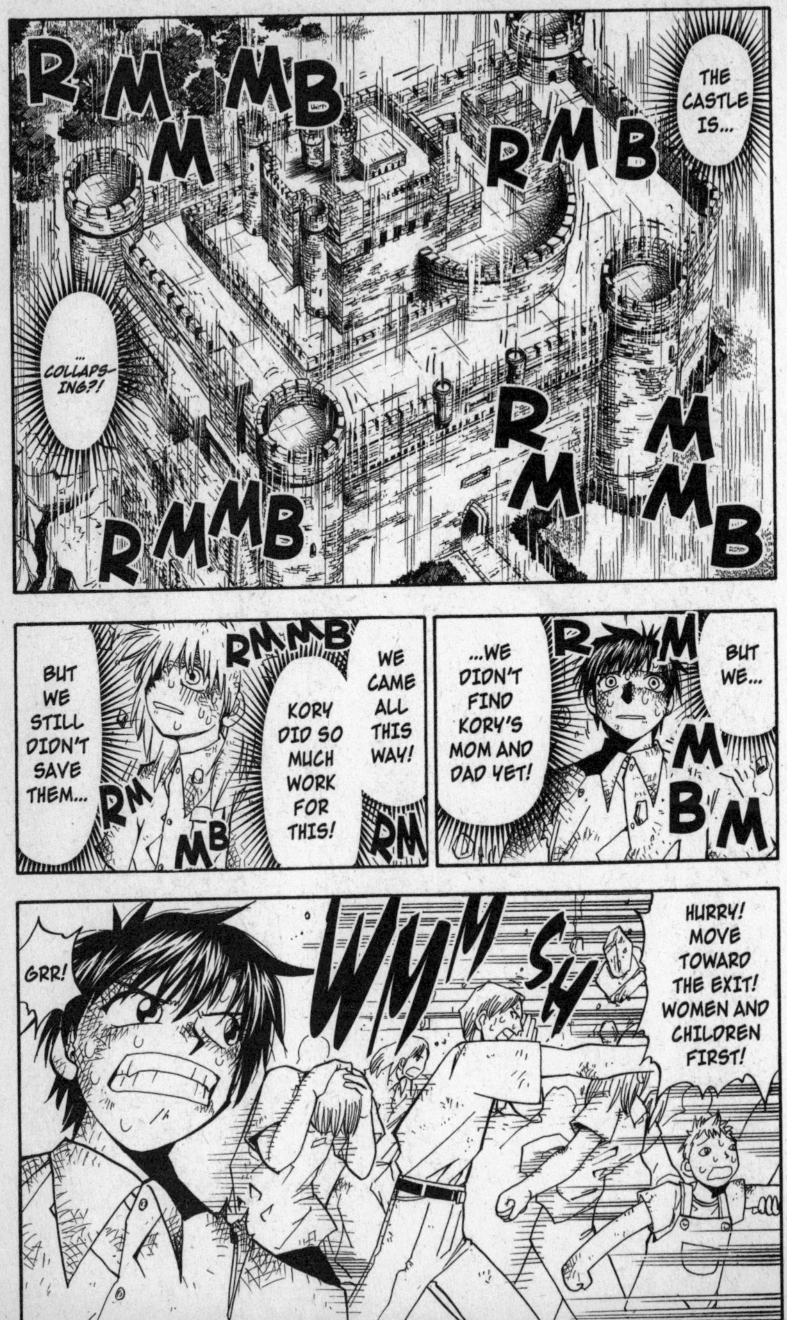
THE CASTLE IS...
RMB
RMMMB
RMMMB
RMMB
...COLLAPSING?!
BUT WE...
RMMMBM
...WE DIDN'T FIND KORY'S MOM AND DAD YET!
WE CAME ALL THIS WAY!
RMMB
KORY DID SO MUCH WORK FOR THIS!
RM
BUT WE STILL DIDN'T SAVE THEM...
RM
MB
HURRY! MOVE TOWARD THE EXIT! WOMEN AND CHILDREN FIRST!
SH
WMMM
GRR!

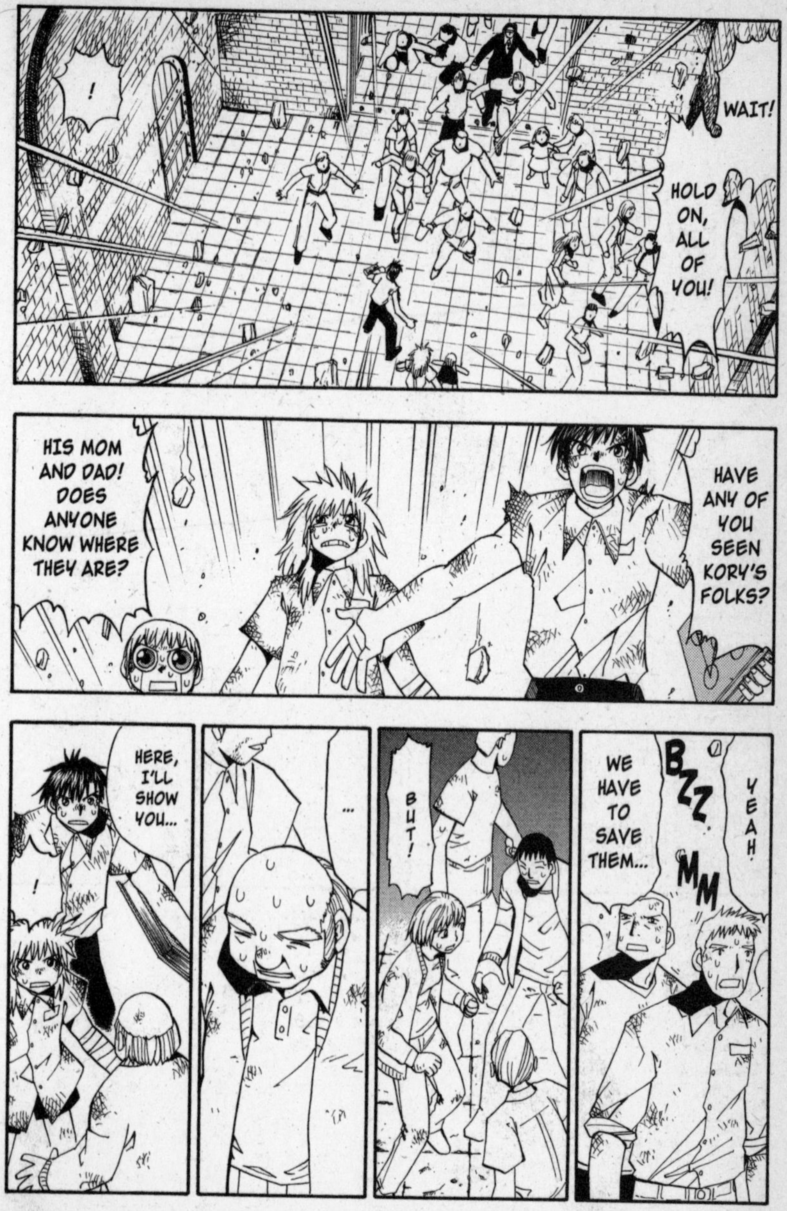
WAIT!
HOLD ON, ALL OF YOU!
!
HAVE ANY OF YOU SEEN KORY'S FOLKS?
HIS MOM AND DAD! DOES ANYONE KNOW WHERE THEY ARE?
YEAH
BZZ MM
WE HAVE TO SAVE THEM...
BUT!
...
HERE, I'LL SHOW YOU...
!

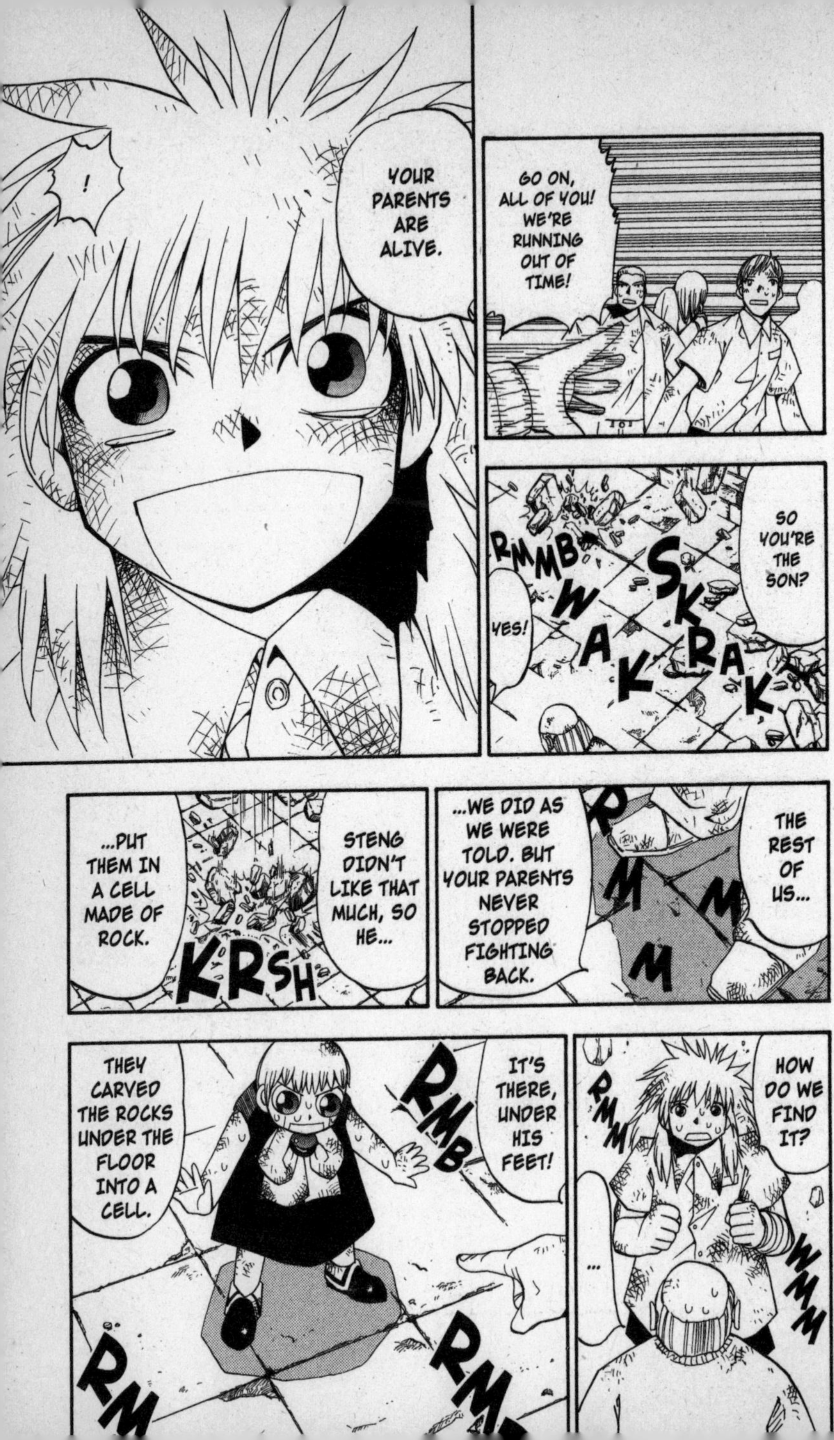
GO ON, ALL OF YOU! WE'RE RUNNING OUT OF TIME!
SO YOU'RE THE SON?
YES!
RMMB WAK
SKRAKRAK
!
YOUR PARENTS ARE ALIVE.
THE REST OF US...
...WE DID AS WE WERE TOLD. BUT YOUR PARENTS NEVER STOPPED FIGHTING BACK.
RMMMM
STENG DIDN'T LIKE THAT MUCH, SO HE...
...PUT THEM IN A CELL MADE OF ROCK.
KRSH
HOW DO WE FIND IT?
RMM
WMMM
...
IT'S THERE, UNDER HIS FEET!
RMB
THEY CARVED THE ROCKS UNDER THE FLOOR INTO A CELL.
RMB
RM

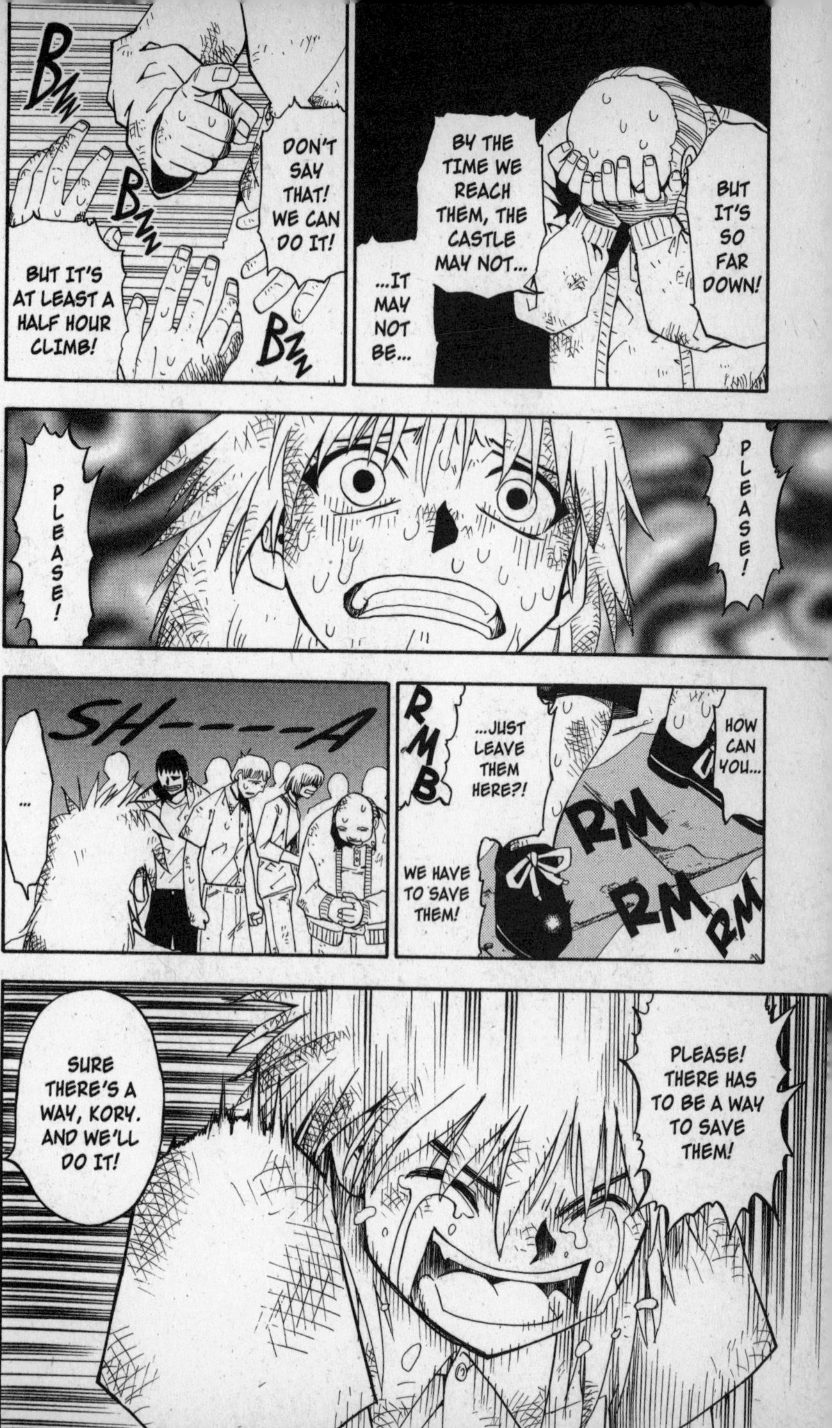
BUT IT'S SO FAR DOWN!
BY THE TIME WE REACH THEM, THE CASTLE MAY NOT...
...IT MAY NOT BE...
DON'T SAY THAT! WE CAN DO IT!
BZZ
BZZ
BUT IT'S AT LEAST A HALF HOUR CLIMB!
BZZ
PLEASE!
PLEASE!
HOW CAN YOU...
RMB
...JUST LEAVE THEM HERE?!
RM RM RM
WE HAVE TO SAVE THEM!
SH----A
...
PLEASE! THERE HAS TO BE A WAY TO SAVE THEM!
SURE THERE'S A WAY, KORY. AND WE'LL DO IT!

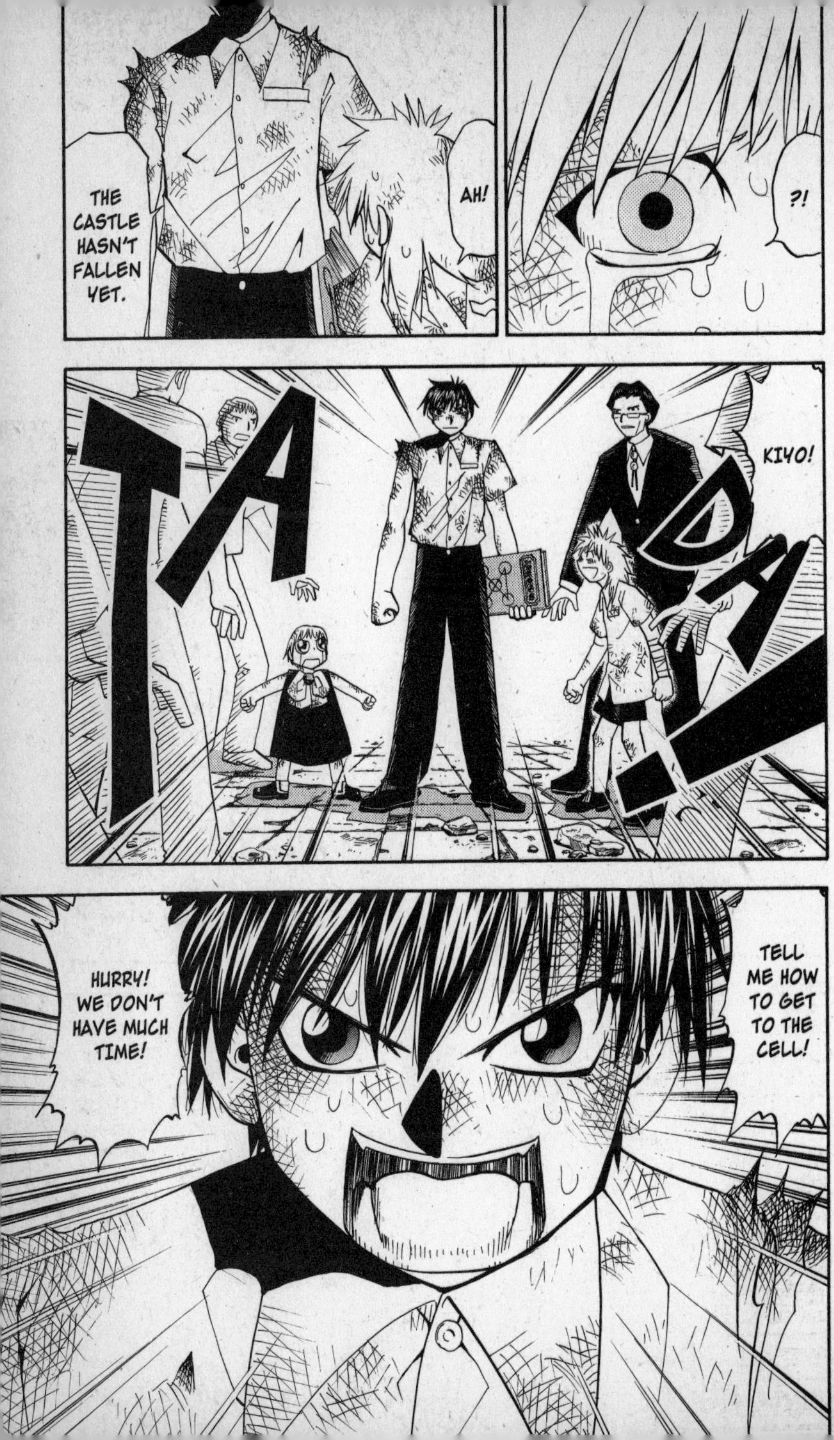
?!
AH!
THE CASTLE HASN'T FALLEN YET.
KIYO!
TA DA..!
TELL ME HOW TO GET TO THE CELL!
HURRY! WE DON'T HAVE MUCH TIME!

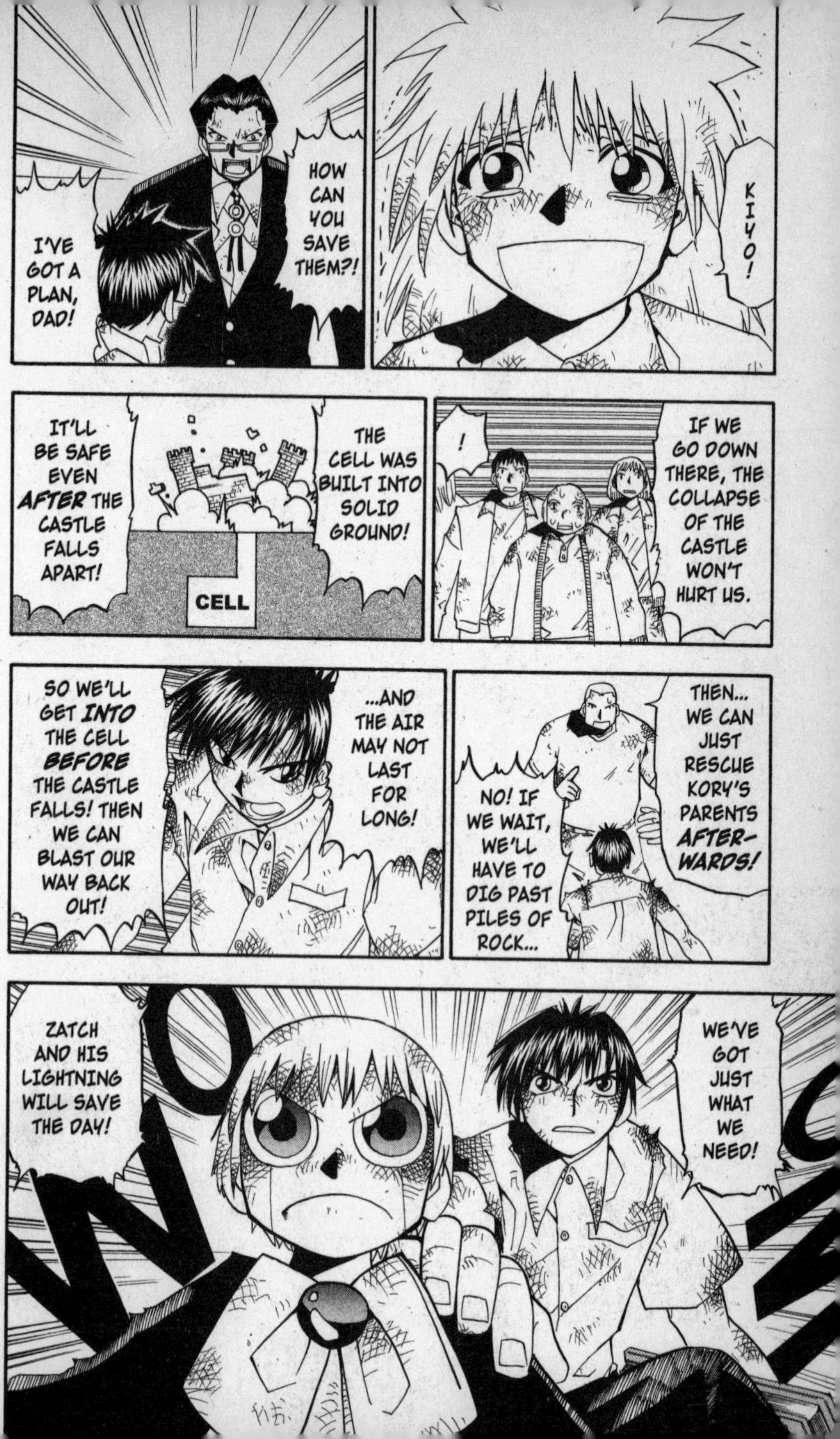
KIYO!
HOW CAN YOU SAVE THEM?!
I'VE GOT A PLAN, DAD!
IF WE GO DOWN THERE, THE COLLAPSE OF THE CASTLE WON'T HURT US.
!
THE CELL WAS BUILT INTO SOLID GROUND!
IT'LL BE SAFE EVEN AFTER THE CASTLE FALLS APART!
CELL
THEN... WE CAN JUST RESCUE KORY'S PARENTS AFTERWARDS!
NO! IF WE WAIT, WE'LL HAVE TO DIG PAST PILES OF ROCK...
...AND THE AIR MAY NOT LAST FOR LONG!
SO WE'LL GET INTO THE CELL BEFORE THE CASTLE FALLS! THEN WE CAN BLAST OUR WAY BACK OUT!
WE'VE GOT JUST WHAT WE NEED!
ZATCH AND HIS LIGHTNING WILL SAVE THE DAY!

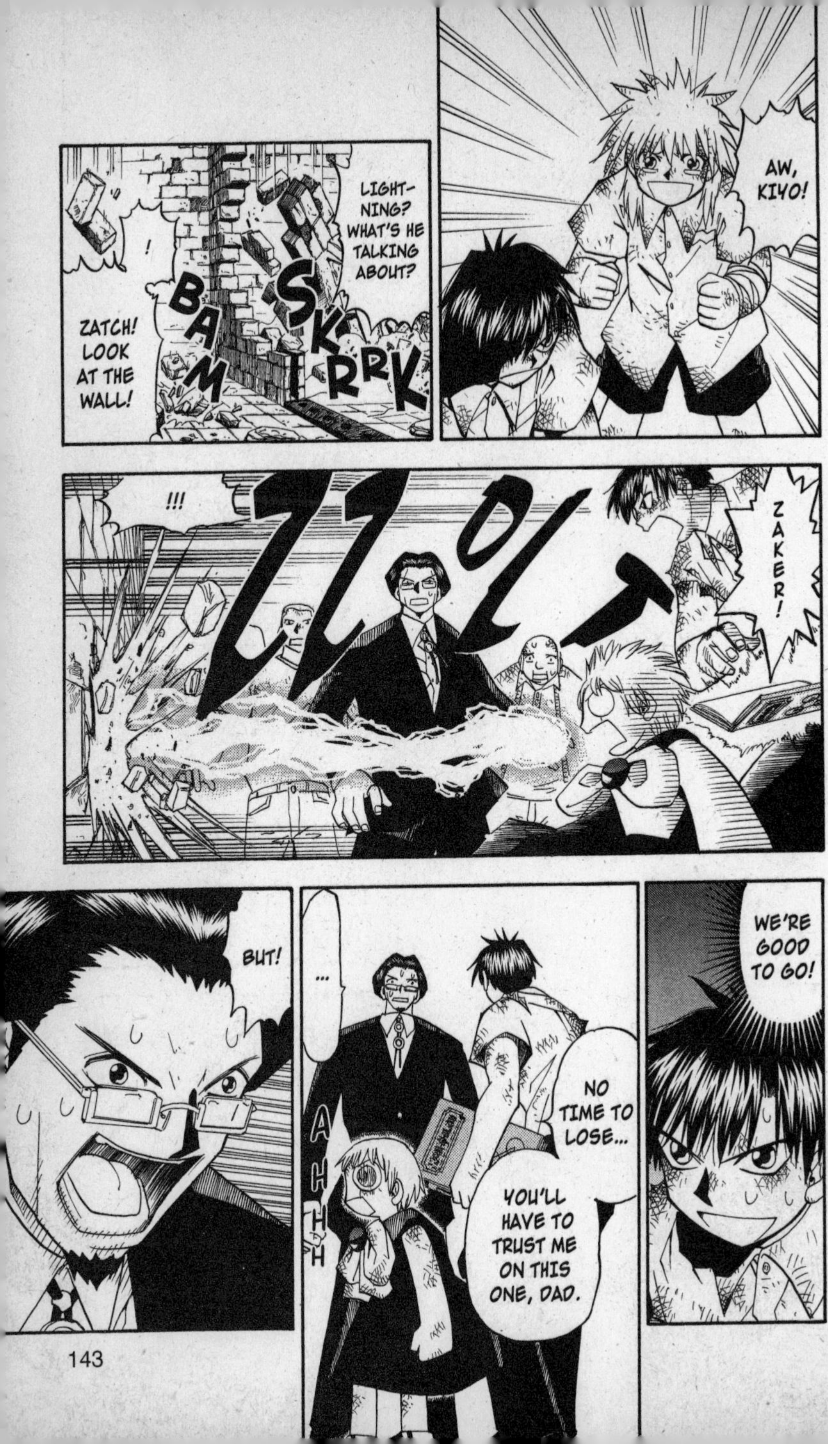
AW, KIYO!
LIGHT-NING? WHAT'S HE TALKING ABOUT?
!
SKRRK
BAM
ZATCH! LOOK AT THE WALL!
ZAKER!
ZZOLT
!!!
WE'RE GOOD TO GO!
NO TIME TO LOSE...
YOU'LL HAVE TO TRUST ME ON THIS ONE, DAD.
...
AHHHH
BUT!

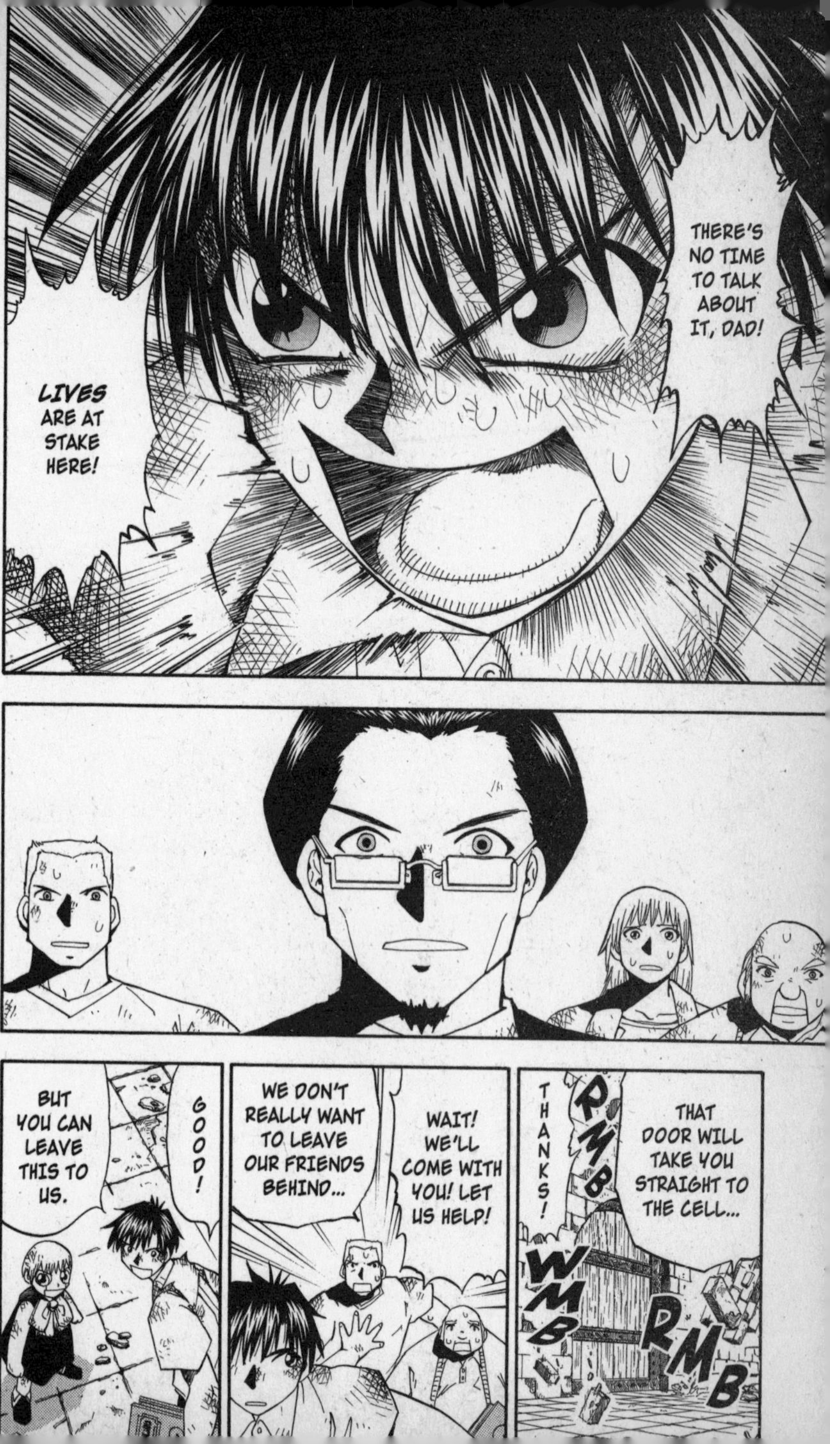
THERE'S NO TIME TO TALK ABOUT IT, DAD!
LIVES ARE AT STAKE HERE!
THAT DOOR WILL TAKE YOU STRAIGHT TO THE CELL...
RMB
THANKS!
WMB
RMB
WAIT! WE'LL COME WITH YOU! LET US HELP!
WE DON'T REALLY WANT TO LEAVE OUR FRIENDS BEHIND...
GOOD!
BUT YOU CAN LEAVE THIS TO US.

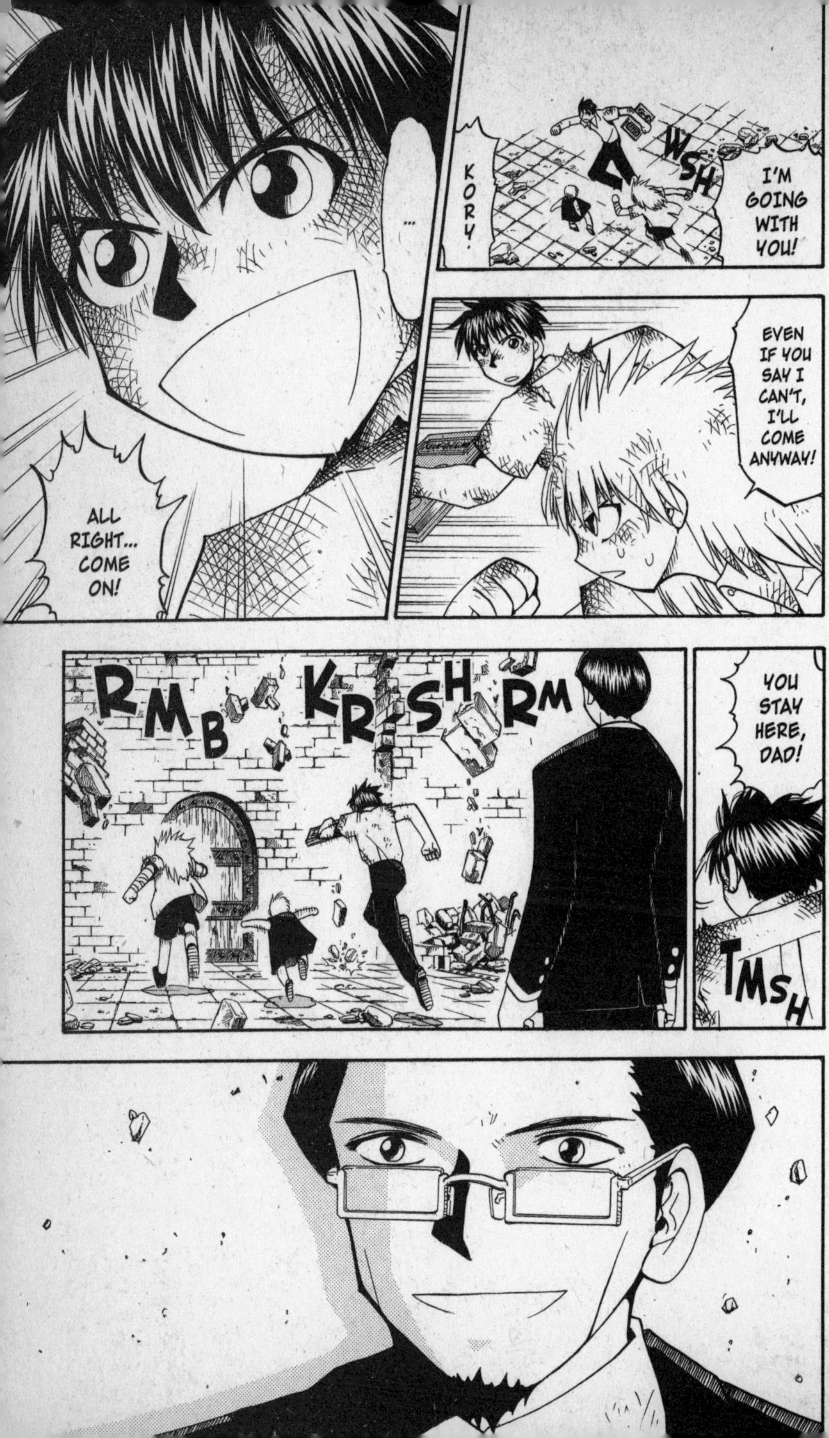
I'M GOING WITH YOU!
WSH
KORY...
EVEN IF YOU SAY I CAN'T, I'LL COME ANYWAY!
ALL RIGHT... COME ON!
YOU STAY HERE, DAD!
TMSH
RMB KRSH RM

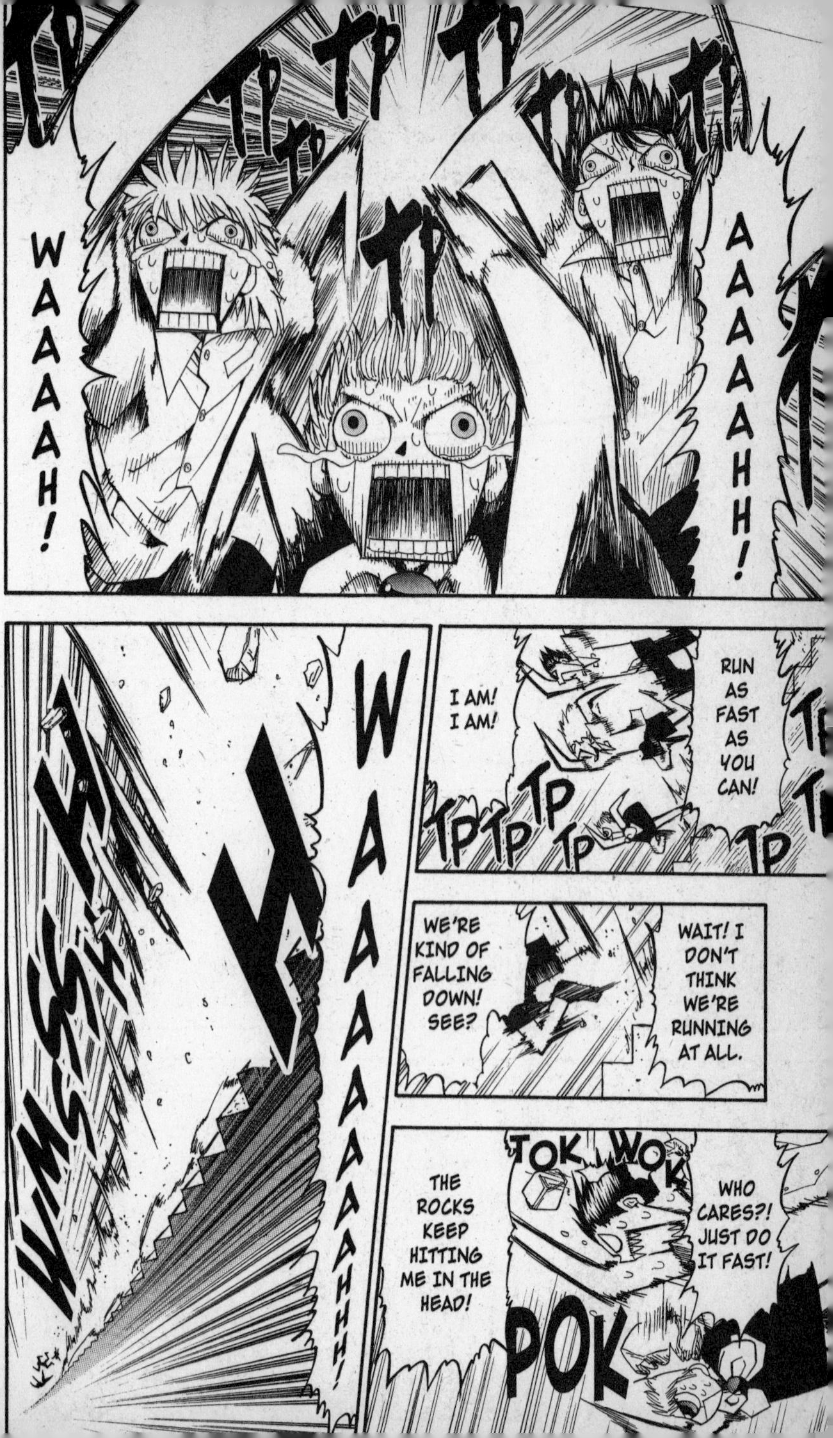
TP TP TP TP TP TP TP TP TP TP
AAAAAAHH!
WAAAAAAH!
RUN AS FAST AS YOU CAN!
I AM! I AM!
TP TP TP TP TP TP
WAIT! I DON'T THINK WE'RE RUNNING AT ALL.
WE'RE KIND OF FALLING DOWN! SEE?
TOK WOK
WHO CARES?! JUST DO IT FAST!
THE ROCKS KEEP HITTING ME IN THE HEAD!
POK
WHSSH
WAAAAAAAAHHH!

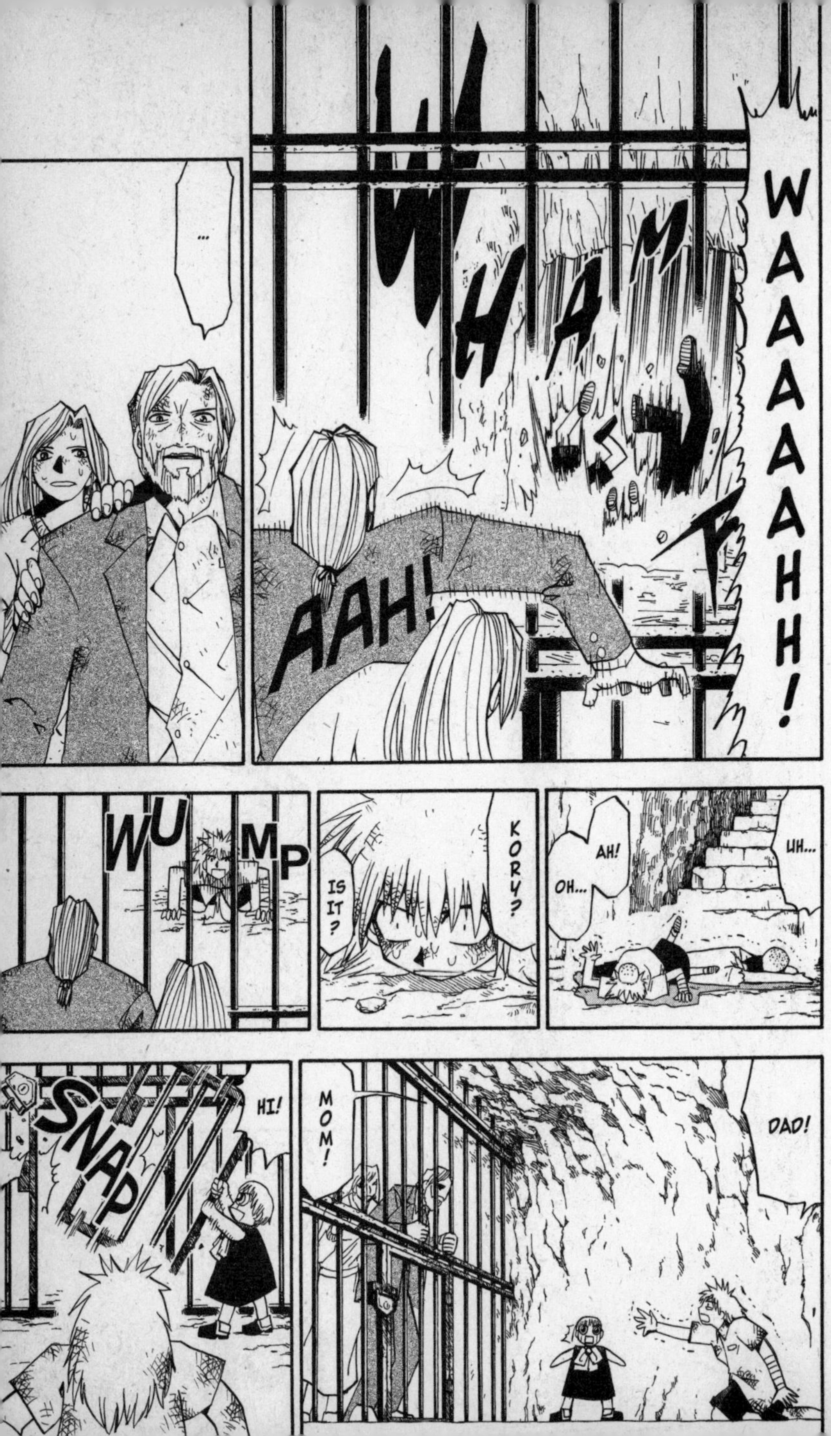
WAAAAAHH!
WHAM
AAH!
...
UH...
AH!
OH...
KORY?
IS IT?
WUMP
DAD!
MOM!
HI!
SNAP

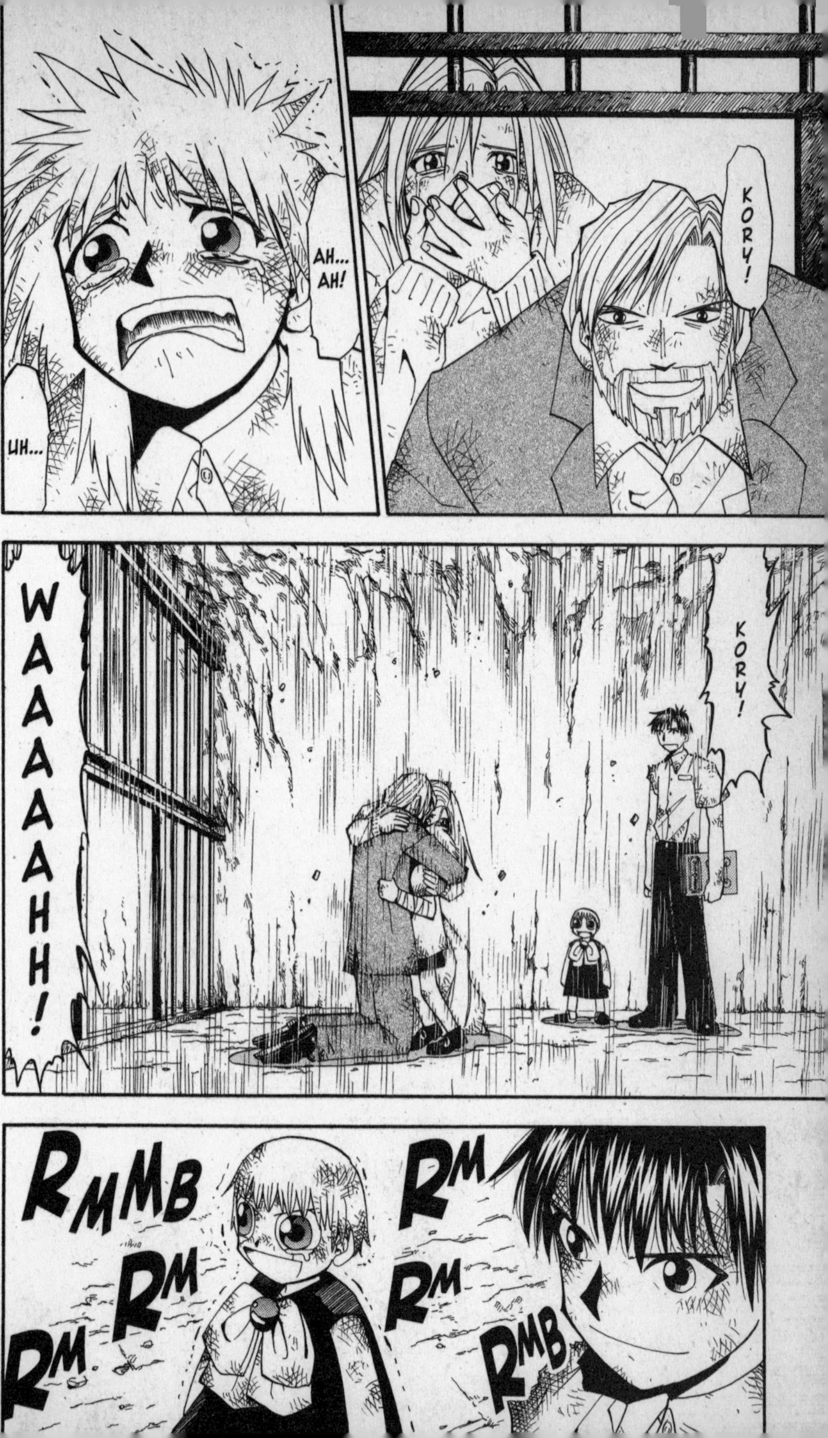
KORY!
AH... AH!
UH...
KORY!
WAAAAAAHH!
RM
RM
RMB
RMMB
RM
RM

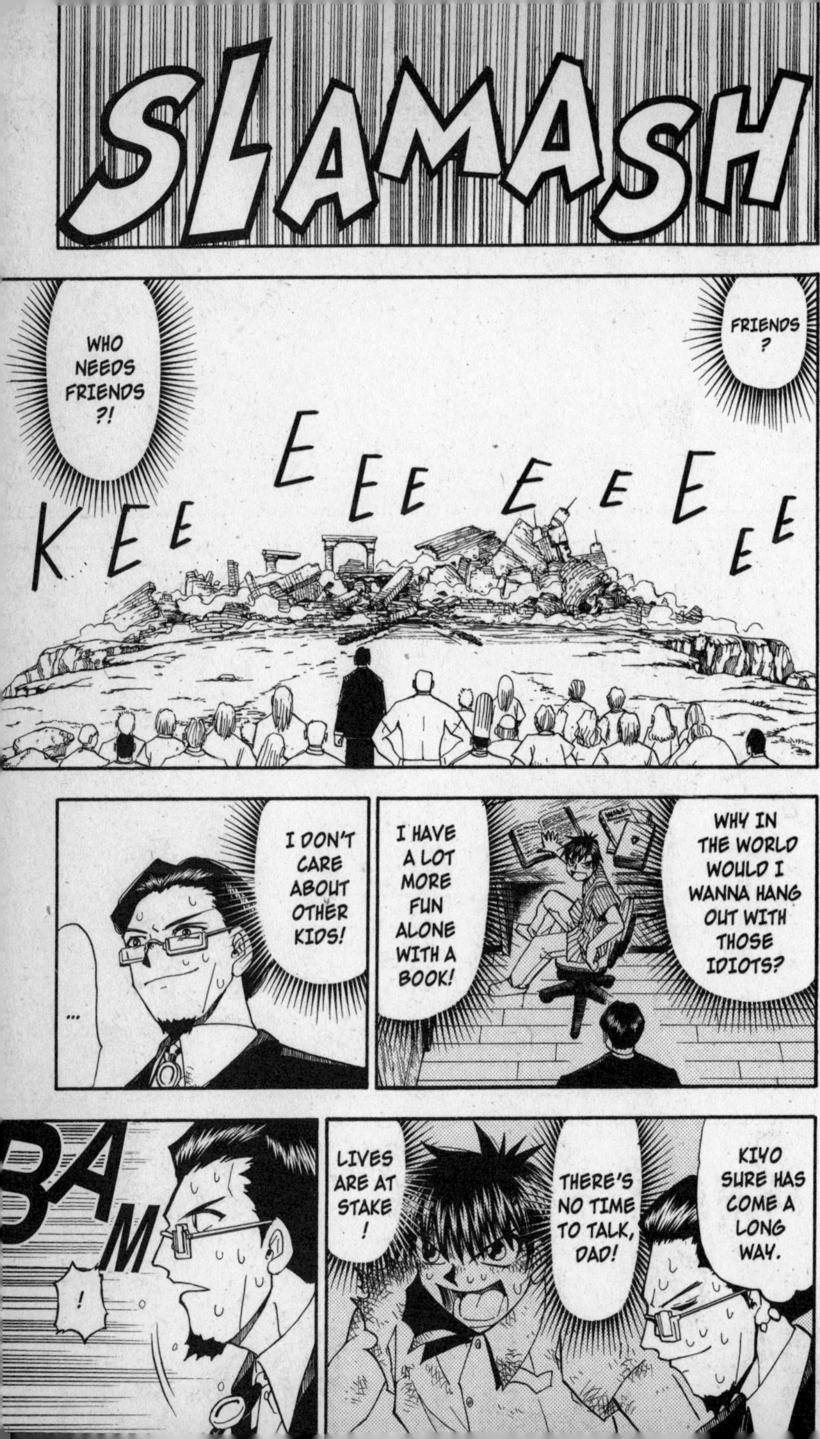
SLAMASH
FRIENDS?
WHO NEEDS FRIENDS?!
KEEEEEEEEEEE
WHY IN THE WORLD WOULD I WANNA HANG OUT WITH THOSE IDIOTS?
I HAVE A LOT MORE FUN ALONE WITH A BOOK!
I DON'T CARE ABOUT OTHER KIDS!
...
KIYO SURE HAS COME A LONG WAY.
THERE'S NO TIME TO TALK, DAD!
LIVES ARE AT STAKE!
BAM
!

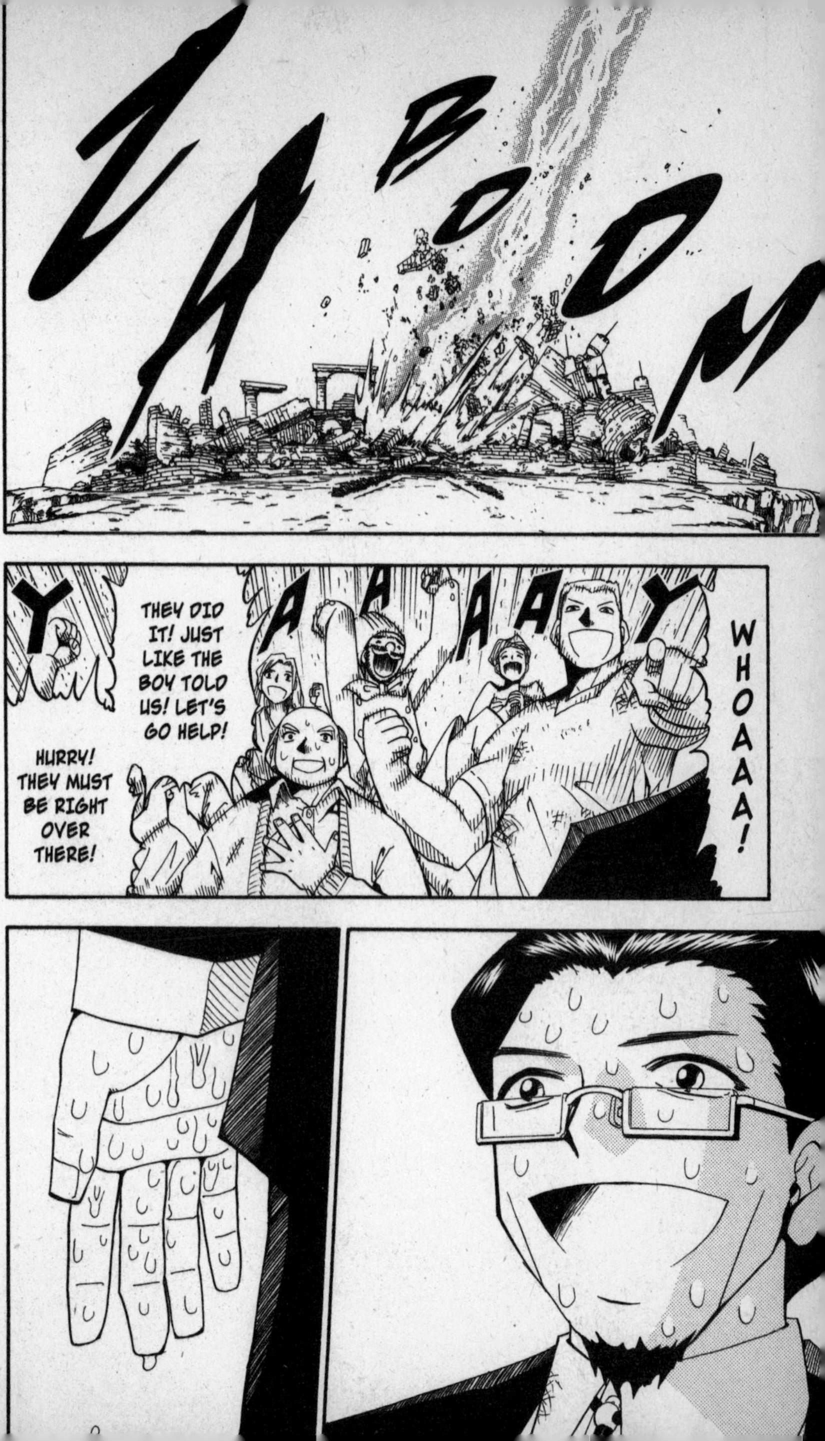
KABOOM
WHOAAA!
YAAAAY
THEY DID IT! JUST LIKE THE BOY TOLD US! LET'S GO HELP!
HURRY! THEY MUST BE RIGHT OVER THERE!

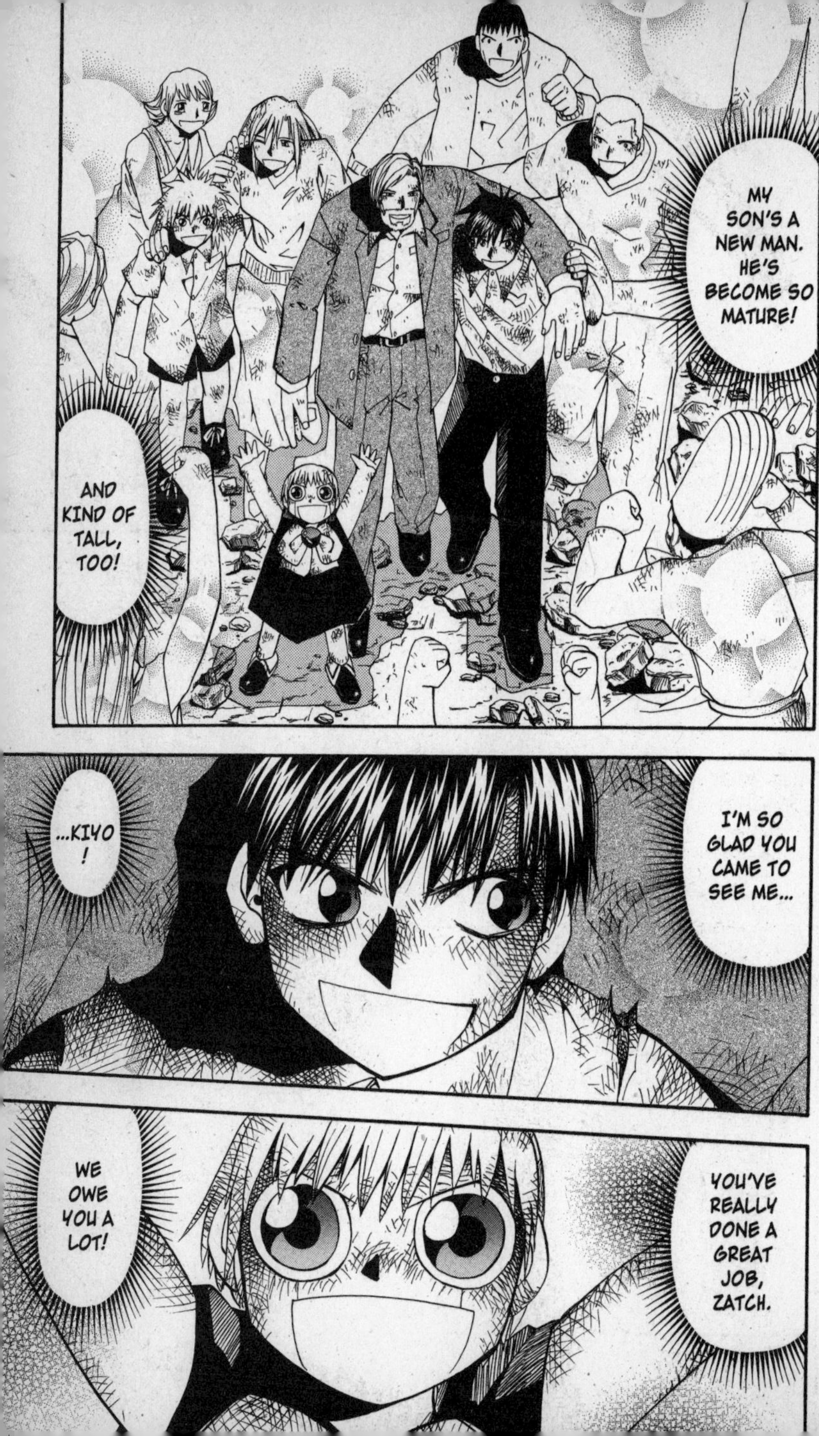
MY SON'S A NEW MAN. HE'S BECOME SO MATURE!
AND KIND OF TALL, TOO!
I'M SO GLAD YOU CAME TO SEE ME...
...KIYO!
YOU'VE REALLY DONE A GREAT JOB, ZATCH.
WE OWE YOU A LOT!

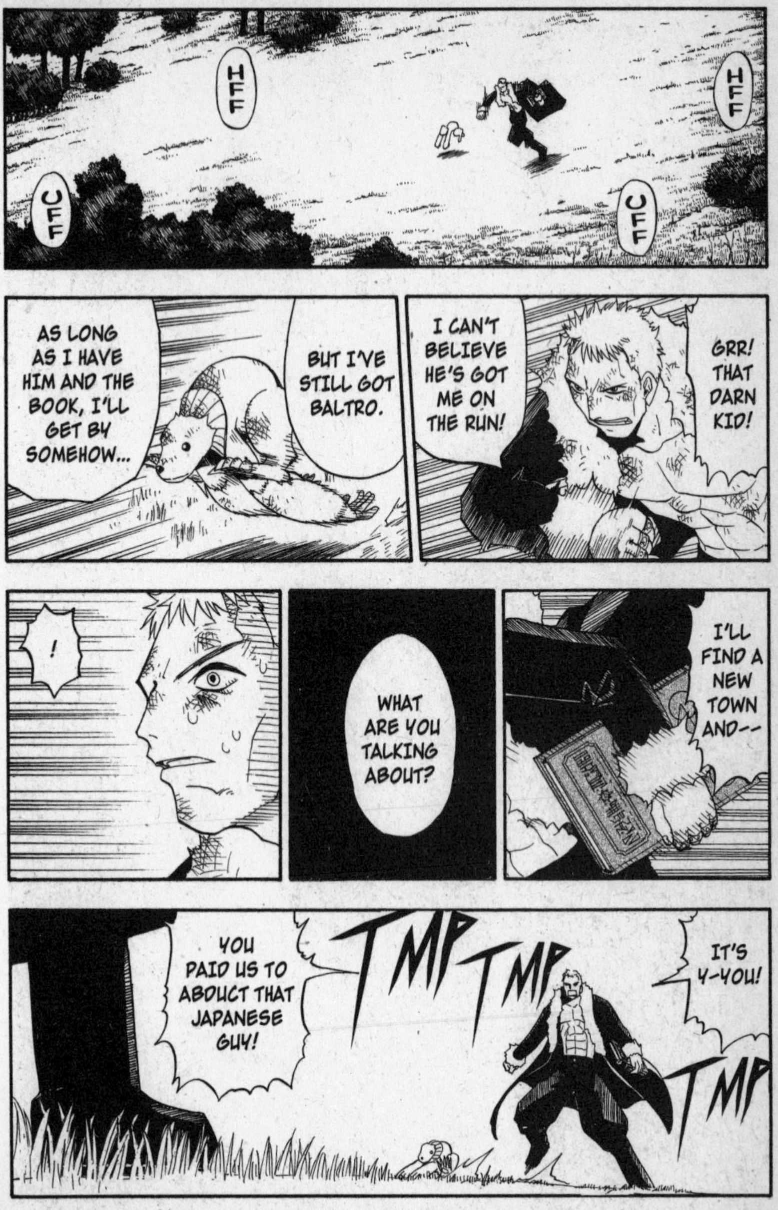
HFF
HFF
UFF
UFF
GRR! THAT DARN KID!
I CAN'T BELIEVE HE'S GOT ME ON THE RUN!
BUT I'VE STILL GOT BALTRO.
AS LONG AS I HAVE HIM AND THE BOOK, I'LL GET BY SOMEHOW...
I'LL FIND A NEW TOWN AND--
WHAT ARE YOU TALKING ABOUT?
!
IT'S Y-YOU!
TMP
TMP
TMP
YOU PAID US TO ABDUCT THAT JAPANESE GUY!

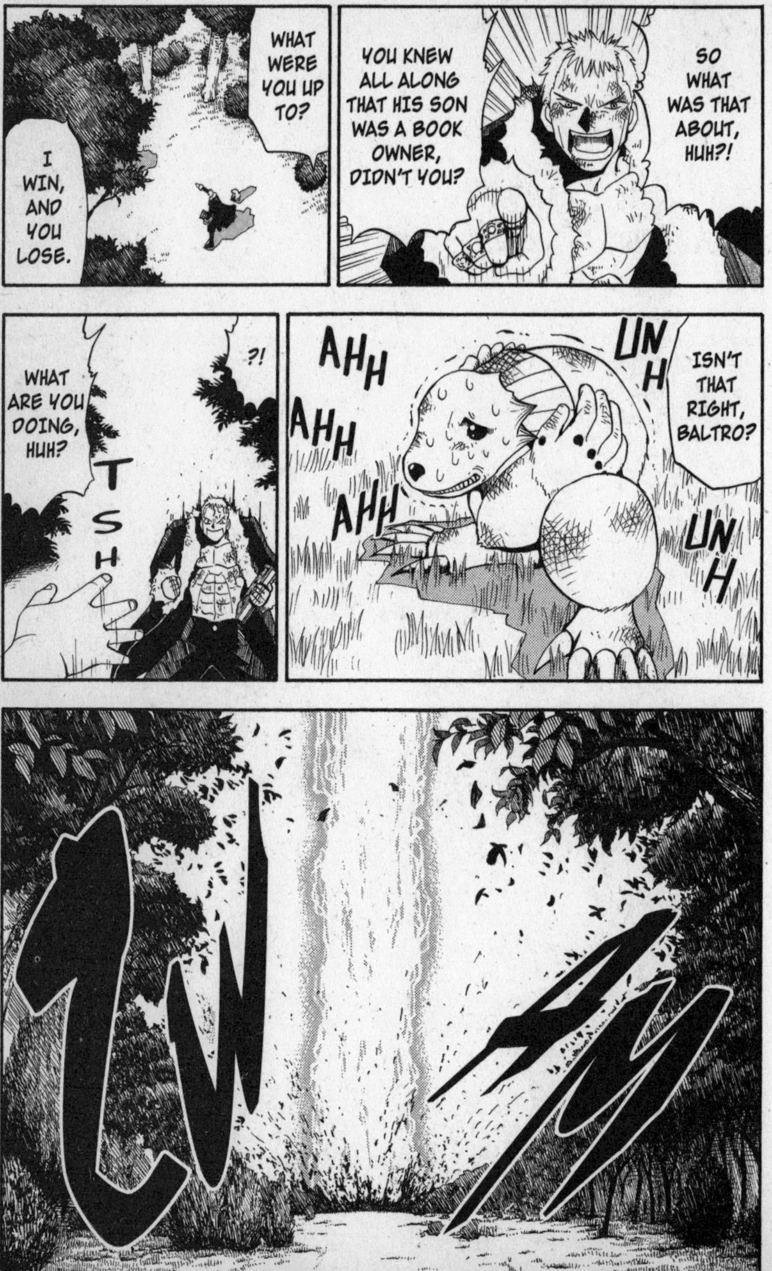
SO WHAT WAS THAT ABOUT, HUH?!
YOU KNEW ALL ALONG THAT HIS SON WAS A BOOK OWNER, DIDN'T YOU?
WHAT WERE YOU UP TO?
I WIN, AND YOU LOSE.
ISN'T THAT RIGHT, BALTRO?
UNH
UNH
AHH
AHH
AHH
?!
WHAT ARE YOU DOING, HUH?
TSH

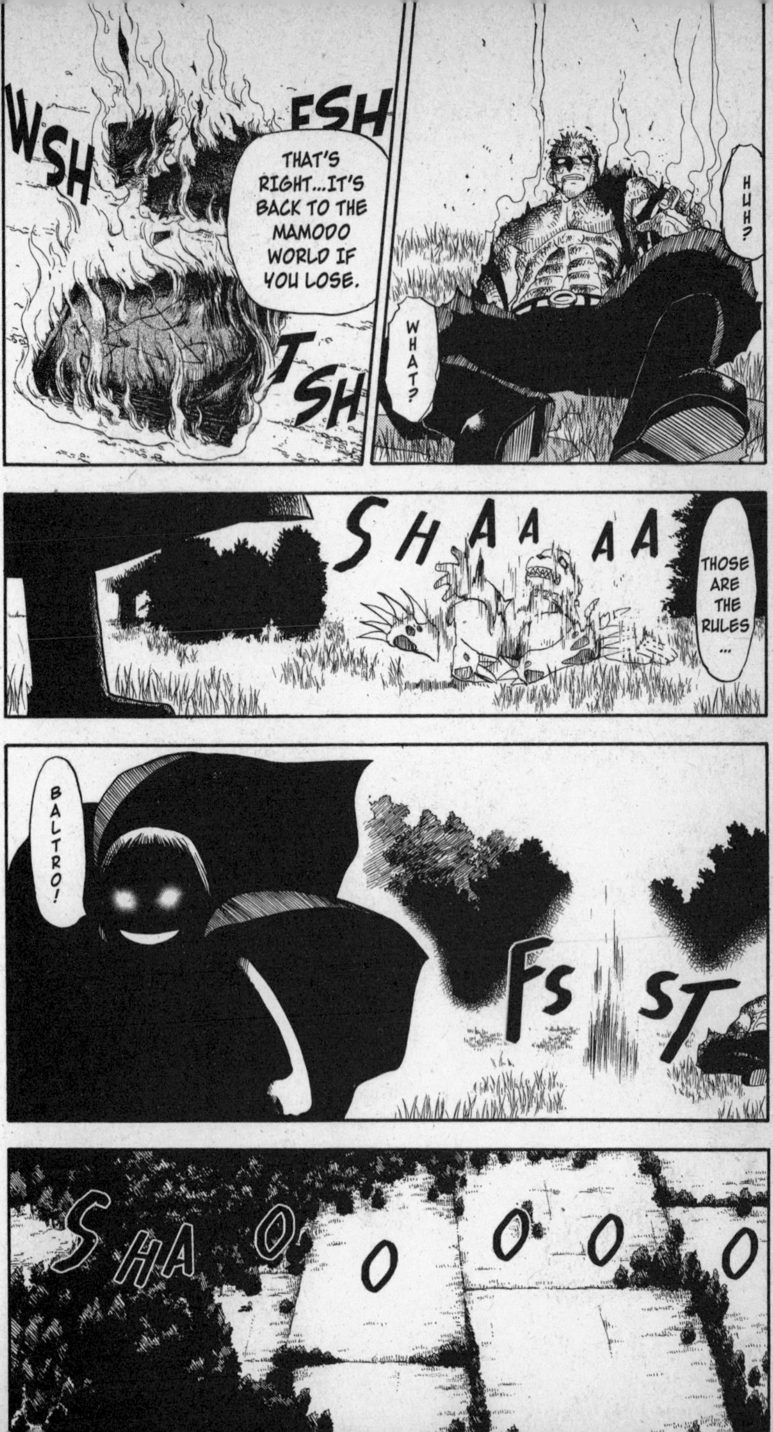
HUH?
WHAT?
FSH
WSH
THAT'S RIGHT...IT'S BACK TO THE MAMODO WORLD IF YOU LOSE.
TSH
THOSE ARE THE RULES ...
SHAAAAA
BALTRO!
FS ST
SHAOOOOO

LEVEL 47: The Forest of Spirits

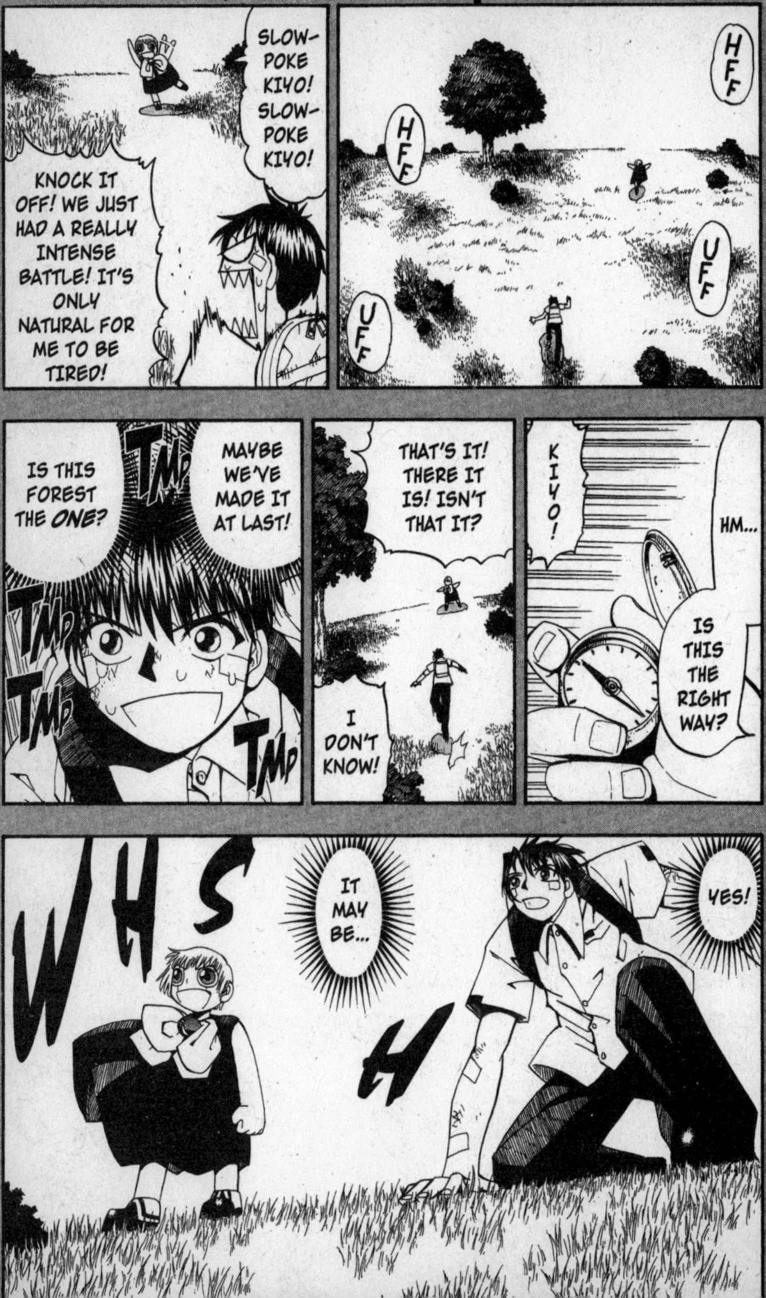
HFF
HFF
UFF
UFF
SLOW-POKE KIYO! SLOW-POKE KIYO!
KNOCK IT OFF! WE JUST HAD A REALLY INTENSE BATTLE! IT'S ONLY NATURAL FOR ME TO BE TIRED!
KIYO!
HM...
IS THIS THE RIGHT WAY?
THAT'S IT! THERE IT IS! ISN'T THAT IT?
I DON'T KNOW!
MAYBE WE'VE MADE IT AT LAST!
TMP
IS THIS FOREST THE ONE?
TMP
TMP
TMP
TMP
YES!
IT MAY BE...
WHSH

LEVEL 47: The Forest of Spirits

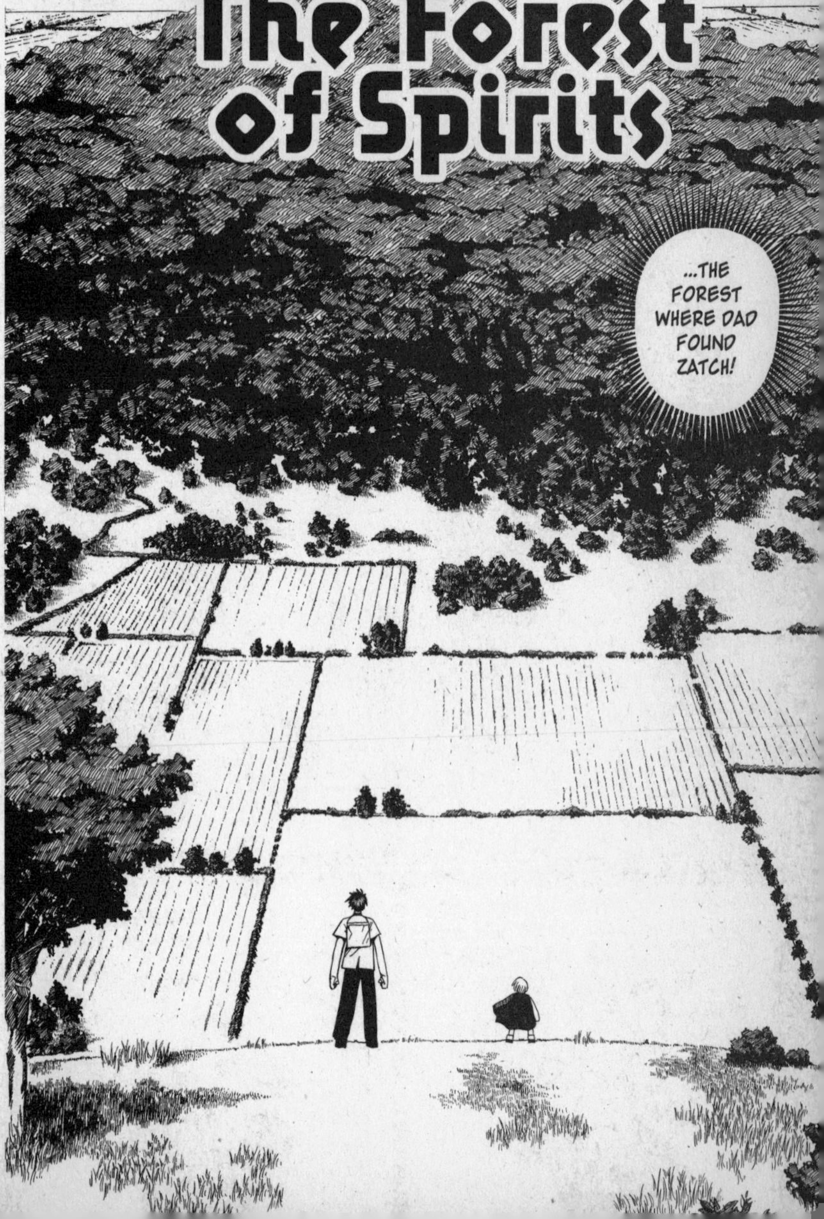
...THE FOREST WHERE DAD FOUND ZATCH!

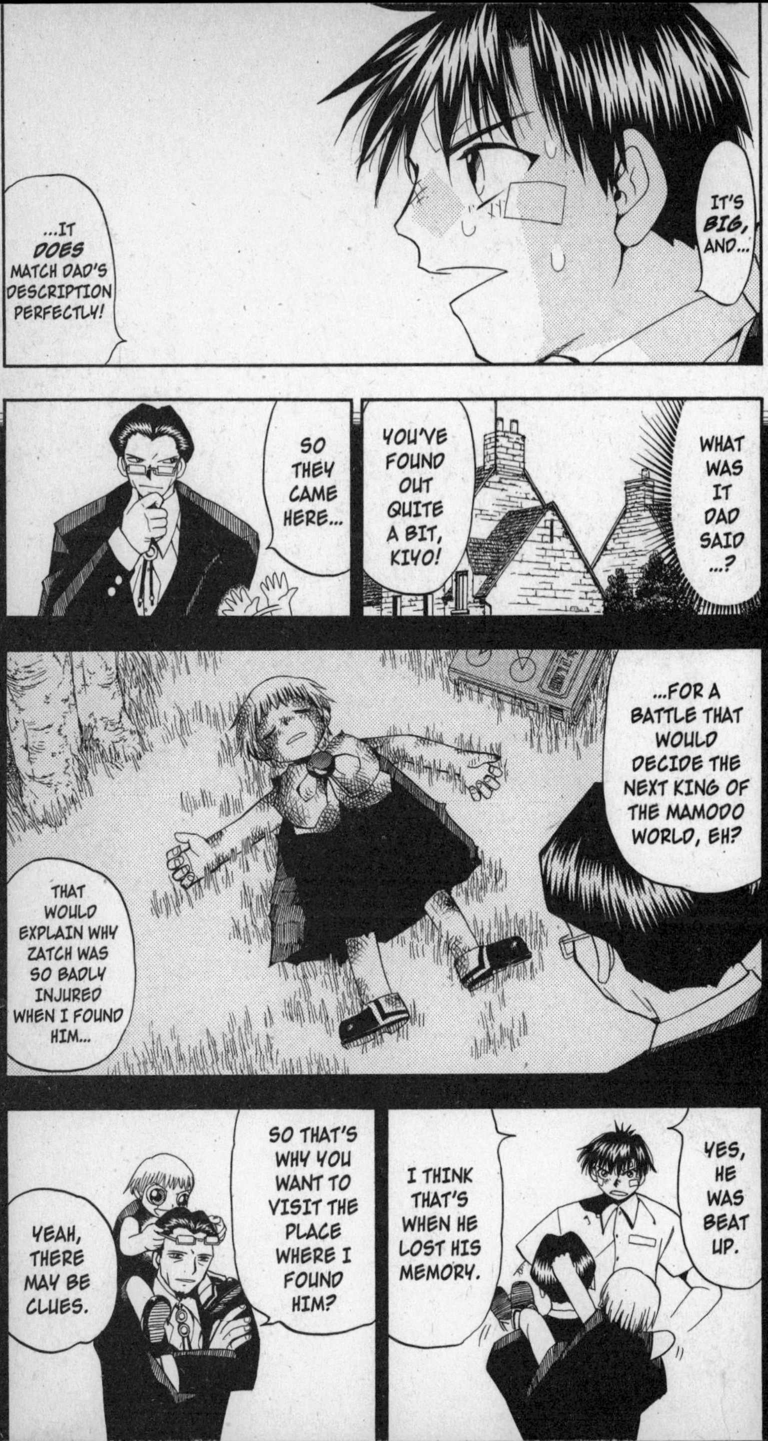
IT'S BIG, AND...
...IT DOES MATCH DAD'S DESCRIPTION PERFECTLY!
WHAT WAS IT DAD SAID...?
YOU'VE FOUND OUT QUITE A BIT, KIYO!
SO THEY CAME HERE...
...FOR A BATTLE THAT WOULD DECIDE THE NEXT KING OF THE MAMODO WORLD, EH?
THAT WOULD EXPLAIN WHY ZATCH WAS SO BADLY INJURED WHEN I FOUND HIM...
YES, HE WAS BEAT UP.
I THINK THAT'S WHEN HE LOST HIS MEMORY.
SO THAT'S WHY YOU WANT TO VISIT THE PLACE WHERE I FOUND HIM?
YEAH, THERE MAY BE CLUES.

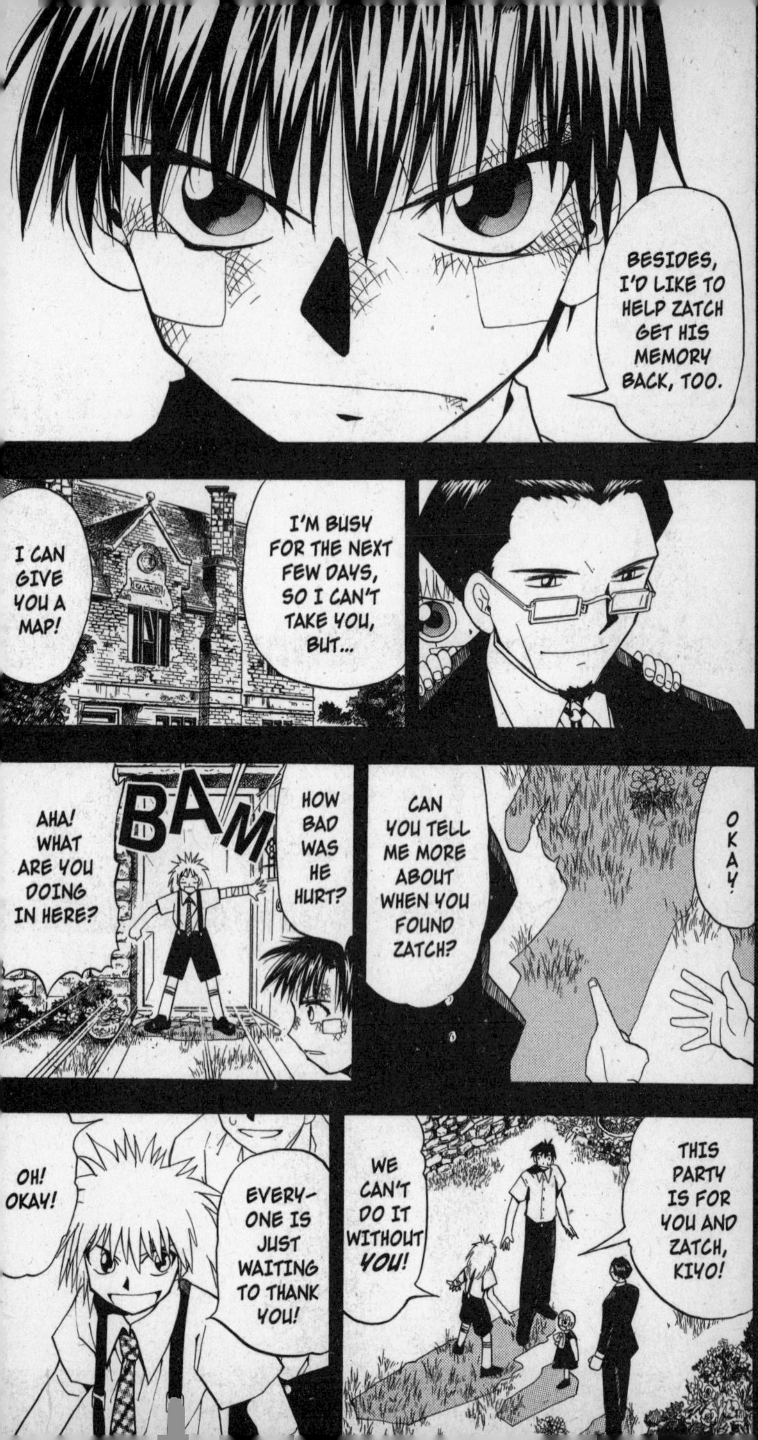
BESIDES, I'D LIKE TO HELP ZATCH GET HIS MEMORY BACK, TOO.
I'M BUSY FOR THE NEXT FEW DAYS, SO I CAN'T TAKE YOU, BUT...
I CAN GIVE YOU A MAP!
OKAY.
CAN YOU TELL ME MORE ABOUT WHEN YOU FOUND ZATCH?
HOW BAD WAS HE HURT?
BAM
AHA! WHAT ARE YOU DOING IN HERE?
THIS PARTY IS FOR YOU AND ZATCH, KIYO!
WE CAN'T DO IT WITHOUT YOU!
EVERY-ONE IS JUST WAITING TO THANK YOU!
OH! OKAY!

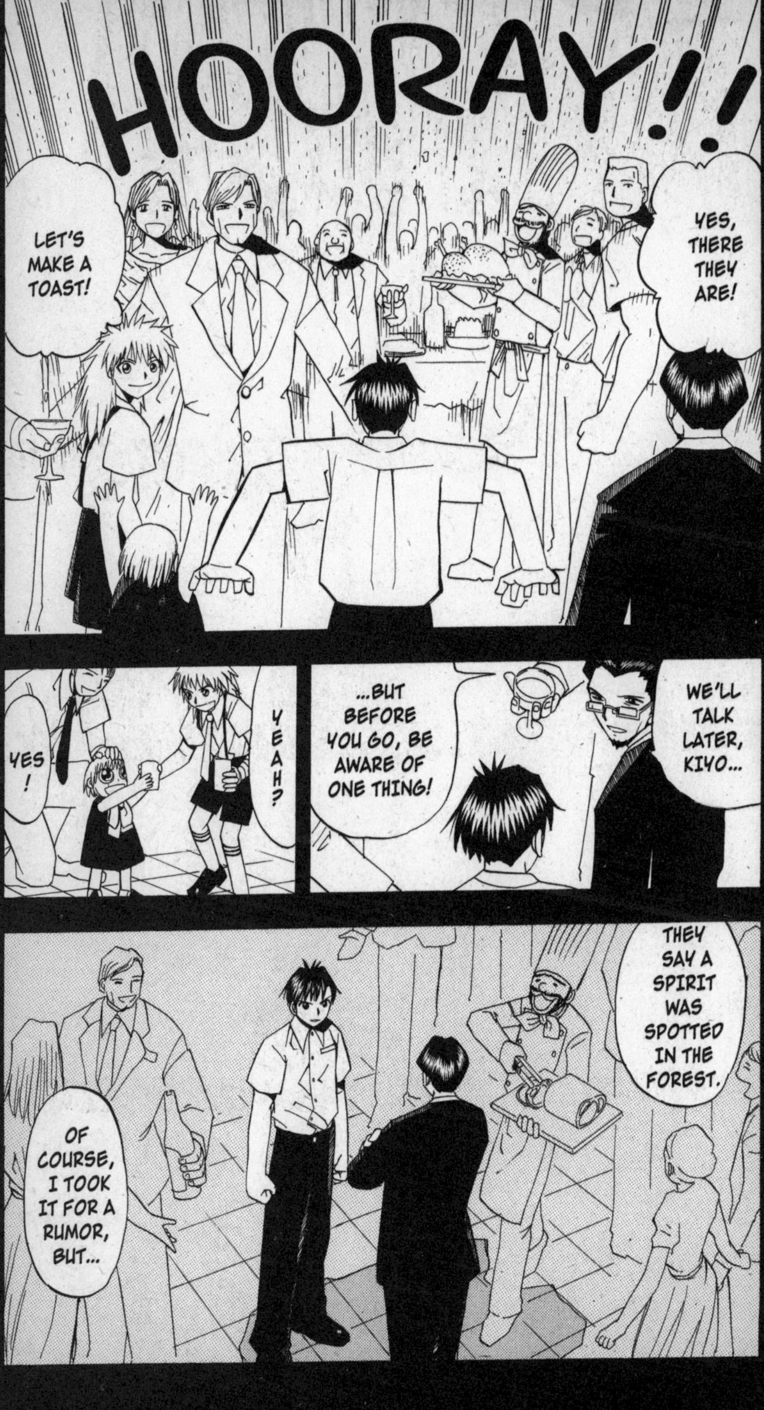
HOORAY!!
YES, THERE THEY ARE!
LET'S MAKE A TOAST!
WE'LL TALK LATER, KIYO...
...BUT BEFORE YOU GO, BE AWARE OF ONE THING!
YEAH?
YES!
THEY SAY A SPIRIT WAS SPOTTED IN THE FOREST.
OF COURSE, I TOOK IT FOR A RUMOR, BUT...

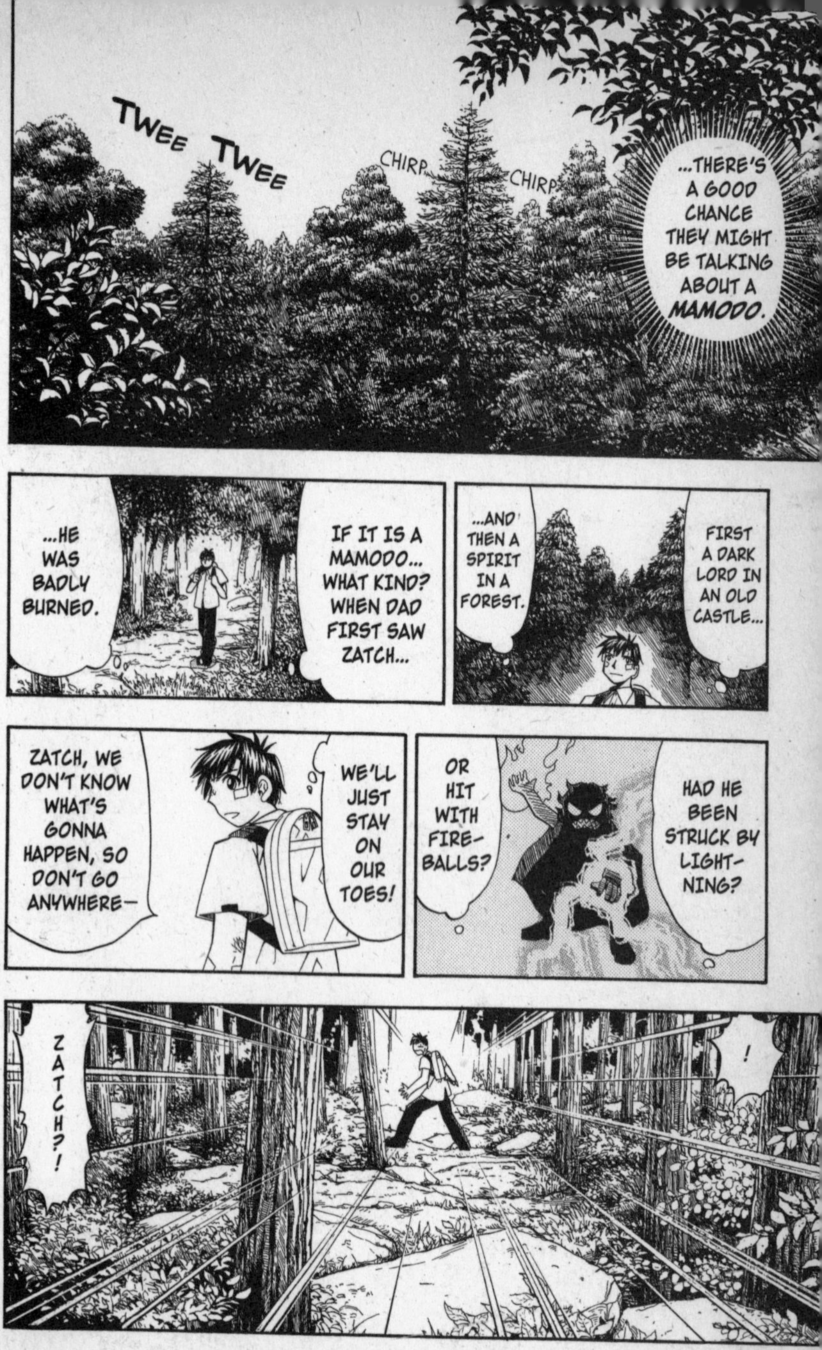

TWEE TWEE
CHIRP CHIRP
...THERE'S A GOOD CHANCE THEY MIGHT BE TALKING ABOUT A MAMODO.
FIRST A DARK LORD IN AN OLD CASTLE...
...AND THEN A SPIRIT IN A FOREST.
IF IT IS A MAMODO... WHAT KIND? WHEN DAD FIRST SAW ZATCH...
...HE WAS BADLY BURNED.
HAD HE BEEN STRUCK BY LIGHT-NING?
OR HIT WITH FIRE-BALLS?
WE'LL JUST STAY ON OUR TOES!
ZATCH, WE DON'T KNOW WHAT'S GONNA HAPPEN, SO DON'T GO ANYWHERE—
!
ZATCH?!

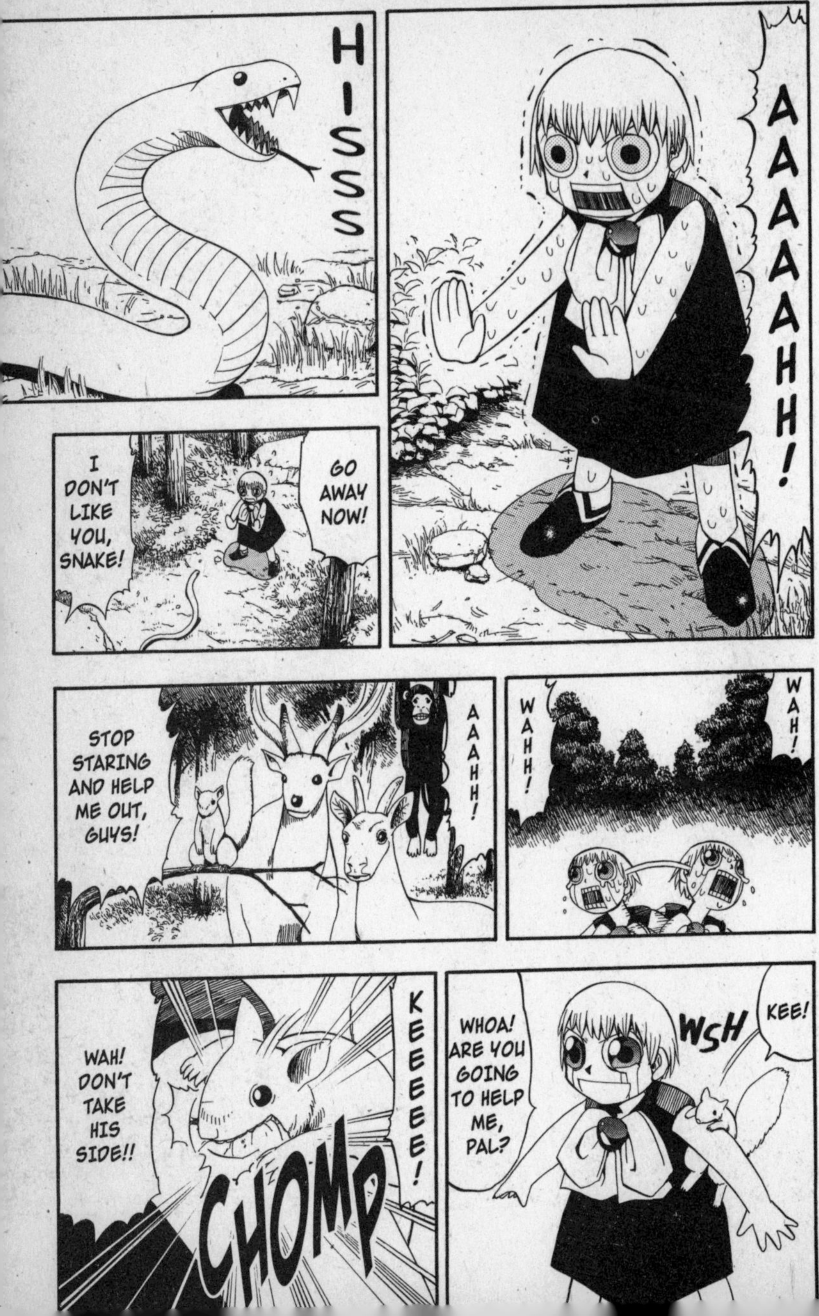
AAAAAHH!
HISS
GO AWAY NOW!
I DON'T LIKE YOU, SNAKE!
WAH!
WAHH!
AAAAHH!
STOP STARING AND HELP ME OUT, GUYS!
KEE!
WSH
WHOA! ARE YOU GOING TO HELP ME, PAL?
KEEEEEE!
WAH! DON'T TAKE HIS SIDE!!
CHOMP

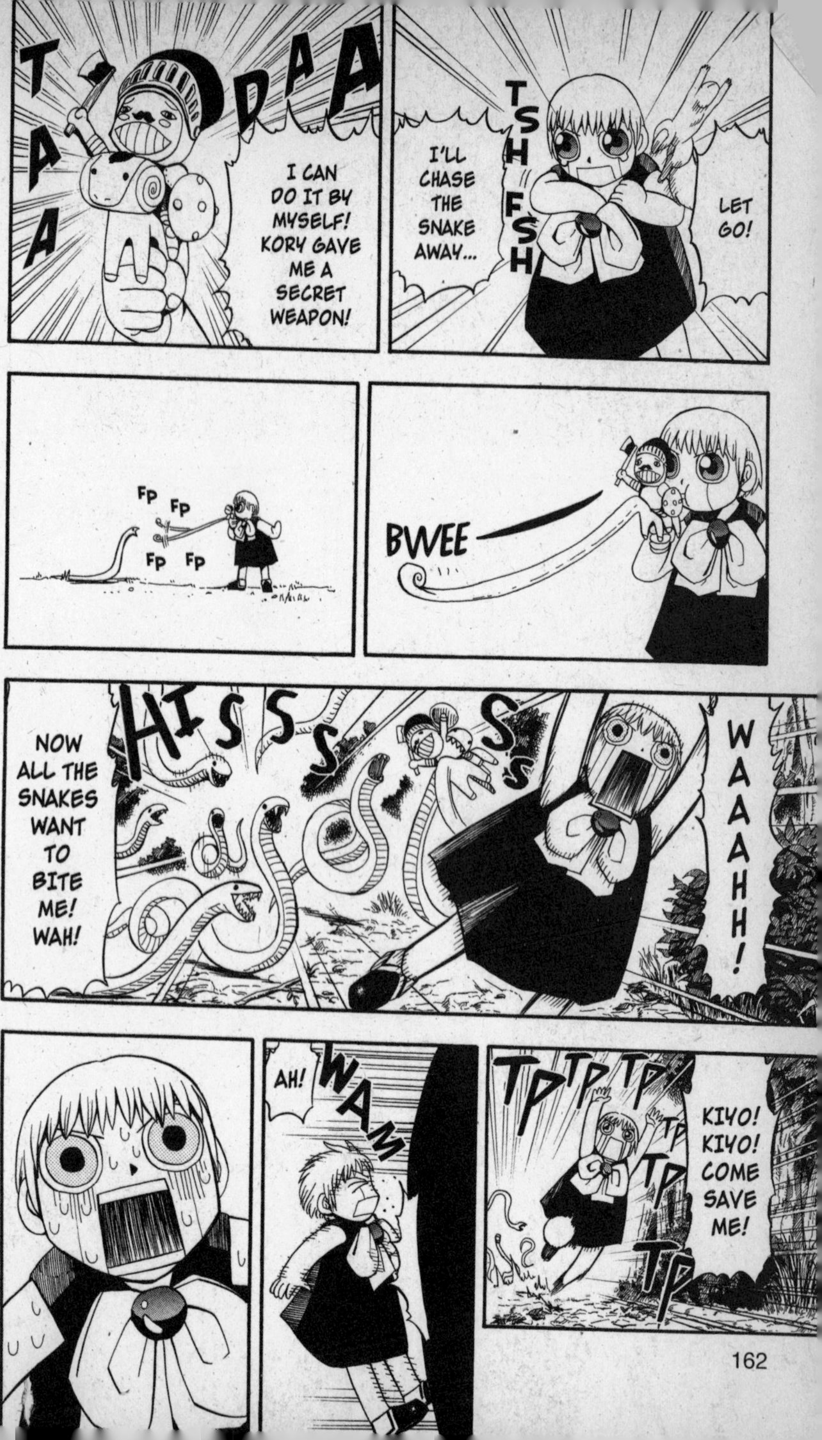
LET GO!
TSH FSH
I'LL CHASE THE SNAKE AWAY...
TADAA
I CAN DO IT BY MYSELF! KORY GAVE ME A SECRET WEAPON!
BWEE
FP FP FP FP
WAAAAHH!
HISSSS
NOW ALL THE SNAKES WANT TO BITE ME! WAH!
TP TP TP TP TP TP
KIYO! KIYO! COME SAVE ME!
WAM
AH!

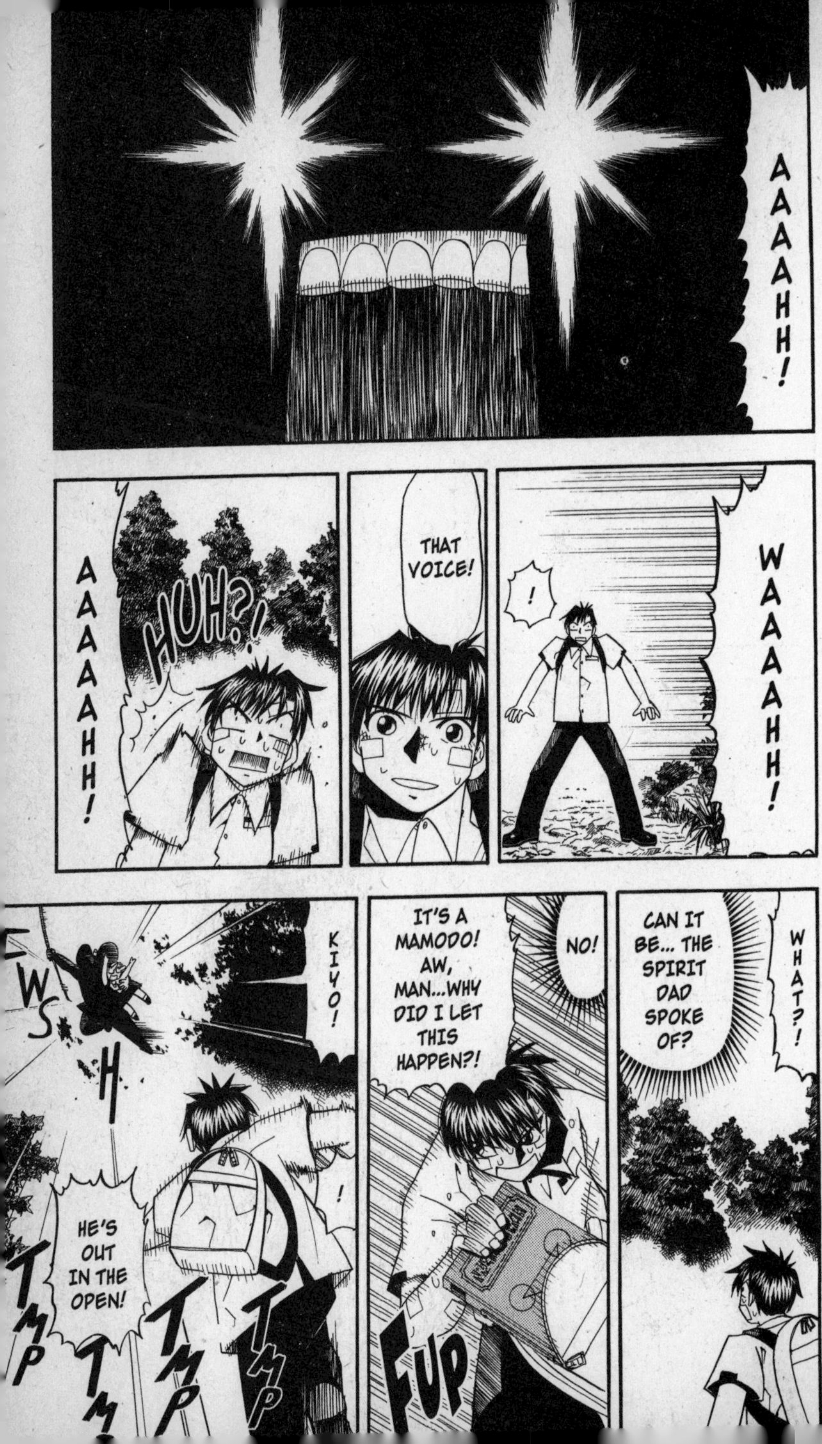
AAAAAHH!
WAAAAAAHH!
!
THAT VOICE!
AAAAAAHH!
HUH?!
WHAT?!
CAN IT BE... THE SPIRIT DAD SPOKE OF?
NO!
IT'S A MAMODO! AW, MAN...WHY DID I LET THIS HAPPEN?!
FUP
KIYO!
!
WSH
HE'S OUT IN THE OPEN!
TMP
TMP
TMP
TMP

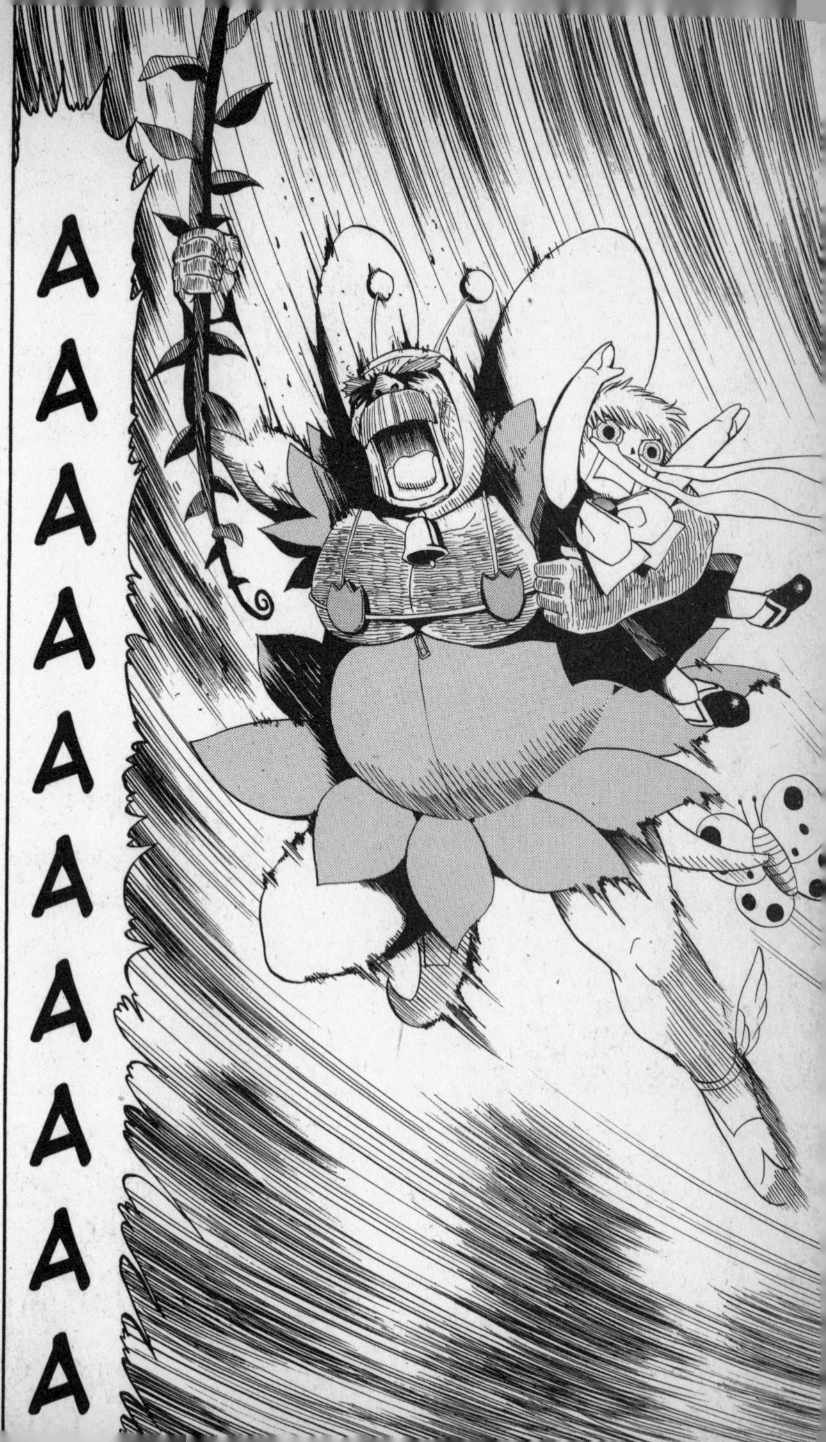
AAAAAAAAAA

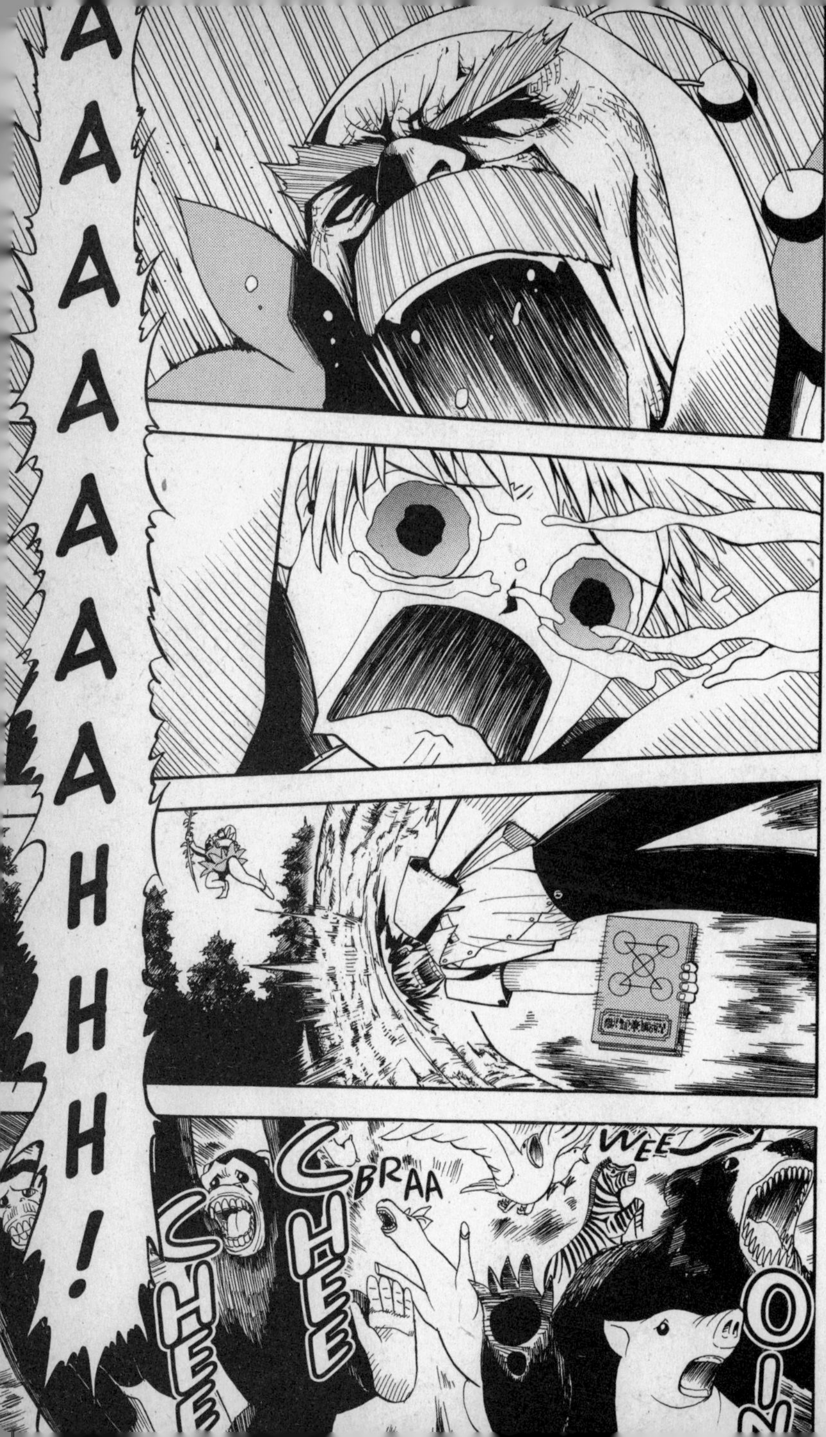
AAAAAAAHHH!
OIN
WEE
BRAA
CHEE
CHEE

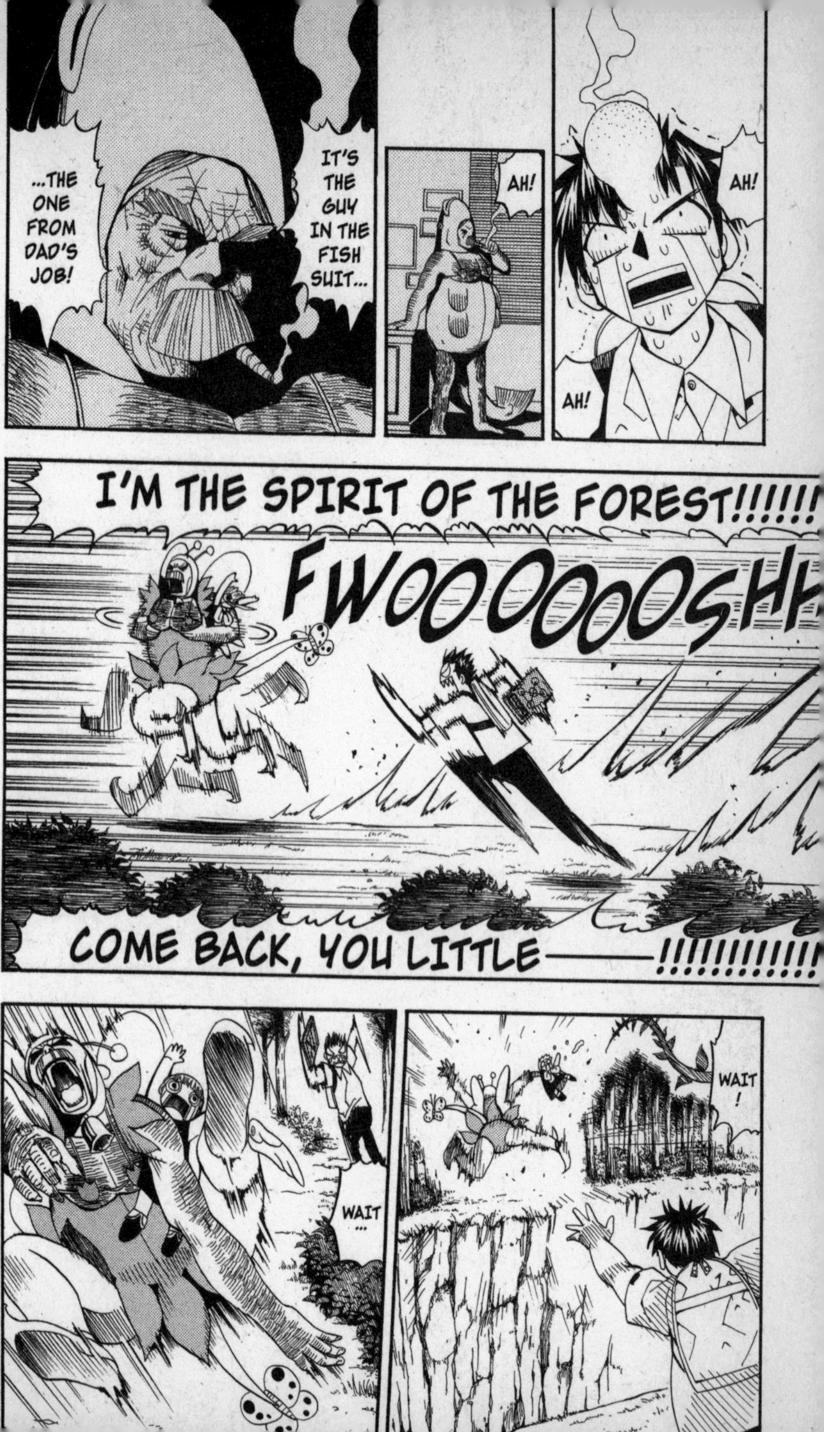
AH!
AH!
AH!
AH!
IT'S THE GUY IN THE FISH SUIT...
...THE ONE FROM DAD'S JOB!
I'M THE SPIRIT OF THE FOREST!!!!!!
FWOOOOOOSHH
COME BACK, YOU LITTLE——!!!!!!!!!!!
WAIT!
WAIT...

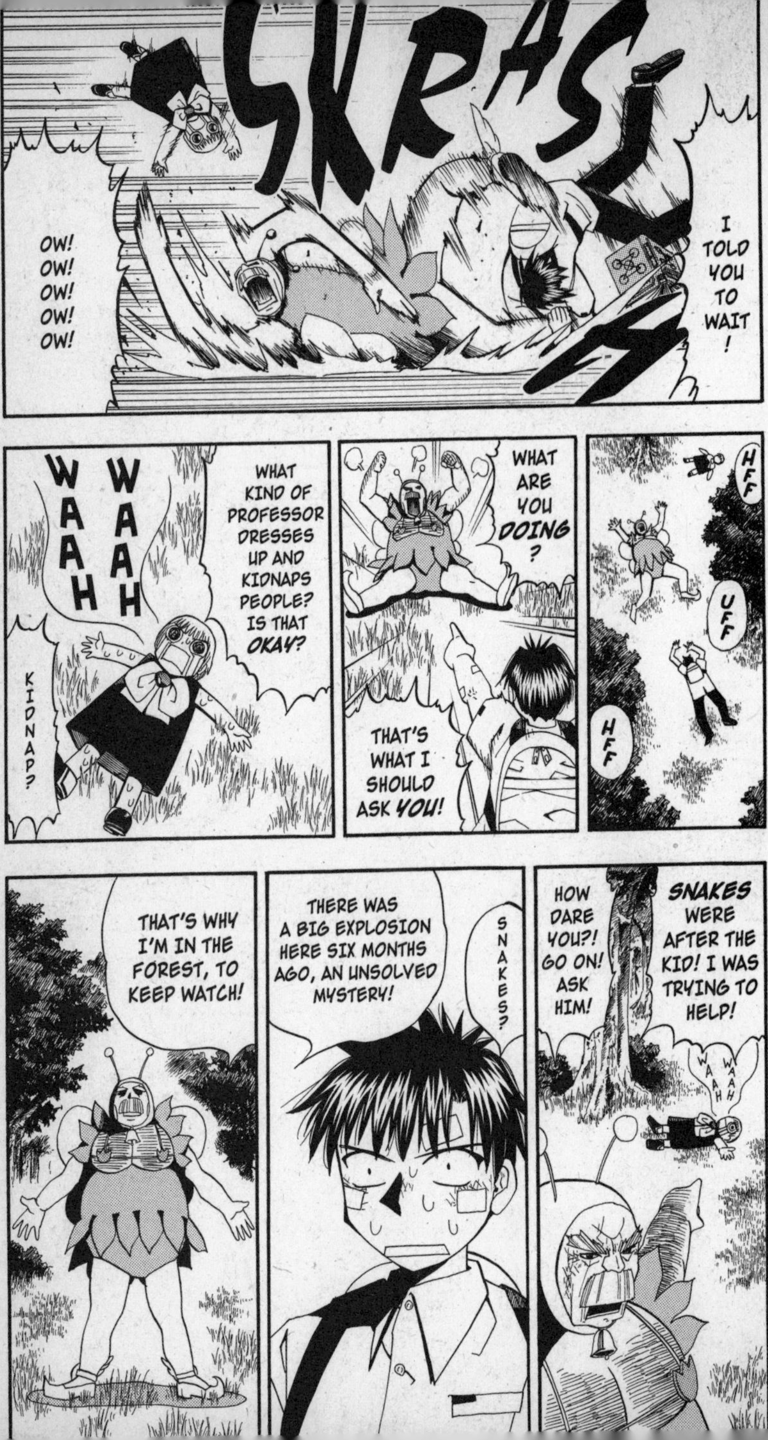
SKRASH
I TOLD YOU TO WAIT!
OW! OW! OW! OW! OW!
HFF
UFF
HFF
WHAT ARE YOU DOING?
THAT'S WHAT I SHOULD ASK YOU!
WHAT KIND OF PROFESSOR DRESSES UP AND KIDNAPS PEOPLE? IS THAT OKAY?
WAAH WAAH
KIDNAP?
SNAKES WERE AFTER THE KID! I WAS TRYING TO HELP!
HOW DARE YOU?! GO ON! ASK HIM!
WAAH WAAH
SNAKES?
THERE WAS A BIG EXPLOSION HERE SIX MONTHS AGO, AN UNSOLVED MYSTERY!
THAT'S WHY I'M IN THE FOREST, TO KEEP WATCH!

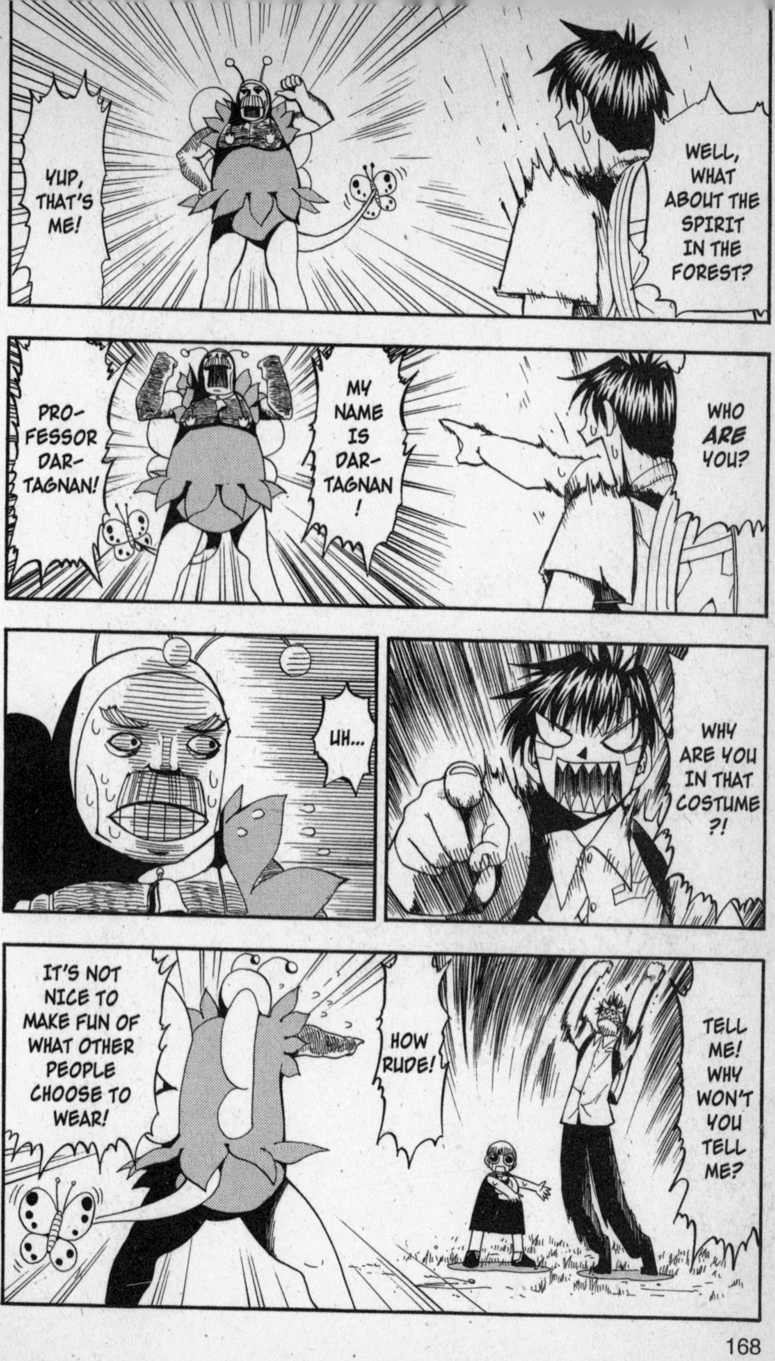

WELL, WHAT ABOUT THE SPIRIT IN THE FOREST?
YUP, THAT'S ME!
WHO ARE YOU?
MY NAME IS DARTAGNAN!
PROFESSOR DARTAGNAN!
WHY ARE YOU IN THAT COSTUME?!
UH...
TELL ME! WHY WON'T YOU TELL ME?
HOW RUDE!
IT'S NOT NICE TO MAKE FUN OF WHAT OTHER PEOPLE CHOOSE TO WEAR!

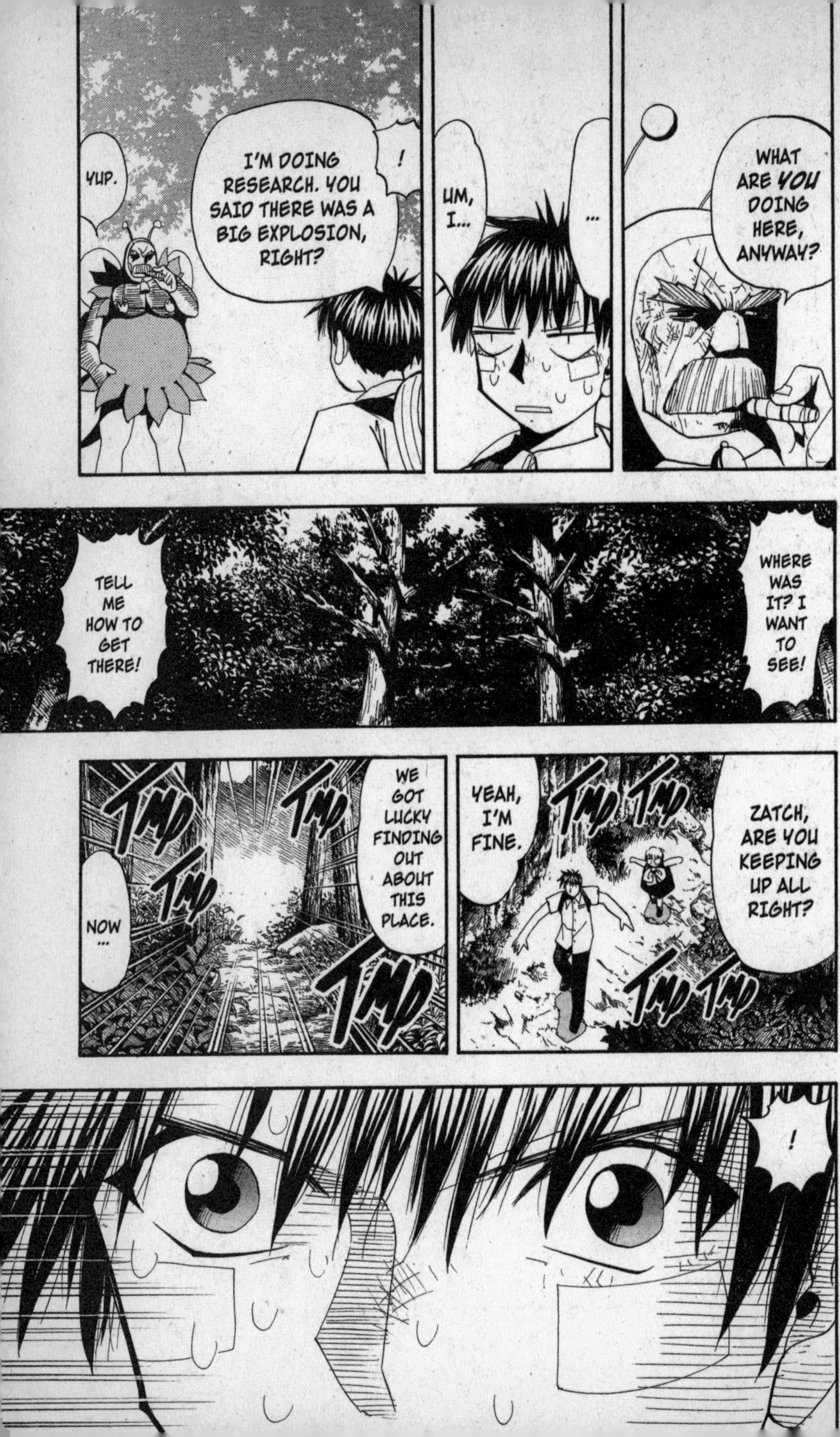
WHAT ARE YOU DOING HERE, ANYWAY?
...
UM, I...
!
I'M DOING RESEARCH. YOU SAID THERE WAS A BIG EXPLOSION, RIGHT?
YUP.
WHERE WAS IT? I WANT TO SEE!
TELL ME HOW TO GET THERE!
ZATCH, ARE YOU KEEPING UP ALL RIGHT?
TMP TMP
TMP TMP
YEAH, I'M FINE.
WE GOT LUCKY FINDING OUT ABOUT THIS PLACE.
TMP
TMP
TMP
TMP
NOW ...
!

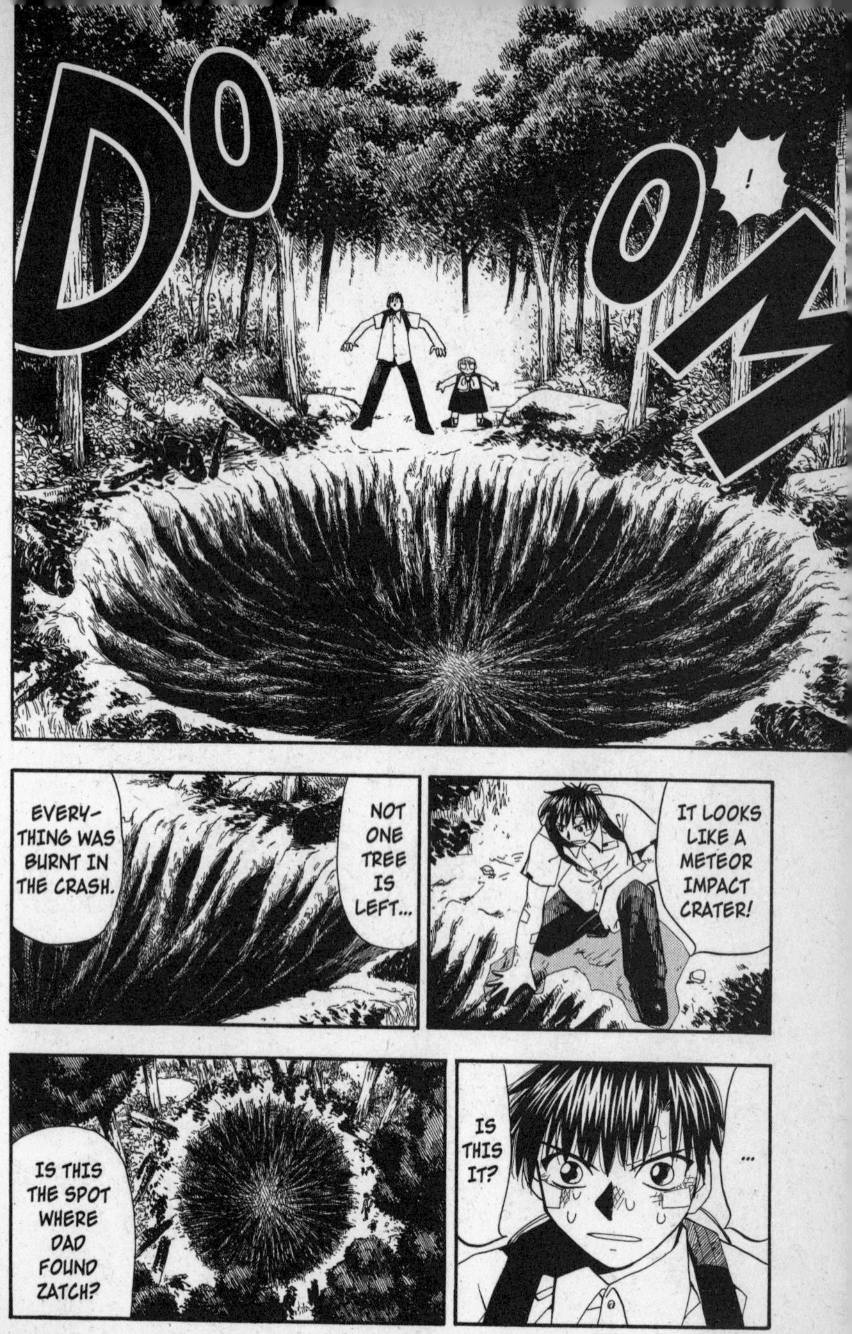
DOOM
!
IT LOOKS LIKE A METEOR IMPACT CRATER!
NOT ONE TREE IS LEFT...
EVERY-THING WAS BURNT IN THE CRASH.
...
IS THIS IT?
IS THIS THE SPOT WHERE DAD FOUND ZATCH?

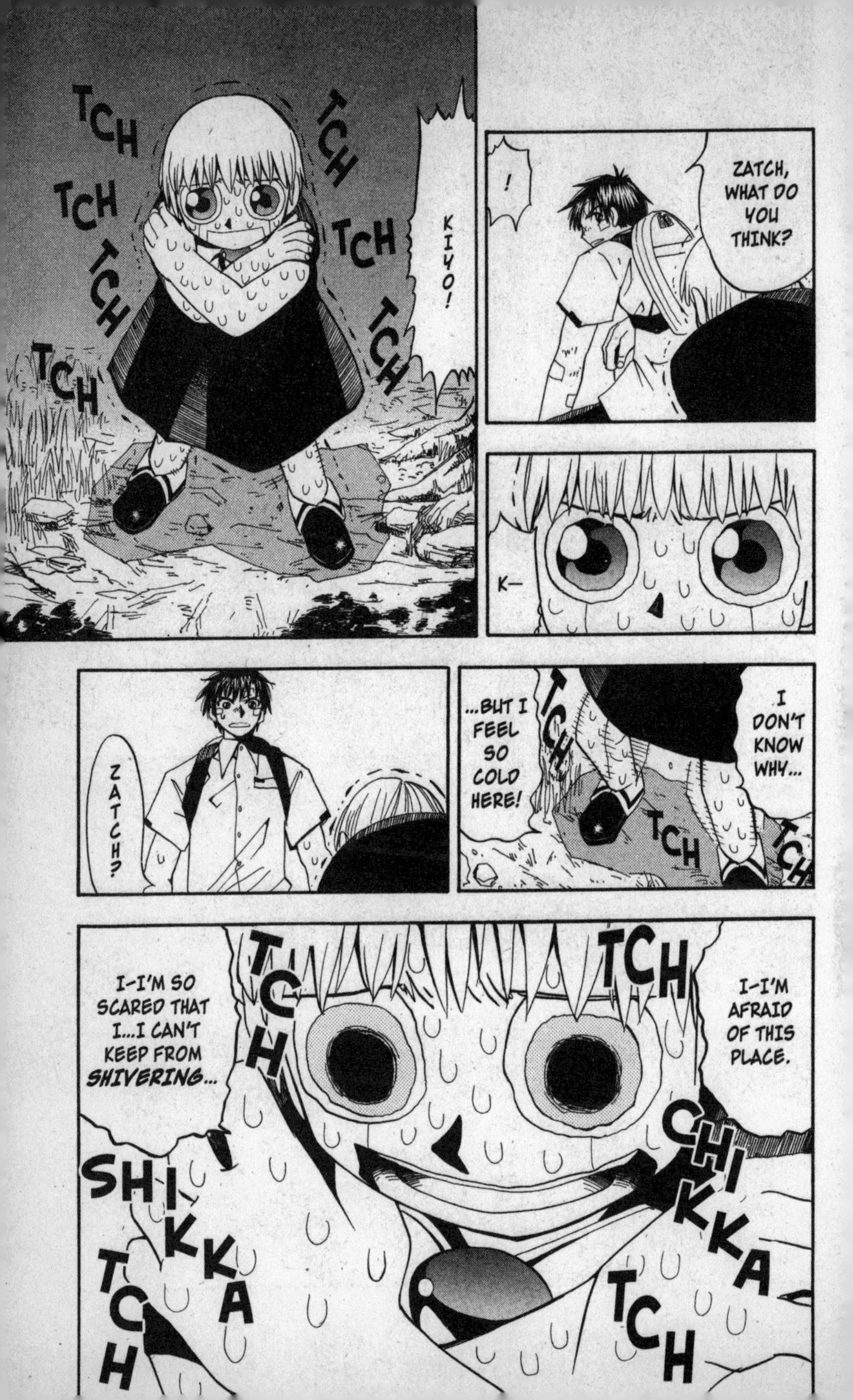
ZATCH, WHAT DO YOU THINK?
!
K—
TCH
TCH
TCH
TCH
TCH
TCH
TCH
KIYO!
I DON'T KNOW WHY...
...BUT I FEEL SO COLD HERE!
TCH
TCH
TCH
ZATCH?
I-I'M AFRAID OF THIS PLACE.
TCH
I-I'M SO SCARED THAT I...I CAN'T KEEP FROM SHIVERING...
TCH
CHIKKA
TCH
SHIKKA
TCH

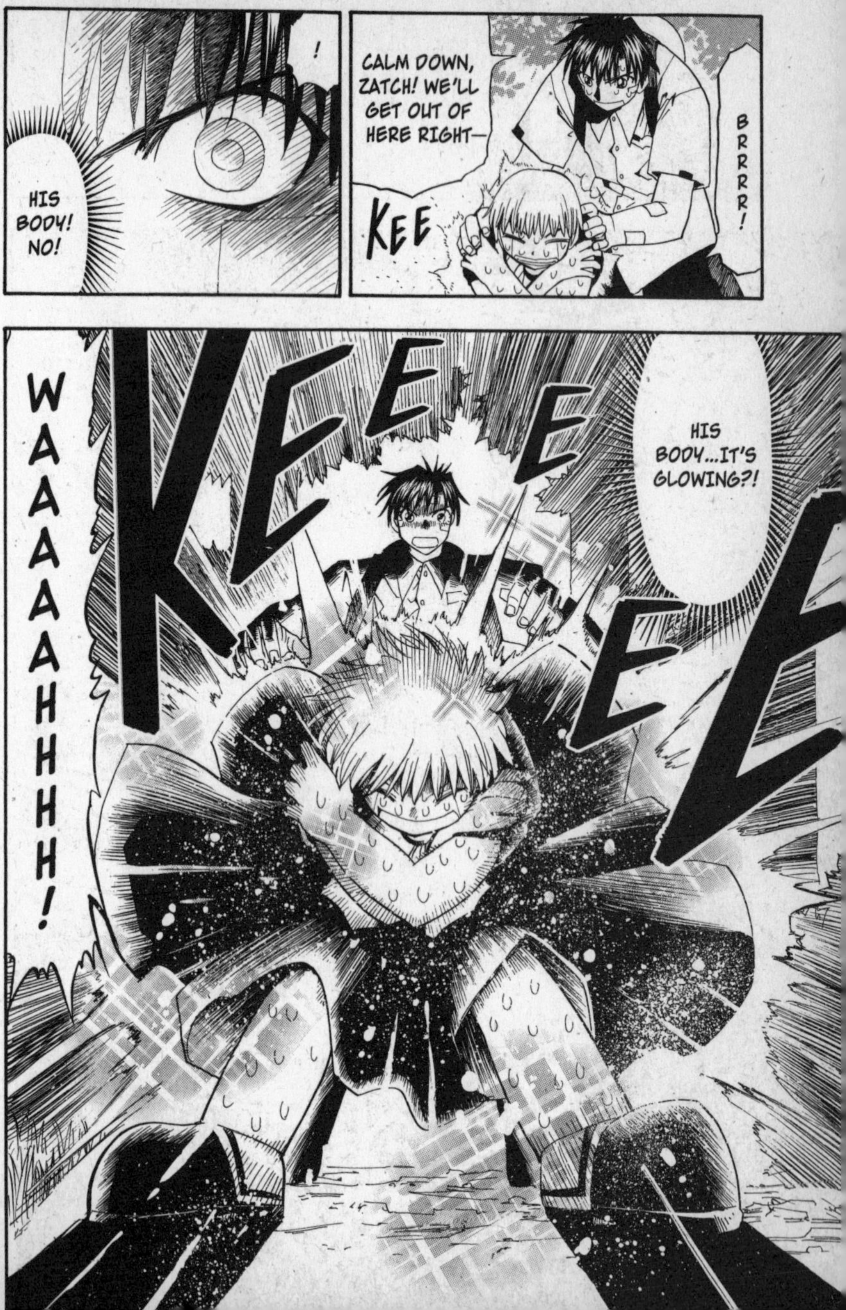
CALM DOWN, ZATCH! WE'LL GET OUT OF HERE RIGHT—
BRRRRR!
KEE
!
HIS BODY! NO!
HIS BODY...IT'S GLOWING?!
KEEEEE
WAAAAAHHHHHH!

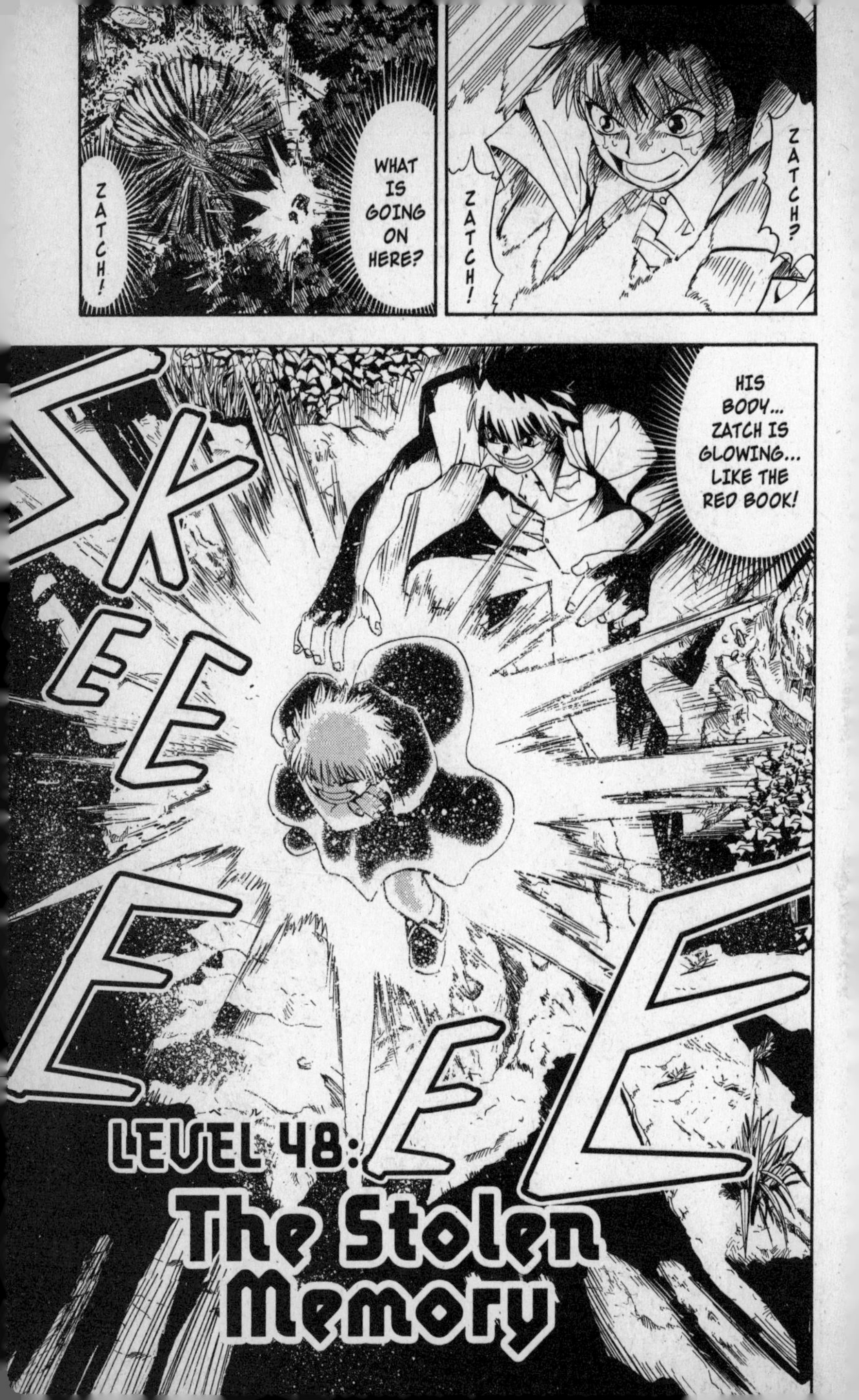
ZATCH?
ZATCH!
WHAT IS GOING ON HERE?
ZATCH!
HIS BODY... ZATCH IS GLOWING... LIKE THE RED BOOK!
LEVEL 48:
The Stolen Memory

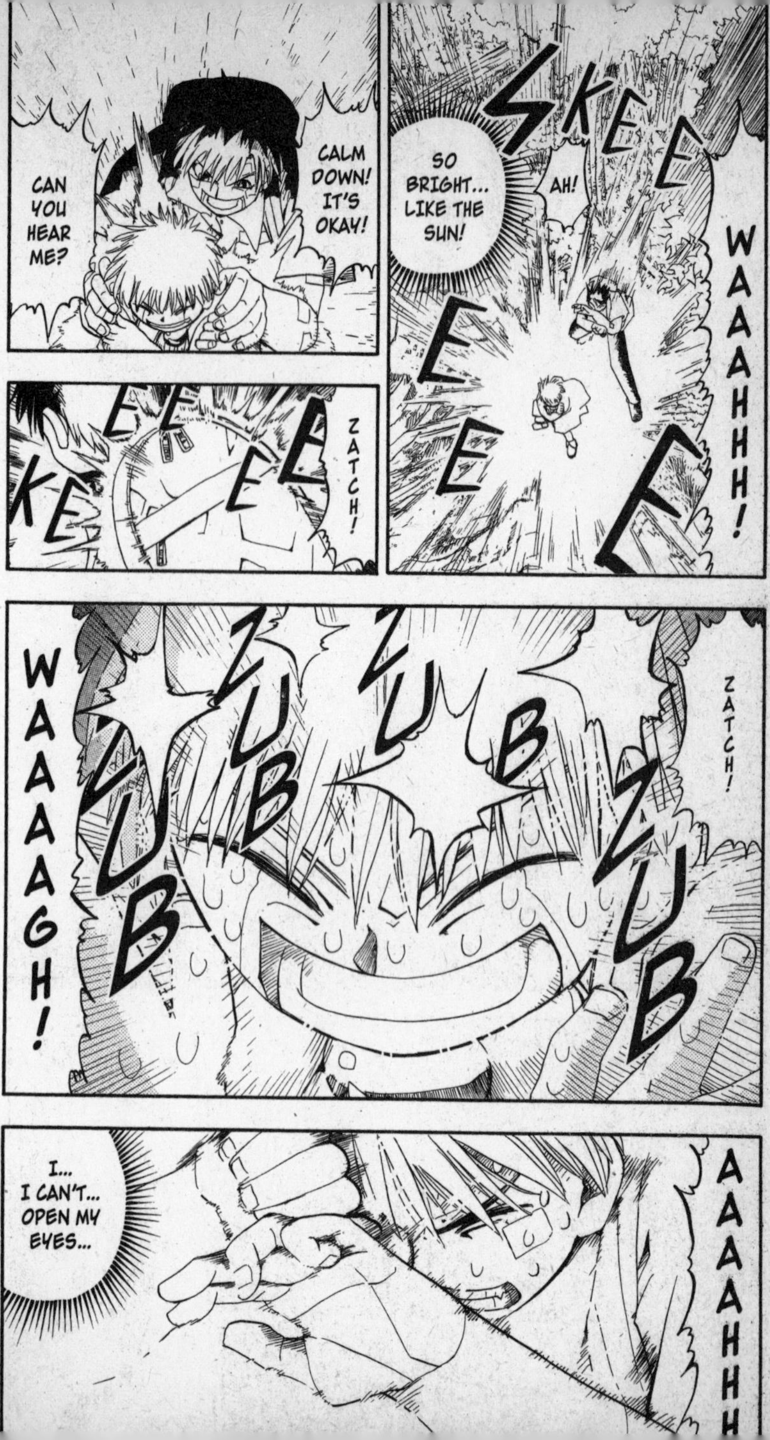
SKEEEEEEE
WAAAHHHH!
AH!
SO BRIGHT... LIKE THE SUN!
CALM DOWN! IT'S OKAY!
CAN YOU HEAR ME?
ZATCH!
KEEEEE
ZATCH!
ZUB ZUB ZUB ZUB
WAAAAAGH!
AAAAAHHH
I... I CAN'T... OPEN MY EYES...

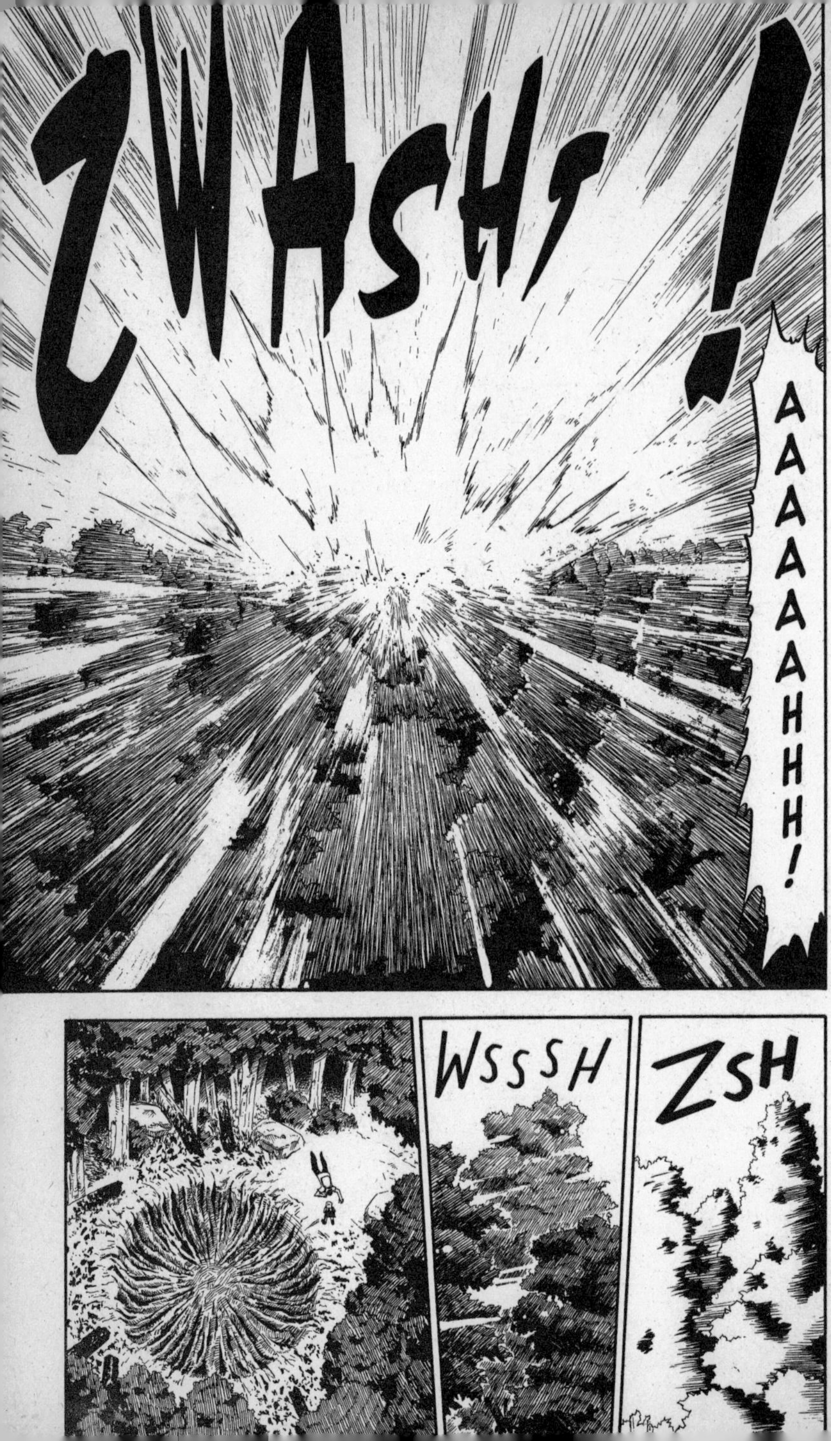
ZWASH!
AAAAAAHHH!
ZSH
WSSSH

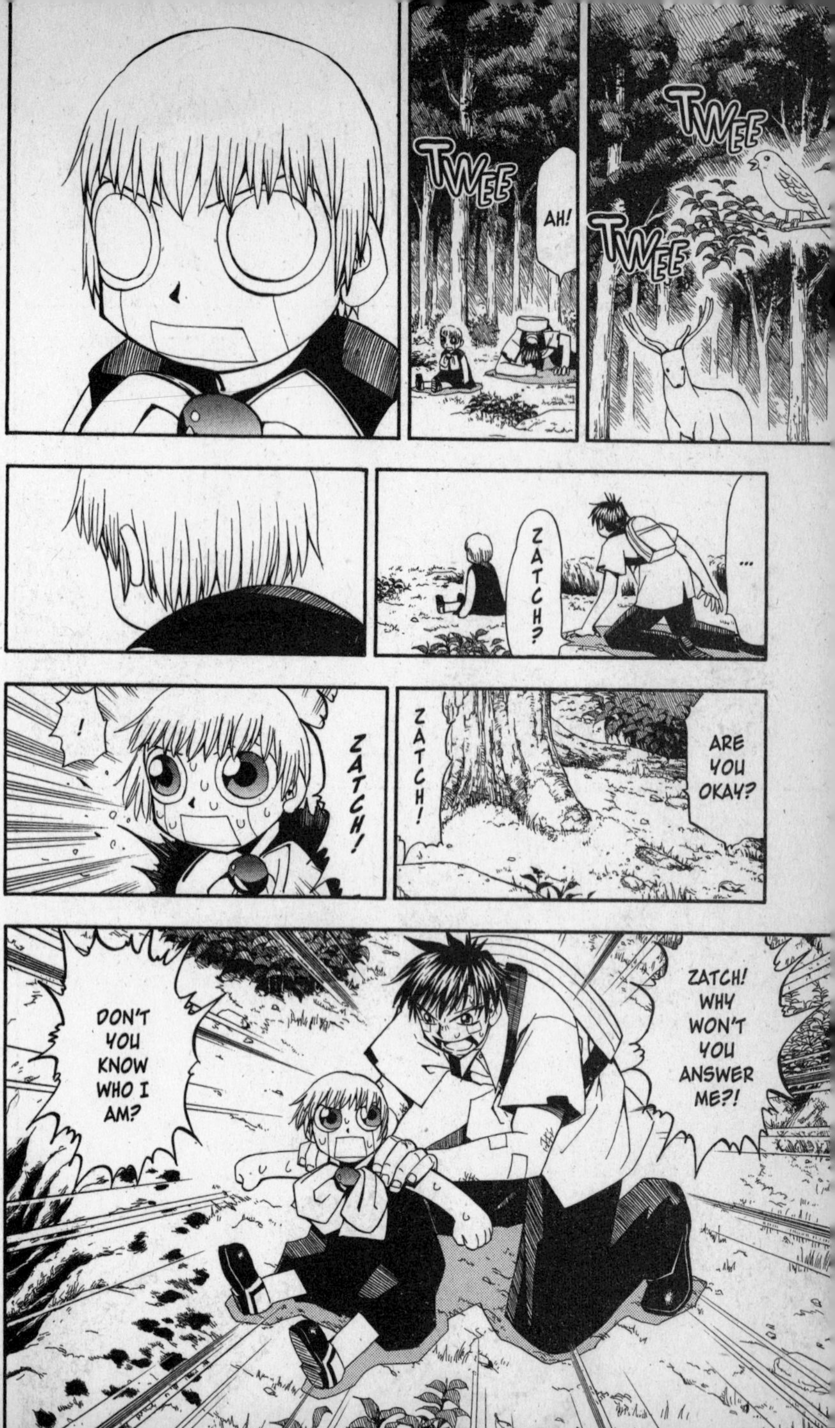
TWEE
TWEE
TWEE
AH!
...
ZATCH?
ARE YOU OKAY?
ZATCH!
ZATCH!
!
ZATCH! WHY WON'T YOU ANSWER ME?!
DON'T YOU KNOW WHO I AM?

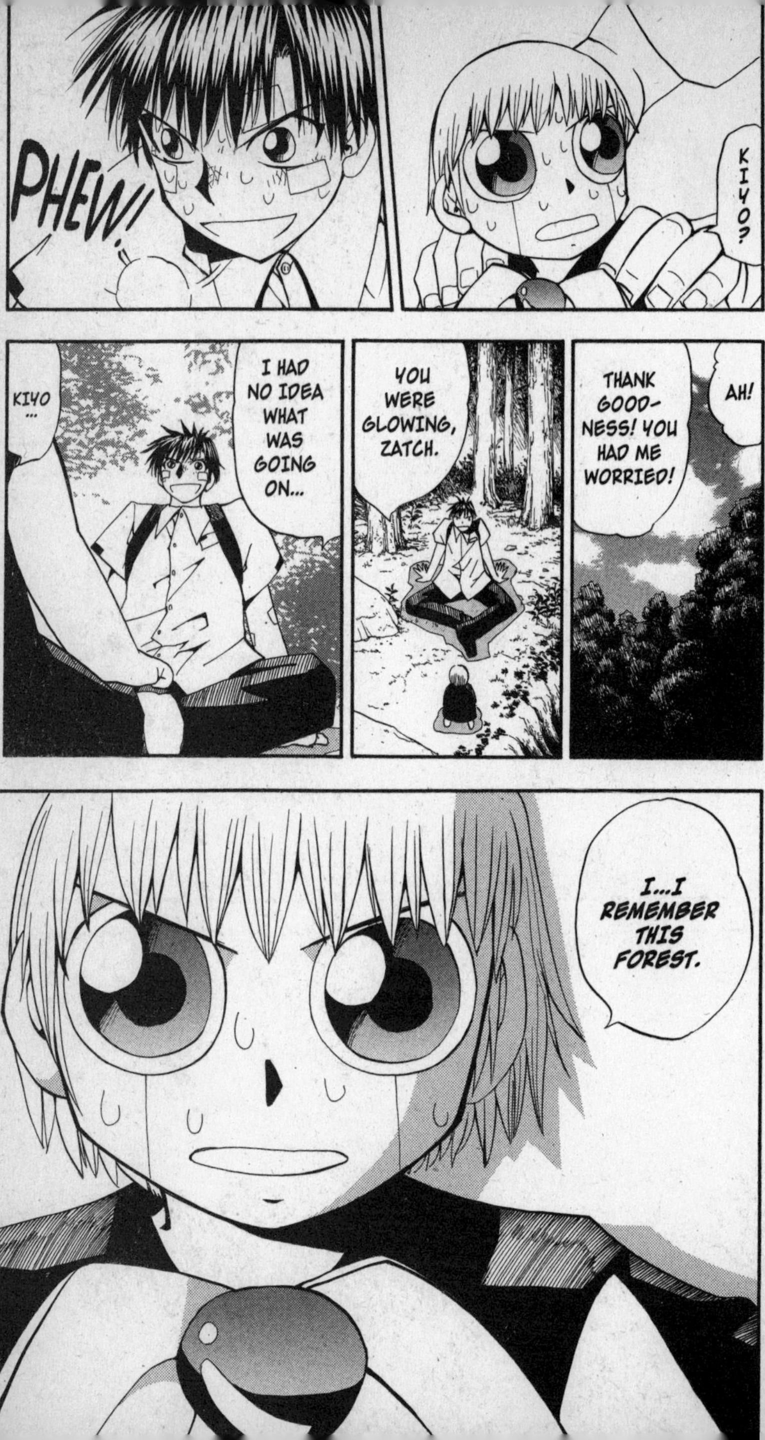
KIYO?
PHEW!
AH!
THANK GOODNESS! YOU HAD ME WORRIED!
YOU WERE GLOWING, ZATCH.
I HAD NO IDEA WHAT WAS GOING ON...
KIYO...
I...I REMEMBER THIS FOREST.

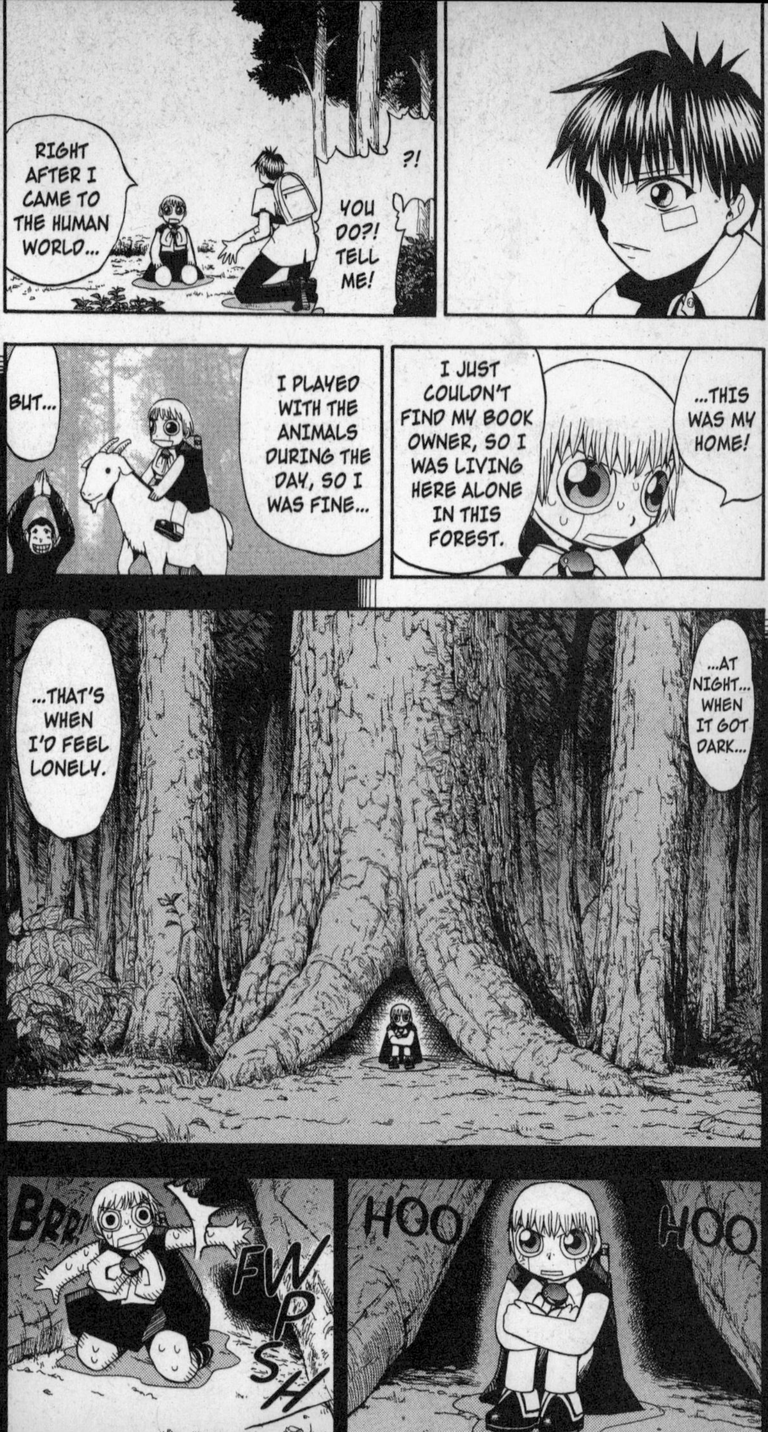
?!
YOU DO?! TELL ME!
RIGHT AFTER I CAME TO THE HUMAN WORLD...
...THIS WAS MY HOME!
I JUST COULDN'T FIND MY BOOK OWNER, SO I WAS LIVING HERE ALONE IN THIS FOREST.
I PLAYED WITH THE ANIMALS DURING THE DAY, SO I WAS FINE...
BUT...
...AT NIGHT... WHEN IT GOT DARK...
...THAT'S WHEN I'D FEEL LONELY.
HOO
HOO
FWPSH
BRR!

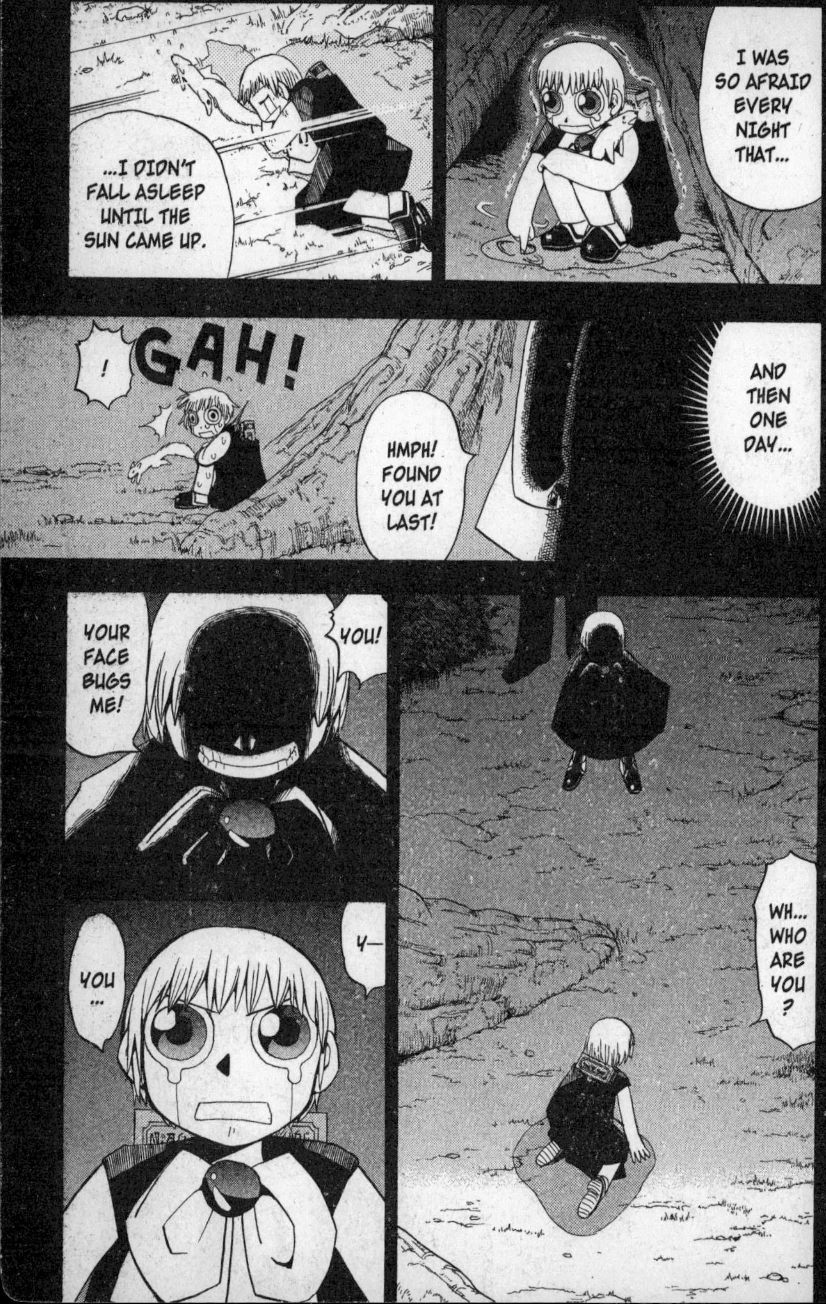
I WAS SO AFRAID EVERY NIGHT THAT...
...I DIDN'T FALL ASLEEP UNTIL THE SUN CAME UP.
AND THEN ONE DAY...
HMPH! FOUND YOU AT LAST!
GAH!
!
WH... WHO ARE YOU?
YOU!
YOUR FACE BUGS ME!
Y—
YOU...

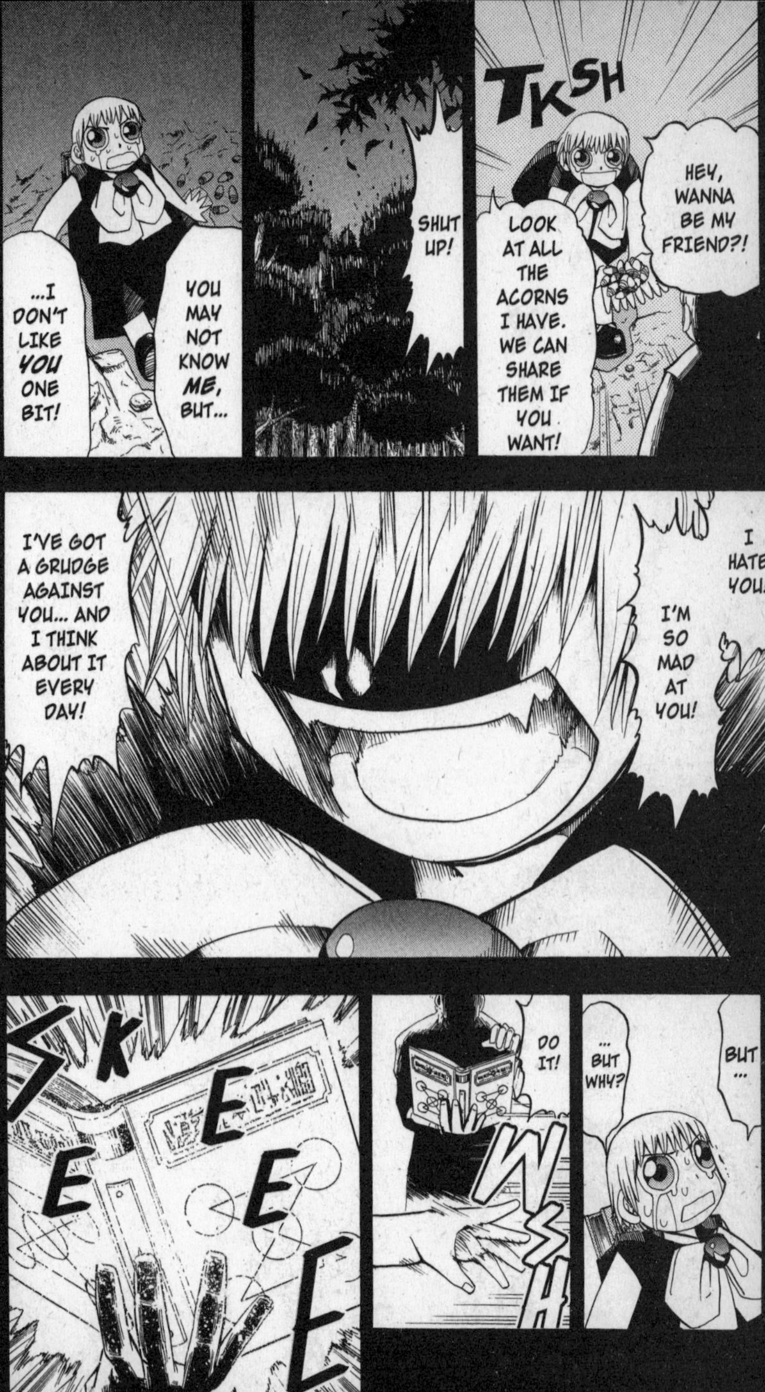
TKSH
HEY, WANNA BE MY FRIEND?!
LOOK AT ALL THE ACORNS I HAVE. WE CAN SHARE THEM IF YOU WANT!
SHUT UP!
YOU MAY NOT KNOW ME, BUT...
...I DON'T LIKE YOU ONE BIT!
I HATE YOU!
I'M SO MAD AT YOU!
I'VE GOT A GRUDGE AGAINST YOU... AND I THINK ABOUT IT EVERY DAY!
BUT ...
... BUT WHY?
DO IT!
WSH
SKEEEEE

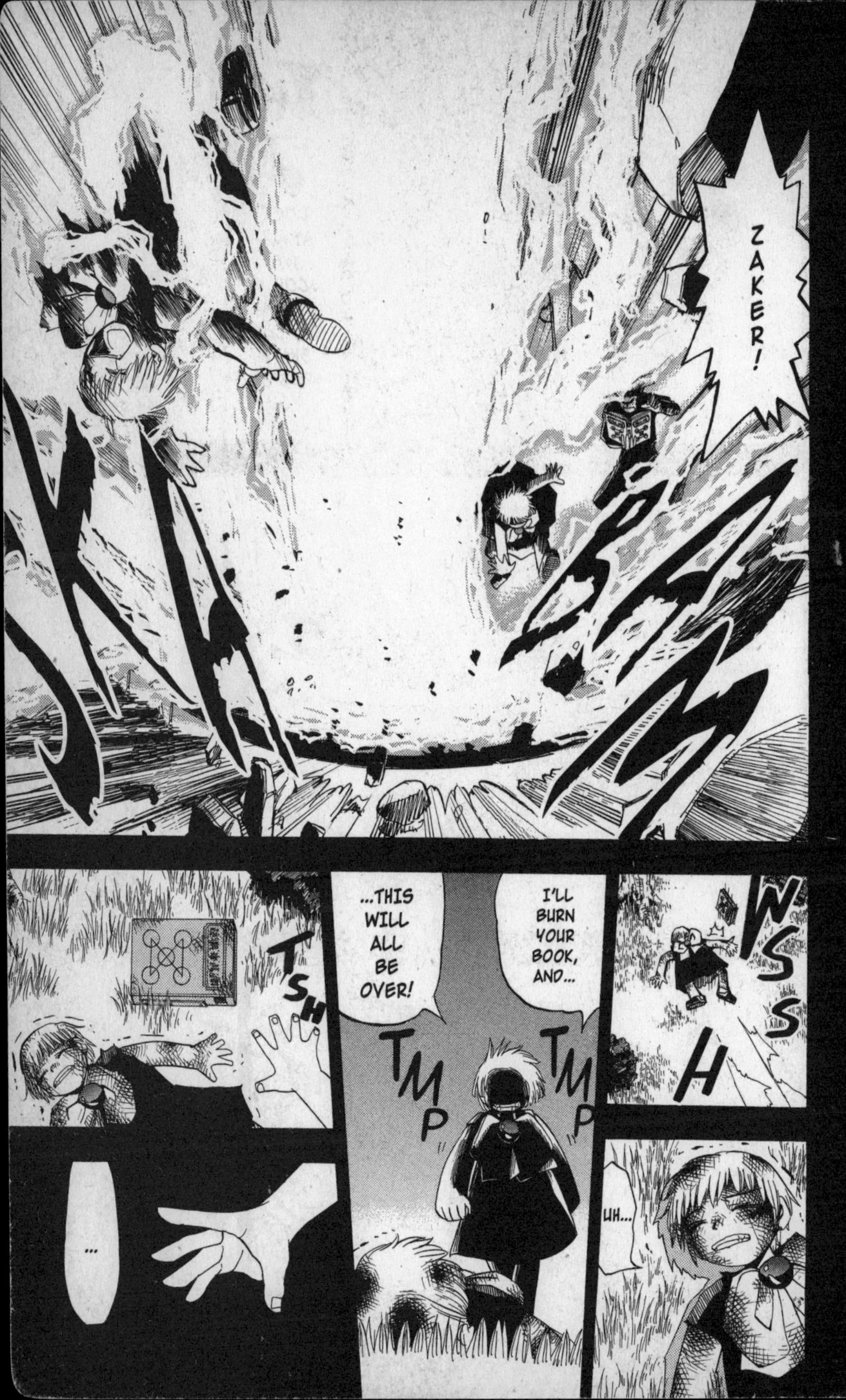
ZAKER!
WSSH
UH...
I'LL BURN YOUR BOOK, AND...
...THIS WILL ALL BE OVER!
TMP
TMP
TSH
...

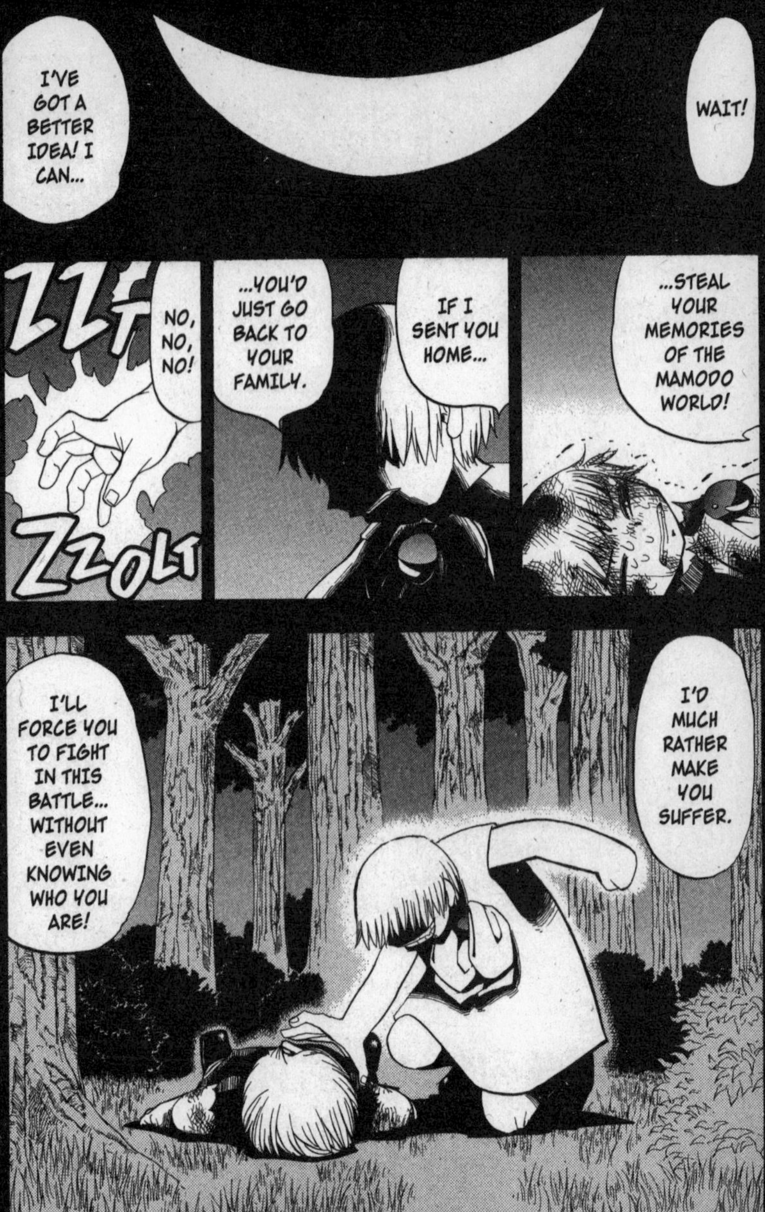
WAIT!
I'VE GOT A BETTER IDEA! I CAN...
...STEAL YOUR MEMORIES OF THE MAMODO WORLD!
IF I SENT YOU HOME...
...YOU'D JUST GO BACK TO YOUR FAMILY.
NO, NO, NO!
ZZT
ZZOLT
I'D MUCH RATHER MAKE YOU SUFFER.
I'LL FORCE YOU TO FIGHT IN THIS BATTLE... WITHOUT EVEN KNOWING WHO YOU ARE!

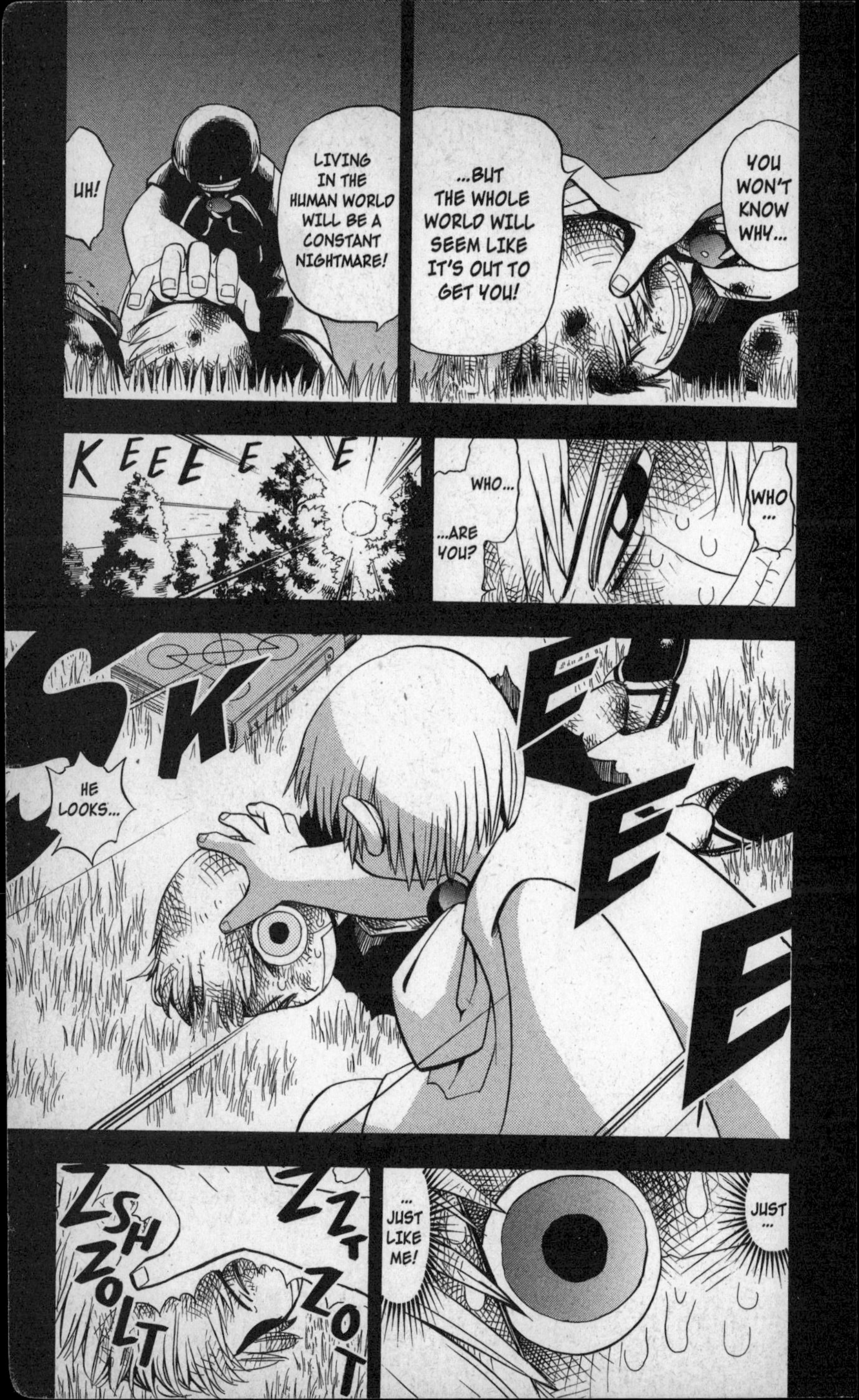
YOU WON'T KNOW WHY...
...BUT THE WHOLE WORLD WILL SEEM LIKE IT'S OUT TO GET YOU!
LIVING IN THE HUMAN WORLD WILL BE A CONSTANT NIGHTMARE!
UH!
WHO...
WHO...
...ARE YOU?
KEEEEE
KEEEE
HE LOOKS...
JUST...
...JUST LIKE ME!
ZZZT
ZOT
ZSH
ZOLT

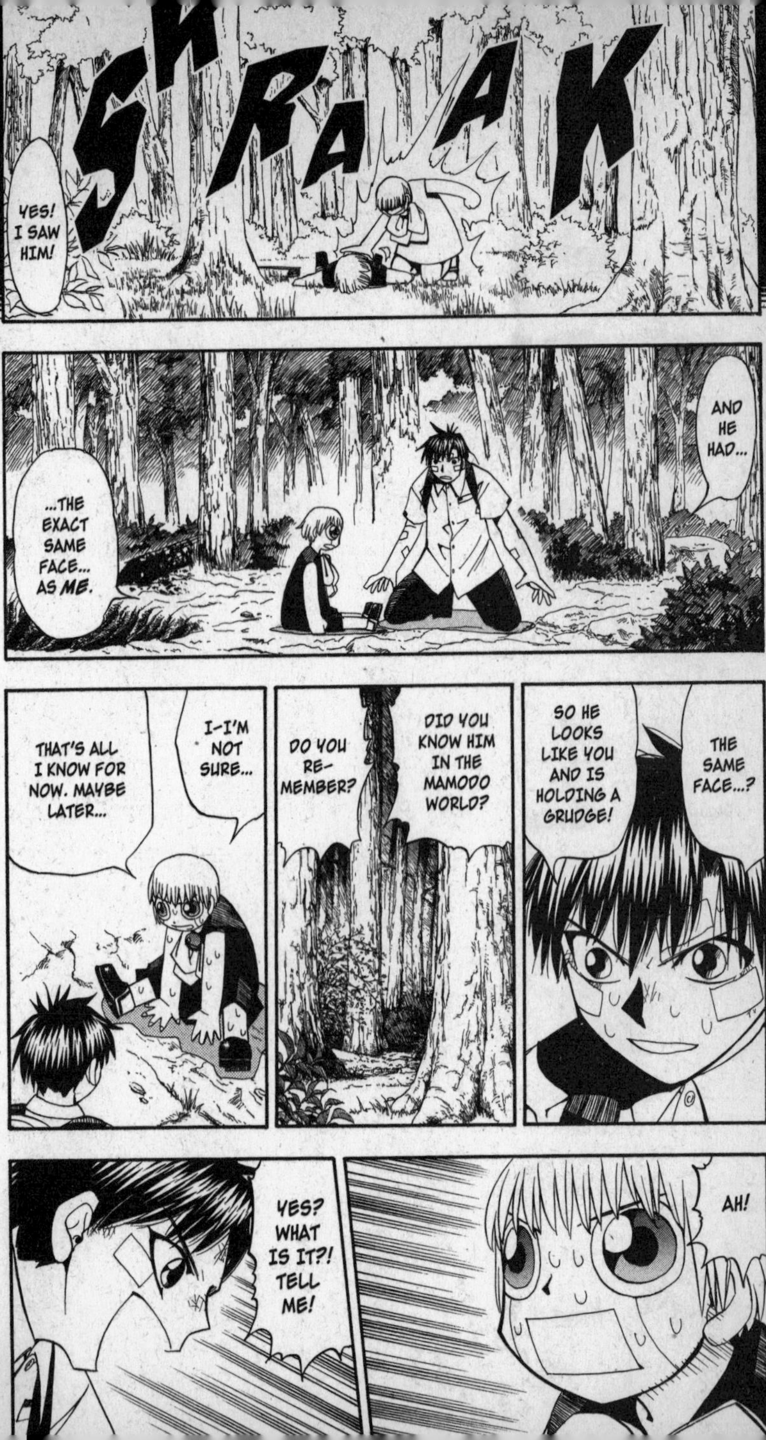
SHRAAK
YES! I SAW HIM!
AND HE HAD...
...THE EXACT SAME FACE... AS ME.
THE SAME FACE...?
SO HE LOOKS LIKE YOU AND IS HOLDING A GRUDGE!
DID YOU KNOW HIM IN THE MAMODO WORLD?
DO YOU RE-MEMBER?
I-I'M NOT SURE...
THAT'S ALL I KNOW FOR NOW. MAYBE LATER...
AH!
YES? WHAT IS IT?! TELL ME!

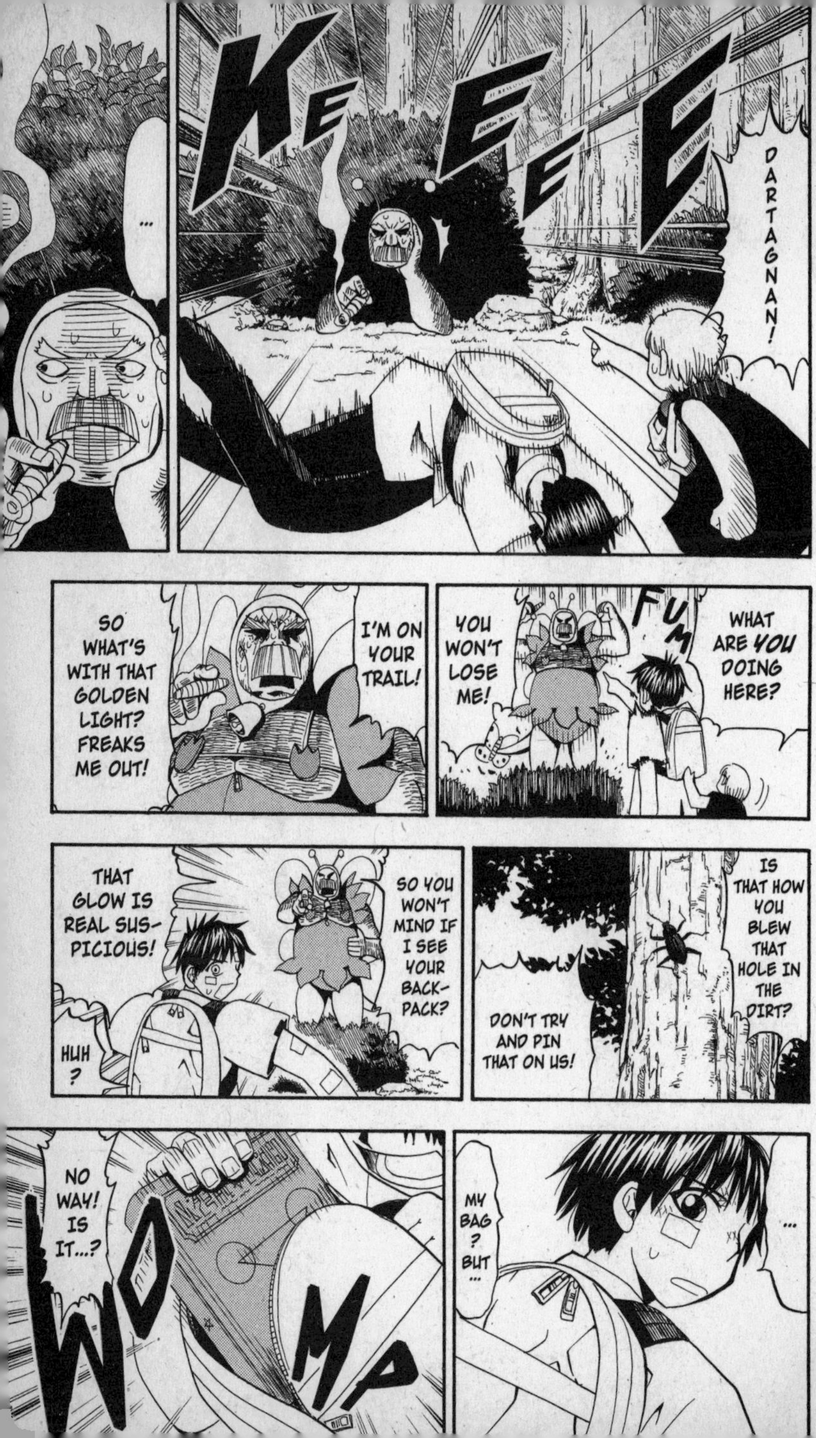
KEEEEE
DARTAGNAN!
...
WHAT ARE YOU DOING HERE?
FUM
YOU WON'T LOSE ME!
I'M ON YOUR TRAIL!
SO WHAT'S WITH THAT GOLDEN LIGHT? FREAKS ME OUT!
IS THAT HOW YOU BLEW THAT HOLE IN THE DIRT?
DON'T TRY AND PIN THAT ON US!
SO YOU WON'T MIND IF I SEE YOUR BACK-PACK?
THAT GLOW IS REAL SUS-PICIOUS!
HUH?
...
MY BAG? BUT...
NO WAY! IS IT...?
WOMP

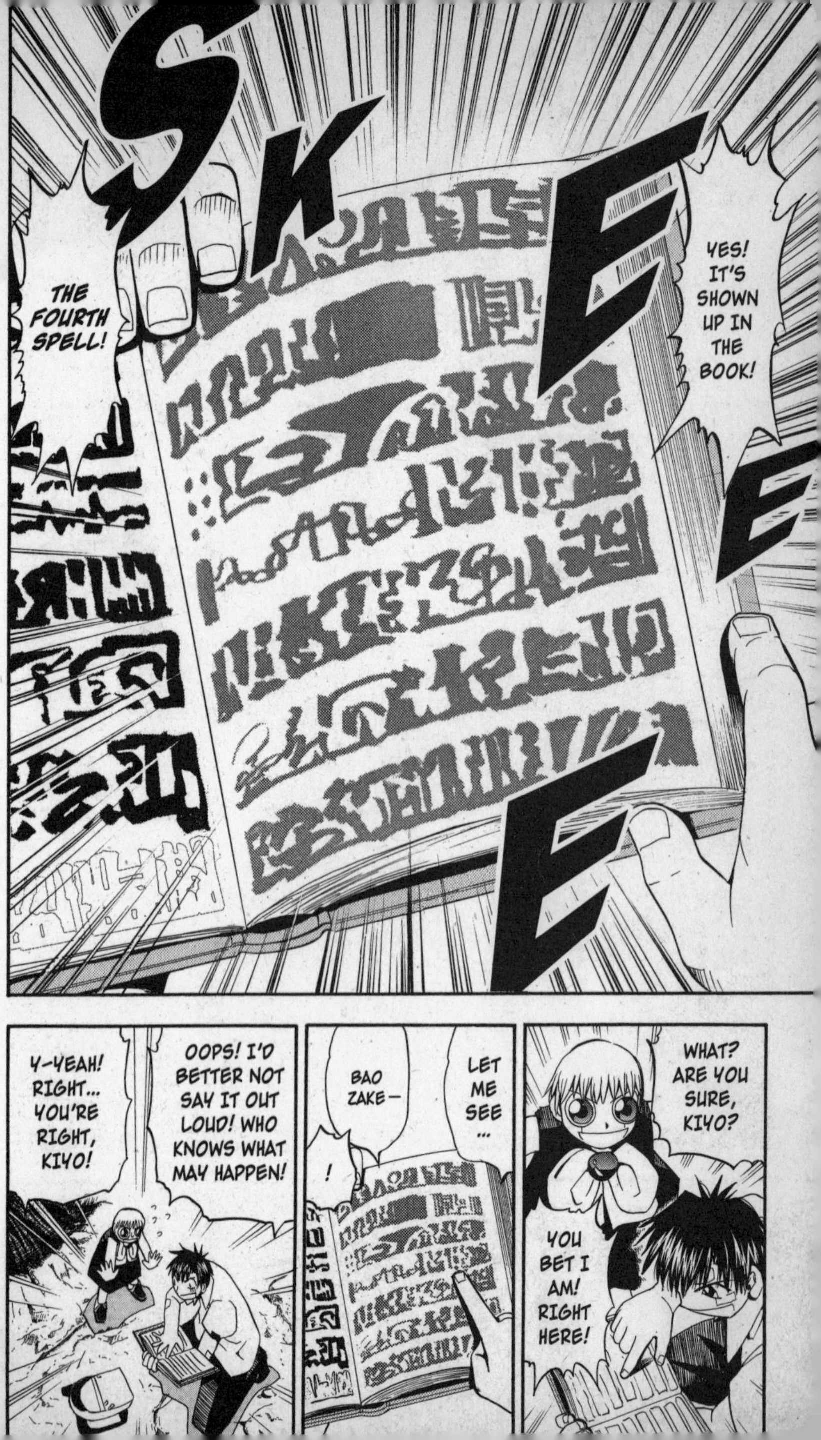
SKEEEE
YES! IT'S SHOWN UP IN THE BOOK!
THE FOURTH SPELL!
WHAT? ARE YOU SURE, KIYO?
YOU BET I AM! RIGHT HERE!
LET ME SEE...
BAO ZAKE—
!
OOPS! I'D BETTER NOT SAY IT OUT LOUD! WHO KNOWS WHAT MAY HAPPEN!
Y-YEAH! RIGHT... YOU'RE RIGHT, KIYO!

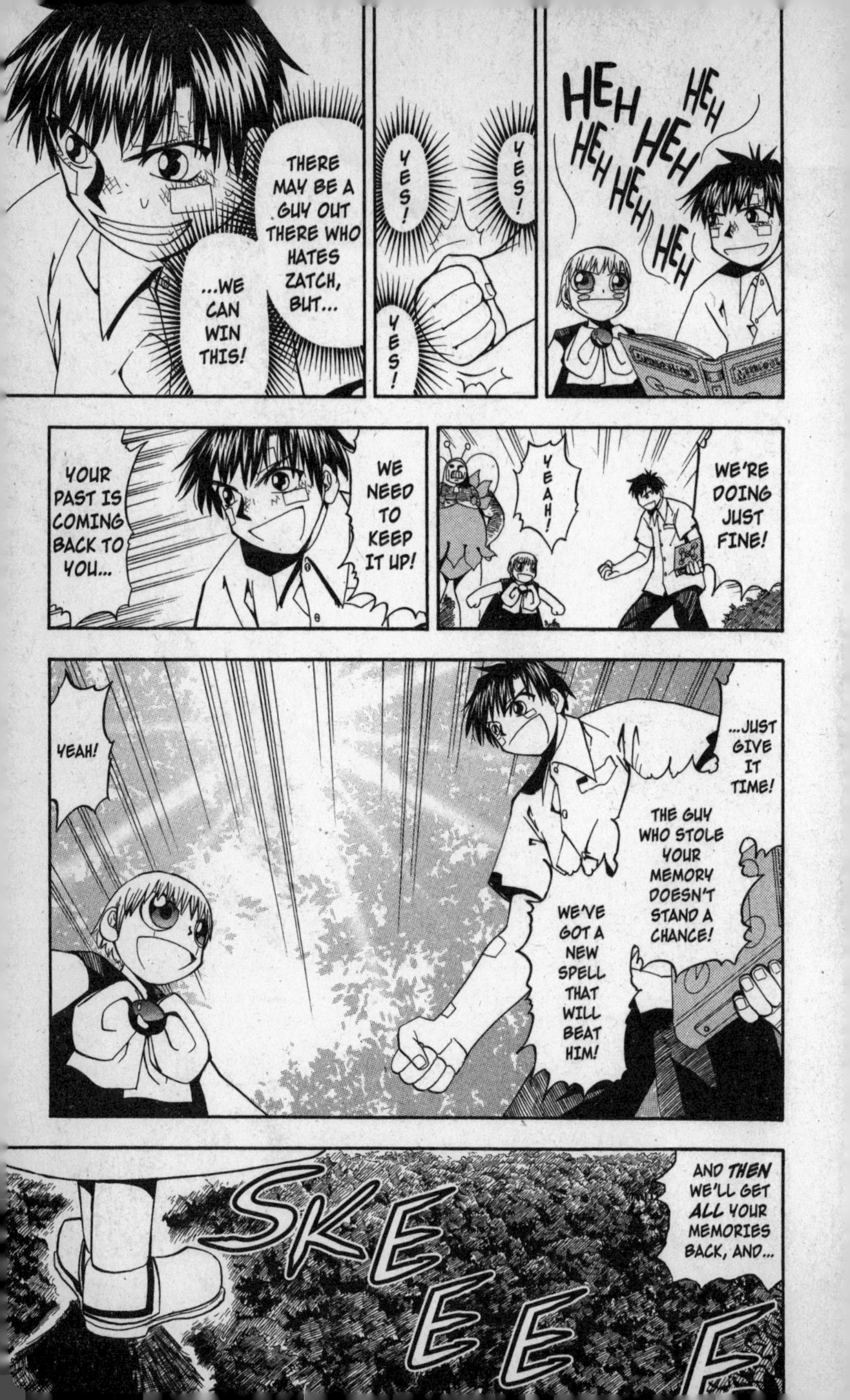
HEH HEH HEH HEH HEH HEH HEH
YES!
YES!
YES!
THERE MAY BE A GUY OUT THERE WHO HATES ZATCH, BUT...
...WE CAN WIN THIS!
WE'RE DOING JUST FINE!
YEAH!
WE NEED TO KEEP IT UP!
YOUR PAST IS COMING BACK TO YOU...
...JUST GIVE IT TIME!
THE GUY WHO STOLE YOUR MEMORY DOESN'T STAND A CHANCE!
WE'VE GOT A NEW SPELL THAT WILL BEAT HIM!
YEAH!
AND THEN WE'LL GET ALL YOUR MEMORIES BACK, AND...
SKEEEEF

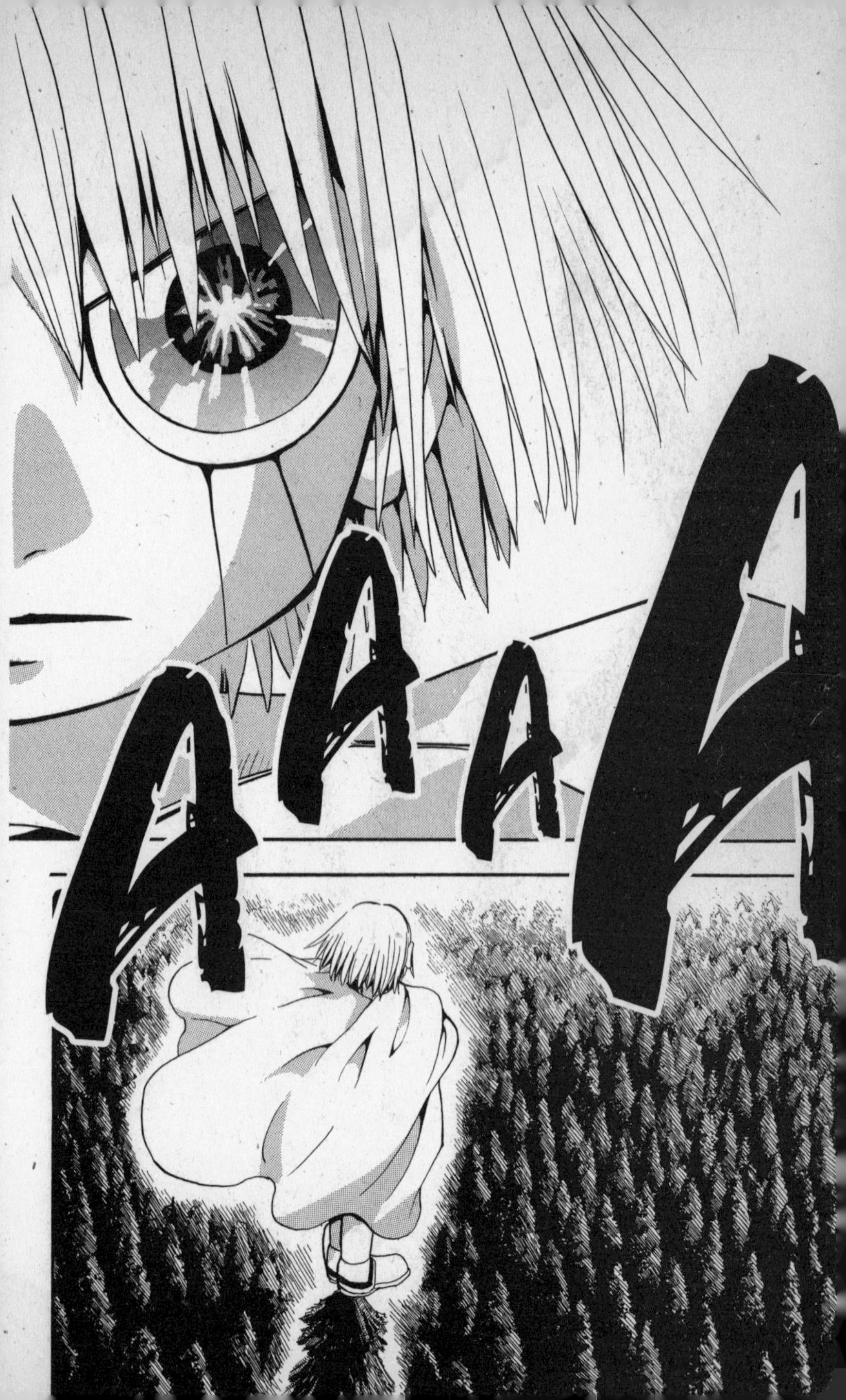
AAAA

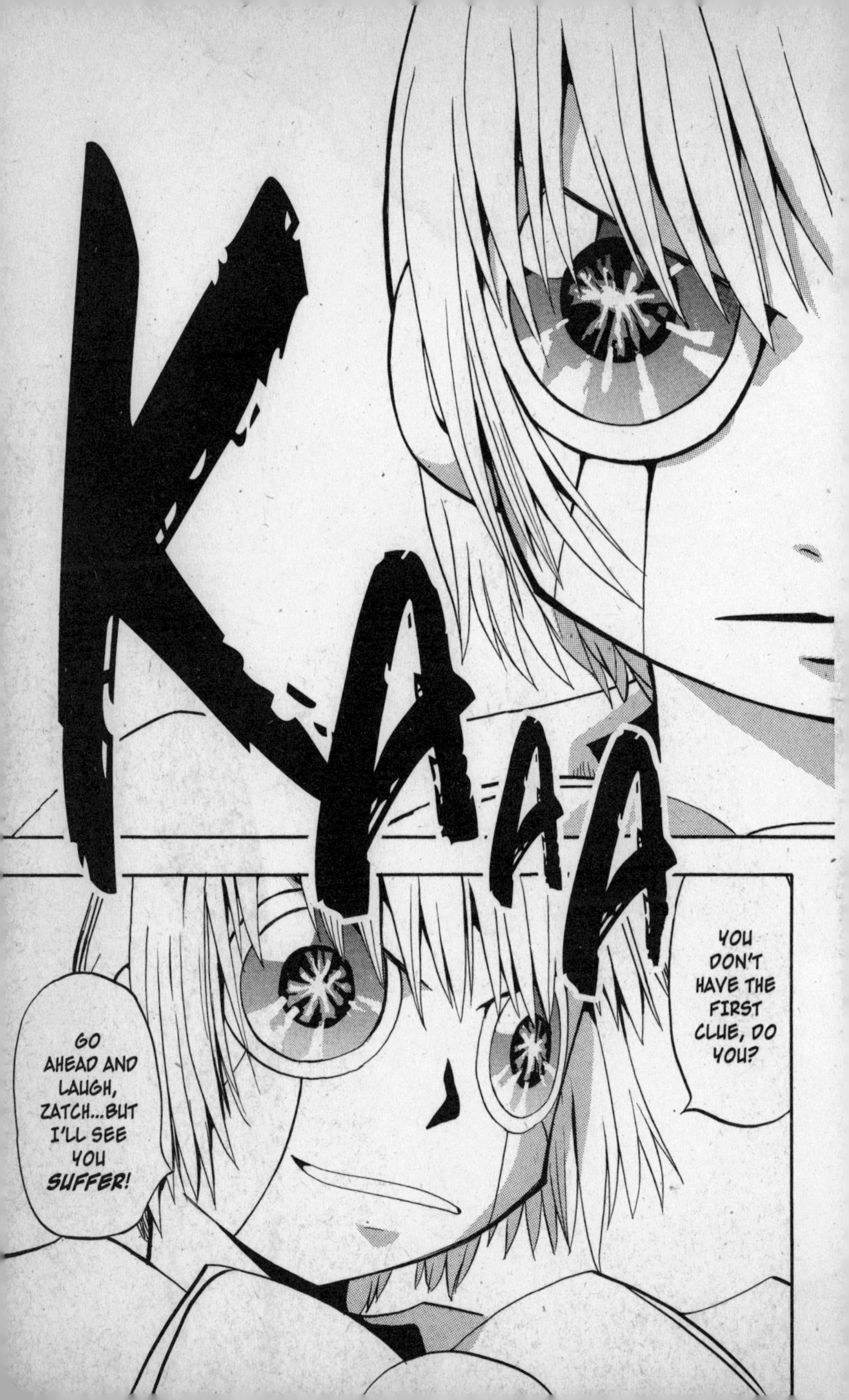
KAAA
YOU DON'T HAVE THE FIRST CLUE, DO YOU?
GO AHEAD AND LAUGH, ZATCH...BUT I'LL SEE YOU SUFFER!

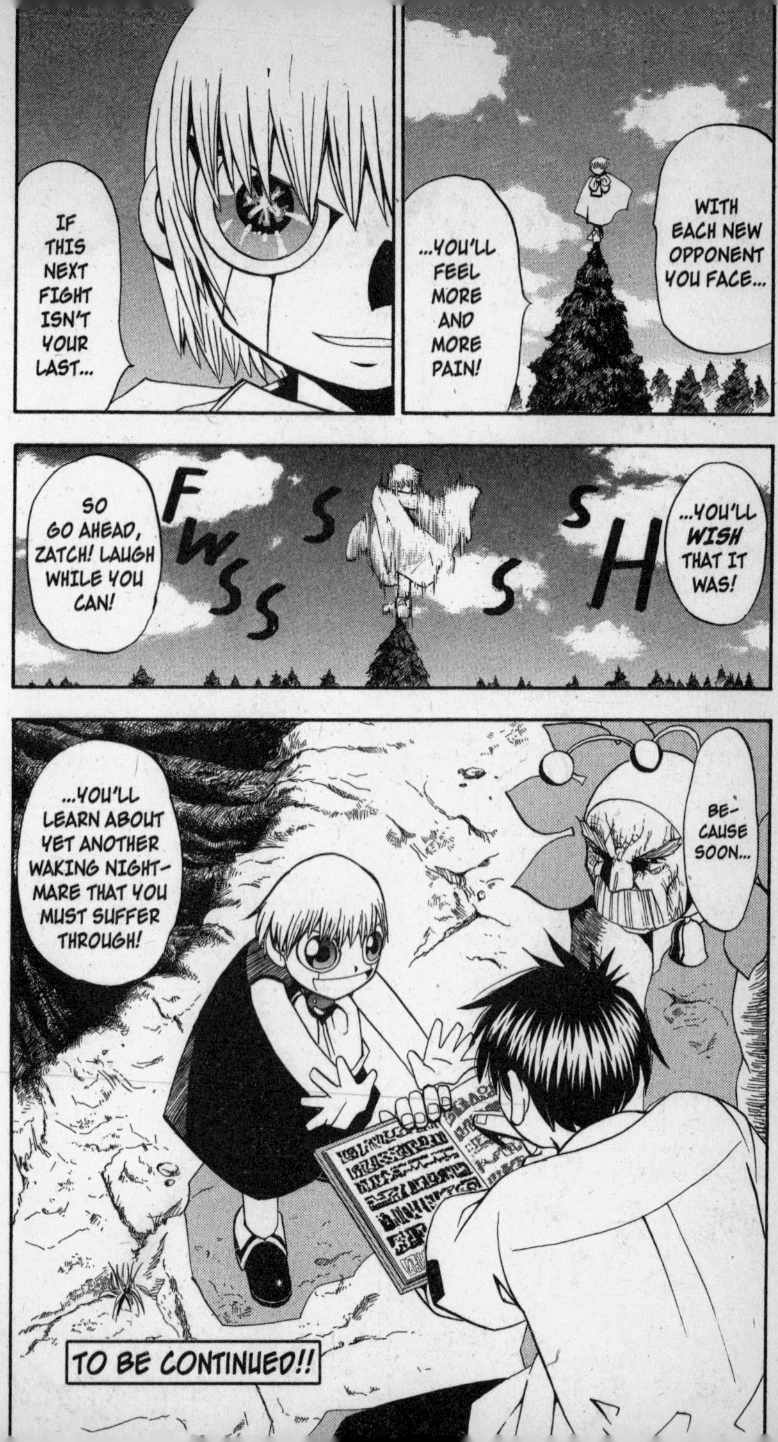
WITH EACH NEW OPPONENT YOU FACE...
...YOU'LL FEEL MORE AND MORE PAIN!
IF THIS NEXT FIGHT ISN'T YOUR LAST...
...YOU'LL *WISH* THAT IT WAS!
FWSSSSSH
SO GO AHEAD, ZATCH! LAUGH WHILE YOU CAN!
BE-CAUSE SOON...
...YOU'LL LEARN ABOUT YET ANOTHER WAKING NIGHT-MARE THAT YOU MUST SUFFER THROUGH!
TO BE CONTINUED!!

BONUS PAGE
~ BEING ON A DIET ~

YOU'LL FAIL!

BY MAKOTO RAIKU

ONE OF THE PRODUCTS THAT I'VE BEEN OBSESSING ABOUT IS...

YES, THAT'S RIGHT!

I'M STILL WORKING ON IT, BUT...

I'M ON A DIET RIGHT NOW.

...I'M STARTING TO BECOME SUSPICIOUS OF ALL THOSE "DIET" FOODS I'VE BEEN DUTIFULLY CONSUMING.

...IT'S NOT GOING SO WELL. IN FACT...

THAT'S WHEN I DECIDED TO WASH MY HANDS IN IT!

PLISH

PLASH

SPLSH

A LIE! IT'S ALL A LIE!

IT'S SO SWEET! HOW CAN THIS BE?

...THE LABEL SAYS IT CONTAINS *ZERO* CALORIES!

THE TASTE IS ALMOST THE SAME AS REGULAR SODA, BUT...

NUTRITION FACTS (100ML)	
CALORIES	0
TOTAL FAT	0G
TOTAL CARB	0G
SODIUM	10MG

OH, WELL...I GUESS IT REALLY IS MY OWN FAULT THAT I'M NOT LOSING WEIGHT...HMPH!

SILKY SMOOTH, LIKE WATER!

BUT MY HANDS DIDN'T GET STICKY AT ALL...

SHA

AA

SHA

AA

AAA

THAT WILL PROVE THERE'S NO SUCH THING AS A DIET SODA!

THAT'S RIGHT! IF DIET COLA CONTAINS SUGAR, MY HANDS WILL BE ALL STICKY!

SPISH

SPASH

ZATCH & SUZY

BY MAKOTO RAIKU

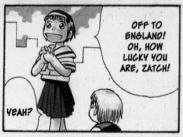

OFF TO ENGLAND! OH, HOW LUCKY YOU ARE, ZATCH!
YEAH?
DO YOU WANT TO GO TOO, SUZY?
YES! FAIRIES LIVE IN THE FOREST THERE, YOU KNOW.
THEY *DO*? YOU MEAN IT?
SURE! SWEET AND TINY AND CUTE!
OH, BOY! WILL THEY LIKE ME?
YOU WILL HAVE *SO* MUCH FUN!

AND SO ZATCH MEETS THE FAIRIES...

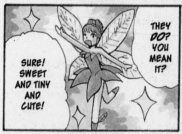

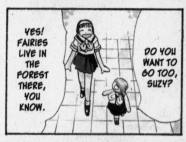

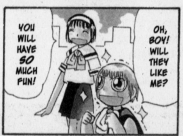

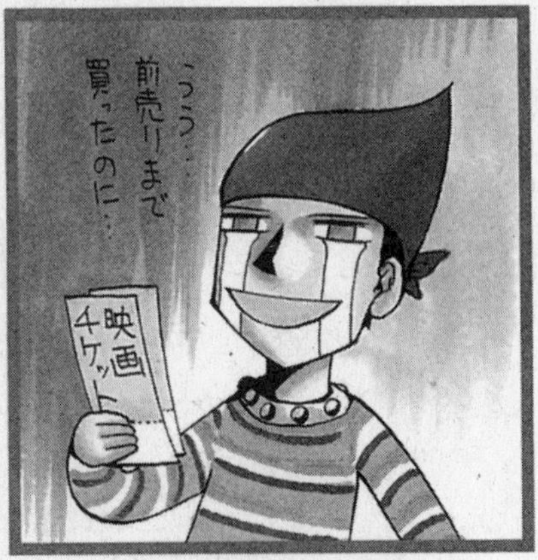
ううう…
前売りまで
買ったのに…
映画
チケット

MAKOTO RAIKU

I even bought movie tickets in advance...

Oh, how I'd love to go to the movies in a real theater!
There are plenty of movies out that I'm interested in seeing, but it seems I never get a chance to watch them. So instead, I bought a bunch of recent releases on DVD...but I still can't seem to find the time...
Sob, sob...

CATCH AN ANIME SPELL!

KIYO'S A GENIUS, BUT THE ONE THING HE DOESN'T KNOW IS HOW TO MAKE FRIENDS. WHEN HIS DAD SENDS A LITTLE BOY NAMED ZATCH TO HELP, KIYO DISCOVERS THAT ZATCH ISN'T EXACTLY HUMAN... SOON MAKING FRIENDS BECOMES THE LEAST OF KIYO'S PROBLEMS!

$19.98!

ZATCH BELL!

THE LIGHTNING BOY FROM ANOTHER WORLD

1

DVD

THE TOP-RATED TV SHOW NOW AVAILABLE ON DVD

ZATCH BELL!™

Visit **WWW.ZATCH-BELL.COM** to find out more!

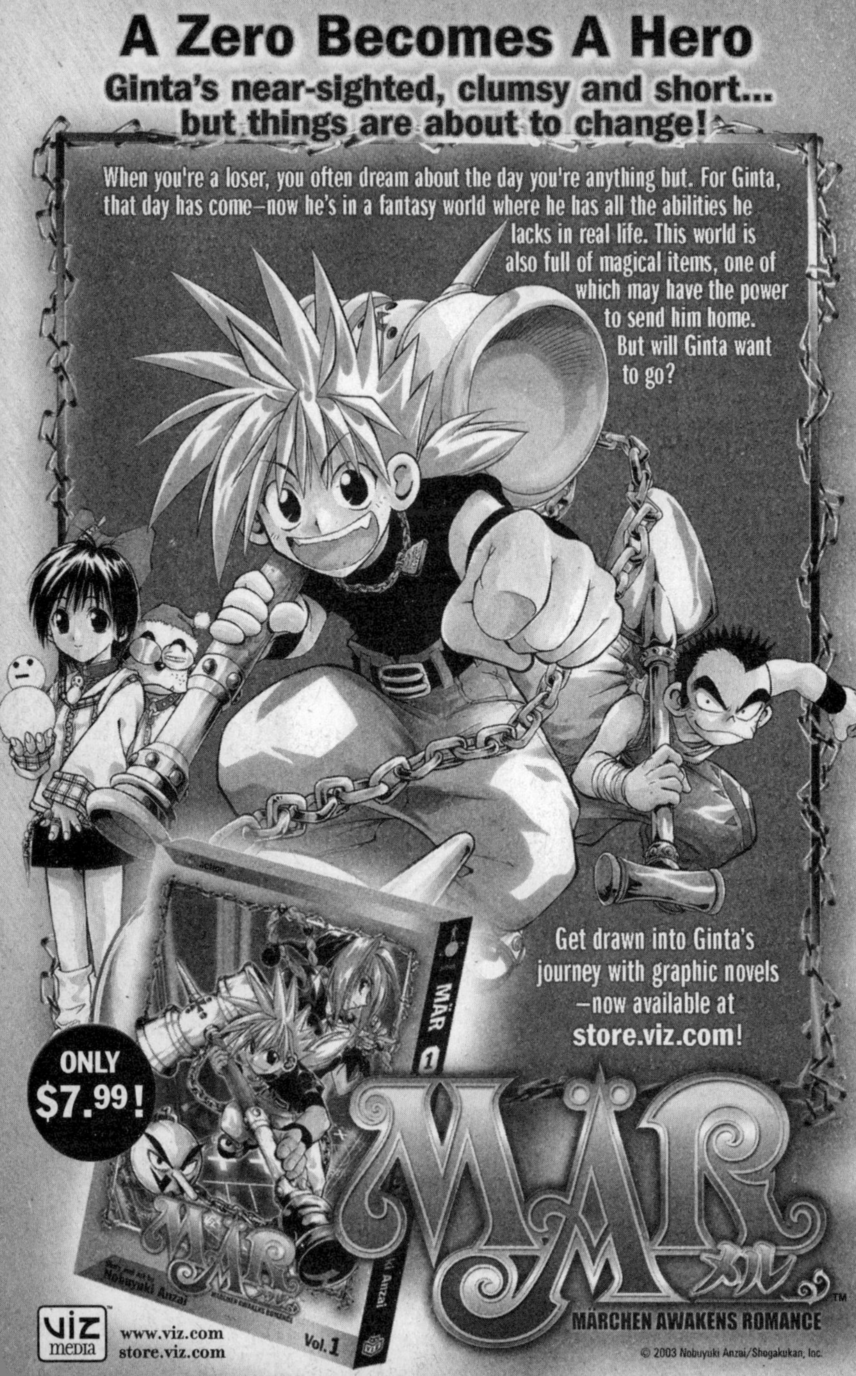
A Zero Becomes A Hero
Ginta's near-sighted, clumsy and short... but things are about to change!
When you're a loser, you often dream about the day you're anything but. For Ginta, that day has come—now he's in a fantasy world where he has all the abilities he lacks in real life. This world is also full of magical items, one of which may have the power to send him home. But will Ginta want to go?
Get drawn into Ginta's journey with graphic novels —now available at store.viz.com!
ONLY $7.99!
MÄR
MÄRCHEN AWAKENS ROMANCE
Nobuyuki Anzai
Vol. 1
viz media
www.viz.com
store.viz.com
© 2003 Nobuyuki Anzai/Shogakukan, Inc.

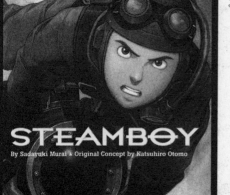

The Evolution of Science...
The Downfall of Man?

Based on the hit movie from Katsuhiro Otomo

STEAMBOY

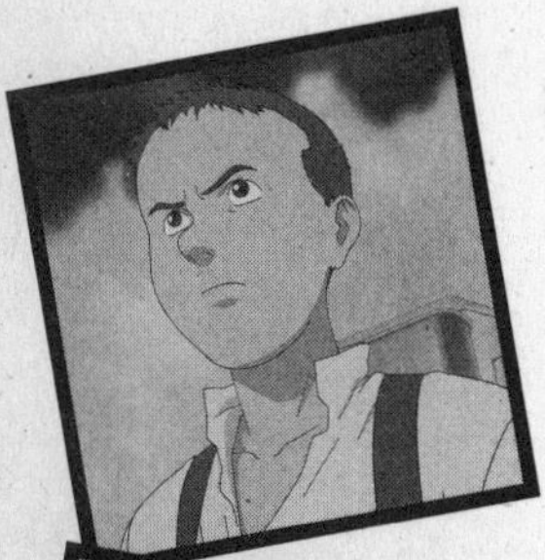

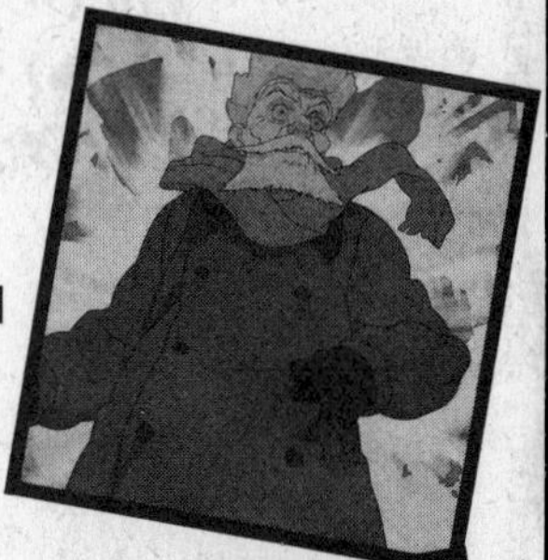

Meet Ray Steam, a resourceful young inventor whose father and grandfather have harnessed the ultimate energy source that will transform the world for better or worse!

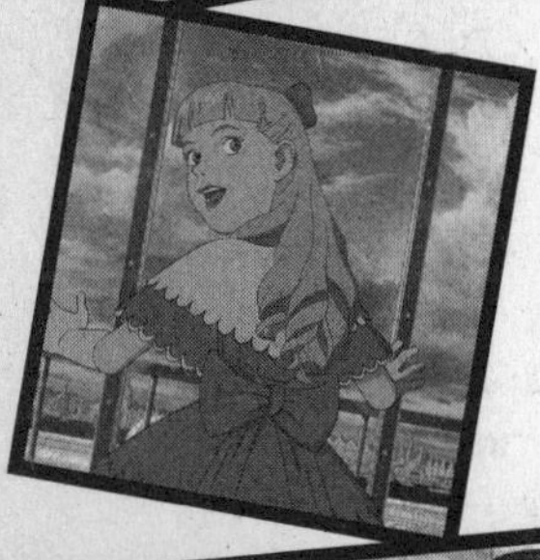

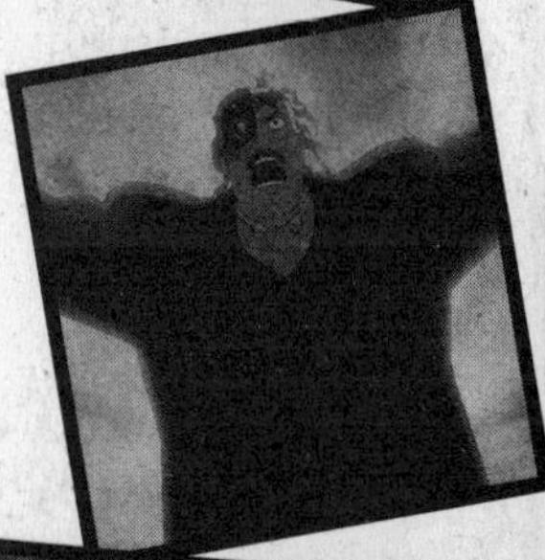

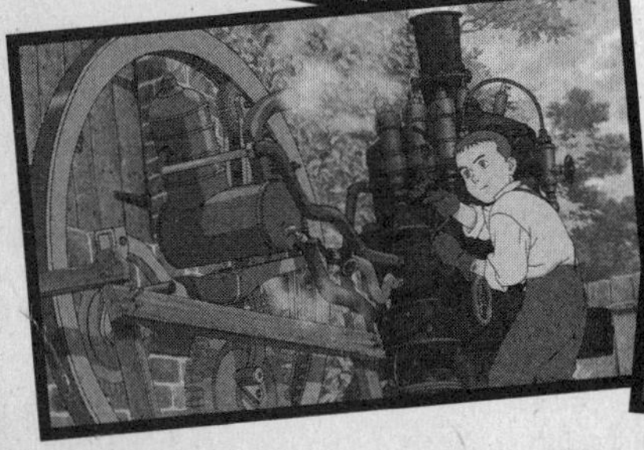

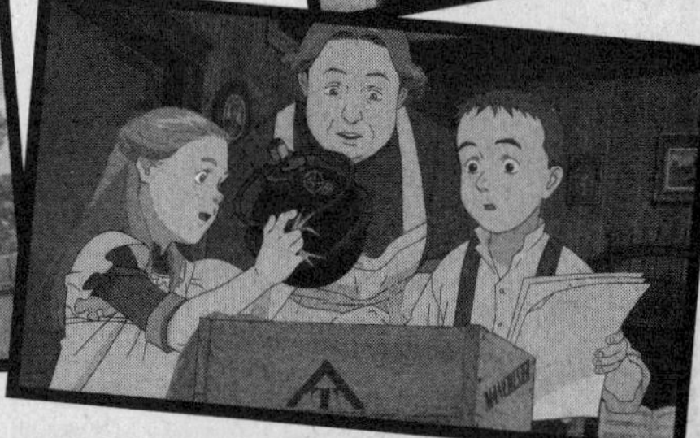